ALSO BY ROBIN WRIGHT

Flashpoints:
Promise and Peril in a New World
(with Doyle McManus)

Sacred Rage:
The Wrath of Militant Islam

In the Name of God:
The Khomeini Decade

THE LAST GREAT REVOLUTION

THE LAST GREAT REVOLUTION

Turmoil and Transformation in Iran

ROBIN WRIGHT

Alfred A. Knopf NEW YORK 2000

This Is a Borzoi Book
Published by Alfred A. Knopf

Copyright © 2000 by Robin Wright
Map copyright © 2000 by David Lindroth Inc.

All rights reserved under International and Pan-American Copyright
Conventions. Published in the United States by Alfred A. Knopf, a
division of Random House, Inc., New York, and simultaneously in
Canada by Random House of Canada Limited, Toronto. Distributed
by Random House, Inc., New York.

www.randomhouse.com

Knopf, Borzoi Books and the colophon are registered trademarks
of Random House, Inc.

Library of Congress Cataloging-in-Publication Data
Wright, Robin B., [date]
    The last great revolution / by Robin Wright. — 1st ed.
      p.   cm.
    Includes bibliographical references (p.   ) and index.
    ISBN 0-375-40639-5
      1. Iran—Politics and government—1979–1997. 2. Iran—
Politics and government—1997– 3. Iran—Social conditions—
1979–1997.   4. Iran—Social conditions—1997–   I. Title.
DS318.8.W75 2000
955.05'4—dc21   99-27798
                                                          CIP

Manufactured in the United States of America
First Edition

FOR MY MOTHER

*who inspired me to taste the world
and who taught me tolerance*

The way of God, who disposes all things with gentleness, is to instill religion into our minds with reasoned arguments and into our hearts with grace. Attempting to instill it with force and threats is not religion, but terror.

—PASCAL

CONTENTS

INTRODUCTION:
A PERSONAL ODYSSEY

One man with beliefs is equal to a thousand with only
interests.
—JOHN STUART MILL

We cannot apply European standards of conduct to
Persia with any expectation that they will furnish a
reliable gauge of action.
—LORD BALFOUR

I FIRST WENT to Iran in 1973 as a young reporter. The fourth modern
Mideast war had just erupted and fury engulfed other parts of the region.
As I wrote home at the time, Iran was then a place that seemed to make
sense. In a part of the world where people were so filled with hate for one
another—and so often for the West as well—Iran was one of the few
comfortable places for foreigners. We were welcome.

Indeed, we were everywhere in Iran—advising its government officials, training its military, building its oil rigs, teaching in its schools and
peddling our cars, language, fashions, industrial products and culture.

My memories of that visit are still strong. I stayed at the new Hilton Hotel, where a recent Miss Iran pageant had selected a candidate for the Miss Universe contest. I swam in the pool. I borrowed a racket and played tennis on the hotel courts. I also had a drink in the hotel bar with an uncle from the University of California who was among some forty thousand Americans working in Tehran at the time. He was advising the government on how to modernize its national library system.

Tehran was the kind of place where foreigners could often find someone they knew or with whom they shared mutual friends.

The images that I stored away of Iran in 1973 were familiar, some even reassuring. I remember a day wandering through the dusty, labyrinthine alleys of Tehran's Great Bazaar and seeing an enormous silk carpet woven in the image of President John F. Kennedy hanging from the vaulted rafters next to a slightly larger carpet of Mohammad Reza Shah Pahlavi. I drove down major boulevards in Tehran named after Presidents Franklin Roosevelt and Dwight Eisenhower, after Queen Elizabeth and Winston Churchill, all of whom had visited the Iranian capital as guests of the shah.

Iran was then an openly inviting place for an American woman. I felt as relaxed about traveling throughout the country as I did in Europe. I could go most places, do virtually anything, talk to anyone and dress in whatever apparel I chose. Short skirts were acceptable. After all, Iranians wore bikinis on the beach.

It was somewhat of an illusion, of course. Through a political sleight of hand that was sometimes masterful and other times clumsy, an autocratic monarchy tightly controlled the environment. The shah wanted to see Iran move in one direction and many who deviated, politically or culturally, paid a price. Some were excluded from the system or publicly denounced. Others went to prison. A few, including Ayatollah Khomeini, were deported from the land of their birth.

Foreigners sometimes felt better about Iran than Iranians did, partly because of a superficial cultural imprint from the West but mostly because we chose to see what we wanted to see. A decade after the revolution, an Iranian journalist tried to explain to me what had happened.

"You thought you understood Iran because the shah spoke English and because his cabinet had read Shakespeare," he said. "You thought he was good because you could see a reflection of yourself in him. But he understood Iran as little as you did, and that's why you both failed."[1]

After that initial trip, I didn't give much thought to going back and I certainly never envisioned making Iran a specialty. I went off and did stints as a foreign correspondent in Africa, then Europe. But the revolution in early 1979 and then the United States Embassy takeover later that year got in the way. For a journalist, Iran became the best story in the world. So I returned.

The images from the revolution's angry early years are also still strong in my mind. I'll never forget my first flight back to Tehran, when the pilot invoked God as he greeted passengers on the intercom.

"In the name of God, the compassionate and merciful," he said, "welcome aboard this flight to the Islamic Republic of Iran."

The same salutation had begun to precede every official's speech and every television broadcast. It became the first line of all public documents, from wills and deeds to marriage licenses. It was incorporated into the new national flag, integrated into business signs, printed atop official stationery and even painted as roadside graffiti. The phrase became a kind of formal public greeting, roughly equivalent to the French Revolution's *citoyen* or the Soviet Union's "comrade."

Its use by the pilot was fair notice that even minutiae had been redefined in religious terms.

Before we landed in Tehran, the flight's lone stewardess helped me tighten a big headscarf and button up a baggy ankle-length coat known as a *roopoosh* to better cover my hair and neck. She also gave me ten Band-Aids to cover the nail polish I'd forgotten to remove.

Once on the ground, I watched and the long line behind me waited as a customs official searching for cultural contraband tore up my deck of playing cards, tediously one by one, to drive home the point that they were no longer allowed. I also went through a body search and a currency check, when I had to declare every penny I brought in so it could later be reconciled with what I took out to ensure I didn't trade in a black market desperate for American dollars.

And those represented only a tiny taste of how much Iran was changing. For anyone who'd been to Iran before, the new Islamic Republic of Iran seemed almost like a different country. All those familiar sights disappeared. So, initially, did most activities beyond work and home life.

Cultural outlets were forcibly closed. University life was suspended while curriculum was reviewed. Bars and nightclubs had their liquor stocks destroyed before being boarded up. Religious vigilantes monitored morality in each neighborhood. Streets were often empty at night, because pedestrians and drivers wanted to avoid searches at impromptu checkpoints set up by the new Revolutionary Guards.

Even fashion had changed. Women were forced behind chadors and *hejab,* the generic term for a variety of body covers. Many simply retreated into their homes. To show loyalty, men grew beards or a permanent three-day stubble. Ties, the epitome of Western style, became taboo.

And there was no question, needless to say, of an Iranian entrant in the 1980 Miss Universe contest.

The turnover of power was reflected in name changes. Royal terms were replaced with unfamiliar religious titles. The *shahanshah,* or "king of kings," was gone. In his stead was the ayatollah, or "mirror of God." The young princes were replaced by *hojatoleslams,* a clerical rank meaning "authority on Islam." The reverence demanded, however, was just the same.

My first journey deep inside the revolution was sometimes bizarre, often challenging, but always interesting. The bottom line is that the story hooked me. For the next twenty years, I went back to the Islamic Republic of Iran as often as I could—more than any American, the Ministry of Culture and Islamic Guidance often complained. My odyssey included virtually all the major highs and lows of the revolution, as well as their spillover on the outside world. Many encounters and events left an indelible impression. The first decade included the most sensational moments.

I still remember the look of both exhaustion and exhilaration on the faces of the fifty-two American hostages as they stepped off the plane to freedom in Algiers. I covered the Carter administration's suspenseful mediation to win their release and I spent that cold, rainy night in January 1981 waiting with a small group of journalists on the Algiers airport tarmac getting wet and wondering if the deal was going to fall through—again.

In an I-want-the-last-word pique, Tehran had waited until after Ronald Reagan was sworn in and Jimmy Carter was no longer president to let the plane fly off.

Watching the hostages' faces as they came down the steps, I fully understood their relief to be getting out of the Islamic Republic. During those intense early years, I felt that way myself whenever the planes I took, preferably foreign carriers, lifted off from Tehran's Mehrabad Airport.

A few months later, I moved from my base in Rome to Beirut, and

Iran became part of my regular beat. Press access, then tightly controlled, opened up a bit because of the grisly war with Iraq that dragged on from 1980 to 1988. After Iraqi atrocities or major Iranian victories, Tehran usually issued visas. So I often traipsed around with Iranian troops, either on the marshy southwest war front holding up my long, bulky coat or in the hot, arid scrublands wishing desperately I could take off the thick extra layer of clothing. I also interviewed victims of Iraq's chemical weapons attacks and Iraqi prisoners of war within hours of their capture.

During the war years, I spent a lot of time at Tehran's Behesht-e Zahra, or Zahra's Paradise, as it grew into one of the world's largest cemeteries, to talk with families of military and civilian war victims.

I still remember the first funeral cortege I saw en route to the graveyard named after the prophet Mohammad's daughter. It was led by a green hatchback. Two men sitting in the open rear were running a large tape recorder from which a man's chanting of Koranic verses was amplified on two loudspeakers strapped to the car roof. On the hood, a garland of flowers surrounded a picture of the deceased soldier. A beige ambulance carrying the body was next. Its back doors were open and young men, probably family members and fellow soldiers, were crowded on both sides of the body. Buses packed with relatives and friends followed. One was plastered with a large banner reading, "Congratulations on your martyrdom."

Traffic was so congested at Zahra's Paradise that a policeman was frantically whistling directions to funeral convoys.

The war, like all my encounters, had its human moments too. I'll never forget meeting up with a group of Revolutionary Guards in 1982 on a battlefield near Dezful. When they asked whether there were any Americans among the reporters, I reluctantly lifted my hand. I was the only one.

As a couple of them took me aside, I thought, Well, it's been a sweet life.

But all they wanted to know was whether Nebraska had beaten Oklahoma in a football game that fall and if Pink Floyd had a new album out. The only thing that made them suspicious was that I'd never heard of Pink Floyd.

During the revolution's first decade, I also covered the emergence and spread of Islamic militancy throughout the Middle East. Much of it was inspired by Iran. Some events were encouraged or directed by Tehran through surrogate militias.

I went through both rage and anguish about Iran's role, direct and indirect, in the deaths of Americans in Beirut. I remember the lingering black clouds of smoke that covered the United States Embassy in April 1983 after a suicide bomber sped a dark delivery van into the driveway and blew away the entire face of a high-rise concrete building overlooking the otherwise tranquil Mediterranean. For days, I watched as Lebanese rescuers picked up small bits of bodies and put them in blue plastic bags for forensic testing and then identification.

One of the enduring memories of my entire career was being jolted awake five months later by a double bombing with sound waves that shattered windows for miles in all directions. This time the headquarters of American and French peacekeepers had been hit. Again, I spent days at the American base on the edge of Beirut's international airport watching as mutilated bodies were pulled from under the huge pile of concrete and twisted metal that had been the Marine battalion living quarters.

It was the largest loss for the American military in a single incident since the Vietnam War.

Six months later, the new United States Embassy, relocated in supposedly safe east Beirut, was also bombed. I lost friends and professional contacts in all three attacks. Iran's allies—clandestine cells widely believed to be under the tutelage of Revolutionary Guards deployed in Lebanon after Israel's 1982 invasion—either claimed credit or were linked to all three bombings. During a subsequent trip to Tehran, I had a surreal discussion with the Revolutionary Guard commander about the way Iran armed, trained and encouraged Lebanon's Shi'ites.

The confrontation between America and Iran became even more personal when the tactics shifted from mass suicide bombings to individual hostage seizures in Lebanon. Terry Anderson and Tom Sutherland, two of the longest-held hostages, were among my good friends during those Beirut years. I also knew many of the other hundred-plus hostages held between 1984 and 1991. Again, Iran's surrogates claimed credit for many of the seizures.

Like most of the rest of the foreign press, I eventually had to abandon my Beirut base because of Terry Anderson's abduction. The press was no longer off-limits. And our offices were in the same building. I assumed—wrongly—that I'd soon be able to go back. But Terry was held seven years, until Iran intervened to facilitate his release. I never did retrieve my furniture, clothing, files or last typewriter.

American–Iranian relations have been a recurrent theme of the revolution's first two decades—and of my encounters with the Islamic Republic. I covered the 1985–86 arms-for-hostages swap from both Washington and Tehran. A manager at the Tehran Hilton, which had been renamed the Independence Hotel after the revolution, even took me on a tour of the suites where Oliver North and the rest of the American delegation had stayed.

"It was all supposed to be secret," he told me with great delight. "But *everyone* knew they were here."

In 1987, I had breakfast at the Waldorf-Astoria Hotel in New York with President Ali Khamenei when he became the first Iranian president to speak at the United Nations. The victim of a tape-recorder bomb in 1980 that cost him the use of one arm, Khamenei had to have his breakfast food of cold cuts and fruit cut up for him by a bodyguard. Later that day, he threw out the prepared text of his speech, which had included a tepid overture to the United States, because American helicopters had just hit and set ablaze an Iranian ship. Three Iranian sailors had been killed, twenty-six captured. Iran claimed the *Iran Ajr* was merely a merchant ship. But the United States had photos of its crew planting mines in Persian Gulf sealanes vital to oil exports. So instead of detente, Khamenei went on the offensive, again, against the Great Satan.

The episode typified the way diplomatic intentions and events on the ground too often ended up colliding—and canceling each other out.

But it was a two-way street. In 1988, I was taken to an Iranian morgue to look at grotesque, water-bloated bodies after the U.S.S. *Vincennes* mistakenly shot down an Iran Air passenger plane flying over the Persian Gulf to the United Arab Emirates. Almost three hundred people, including sixty-six children, had plummeted to their deaths.

The drama, passions and extremism of that tumultuous first decade led to my first two books. *Sacred Rage* chronicled the rise of militant Islam across the region. *In the Name of God* covered the revolution's first ten years, from Ayatollah Khomeini's return in 1979 until his death in 1989.

But I was drawn to Iran by more than just specific news events, which was why I ended up going back and back again during the revolution's second decade, when the headlines weren't as flashy, the threat not quite so blatant. The fascination ran deeper for several reasons.

First, the revolution is one of the century's seminal turning points. For the Mideast, only two events have had comparable impact: the creation of the state of Israel and the Ottoman Empire's collapse after five centuries, in turn triggering the creation of modern Arab states. Iran's revolution has also had a rippling impact felt far beyond the Middle East, because of its influence on oil prices, the patterns of warfare and terrorism and the broader use of religion in politics worldwide.

Second, Iran is too valuable to ignore, at least for long. Its resources, size, geostrategic location and markets have always made it one of the world's prime properties. Dating back to the fourth century B.C., an array of historic figures sought to conquer the land because it's a critical crossroads. Those who became enthralled with Iran ranged from Alexander the Great to Josef Stalin and included the armies of the prophet Mohammad, Genghis Khan and Tamerlane.

Modern Iran's location is just as pivotal. Its land borders include Turkey, Iraq, Pakistan, Afghanistan and the former Soviet republics of Azerbaijan, Armenia and Turkmenistan. It also has, by far, the longest border with the Persian Gulf—hence the name—through which more than 40 percent of oil bound for Western industrialized countries passes daily. And a hop, skip and jump across those blue-green waters are Saudi Arabia, Kuwait, Qatar, Bahrain, the United Arab Emirates and Oman, some of the world's richest but most vulnerable states.

Third, Iranians are special people. I've gone through an array of emotions about the governments in Tehran over the years—angered by the injustices at home, alienated by the arrogance, frustrated by the corruption and astonished at the inefficiency. Yet I've developed an enduring admiration for Iranians. As much as many Persians and Americans might disagree, I've often been struck by how similar they are, despite vastly different histories. Both are generous, eager, inquisitive, fiercely proud, often a little naive, insecure, vulnerable and incredibly hospitable.

"Iranians are on the whole extremely hospitable to foreigners— almost embarrassingly so sometimes," wrote David St. Vincent, the British author of the Lonely Planet travel guide to Iran.[2]

St. Vincent wrote that in 1992 despite the fact he had been brought before a revolutionary court on the imaginative charge of plotting to import Salman Rushdie's controversial *Satanic Verses*. One of his four trips to Iran for the guidebook was also cut short when he was deported in retaliation for the expulsion of some Iranians from Britain.

Yet St. Vincent still advised, "Don't be afraid to accept invitations from Iranians. Iranians have always entertained predominantly at home and you will never understand Iran if you don't make an effort to meet Iranians on their own terms."[3]

He's right. And encounters with Iranians are about more than mere hospitality. Over a typical meal of grilled lamb or chicken and saffron rice, goat cheese, flat bread and onions, they love to discuss and feistily debate. Some subjects—such as atheism—are best avoided, at least at first. Yet politics, religion, women's rights, money and even sex, including birth control, can be dinner table conversation. Curiosity and candor are two strong Iranian traits. They'll probe virtually any subject—and in the privacy of their homes, the revolution has not kept them from doing so.

And oh, how they love to weave intricate conspiracy theories! Among my favorites over the past twenty years have been an array of amazing scenarios—despite abundant and indisputable evidence to the contrary—about how the CIA secretly arranged for Ayatollah Khomeini to replace the shah. Hundreds of Iranians I know contend to this day that the United States played a role in the revolution. Some have no proof except their belief that it couldn't have happened unless Washington allowed or arranged it.

But Iranians are hardly uniform in thought. An old saying about diversity applies in Iran more than anywhere else: If there are five people, there are at least six different opinions.

Despite the lingering images from the revolution's early days, it's also unfair to stereotype Iranians generally, for they also can vary widely in ethnicity, language and even religion.

Ethnically, Iranians reflect the geographic crossroads of Iran where Arabia, the Caucasus, Central Asia, Turkey and the Asian subcontinent meet. Iranians are Turkoman farmers and horse traders in the northeast, western Kurds, Baluchis (or "wanderers") who straddle the arid and unruly southeast border with Pakistan, Arabs on the southern coast, mountainous Lors (an Arab-Persian mix), nomadic herding tribes in the south and, in the cities, an array of Armenians, Mongols, Afghans and Indians—plus, of course, the majority Persians, who are everywhere, and the Turkish-speaking Azeris from the northernmost province of Azerbaijan, who account for up to a quarter of the population, making them the largest minority.

Although Iran is now an Islamic republic with an overwhelming Muslim population, there is variety in religion too. The largest group is made up of Shi'ite Muslims of the Twelver sect, so-named because they believe in the twelve imams who ruled successively after the prophet Mohammad's death until the twelfth one disappeared—or went into "occultation." Twelver Shi'ites now await the return of the Mahdi, or twelfth imam—an idea not unlike expectations in other major faiths.

But Iran is also home to mainstream Sunni Muslims as well as other smaller Muslim sects. And there are enough Iranian Christians, Jews and Zoroastrians to have their own special seats in Parliament. Most big Iranian cities have at least one church, synagogue and fire temple. The one faith shunned politically and persecuted exclusively on religious grounds is that of the three million Baha'is, whose break from Shi'ite Islam in the nineteenth century is still viewed as heresy.

Iran is diverse politically too. Again despite stereotypes that haven't changed much since 1979, Iran has actually evolved a great deal since the shah departed. In some ways it is unrecognizable from the early days, and not only because the revolution's rigid rules relaxed enough to allow nail polish to be sold at every salon, perfumerie and department store, often in outrageous shades.

So much has changed that, as Iran celebrated its twentieth anniversary in 1999, I decided another book was needed to put an extraordinary event into the broader perspective of modern history. But this book is quite different from my earlier book on the Iranian revolution's first decade. The first one was a chronological account of key events and major players. The voice and analysis in that volume were my own.

This book is a human journey inside twenty years of Iran's revolution. It's about the people and places that make up Iran and it unfolds through the pressing issues in Iranian life, from love and family to freedom of expression, from religious reform to women's rights, from culture to economics.

This time, Iranians speak for themselves about their ideas, experiences, dreams and frustrations. The issues and individual stories chronicle how the world's only modern theocracy gradually adapted—and how the revolutions within the revolution helped Iran become more modern and less theocratic. Together, they also offer a prognosis about the Islamic republic's future.

Needless to say, a lot still hasn't changed. Many of the unusual rules—unusual in Western eyes, anyway—still apply.

As the Lonely Planet guide advises a new generation of foreign tourists daring to visit Iran, "When making a personal compliment about someone—such as when telling a mother how handsome her child is— always say *mashallah,* or "God has willed it," for fear of invoking divine retribution. The idea is that all beauty and goodness are gifts of God— and can be taken away by Him at any time."[4]

Understanding Iran isn't as easy as it once was—or at least as outsiders thought it was. But given Iran's history, resources and location, the country is no less important today than it was during the monarchy. The system has changed, but Iranians haven't. This book is written in the hope that sharing a personal odyssey through twenty years of Iran's historic revolution will help outsiders see what is there, not just what they want to see.

SOME FACTS ABOUT IRAN

GEOGRAPHY | Iran is the crossroads for Arabia, the Caucasus, Central Asia, Turkey and the Asian subcontinent. For millennia, it has been an important geostrategic property. In size, it covers about 650,000 square miles, slightly larger than Alaska.

The topography is largely a high plateau bordered by a rugged mountainous rim, deserts and bodies of water that have allowed Iran to maintain a separate identity for thousands of years. To the north are the Caspian Sea and the Alborz Mountains. To the east are mountains and salt deserts, including the Kevir Desert. The Persian Gulf stretches along the southwest border and the Arabian Sea is to the south.

Iran is bordered by Iraq, Turkey, Afghanistan, Pakistan and the former Soviet republics of Armenia, Azerbaijan and Turkmenistan. Across the Persian Gulf are Saudi Arabia, Kuwait, the United Arab Emirates, Oman, Qatar and Bahrain.

POPULATION | In 1979, Iran had a population of around 34 million. On the twentieth anniversary of the revolution, Iran had more than 62 million.

About half the population is Persian, an ethnic group descended from Indo-European Aryans, from whom Iran derived its modern name. The second-largest ethnic group, about a quarter of the population, is Azeri. Iran is also home to significant groups of Turks, Kurds, Arabs, Turkomans, Armenians, Mongols and Afghans.

CITIES | Tehran is the modern capital. Historic capitals include Persepolis, Shiraz and Isfahan. Other major cities include Mashhad, Tabriz, the religious center of Qom, Yazd, Kerman, Bandar Abbas, Bushehr, Khorramshahr and Abadan.

RELIGION | Iran is overwhelmingly Muslim, and more than 90 percent Shi'ite Muslim. About 5 percent are Sunni Muslim. Iran is also home to small communities of various Christian faiths, Jews, Baha'is and Zoroastrians.

LANGUAGES | Farsi, or Persian, is the dominant language. But Iran also has more than seventy minority languages, including large communities who speak Azeri and Kurdish.

ECONOMY | The country is heavily dependent on revenue from oil exports—Iran is the world's third-largest exporter after Saudi Arabia and Norway. It has about 90 billion barrels of proven oil reserves—roughly 10 percent of the world total. After Russia, Iran also has the second-largest proven gas reserves, about 15 percent of the world's total. Only about 8 percent of Iran's land is arable. Its currency is the rial.

THE LAST GREAT REVOLUTION

CHAPTER I

THE LAST GREAT REVOLUTION

Never was any such event so inevitable, yet so completely unforeseen.
                    —ALEXIS DE TOCQUEVILLE,
                        on the French Revolution

We will create a strong new current of thought and a
powerful popular movement that will result in the
establishment of an Islamic government.
                    —AYATOLLAH KHOMEINI

ON THE DUSTY HIGHWAY south from bustling Tehran, an enormous
gold dome rises importantly across the horizon. Heat from the surrounding desert makes it shiver like a mirage, even in winter. Four spiny
minarets quiver rhythmically alongside it.

The most ornate shrine in Iran—and one of the largest monuments
ever constructed in the Muslim world over the past thirteen centuries—
was built in record time above the burial site of Ayatollah Ruhollah Khomeini after he died abruptly from a heart attack in 1989. Disgruntled
Iranians complained at the time that its cost was greater than the annual
budget of Tehran, a city of some 13 million people. Iran's devout boasted

3

that it was finer than both the Grand Mosque in Mecca and the prophet Mohammad's tomb in Medina, Islam's two holiest sites. Their message was implicit.

The trip to Khomeini's tomb and the nearby Paradise of Zahra has always served as a barometer of Iran's revolution. I've stopped there on every visit. The last time was almost twenty years after the revolution—and a decade after the ayatollah's death—when I sat in the back seat of a boxy white Paykan taxi, a warm wind threatening to blow off the big scarf that hid my hair and a tape of the Spice Girls booming from the taxi's tape deck.

En route, my old friend Lily Sadeghi and I made plans to see a Molière farce that night at one of Tehran's new cultural centers. We regretted having missed a local production of *Les Misérables,* in Persian, that had just closed after a six-month run.

"We probably wouldn't have gotten in anyway," Lily said. "It was very popular. It was always sold out."

Then we laughed about all the American tourists who had started coming to Iran again. Another group had just checked into the Laleh Hotel, the former Intercontinental renamed for the tulip, a national symbol.

Until just a few months earlier, the Laleh and most other hotels had big signs emblazoned across lobby walls or on entrance walkways for visitors to tread on that declared, in English, "DOWN WITH THE USA." They'd been put up in the heady days of 1979 after the United States Embassy seizure, at the same time that Khomeini's pledge "America will face a severe defeat" was painted across the embassy's high brick wall.

But that morning, two decades after the revolution, I'd watched a group of American tourists assemble in the Laleh's redecorated lobby. They, too, were going to visit Khomeini's tomb.

Like the world around it, Iran has been—and still is—going through a transformation. Early passions have been replaced by a hard-earned pragmatism, produced in part by revolutionary excesses that backfired against the clerics and exhausted the population. Arrogance has given way to realism. The "government of God" is ceding to secular statecraft. The passage of time has also helped to restore perspective. The shift is visible even at the tomb of the soulful Imam* who in 1979 led a widely

---

*"Imam" is a term of reverence given a Shi'ite religious leader by popular consensus rather than by formal appointment or vote. Its use is rare.

disparate movement that ended 2,500 years of monarchy and then, over the next decade, defined what would replace it.

The main chamber in the domed tomb is, indeed, magnificent. The foundation, walls and massive pillars are a polished white marble that reflects the light of chandeliers and gives the tomb an airy feeling. Persian carpets, all handwoven silks in richly textured designs denoting Iran's different provinces, adorn the floors.

In the center is a cage-like chamber of glass big enough to be a room. It is canopied in green, the color of Islam. Inside, the ayatollah lies under a six-foot-high block of marble, also covered by a green cloth. Next to the Imam, under a smaller block of marble, is his son Ahmad, who died in 1995. The official version is that Ahmad died of a heart attack, although the grapevine in conspiracy-crazed Iran claimed a variety of more sinister causes, each of which was fueled largely by the fact that Ahmad was only in his late forties.

The chamber's glass walls are covered with a silvery-metal grid, in no small part to prevent the large crowds that once assembled here from breaking through to the Imam's remains. The faithful still shudder at the memory of the chaos at Khomeini's funeral, when his shrouded body was uncovered and tossed around by mourners vying to get a last look or touch. On each side of the chamber, at eye level, is a slit through which to pass money. Rial notes used to be piled high inside around the edges. Inside the octagonal dome above Khomeini are somewhat incongruous stained-glass windows of giant red tulips with green stems crafted artistically in the simple modernistic style of New York City's "big apple." In Iran, the tulip is the symbol of martyrdom as well as the national flower.

For all its splendor, the tomb is now a place of unusual informality. Non-Muslims and foreigners are welcome; unlike in mosques, men and women mix freely together here. Out of either reverence or curiosity, almost everyone who enters heads first for Khomeini's chamber.

As I peered inside it, a small middle-aged woman next to me wept softly, reciting a prayer and touching the metal with rough hands stained with henna. Then, having paid her respects, she walked over to join a group having a picnic lunch.

Throughout the cavernous tomb, groups were spread across the carpets, eating or chatting, while children played tag or raced to slide across the marble floor in their stocking feet; two boys even kicked around a small soccer ball. Some loners, mainly but not exclusively men, were curled up against the wall napping.

Outside, on the vast plaza that surrounds the tomb, the atmosphere was quite social, almost festive. A row of outdoor cafés offered an assortment of sweet delicacies. On the other side of the plaza, souvenir kiosks sold T-shirts, beach towels, key rings, pinup posters and even large bamboo blinds featuring Khomeini's image, as well as cassette tapes of the ayatollah's last will and testament—in Persian, English, French, German and Arabic.

"With a tranquil and confident heart, joyous spirit and conscience hopeful of God's grace, I leave you, sisters and brothers, and depart for the eternal abode," one poster proclaimed, quoting Khomeini, who is depicted ascending to heaven on a rainbow.

Judging from the purchases, T-shirts were clearly more popular than the Imam's last will and testament.

Like the crumpled rials around the grave, profits from memorabilia were being used to expand the complex. Construction was already under way on an addition designed to spread across some five thousand acres and include an Islamic studies university as well as a seminary, hotels for pilgrims and a shopping mall, all at a cost of at least $2.5 billion. The tomb will eventually become the center of a suburb, complete with its own metro stop.

For a weekend afternoon, the tomb was lightly populated—roughly two hundred people in a facility that could hold several thousand. The count went up when a class of preteen girls, just old enough to don the headscarf and body cover of Islamic modesty, filed in with their teachers. The tea men at the outdoor café said the tomb still bustled at holidays and revolutionary anniversaries and during various pilgrimages.

"They keep coming and coming," said one, shaking his head, in a tone of curious disbelief that once might have been considered dangerously irreverent.

The last stop for many visitors before leaving the plaza is a large chunk of smoothed white stone that features an embossed bust of Khomeini. The image is almost translucent. That day, a few Japanese tourists and several Iranian schoolgirls were lined up to have their picture taken in front of it. With the Imam peering across their shoulders and the domed shrine in the background, the photo is the ultimate souvenir in the Islamic republic. It captures what even the most dogmatic clergy now concede is part of Iran's past.

———

THE PASSIONS once evoked by Ayatollah Khomeini may have waned, even withered, as the tough realities of running a large country with a complex economy have taken precedence. But the idea behind the revolution led by the Imam still had historic importance two decades later—perhaps in some ways even more than when it started.

Its significance also extended far beyond Iran, the Middle East, the broader Islamic world and even the twentieth century, for one simple reason: It is the last great revolution of the Modern Era.

The singular political theme of the Modern Era—and particularly the twentieth century—has been empowerment, or the spread of political, economic and social rights to the earth's farthest corners, to all its diverse ethnic groups, races, religions and, perhaps last of all, to both genders. Dozens of countries can claim revolutions in the name of empowerment since the English Revolution of the 1640s created a modern precedent. But fewer than a handful represented seminal turning points. They set the pace, defined goals, provided justification and, most important, introduced a viable new idiom of opposition later adapted or imitated elsewhere.

Two revolutions particularly shook political conventions by introducing new ideologies: In toppling the Bourbons of France, the Jacobins of the eighteenth century introduced equality and civil liberty as the basis of modern democracy. In the early twentieth century, the Bolsheviks overthrew the Russian Romanovs in favor of classless egalitarianism.

The ideas that emerged from both revolutions in turn helped to topple monarchies and petty tyrannies worldwide and then defined the political spectrum that replaced them. The pace accelerated as demand for political participation spread after World War II. However misguided in application, the empowerment embodied in democracy and socialism inspired popular uprisings from China to Cuba in the 1940s and 1950s, independence movements from Algeria to Zambia in the 1960s and 1970s and, finally, the penetration of democracy from the Soviet Union to South Africa in the 1980s and 1990s.

But that pattern of global change has had one large gap: the Islamic bloc.

The Muslim world is a vast and vital area that accounts for more than 50 of the world's 191 countries. It stretches from Indonesia on the Pacific Ocean to Morocco on the Atlantic, from Kazakhstan in chilly Central Asia to Saudi Arabia on the warm Persian Gulf, from Somalia in drought-plagued east Africa to Nigeria on Africa's fertile west coast and from Yemen on the Red Sea to Lebanon on the Mediterranean.

The Islamic bloc also accounts for one of every five people on earth—or more than one billion who have been excluded from the political process for most of the Modern Era. As home to the final functioning monarchies and the largest number of authoritarian regimes, it is today the last bloc to hold out against the tide of democratic reform that has swept the rest of the world.

In this context, Iran's upheaval is arguably the Modern Era's last great revolution. It effectively completes the process launched in the West by other ideologies that were adopted by or adapted to all other parts of the world.

Like its earlier counterparts, Iran's Islamic revolution introduced a new ideology to the world's modern political spectrum.* In a region where members of the opposition have often been imprisoned or exiled, it established the precedent of using Islam—a familiar, legitimate and widely available vehicle—to push for empowerment. It provided a format, if not a precise formula, for the last group of undemocratic regimes to make the transition. And despite Western portrayals of it as a force spinning Iran back thirteen centuries in time, the sixteen-month upheaval in Tehran demonstrated that Islam could be a distinctly modern idiom of political opposition in both tactics and goals.

The product has been unique: Although thoroughly Islamic with several unique twists, Iran has become a modern republic based on a unique blend of Islamic and European law, most notably borrowing ideas from France and Belgium. It calls for national, provincial and local elections in which all males and females vote as of age fifteen. It stipulates term limits for the presidency and allocates parliamentary seats for Christians, Jews and Zoroastrians—at least token acknowledgment of individual or minority rights.

The impact of Iran's revolution on its brethren has also been obvious: It ignited the budding Islamic movement that emerged out of the 1967 and 1973 Arab–Israeli wars and spurred on opposition movements

---

*In 1984, the State Department held a closed-door conference on Iran. Marvin Zonis, director of the University of Chicago's Middle East Institute, concluded at the time, "The message from Iran is in my opinion the single most impressive political ideology proposed in the twentieth century—since the Bolshevik Revolution. And if we accept that Bolshevism is a remnant of the nineteenth century, then I argue that we've had only one good one in the twentieth—and it's this one. . . . This powerful message will be with us for a very long time—no matter what happens to Ayatollah Khomeini."

throughout the Muslim world. In the 1980s, the trend was most visibly linked to radicalism, from plots to overthrow the emir on the tiny Persian Gulf island of Bahrain to the Islamic takeover in Sudan, Africa's largest country, from the assassination of President Anwar Sadat in Egypt to the campaign against American diplomats and Marines in Lebanon.

Less visible and more important, however, were the quiet efforts to produce Islamic alternatives to failed state institutions, from schools and clinics to farm co-ops and welfare agencies. Islamic groups struggled to create a new civil society—the network of associations, unions and clubs for workers, teachers, engineers, women, doctors, youth and other sectors that became a means of addressing problems their governments ignored.

In the 1990s, tactics among key political groups increasingly shifted from the bullet to the ballot, with the rise of political parties trying to work within the system rather than from outside it in countries such as Egypt, Jordan, Algeria, Yemen and Kuwait.

At the beginning of the twenty-first century, the trend is far from climaxing. For years, empowerment in the Islamic world will be a major theme of political change—be it peaceful as in Jordan, bloody as in Algeria, or tumultuous as in Indonesia. Iran's revolution may therefore not be the last revolution; other societies may well have national revolts that topple outdated ideological systems.

And in the end, no Islamic country is likely to duplicate the Iranian experience. Its excesses diminished interest in emulating Tehran, except among a tiny corps of extremists. The costs were too high, the results too controversial. The Shi'ite character of the revolution also makes it unlikely to be repeated among Sunni governments, which most other Muslim governments are. Finally, strong indications that the specific Iranian model may yet fail—albeit for economic rather than ideological reasons—will make other societies wary of imitating the Islamic Republic.

Yet whatever happens, Iran's revolution will still rank as the Modern Era's last great revolution, because Tehran paved the way for using Islam to push for empowerment—not only politically. Just as the Reformation was critical to the Age of Enlightenment and the birth of modern democracy in the West, so too have Iranian philosophers advanced a reformation within Islam that is critical to lasting political change.

In some ways, Iran might seem an unusual place for the last great revolution. The Islamic world is as diverse as it is vast.

But Iran is particularly unique. It is the only overwhelmingly Shi'ite country in a bloc that is some 85 percent Sunni Muslim. It is an aberration from both the Middle East and south Asia, the two regions it bridges. It is the only Muslim state of Aryan people, the Indo-European race whence Iran gets its modern name.

Ethnically it also stands alone, with Arabs to the west, the Central Asian mix to the north, Indo-Afghan-Pakistanis to the southeast and assorted Asian Muslims to the far east. Even Tajikistan, a northern neighbor and the only other Farsi-speaking country in the world, is Sunni Muslim.

Iran stands apart geographically, too, because of two great mountain ranges, the Alborz and the Zagros, and three great bodies of water, the Caspian Sea, the Persian Gulf and the Indian Ocean.

Yet those attributes are also reasons why Iran was a logical place for such sweeping political innovation.

First, Shi'ite Islam demands that the faithful fight against injustice and tyranny, even if it means certain death. Islam's so-called second sect was born out of a sense of persecution by a seventh-century dynasty that usurped leadership of the new Islamic world—and spawned a sense of outrage that lives on today. Shi'ite clerics also have a mandate to mobilize and direct their flocks into action, not just to advise them. That power explains why Ayatollah Khomeini emerged as a natural leader to unite both secular and religious opposition against a twentieth-century dynasty.

Islam, which makes no distinction between the powers of Caesar and God, had also long been a nationalist force in Iran. Shi'ism had been a source of national identity—even among those less than devout—since it was introduced in 1501 by the new Safavid Dynasty to create a sense of common identity separate from the Ottoman Empire, which was ruled by Sunni Muslims. And even into the twentieth century, Iran was a country of feudal fiefdoms, tribes and ethnic groups whose rivalries ran deep— hence the historic need for strong leadership or a binding social force, or both.

Second, Iran was politically more experienced than virtually any other Muslim state. Most countries were created or gained independence from European colonial powers only in the twentieth century. But Iran had a long, if somewhat varied, history of sovereignty.

Third, with more than 2,500 years of civilization, Iranians have a sense of historic importance and of a role in shaping the world. Iran has produced centuries' worth of great writers and philosophers. It also had the intellectual environment that stimulated questioning, new ideas and, eventually, a revolutionary spirit.

Fourth, as a crossroads between East and West and a target of invading armies from ancient Greece to contemporary Britain, Persia had long exposure to ideas from the outside world. Iranians absorbed and adapted many of the traditions, ideas and skills from other cultures to their own ways, from the early medicine of the Jews and the religion of the Arabs to English as a second language. Along the way, they were also influenced by the Greco-Roman legacy and the Judeo-Christian values that, together, formed the basis for Western revolutions since the Age of Enlightenment.[1]

Fifth, the quest for empowerment in Iran did not simply explode unpredictably in 1979. The trend of the entire century, particularly two earlier upheavals, centered on ending dynastic rule.

The Constitutional Revolution of 1905–11 was sparked by the weak Qajar Dynasty's decision to dole out political and economic concessions to Britain and Russia. Britain won the exclusive right to tap Iran's oil. To curtail powers that allowed the king to give away the country and to rid Persia of foreigners who challenged religious and social traditions, a powerful alliance of the clergy, the intelligentsia and the bazaar merchants launched a protest.[2] Prolonged instability forced the Qajar monarch, in 1906, to accept demands for Persia's first constitution and its first parliament—both of which limited the king's powers.[3]

In 1953, the last Pahlavi shah, also weak and also heavily influenced by foreign powers, faced a similar challenge from the National Front. The front, led by Prime Minister Mohammad Mossadeq, was a four-party coalition that advocated constitutional democracy and limited powers for the monarchy. But the shah's attempt to have Mossadeq dismissed backfired, forcing the monarch to flee to Rome. The last dynasty looked as if it had fizzled—until the CIA and British intelligence orchestrated riots that forced Mossadeq to resign and allowed the young king to return to the Peacock Throne for another quarter century.[4]

The revolution was thus an extension of earlier challenges. With attempts at evolutionary change repeatedly blocked, revolution became the alternative route to empowerment.

But the political endgame in 1979 marked the Modern Era's last great revolution not only because of its success in scrapping one of the world's oldest kingdoms. What happened after the revolution may be even more important, particularly the way Iranians, often in defiance of the government, adapted the Islamic system in creative and progressive ways.

During the Islamic republic's first two decades, new approaches to everyday issues produced everything from an internationally acclaimed cinema to an alternative press, from novel family-planning programs to women's activism. These nonpolitical innovations are virtually certain to produce the revolution's real legacy—and to have a far more enduring impact in the wider Islamic world than Iran's political system will have.

REVOLUTIONS ARE like fevers, Crane Brinton wrote in his classic work *The Anatomy of Revolution*. And like fevers, they progress through stages. The initial phase is marked by the onset of a raging temperature and other extreme conditions, including delirium. The next stage witnesses the breaking of the temperature and a long and fitful convalescence, often marked by a relapse or two. Finally comes the recovery and restoration to normal health.[5]

Iran's revolution may have been groundbreaking in its use of Islam as a political idiom. But when judged by Brinton's criteria, the upheaval was no different in goals or stages from the other great modern revolutions in the West, most notably in England, France and Russia. The popular uprisings led by the Independents, the Jacobins and the Bolsheviks all demanded freedom and empowerment from a privileged royal minority. So did Iran's Islamic revolutionaries.

Iran's use of religion was not even novel. It was also part of the political uprisings in Western societies.

"With the Reformation and the Renaissance, men began to think more earnestly about bringing part of heaven to this earth," Brinton wrote in 1952, a quarter century before Iran's uprising.

The Modern Era's revolutionaries were motivated by "a flaming sense of the immediacy of the ideal, a feeling that there is something in all men better than their present fate and a conviction that what is, not only ought not, but need not, be."[6]

After *anciens régimes* were ousted, earlier revolutions also invoked religious values or ideals to define goals and justify revolutionary behavior, especially during the angry early years.

"The little band of violent revolutionists who form the nucleus of all action during the Terror behave as men when under the influence of active religious faith. Independents, Jacobins, Bolsheviks all sought to make all human activity here on earth conform to an ideal pattern," Brinton wrote.

"A striking uniformity in all these is their asceticism or their condemnation of what we may call the minor as well as the major vices. Essentially, however, these patterns are a good deal alike, and all resemble closely what we may call conventional Christian ethics."[7]

During its first two decades, Iran went through all three stages of a classic revolution. By its twentieth anniversary, the process was still not quite complete, but it appeared to be headed toward some sort of climax.

The revolution's opening phase covered a full decade, from 1979 to 1989, and is often referred to as the first republic.[8] It began when Mohammad Reza Shah Pahlavi, with a small jar of Iranian soil in his hand and Empress Farah Diba at his side, reluctantly abandoned the Peacock Throne and flew off to become a political vagabond on an "open-ended vacation." The first republic lasted the entire final ten years of Ayatollah Khomeini's life, ending only with his sudden death of a heart attack.

It marked the period when the fever raged most wildly, especially between 1979 and 1982.

The strongest images of Iran's revolution come from those early years. Many still linger in the minds of outsiders: The demonstrations by rifle-toting mullahs and chador-clad women. The morgue slabs with bullet-riddled bodies of officials from the monarchy and other loyalists who were summarily executed in the course of revolutionary justice. The seizure of the United States Embassy and fifty-two hostages who, over the next 444 days, were often paraded with crude blindfolds in front of cameras as effigies of Uncle Sam were burned in the background by angry youths. This was the delirium.

It was also the period of the toughest challenges. In a lightning 1980 invasion ordered by President Saddam Hussein, Iraq swiftly captured thousands of square miles of Iran, including several strategic oil fields. Since Iraq invaded shortly after most of the shah's military had fled or been imprisoned or executed, Iran's physical survival was suddenly precarious.

But the greatest trauma was the political bloodshed and turmoil as the fragile young Islamic Republic of Iran struggled to create a whole new system of rule. The revolutionaries who came to power knew virtually nothing about running a state. A lot was improvised.

"The important thing about this revolution is that it didn't have any prepared plan, what was *exactly* planned for the economy or industry or anything else," Kamal Kharrazi, chief of the Islamic Republic News Agency, told me in the 1980s.

"We've been developing experience as we go along," added Kharrazi, who went on to become Iran's United Nations ambassador and then foreign minister.

Iran's emergence as a modern theocracy was never written in the heavens. Quite the contrary. In earlier pronouncements about a just government, Ayatollah Khomeini actually said he didn't advocate clerical rule.

"Rather we say that government must be run in accordance with God's law," he wrote, referring to Islamic laws known as the Sharia.[9]

And in one of his last interviews before leaving Paris, Ayatollah Khomeini told *Le Monde,* "Our intention is not that religious leaders should themselves administer the state."[10]

Once the tumultuous fanfare of his return died down, the Imam seemed almost uninterested in day-to-day government affairs. The ayatollah, already in his late seventies, instead went back to the dusty theological center of Qom. He seemed content to leave politics to the first revolutionary government of secular technocrats. His role was limited to settling disputes, with guidance relayed either through his son Ahmad or to government officials who made the pilgrimage to Qom.

The very idea of mullahs involved in government was actually anathema among Shi'ites, who historically were wary of political power.

The turning point was the furor over a new constitution in the autumn of 1979. The disparate parties to the revolution had vastly different visions of a new state.

The first two formal drafts called for a strong president, based on the French model, to lead the nation. Both were largely secular in structure. Neither mentioned special powers for the clergy. But secular parties balked. They wanted other changes or further reviews or simply more input. So Iran was thrown into even deeper debates. The compromise was a proposal to elect an Assembly of Experts to sort through the differences and to write a final draft for the nation to vote on.

That was the moment Iran's future was formally hijacked by the clergy.

Fearful that other changes might further marginalize or even exclude them, Ayatollah Khomeini's followers introduced a process to vet candidates' credentials—a precedent that time and again allowed them to manipulate future elections too. It worked. They won a majority. And the final draft ended up thoroughly Islamic.

The most important change was at the top. The presidency was weakened to titular status—to avoid a strong head of government creating a new dynasty, as had happened with the first Pahlavi king. Real leadership was instead invested in a Supreme Leader, a Velayat-e Faqih, commonly called a Faqih.

The position was created to check secular influences in all branches of government and to keep the revolution on an Islamic course. But it also had appointment powers over the judiciary and the military. It had ultimate veto power over candidates. It included the title of commander in chief. And in a departure from the rules established for the other branches of government, the term was for life.

The Supreme Leader was the closest thing to a political papacy in any government in the world.

The idea grew in part out of Ayatollah Khomeini's fascination with Plato's *Republic,* which he'd studied as a young theologian. The Faqih was adapted from Plato's idea of a philosopher-king—with an Islamic twist.[11]

The overall product was also one of the world's most unusual political systems.

Borrowing from Western models, the republican constitution called for three separate branches of government—executive, judicial and legislative—to provide checks and balances. But the theocracy also had another parallel layer of power: Virtually every branch of government had a shadow position or institution with equal power—at *least* equal—usually led by, loyal to or largely made up of clerics.

In the military, the regular army, navy and air force had shadow counterparts in the Revolutionary Guards and the Basij, the militia of young volunteers later made famous when dispatched in human waves against Iraqi tanks and artillery.

In law enforcement, the police for years had a counterpart in the *komitehs,* the neighborhood committees that served as watchdogs—more like rottweilers, actually—on social behavior. The two forces were eventually merged. But after the war, the Basij often stepped in to perform the same kind of jobs.

In the judiciary, the civil and criminal courts had counterparts in the

Revolutionary Courts headed by clerics that tried subversive crimes considered to be challenges to the revolutionary system—always in closed-door proceedings.

In the legislative branch, the Iranian Parliament's 270 members were shadowed by the 12-member Council of Guardians, which was empowered to veto new laws if they were deemed un-Islamic and to vet the credentials of candidates for public office. The conflicts between the two bodies became so heated that Ayatollah Khomeini created the Expediency Council in the mid-1980s to arbitrate between Parliament and the Council of Guardians. Along the way, however, it has also become a policymaker, advising the Supreme Leader on major controversies and offering verdicts on issues that couldn't be solved through regular channels.[12]

In local government, the provincial governors, appointed by the Ministry of Interior in Tehran, had to watch over their shoulders for what was said by the local Friday prayer leaders appointed by the Supreme Leader.

Even the formal economy had its counterpart in the myriad foundations that were technically offshoots of government but in fact operated on their own—and controlled an extraordinary percentage of the Iranian economy.

Last but not least, the presidency had its shadow in the Supreme Leader.

But the constitution didn't mark the end of the transformation—or the turmoil.

For the first presidential election in January 1980, a full year after the revolution, Ayatollah Khomeini decreed that no clerics could run for president—further proof that he still didn't intend to establish a total theocracy.

Over the next eighteen months, however, Iran was racked by bloodshed as the ruling clergy and their adjutants gradually eliminated former partners—leftists, nationalists and intellectuals—from any claim to power. The reign of terror sparked equally bloody counterattacks. In 1981, more than a thousand officials were killed by former allies who'd turned against the revolution.

The Islamic republic had a particular problem keeping its presidents. In June 1981, its first president, Abolhassan Bani-Sadr, was forced to go underground, dressed as a woman. He later fled the country altogether when heated clashes with the clerics led Parliament to declare him "politically incompetent." The second president was killed in an August 1981 bombing only five weeks after his election. The bomb went off, ironically, during a secret meeting to discuss attacks that had killed two hundred officials, including ten cabinet ministers and twenty-seven members of Parliament in a June bombing.[13]

So for the third time in twenty-one months and the second time in ten weeks, Iranians went to the polls to elect a new president in October 1981. This time, using his powers as Faqih, the Imam reversed his ban. The clergy was allowed to run.

The victor was Ali Khamenei, a taciturn cleric with oversized black glasses and a bushy salt-and-pepper beard extending onto his chest whose rise to power was due more to connections and accidents of history than scholarship. A former Khomeini student and disciple jailed three times by the shah, he'd also been in the headlines. He'd been seriously wounded as he led a Friday prayer service in Tehran the day before the mass bombing in June. A small bomb had been planted in a tape recorder on the dais.

President Khamenei's election marked a critical turning point. As of October 1981, the mullahs were no longer only the supervisors and shadows of the state. They now dominated all its branches.

Iran, officially, had a government of God—a process that had taken more than two and a half years.

As it tightened its hold on power, the new Islamic government also moved, between 1979 and 1982, to reshape every aspect of Iranian society, from schoolbooks and dress codes to music. There were few exceptions.

Changes were visible even on Tehran's streets. During rush hour on a dusky summer evening, I once watched an old blind violin player, led by a young boy, work his way down the middle of Tehran's busiest intersection. As the blind beggar played, the boy temporarily abandoned him in traffic to dart to car windows for coins.

"He's been here forever, since I was fifteen," said my driver, then well into middle age, as he handed money to the child. "He used to play jazz and popular Iranian music," the lilting love sonnets by great Persian lyricists, such as fourteenth-century poet Hafez, whose words were set to music.

"But since the revolution all that's forbidden," the driver said. "Now he plays only Islamic music and the anthem—mostly the anthem."

The streets themselves also became vehicles for the revolution. Wide boulevards honoring Roosevelt, Eisenhower and Elizabeth, the British queen who once visited Tehran, had been renamed, some with wry touches. Elizabeth Street, near the British Embassy, was renamed for Bobby Sands, after the Irish Republican Army leader who fasted to death in prison to protest British rule. The street named for Los Angeles, home to Hollywood, had been changed to Hejab, the name for modest Islamic dress required of all women.

Lest Tehranis forgot what the revolution was about, the revolution even had its own street graffiti to remind them. On the brick walls downtown, neat calligraphy repeatedly pronounced, "Our duty is to protect Islam." At Niavaran Palace, one of the shah's former residences, the exterior wall was adorned with instructions from Ayatollah Khomeini: "Talk about God and don't think about anything else."

During the first republic, Iran also pushed to expand its Islamic ideology and influence beyond its borders. The years 1983 through 1986 were the most aggressive. At home, the mullahs completed the process of "cleansing" schools and universities, penal codes, banking laws, cultural outlets and the media of non-Islamic practices. People who would not conform were next.

They also radically altered the status quo in the region. Once the protector of the Persian Gulf, Iran became its biggest threat as it sought to propagate militant Islam through a wide network of allies and surrogates. The challenge extended beyond states in the vicinity to others farther afield in the West, as Iran helped redefine terrorism and its tactics. Terms such as "suicide bomber" entered the lexicon of conflict.

On the war front, Iran began to turn the tide in a series of bold counteroffensives against Iraq's better-equipped and better-trained army. Tehran's only edge was a corps of young volunteers wearing headbands that declared their desire to become martyrs. Many eventually became human minesweepers, and the conflict soon became the bloodiest of modern Middle East wars. But not even Baghdad's introduction of chemical weapons could stop the Iranians.

At one point in 1986, a U.S. intelligence estimate suggested Iran might actually be capable of winning the war.

But the costs of Iran's expansionist goals, political arrogance and economic isolation were high. The revolution began to falter in late 1986. At home, public sentiment grew restless and then angry from the combined toll of the war, rationing of basic foodstuffs and internal wrangling. New U.S. embargoes on oil and other Iranian exports after the disastrous arms-for-hostages swap collapsed added to the growing economic squeeze. Iran lost ground against Iraq, until, by mid-1988, the front line was back to where it was in the war's early days.

The impact was widely visible in Tehran. Elaborate portraits of the Imam, his dark brow furrowed and his hand raised in exhortation, began to fade from billboards and the sides of high-rise buildings. To ensure a decent turnout at Friday prayers, public rallies and even elections, the faithful often had to be rounded up or prodded into attending. Graffiti on fences, highway underpasses and public walls dared to criticize the regime. Even clerics were disgruntled.

A conversation overheard at a Tehran pharmacy between the chemist, a female customer and a cleric waiting for a prescription was telling. As the woman paid her bill, she complained to the chemist about rising prices.

Pointing at the mullah, the chemist replied, "Don't tell me, tell him."

"It's not my fault. It's the fault of this regime," the mullah said. "I'm only responsible for a poor group at a mosque. I get a small salary and I have to feed my family too."

Clearly frustrated himself, he then blurted out, "We really had better conditions during the shah's time."

The revolution reached the first of two near-breaking points in the final year of Khomeini's life. To survive, the regime was forced from mid-1988 to mid-1989 to end its aggressive thrusts on several fronts and begin a retreat. It started when Tehran accepted United Nations terms for a ceasefire in August 1988. The Imam said the decision was like drinking from a poisoned chalice. But he had little choice.

With the war over, the regime then turned inward. To ease public discontent at home, rigid strictures both big and small were relaxed. Revolutionary committees, or *komitehs,* that monitored public compliance with Islamic regulations were reined in. Sporadic nighttime roadblocks were eased. Iran's movie industry moved from themes of war and revolution to love and adventure. The *bazaaris,* or merchant class, won guarantees that foreign trade would not be nationalized. Chess, once forbidden as a form of gambling, was again permitted. And pale nail polish became permissible.

Tehran even made overtures to Western capitals and used its leverage to help win release of Western hostages in Lebanon. Through trade, relations began to improve. The revolutionary fever looked as though it was about to break.

But while the vast majority of Iranians both inside the regime and outside were ready to move on, Khomeini was apparently not willing to compromise his vision. As Iran celebrated its tenth anniversary, in early 1989, the ayatollah abruptly issued a fatwa sentencing Salman Rushdie to death for his controversial book *The Satanic Verses*. The Imam decreed that the novel, which had fictional dream sequences attributed to the prophet Mohammad, was blasphemous against Islam and all Muslims. Ayatollah Khomeini's death sentence froze rapprochement with the outside world.

In a second move that threatened the revolution's own future stability, the Imam then fired his handpicked successor, Ayatollah Ali Montazeri. On the revolution's tenth anniversary, Montazeri had dared to criticize it. He publicly conceded that the Islamic republic had failed to fulfill much of its early promise. He condemned the mass executions. And he called on the government to "correct past mistakes."

After the Imam's fatwa against Rushdie, he also warned, "People in the world are getting the idea that our business in Iran is just murdering people."[14]

Ayatollah Khomeini had a broader goal in both draconian steps: He wanted to steer the revolution back onto its original course. The singular theme of the Khomeini decade had been deconstruction—of the monarchy, of foreign influences that flavored everything from education and business priorities to fashion, of the regional balance of power and of longstanding diplomatic and economic alliances. The Imam feared any relaxation might eventually dilute the Islamic agenda. So he pulled in the reins. Then he died.

The Islamic Republic did manage to survive the first republic and its most radical phase, despite stiff odds. But the sudden death of the Imam, whose unparalleled power and charisma could not be replaced by any single individual, left the Islamic Republic facing very mixed signals about what was supposed to happen next.

THE REVOLUTION'S second phase began after Ayatollah Khomeini's death and covered the next eight years, from mid-1989 to mid-1997. It basically coincided with—and centered on—the two presidential terms of Ali Akbar Hashemi Rafsanjani, whose wily charm, accessibility and Cheshire cat grin made him Iran's most popular and able politician. The so-called second republic marked the period of attempted convalescence.

The core issue of the second republic was whether the Islamic Republic would—or even could—move beyond Khomeini-ism. The shift didn't necessarily mean rejecting the Imam or denying the importance of Islam, but it did mean changing priorities and practices.

President Rafsanjani started out strong. Shortly before being elected, he redesigned the power structure and strengthened his own position by orchestrating constitutional amendments while he was speaker of Parliament. One change scrapped the prime minister's job and converted the presidency, a former figurehead position, into the top government job. The other major change weakened the role of Ayatollah Khomeini's successor.

The hastily selected new Supreme Leader was the former president, Ali Khamenei, a mid-ranking cleric who had just as hastily been elevated to the rank of ayatollah. He retained political powers but lost the role of top religious authority.

The new balance of power effectively positioned President Rafsanjani to define the post-Khomeini era. But the changes also reflected his goals. Iran's fourth president sought to fashion a durable state as the basis of authority and to make its survival less dependent on the credentials, personality or clout of the Supreme Leader.

President Rafsanjani then moved to change the other political players. During his first term, from 1989 to 1993, he expended much of his clout purging radicals who had a stranglehold on policy and who were most tied to the militancy that had ruined Iran's reputation abroad. The process took the better part of three years, but he eventually replaced the angry ideologues of the first republic with technocrats holding Western Ph.D.s and, in Parliament, with conservatives. Efficiency became a more important qualification than piety.

President Rafsanjani didn't intend to abandon Islam, but he did want to introduce pragmatism and soften the Islamic Republic's sharp ideological edge. He also wanted to shift the emphasis from deconstruction to reconstruction—of the physical and psychological damage from the war with Iraq, of the tattered economy and of an inefficient political system. That meant less interest in how many people went to mosques and more concern about how many people had jobs, homes, schooling or health care.

A free-market mullah and son of a major pistachio producer, President Rafsanjani fashioned an agenda centered on reform, including privatization of many businesses nationalized after the revolution, opening up the country to foreign investment forbidden since the revolution and stronger diplomatic ties with the outside world, eventually including the United States. The shift was in many ways comparable to the overhauls in Eastern Europe after the demise of Communism. The new president was actually trying to move Iran into a groove with the rest of the world.

In some cases, the changes marked virtual reversals. The stock market started by the shah reopened in new offices fitted with a gleaming marble, glass and brass decor and Western computers. A lottery was launched, indicating that Iranians were no longer required to depend only on the benevolence of God for good fortune. Free-trade zones were created to encourage foreign capital. And diatribes about the need for social justice were replaced with detailed plans for "shock therapy" and belt-tightening in language right out of the International Monetary Fund in Washington, D.C.

The shift was reflected in the signs along Vali-e Asr Street, Tehran's main drag. Graffiti on a concrete wall quoting the Imam—"Defending Islam is as important today as it was when the religion was founded and it requires sacrifice"—were barely readable. Next to the wall was an enormous new billboard with a picture of actor Donald Pleasance advertising Swatch watches.

At first, Tehran did exude a new sense of energy and mission. Sandbags from the war years disappeared and windows boarded or taped to minimize the impact of broken glass from incoming Iraqi missiles were cleaned off. New housing projects, shopping malls, office blocks and even private villas shot up. Billboard space that had for years extolled the revolution or condemned the greater and lesser Satans started advertising European appliances and Japanese electronics. Empty lots were converted into public parks. Western plays, from Chekhov's *Uncle Vanya* to Arthur Miller's *The Crucible,* opened in Tehran theaters.

The regime would have denied vehemently that it had abandoned so-called "barefoot Islam" for "American Islam" or "capitalist Islam," in the jargon of the time. But President Rafsanjani's plans did effectively desert the oppressed masses, or *mostazafin,* in whose name the revolution had theoretically been undertaken. They stood to lose the most, especially after the technocrats proposed eliminating subsidies for basic foodstuffs badly needed by a burgeoning population under ever greater economic pressure.

But the convalescence proved fitful. The momentum behind recovery faced repeated challenges—and relapses. The system simply was unwilling to tolerate the medicine required to strengthen the regime and return Iran to normal health.

And without Ayatollah Khomeini's balancing act, the long-simmering divisions among the disparate revolutionary factions came to a boil.

President Rafsanjani's masterful purge of radicals also backfired. The new crop of political, social and fiscal conservatives who replaced the militants in 1992 parliamentary elections turned out to be as much of a problem—at least. They obstructed new laws needed for reform. They removed key technocrats, including the minister of finance, for trying to restore Western-style capitalism, and the culture and Islamic guidance minister, a little-known figure named Mohammad Khatami, for tolerating too much internal cultural expression and too much of everything from the outside world. In the end, the conservatives blocked the big cuts in subsidies too.

The clampdown hit society hard. After President Rafsanjani's social relaxation led women to wear scarves pushed back so a little hair showed, gangs of young zealots went on the rampage through several Tehran hairdressers' shops, ripping hairstyle photos from the wall.[15] When Iranian television, then headed by the president's brother, attempted to introduce more entertainment, conservatives protested in Parliament.

Progress was soon paralyzed. And public disillusionment set in.

In 1993, halfway through the second republic, disappointment was tangible when President Rafsanjani ran for a second term. Public apathy was so high that only 57 percent of the electorate showed up at the polls—for a leader who was widely seen as more of a politician than a cleric and who had once been heralded as Iran's political healer. Even among those who voted, President Rafsanjani hardly scored the kind of landslide victory he had won in 1989.

The sense of hope that the "Teflon mullah" had once represented was replaced by feelings of indifference, even betrayal.

During President Rafsanjani's second term, from 1993 to 1997, the revolution began to turn on itself. Divisions penetrated even deeper. The increasingly tense alliance between the president and the Supreme Leader often broke down. As debate erupted over the powers of a Supreme Leader and even the need for one, Ayatollah Khamenei cozied up to the conservatives led by Parliamentary Speaker Ali Akbar Nateq-Nouri. Together they stymied the executive branch—and debate about reform.

The system began to atrophy—and then unravel. President Rafsanjani was gradually rendered politically impotent. Meanwhile, Parliament passed no major legislation from 1992 to 1996. It was instead self-absorbed by moral issues, such as the impact of videos on public mores.

Daily life once more became more restricted. In the mid-1990s, tens of thousands were arrested for "social corruption," while more than a million were warned about errant behavior—from improper Islamic attire to possession of illegal videotapes.[16] In 1995, despite President Rafsanjani's opposition, the Parliament also outlawed satellite dishes.

The government of God had reasserted itself and then declared its monopoly on truth. The tentative openings of the late 1980s and early 1990s ended. Major problems went unanswered. Per capita income, halved during the first republic, sank further.[17] Iran's Chamber of Commerce admitted that by 1996 up to 40 percent of Iranians lived below the poverty line or barely above it; diplomats pegged the figure closer to 60 percent.[18] The middle class—the essential element in the survival of any revolutionary ideology and especially any democracy—began to dwindle.

Young men in military fatigues once again appeared on Tehran's streets, although not to indicate a security threat or revolutionary zeal. Military wear became popular because it was the cheapest clothing available due to overproduction during the war with Iraq. Fatigues became a sign of poverty.

Even some of the regime's most ardent supporters began to believe that the Islamic leadership had left them behind. Sporadic unrest erupted in Tehran, Mashhad, Shiraz, Qazvin and Arak. Thousands were involved in smaller pockets of unrest over high prices and housing shortages. Despite the stiff Islamic penal code, crime soared. Even diplomats were victimized at their guarded residences.

The end of the second republic marked the second near-breaking point. Indeed, on the eve of elections to replace President Rafsanjani, the revolution was on the verge of imploding. Instead of an idyllic state with godly virtues, Iran in mid-1997 was a country rife with corruption more extensive than during the Pahlavi Dynasty, paralyzed politically by irreconcilable factional disputes and sinking fast economically. It was, in many ways, in worse condition than at the end of the first republic.

The Islamic Republic was on a precipice.

———

A FUNNY thing then happened on the way to the polls. In May 1997, Iran's political pendulum seemed about to swing to the far right. The first republic had been dominated by radicals. The second republic was led by pragmatic technocrats in the political center. The poll to elect President Rafsanjani's successor appeared to be headed toward a conservative victory, consolidating the right's hold on power.

Indeed, the election had widely been considered a done deal more than a year before it took place. The Supreme Leader, senior judges, top military officers and a majority in Parliament all backed Speaker of Parliament Nateq-Nouri, one of the half-dozen leading conservatives. Then more than two hundred other candidates who registered to run were disqualified by the Council of Guardians. Never had Iranian officials been so blatant in their backing of a single candidate.

But the strategy backfired.

Public disgust was so deep that Nateq-Nouri was trampled at the polls by a dark-horse candidate named Mohammad Khatami, who campaigned for restoration of the rule of law and the creation of a civil society. Khatami, ironically, had also been the minister of culture and Islamic guidance purged by conservatives for his tolerance of diversity. In 1992, he had been almost literally shelved, forced into intellectual exile as head of the National Library.

But in 1997, after a twelve-day campaign, he swept the four-way race with just under 70 percent of the vote. Voters turned out in greater numbers than at any election since the first poll a generation earlier to endorse the revolution.

"Voting for Khatami was like falling in love. You don't quite know how it happens. You can't explain the reasons," reflected Nasser Hadian, a thoughtful Tehran University political scientist with a bushy mop of black hair who'd long been one of my guides in the maze of Iranian politics.

"Some of the vote was a no vote against Nateq-Nouri and the conservatives. But most were yes for Khatami. It was the way he talked, the way he looked, the way voters identified with him, the way they felt they could trust him.

"Five or six people in my family had never voted before, in twenty years, but this time they went to the polls. They wanted to vote," Hadian added.

Iranians had embraced the idea of reform and rejected an increasingly abusive and authoritarian regime. En masse, Iran had voted for change—a first.

The election put an abrupt end to eight years of the second republic.[19]

The election may also have marked the onset of recovery—a revolution's third and final phase. President Khatami certainly started off in a healthy direction. During his first eighteen months, he launched new initiatives and encouraged or tolerated many others generated outside government. The revolution's red lines began to be eased and even erased.

He also called for the formation of political parties to enshrine diversity. Local elections were held in early 1999 to disperse power at last beyond the center, as was originally mandated in the constitution but had never been carried out. Movies and books once banned were released. Licenses were granted to dozens of newspapers and magazines, many of which defined the new cutting edge of freedom in Iran with exposés on senior military officers, satires on the system and even interviews with American officials. Most important to the average Iranian, fear and tension were replaced with prospects of change and hope.

Iran's new president also took bold steps to improve relations with the outside world. In a widely watched CNN interview with Christiane Amanpour, President Khatami called for cultural exchanges between Iranians and Americans and other steps to bring down the "wall of mistrust." The first exchange was, perhaps appropriately, between championship wrestlers—first in Tehran, then in Stillwater, Oklahoma—in a mimic of the Ping-Pong diplomacy that had launched detente between the United States and China in the 1970s. His foreign minister also orchestrated an end to tension with Arab neighbors, most notably Saudi Arabia, and the decade-long impasse over Salman Rushdie. Both steps paved the way for detente with Europe.

President Khatami didn't deserve full credit for Iran's movement, since he didn't initiate the trend. His actions were a response to a popular mandate. Indeed, what most distinguished the third republic from the two earlier phases—and what gave it the greatest prospect of enduring—was the fact that leadership increasingly came from the streets, not mosques or political offices.

Like other revolutions, Iran's upheaval was about empowerment, and arguably for the first time since the shah's overthrow people had the power in the 1997 election to change the leadership—and potentially some fundamentals of the system. That's why they turned out in droves to vote. With the electoral upset, the process of empowerment looked as if it had finally begun.

But President Khatami was the one to pay the price for attempting change. Almost immediately, he faced a backlash from conservatives who had not only lost, but who also suddenly faced the possibility of being marginalized without even having had their turn at the top.

Some of the problems were the same President Rafsanjani had encountered: The Supreme Leader was unwilling to cede control of Iran's agenda to the president. The gap between the two men's positions quickly reached an unprecedented divide, even though both clerics were former protégés of Ayatollah Khomeini whose families once vacationed together. Parliament's conservative majority was also unwilling to tolerate changes that would decentralize power to the masses.

To keep the new crop of reformers off-track, conservatives in several government branches diverted political attention with a slew of trumped-up crises: Tehran's popular mayor, who also had helped run President Khatami's campaign, was convicted of graft in a transparently political trial. Student rallies to back Khatami were disrupted by gangs of political thugs. A parliamentary petition proclaimed that the Rushdie death sentence still applied and a foundation upped the multimillion-dollar bounty on his head. New media voices were silenced for not being Islamic enough. And in the most ominous development, five dissident writers and thinkers were found brutally murdered.

Once again, the revolution appeared to be suffering a relapse.

On its twentieth anniversary, in 1999, Iran faced real questions about whether Khatami's election would ever produce a real recovery. If it didn't, the Islamic republic faced the strong prospect of a serious setback that, if untreated, could even prove terminal. As in the Soviet Union and Eastern Europe, once the idea of change was introduced the public quest for reform was simply too strong to prevent it from continuing—one way or another. The impact of small openings had been to further whet the public appetite, not sate it.

The ability of a minority within the regime to block an overwhelming popular mandate certainly offered strong reasons for pessimistic predictions, at least in the short term. But from a historic perspective, the course of other modern revolutions also suggested that Iran, eventually, could recover and evolve into a more normal state—perhaps even in a somewhat different form from that of the current Islamic republic.

Brinton explained the pattern: "In all our societies, the crisis period was followed by a convalescence . . . [when] the religious lust for perfection, the crusade for the Republic of Virtue, died out, save among a tiny minority whose actions could no longer take place directly in politics. An active proselytizing, intolerant, ascetic, chiliastic faith became fairly rapidly an inactive, indifferent, worldly ritualistic faith."[20]

As the Islamic Republic began its third decade, vast numbers of Iranians were indeed indifferent about an ideology that once inspired them to revolt. Public zealotry and passionate displays of piety had largely disappeared. As faith once again became a private rather than a public practice, Iran's mosques were virtually empty. Widespread complaints about the noise from mosques even forced the office of Ayatollah Khamenei to appeal to clergy throughout Iran to turn down their muezzins.

Mosque services "should not be a nuisance to the public," said a statement released on the anniversary of the prophet Mohammad's birth in mid-1998. "Loudspeakers should not disturb neighbors and should be turned up only during calls to prayers."[21]

Islam began to bear the brunt of the blame for the clerics' failures. A noble religion was hurt by the practitioners' clumsy and ineffective tactics. By 1999, Iranians were far more absorbed in the basic issues of daily survival than in grand ideology.

"None of our revolutions quite ended in the death of civilization and culture. The network was stronger than the forces trying to destroy or alter it,"[22] Brinton wrote of the final stage of revolutions.

"Societies which undergo the full cycle of revolution are perhaps in some respects the stronger for it. But they by no means emerge entirely remade."[23]

As the twenty-first century began, the Islamic revolution appeared to be right on course.

ONE WAY of judging the impact of the revolution—and its success or failure—was by probing Iranian feelings about the monarchy it replaced. It served as a barometer.

Stories abounded. I knew the theocracy was in trouble in 1992 when I met a taxi driver who so disliked the regime that he had named his first son Mohammad and the second one Reza—after the last shah.

As Iran's economy crumbled, as hardships increased and as people started taking second and third jobs, I often heard irreverent Iranian humor offer a cynical spin. One popular story involved a conversation between Imam Khomeini and a martyr—or, in Persian, *shahid.*

"Tell me about paradise, Imam," said the *shahid.*

"Well," replied Ayatollah Khomeini, "there's always wonderful weather in paradise. There are lots of trees and the water is very pure."

"What else?" asked the *shahid.*

"All the foods, including the finest meat and lots of fruit, are available," the ayatollah said. "People have only one job and there are many ways to engage in pleasure."

The *shahid* pressed for more, so Khomeini continued, "There's no tension with anyone and everybody's happy."

"So how would you characterize paradise?" asked the *shahid.*

"Well," said Khomeini, "it's very much like the time of the shah."

The context of the joke was the shah's time, when oil prices were high, trade bustled and Iran was at peace with the outside world. Proud to the point of arrogance about their millennia-old civilization, Iranians have been particularly bothered about being spurned by the outside world—and lesser civilizations—since the revolution.

"A lot of people would like to return to the times of the monarchy. Iran was prosperous and popular then. Everyone came through Tehran," a young man who worked as both a bus driver and shoe salesman once told me.

Indeed, I remembered the days from my first trip to Iran in 1973, when jumbo jets landed daily in Tehran from both major Western cities like Paris and New York and Eastern capitals such as Beijing and Tokyo. Big hotel chains—Hilton, Sheraton, Hyatt and Intercontinental—teemed with tourists, businessmen, diplomats and literati.

"Now we're treated as outcasts," the bus-driving shoe salesman lamented. "Few foreigners come here anymore, and it's almost impossible for ordinary Iranians to get visas to go abroad. We'd probably be all alone if it weren't for our oil."

But the nostalgia is distinctly not for the shah or his family, as I learned when I visited Saadabad, a compound of palaces and villas that were once inhabited by the Qajar and Pahlavi Dynasties, the last two families to sit on the legendary Peacock Throne.

After the 1979 revolution, Saadabad was opened to the public. The crowds were initially large. A visit was a tangible symbol of empowerment. Many years later, it still was. On the day I visited in 1995, a class of schoolkids played on the grounds inside the high fences that once held off the public. The people were sharing in the monarchy's wealth.

"I saw the shah pass by every day," a gardener who had worked there for a quarter century told me as he washed away leaves and debris with a thick fire hose.

"He never waved, smiled or said anything to any of us. I don't think he even saw us. We were like slaves, so I was happy about the revolution. Now I do the same job, but when I plant flowers in the spring and fall it's for everybody."

Saadabad was supposed to expose the extravagance and elitism of the monarchy. And to a certain extent, it achieves that goal. The sprawling sanctuary, spread out in a forest of white birches and towering pines, is in wealthy north Tehran as it rises into the foothills of the Alborz Mountains. The sweet air is refreshing compared with the clouds of pollution sitting low over the city center or the searing heat in the southern desert around Khomeini's tomb. The sounds of birds and geese are a relief from honking taxis and muffler-challenged trucks that crowd the capital's streets. The compound is so large that it's a virtual suburb unto itself, complete with its own bus system. It's probably the only suburb in the world made up only of museums.

The first attraction at Saadabad is a massive pair of bronzed boots, eight or so feet high, just inside the entrance. They're all that's left of a giant statue of Shah Reza Pahlavi, the founder of Iran's last dynasty and the father of the last shah. A self-educated army colonel, Reza Khan wrested power in 1926 from an interim government that ruled after the Qajar Dynasty's collapse. Reza Khan took the name Pahlavi, crowned himself king and went on to forcibly modernize Iran. For his pro-Nazi sympathies, the Allies forced him to abdicate in 1941 in favor of his son. He died in exile in South Africa. Years later, the revolution literally cut him off at the knees.

Saadabad's centerpiece is one of the two major palaces used by the last shah, Mohammad Reza Pahlavi. It's an undistinguished modern building of dull concrete and rather boxy in shape that reflects none of Persia's grand contributions to architecture. Inside, the dated decor imitates Western tastes, from gold flocked wallpaper and copies of Louis XIV furniture to Italian chandeliers and mediocre European art from the late nineteenth and early twentieth centuries on the walls.

"The shah's bed, in gold satin, is a replica of the one used by Napoleon. The cream-and-blue bed in Empress Farah's room duplicates Josephine's," explained a young docent named Mariam, a student in museum studies who was a toddler when the shah and his wife fled. I fully expected her to add, "What else would you expect?"

For many Iranians, the Pahlavis were the antithesis of the country's proud traditions. They secularized society, diminishing Iran's Zoroastrian and Islamic past. Rather than interacting with the outside world, they copied it. Reza Shah even changed the country's name, from Persia to Iran, after the Indo-European Aryans who settled in Iran before Christianity.

But Saadabad was actually more pitiful than impressive. Many of its precious pieces were nicked in the revolution's chaotic early days. Replacements were brought in from other palaces or wealthy homes confiscated from Iranians who fled the revolution. Among the few valuables left behind were three porcelain birds by Edward Marshall Boehm given to the shah by President Nixon in 1972 and an intricate Kerman silk carpet of over 435 square feet. But even the rug was merely a copy of a famous sixteenth-century carpet. Perhaps deliberately, the only gold left in the main palace, in an overwhelmingly Muslim land where liquor was illegal, was on the rim of the shah's wineglasses.

Saadabad was also a lonely place. Besides the schoolchildren and a handful of out-of-towners, the few others wandering the empty halls of its palaces when I was there were also foreigners—Indian diplomats, Canadian businessmen and Japanese tourists.

"In the early days, there were many visitors. People were curious," a guide told me, offering a probable explanation for the layers of dark finger smudges on the wall. "Now there are only a few. There's not much interest anymore." His comment seemed to be a political assessment as well as a tourism head count.

Whatever the public's frustrations with the revolution, Iranians generally had so little feeling about the monarchy in the late 1990s that they didn't even have much anger or curiosity anymore. The image that summed it all up was in the imperial dining room, where a long table had been lavishly set for sixteen years. But the fine crystal and china were now covered with a light film and the candles had bent over like wilted flowers. The dust had long settled on the monarchy.

CHAPTER 2

THE ISLAMIC REFORMATION

Cling to freedom, because among God's favorite cre-
ations, freedom is most beautiful and delicate. Tolerate
the thorn for the sake of the beauty of the flower.
—ABDUL KARIM SOROUSH[1]

Much too often, will and freedom of thought have
been frustrated and liberty suffocated in the name of
salvation.
—PRESIDENT MOHAMMAD KHATAMI[2]

ABDUL KARIM SOROUSH IS an unassuming figure. He's small and
his brown beard is neat. His hair is receding, although he looks a decade
younger than he is. And he's so soft-spoken that hearing him is sometimes
difficult.

The first time we talked, in 1994, Soroush was seated behind a fat oak
table amid stacks of precisely piled books that made him seem almost
fragile. Soft music hummed in the background of his Tehran office as he
discussed the lilting Persian poetry of Hafez and Rumi that he'd memorized as a youth and the work of Western philosophers that he'd studied

at the University of London. He quoted easily from Descartes and Locke and Hegel and Kant.

"I'm not an important man," he insisted when I asked about the impact of his work. "I'm just a writer and a thinker and I'm just toying with ideas about religion."

But Iran's leading philosopher was by then already emerging as one of the most provocative figures in the country, both for his ideas and for the change he symbolized. Both supporters and critics compared him to great reformers within Christianity.

Some even called him the Martin Luther of Islam, after the sixteenth-century German maverick who revolutionized Christianity.

I'd first heard about Soroush in a Tehran University classroom a couple of years earlier. Students in a political science class talked excitedly about his latest writings. A magazine called *Kiyan,* which means "source" or "foundation," had just been launched to publish his columns—and the fiery debates they ignited. During subsequent visits to Iran, his name came up more and more often in discussions at coffeehouses, seminaries, bookshops, think tanks and newspaper offices. His work was at the heart of a growing debate within Iran about both its political future and the evolution of Islam as a faith.

By the mid-1990s, Soroush was pulling in overflow crowds wherever he appeared. Friends and young clerics organized informal talks at various mosques on Thursday evenings, the equivalent of Saturday night for Muslims, that attracted hundreds who spilled onto surrounding streets and alleys. Loudspeakers eventually had to be installed. Whether they sat at his feet or on the curb outside, most who came furiously took notes. And at Tehran University, where he taught a seminar, students acted starstruck. When I went to sit in on one of his lectures, I watched as they gathered quietly in the drab hallways just to watch him walk to class.

"He's so eloquent when he speaks in Persian that it's like listening to poetry," a female student whispered to me.

Tape cassettes of his lectures began circulating on an informal network with the same enthusiasm, if not the same magnitude, as had the clandestine recordings of Khomeini's lectures before the revolution.

But by the mid-1990s, Soroush also had a growing number of enemies. Among them were many of Iran's highest-ranking clergy, who viewed the diminutive academic as a serious threat because he'd committed the ultimate offense: He was one of the revolution's own who'd turned against them.

The emergence of Soroush symbolized a turning point, a sort of dividing line between two different parts of the revolution. The Islamic republic's first decade had been absorbed in ending a millennia-old form of government, crafting a unique political system to replace it, aggressively promoting Islam at home and abroad and then surviving political isolation, economic sanctions and a prolonged war with Iraq. Iran proved during those first ten years that it could survive staggering odds—and all the pundits' predictions of an early demise. But it only barely squeaked through the most radical period of the first republic.[3]

The second decade got back to the revolution's original mission. With the war's end and Khomeini's death in the late 1980s, diverse segments of Iran's complex society, including many who took to the streets to celebrate when the monarchy ended, began to seek answers that the Islamic republic had not yet provided. Disillusionment was running deep. Attention focused particularly on two issues at the heart of the revolution: empowerment and the role of Islam in a modern state.

In other words, by the 1990s Iran was ready for Soroush. His ideas served as a catalyst for change.

The evolution in Soroush's thinking is also a microcosm of the diversity—some insiders called it heresy—that emerged from within the revolution.

He'd been, after all, a staunch early supporter of the world's only contemporary theocracy. His participation had helped to provide the Islamic republic with an intellectual dimension. He's not a cleric, but he is deeply versed in Islamic law and recognized as a pious thinker. So when Iran's universities were shut down and overhauled in the early 1980s, he was the youngest of seven men appointed to the Committee of the Cultural Revolution to conform courses to Islamic tenets. That was the most controversial time in his life.

"I was appointed to arrange the curriculum, to correct the way of the cultural revolution so the universities could reopen," he told me at that first meeting.

"Even then my main emphasis on freedom of speech made me sometimes not very dear to the hearts of people in charge of the revolution. I tried to rescue the human sciences from attacks made against them because the revolutionaries thought the humanities were handmade by Westerners."

He'd argued often and forcefully not to exclude non-Islamic works, particularly those from the West, he said.

"In the end, we managed to insert many more modern subjects," he explained.

But hundreds of professors and staff were also fired before the universities reopened in 1983, and anyone linked to the purge was tainted by association. During Soroush's lectures in Europe and the United States years later, exiled Iranian intellectuals made bitter accusations about his early activities. Most other Iranians first knew Soroush, however, because he hosted one of the regime's new television shows, a rather serious program on the great mystics of medieval Iranian poetry.

The turning point for Soroush was in the late 1980s. As Khomeini's death coincided with sweeping political changes in the outside world, Soroush started to challenge the untouchable core of ideas at the heart of the revolution and even of Islam itself. He began testing his ideas, tentatively at first, at those informal Thursday-night talks organized by his followers. Very soon, his work redirected intellectual discourse.

By 1995, at the rowdy sixteenth anniversary of the American Embassy takeover, Iran's Supreme Leader spent more time castigating Soroush's ideas than condemning either the "Great Satan" or the "Zionist entity"—the code names for the United States and Israel.

"It makes me very sad when I see people who seem to be one of us . . . understanding truths in such a distorted way and publishing them," Ayatollah Khamenei warned.

"Interpreting religion isn't something that can be carried out by just anyone. Jurisprudence is the main science of the clergy. . . . If someone confronts the clergy, he gladdens the Zionists and the Americans more than anything else . . . because they've set their heart on the destruction of the clergy," he said.

"Well, the Islamic system will slap these people hard in the face!"

By then, however, Soroush's reach extended far beyond Iran. He was being invited to speak throughout the Muslim world as well as in Europe, Canada and the United States. *Kiyan* had subscribers on four continents. Followers in London set up a Web site under the name Seraj, or "guiding light," with news of his lectures, interviews and rapidly growing list of books. Graduate students from Georgetown University in Washington to the University of Malaya in Kuala Lumpur were writing dissertations about his work.

Along with a handful of other Islamic philosophers and reformers,

Soroush had begun to shake the foundations of a faith with a billion followers.

"Soroush is challenging thirteen centuries of thinking," Nasser Hadian, the congenial Tehran University political scientist, told me during one of the many long conversations we always had during my visits. Like the students, he too spoke about Soroush with the same animated energy.

"Soroush is profoundly important to an issue facing the entire Muslim world, because he says Islam can be interpreted in a way that's compatible with democracy. And he shows how. He proclaims that the understanding of religion is all relative. Put another way, he says no one interpretation is absolute. It's not fixed for all time and place. Who can say what God meant?" Hadian said.

"This opens the door to *all kinds* of new ideas—political as well as religious."

Soroush's following grew so quickly because he addressed diverse audiences. He appealed to a secular crowd that wanted greater participation in a religious system. Yet unlike the secular opposition, he didn't reject blending Islam and politics, so he attracted many of the faithful. He particularly tweaked the imagination of young clerics and intellectuals, because he didn't simply modify religious traditions, as other reformers did. Soroush boldly reconciled Islam and modernity.

"There's nothing heretical about new interpretations of Islam that differ from interpretations of the past," Soroush once told me. "Adaptation doesn't change the essence of religion."⁴

Soroush also appealed to Iranian cultural pride, because he argued that freedom is not a concept borrowed from the West. Liberties are compatible with religion generally, he said. They're inherently Islamic too.

In questioning rigid traditional Muslim thinking, particularly about political and human rights, Soroush created a twenty-first-century worldview that was both authentically Islamic and authentically modern. He made it possible to be Islamist without being fundamentalist,* to be reverent but free.

---

* "Fundamentalism" is in many ways a misnomer in describing Islamic activism. The term was actually first used in the West to describe a movement among Protestant Christians at the turn of the century. It referred to people who adhered to the literal reading of Scriptures and were passive in accepting their lot in life. They did not seek to change the status quo. In contrast, many of today's Islamic movements are more like Catholicism's Liberation Theology. Many urge active use of religious doctrine to improve the social and political order of temporal existence—usually including greater participation in a country's political and economic life.

The emergence of Soroush and a new genre of reformers underscored two pivotal facts about Iran's revolution: First, it had always been about more than simply getting rid of a particular tyrant or even ending 2,500 years of monarchy. It was part and parcel of the main theme of the twentieth century worldwide—empowerment.

After two earlier attempts at evolutionary reform in Iran were aborted—the 1905–11 Constitutional Revolution and the 1951–53 rule by nationalists, when the shah was forced into a brief exile—the disparate movements seeking a greater say in public life resorted to revolution in 1979.

In its goals, Iran's revolution was also consistent with broader global changes at the end of the twentieth century, including the demise of Communism in Europe, racial rule in Africa and military dictatorships in Latin America.

Second and more critical to the region and the outside world, the revolution's use of religion was part of something bigger that had long been rumbling in the Islamic world, something far more complex than renewed piety and more subtle than a jihad, or holy war.

Iran's political upheaval went hand in hand with a religious reformation, a process similar to that of the Christian Reformation four hundred years earlier, which redefined the relationship between the individual and God and between the individual and the state. For believers of Islam—the only monotheistic religion that offers a set of rules by which to govern society as well as a set of spiritual values—political change and religious reform are parts of a single, inexorably intertwined process.

Iran is not the only country to undergo that simultaneous challenge or change. Indeed, Iran became the Islamist front line only after the 1979 uprising assumed leadership of a movement with roots throughout the Muslim world. The disparate groups that first arose in the early 1970s never constituted a monolithic front. But they did share several common denominators.

They emerged from a common disillusionment with decaying, ineffective or incompetent governments that included the world's largest

---

Soroush describes the difference another way. A fundamentalist is one who uses religion as a form of identity rather than as a set of truths. "True believers are to be separated from fundamentalists," he says.

Most scholars and foreign-policy experts within the U.S. government now prefer the term "Islamist" to "fundamentalist" in describing these movements. The real "fundamentalists" are those like the repressive Taliban government in Afghanistan and the government of Saudi Arabia, which is ruled by a strictly traditional brand of Wahhabi Islam. Both authoritarian regimes seek to limit human rights—and thus actively oppose Islamist activity.

remaining crop of autocrats and monarchs. Intellectuals weren't imaginative, important or numerically strong enough to offer alternatives. Other types of opposition were effectively outlawed. In the search for an alternative, Islam was logical and legitimate—and available.

The diverse groups also emerged out of economic systems either unsuccessful in generating wealth or, in the case of oil-rich states, uneven in distributing it. Most Muslims live in Third World societies where the majority, often the vast majority, still live below the poverty line and where corruption, unemployment, inflation and housing shortages are ever-increasing problems. Islam counters decline and despondence with at least a sense of hope.

The Islamist movement of the late twentieth century also grew out of an identity crisis. It was spawned by a combination of elements: European colonialism, heavy-handed foreign influence and decades of troubled rule by local elites whose agenda and style were shaped by foreign ways. In looking for new inspiration and role models in a rapidly changing world, Islam was one of the few sources with an indigenous identity. It drew on accepted values. And it drew on a proud cultural past of rich literature, scientific greatness and grand achievements in art and architecture.

The new Islamists haven't been unlike other societies that turned to religion to induce change. At one time or another, virtually all the world's great faiths—Christianity, Judaism, Buddhism, Hinduism, Sikhism and others—have provided ideals such as universal equality and individual dignity. They've helped define goals. They've offered an infrastructure to mobilize opposition. And they've helped shape a new order.

The use of Islam differs from the politicization of other faiths, however, in that religion actually offers an alternative framework for ruling society.

Iran's angry revolution was the most energetic response to all of those factors. It was not the first Islamist political force to challenge the status quo. But it was the boldest. So from the late 1970s to the late 1980s, it most typified the kind of rejection that swept the Middle East in sporadic bursts in Lebanon, Egypt, Kuwait, Saudi Arabia, Jordan, Bahrain, Algeria, Tunisia and Sudan and among the Palestinians.

The early turmoil and fury in Tehran also provided the enduring imagery for the broader phenomenon, obscuring the fact that most Muslims attracted to these movements were peace-loving people simply in search of change. To the outside world, that decade is instead best remembered for its darker symbols—scowling mullahs, clandestine extremist groups, hostage traumas, bombed-out embassies and scruffy, bearded gunmen holding pistols to the heads of pilots in hijacked airplanes. Fear of the wider Islamist trend became so pervasive that even muezzins summoning the faithful to prayer from spiny minarets, as they'd done for thirteen centuries, became threatening. To outsiders, they symbolized calls to action.

But beginning in the late 1980s, the emergence of Soroush reflected a broad new phase of activism throughout the Muslim world.

The wider movement began to graduate from reacting against the past to proactively searching for practical solutions to the problems of the late twentieth century—and others that loom ahead in the twenty-first. The new activists were thinkers, civic organizations, unions and registered political parties. Their agenda was to create pieces of a new social order. Their tactics shifted from fanatics' bullets to the ballots of participation. Many of the groups were flawed, some deeply. Their longevity was uncertain. And the course along the way, as the reaction to Soroush demonstrated, was often rocky.

But the bottom line was that Iran, once again, was in the forefront.

The new breed of Islamists could eventually help provide the justification for genuine empowerment in Iran and potentially in other Islamic countries. Whether or not it succeeds, Iran's revolution may someday even be viewed by history as the first major experiment in trying to blend Islam and democracy.

That's no small challenge in the Muslim world, a vast terrain stretching from Indonesia on the Pacific Ocean to Morocco on the Atlantic, from Kazakhstan in Central Asia to Saudi Arabia in the Persian Gulf, from Sudan in east Africa to Nigeria on Africa's west coast, and from Yemen on the Red Sea to Lebanon on the Mediterranean. Accounting for more than fifty countries, it's the last bloc to hold out against the tide of democratic reform that has swept the rest of the world.

Ironically, the country that contributed the most to post–Cold War theories about a new global division between Islam and the West could actually be the breeding ground for ideas that eventually do the most to defuse or prevent that confrontation.

SOROUSH HAS ALWAYS been a reclusive figure. Soroush is not even his real name. When he began writing poetry decades ago, Hossein Dabbagh composed a pseudonym from the names of two now-grown children. Abdul Karim means "servant of God," while Soroush means "angel of revelation." To protect his family and his private life from the controversy and dangers of his work, Soroush now uses only his pen name.

For the same reasons, getting the first of more than a dozen interviews and conversations took a couple of years of appeals and pulling strings with intermediaries. Except for his *Kiyan* columns, Soroush at first shunned the media.

Our first meeting was in November 1994 at the Research Institute for Human Sciences, an old red-brick structure with thick columns near campus where Soroush was then a dean of faculty. Against the honking din of Tehran's late-afternoon traffic, his modest chambers, filled with soft music, seemed like a sanctuary. He welcomed me with warm politeness and invited me to sit with him at the round oak table in the middle of his small office.

But he didn't shake my hand. In Islamic Iran, touching a woman to whom a man is not related is unacceptable. It was the same at every subsequent meeting, even when we met outside Iran.

I'd asked to see him to talk about Islam and politics, the combination that made Iran such a fascinating place in what has arguably been history's most secular century. So I began by asking him if Islam could ever be reconciled with individual freedoms and particularly democracy. After all, Islam literally means "submission."

Isn't there an inherent contradiction? I asked.

"Ah, Islam and democracy are not only compatible. Their association is inevitable. In Muslim society, one without the other is not perfect," he replied, smiling with easy certainty.

"To be a religious man necessitates being a democratic man as well. An ideal religious society can't have anything but a democratic government."

Over the next two hours, Soroush outlined a sophisticated philosophic argument in the simplest terms. He rarely moved as he sat at the oak table sifting through revolutionary ideas in quiet and orderly progression. A yellow legal pad, the kind on which he wrote essays and books in longhand, lay in front of him. It went untouched.

Just listening to Soroush helped explain his following. Although an Islamic reformation has slowly been gaining ground for a century among thinkers from Egypt to India, the language of most intellectuals has been beyond the grasp of the Muslim masses. But Soroush is more accessible, at least to the educated. His books—which covered everything from poetry to the history of ideas and had intriguing titles like *The Story of Love and Servitude* and *Wisdom and Subsistence*—all went into multiple printings. At the same time that literacy and a middle class were growing throughout the Islamic world, his quiet charisma and ability to communicate helped to popularize the idea of religious reform.

"I give two bases for Islamic democracy," he continued. "The first pillar is this: In order to be a true believer, one must be free. To become a believer under pressure or coercion won't be true belief.

"This freedom is the basis of democracy."

To have true belief, one must also live in an environment with universal human rights.

"The idea of human rights prefigures religion or lies outside religion. In order to follow a particular religion, the freedom to exercise that option must be open to you," he said.

Soroush often paused briefly, as if to turn a mental page or allow a listener to absorb his words. He then resumed in the soft but precise English he had perfected in London.

This time, he turned to the heart of my question. The idea of submitting to Islam is fully reconcilable with freedom, he offered.

"To freely surrender or submit doesn't mean that you've sacrificed your freedom. You should be free as well to leave your faith or belief," he said.

"It's a contradiction to be free in order to believe—and then afterwards to abolish that freedom."

Pushing his glasses to his forehead and rubbing his eyes, he conceded, "This is something which is sometimes very difficult in our religious society, because usually a believer can't declare nonbelief. But that's something I'm tackling in my articles. I don't think that it's a part of Islam.

"It might have been some kind of regulation during the Prophet's time because of a political situation," he continued. "It may be. I'm not sure. But it's incompatible with religious freedom and Islamic democracy. Since you're free to become a believer, you should be free to leave your previous faith or to change your religion or to convert to another religion.

"So submission is still there. But if you want to surrender or submit to another faith, you should be free to do that too. Do you see?" he paused again, and smiled as if to say, "It's all so marvelously obvious."

The second pillar of Islamic democracy grows out of the gap between human imperfection and the sacred books—and the effort to bridge it.

For Soroush, the texts of the Koran and the Bible, which Muslims accept as the precursor to Islam, don't change. They're both the essence of religion. And they're sacred.

But human understanding of what is in those texts is imperfect. Exploring what they mean is an ongoing process.

"Nothing is sacred in human society. All of us are fallible human beings. Though religion itself is sacred, its interpretation is not sacred and therefore it can be criticized, modified, refined and redefined," Soroush explained.

"The interpretation of religious texts is thus always in flux. There's no single, inflexible, infallible or absolute interpretation of Islam. Interpretations are also influenced by the age you live in, by the conditions and mores of the time, and by other branches of knowledge. The way Islam was interpreted in the seventh century, when it was established by the prophet Mohammad, also differs from the way it was interpreted in the eleventh or fourteenth or seventeenth century.

"In other words, interpretations evolve with time," he added, rubbing the bridge of his nose under his glasses as he spoke. "Any fixed version would effectively smother religion. It would block the rich exploration of the meanings in the sacred texts."

Soroush then returned once again to my original question about submission—and the crux of his argument for reform.

"In the Muslim world we've talked only of duties, not of rights. In modern civilizations, however, believing in God isn't a duty, but a right."

For a growing group of followers—ranging from young mullahs to regime opponents, intellectuals to government technocrats—the reformist ideas of Soroush and his peers represent the hope of reconciliation, both within Islam and between Islam and the outside world.

But Soroush preferred to avoid parallels with Martin Luther.

"This comparison is an exaggeration. I'm not thinking of doing things like Luther did," he mused, in that even-toned voice.

Then he added with a coy smile, "Though perhaps Luther himself didn't know what he was doing at that time.

"And I am aware that these ideas, if taken seriously, might produce some radical change in the way we look at religion."

THE TRANSFORMATION of Abdul Karim Soroush is in many ways the story of Iran.

Soroush was born into tradition in the old part of Tehran, where homes crafted of raw mud brick and concrete were tightly packed along narrow, dusty alleys. Some of it still stands today along the arid southern fringe of the capital near the desert. Most homes then were just a large room or two and had no bathrooms. Some were interconnected and shared cooking facilities. Hard floors were usually covered with kilims or inexpensive carpets of deep ruby reds and browns with blue accents. Furniture was sparse, often limited to large padded cushions. Meals were eaten sitting on the floor, one reason shoes were left outside. In close-knit quarters, sense of family and community ran strong.

When Soroush was born in 1945, the fundamentals of life in this part of the capital pretty much hadn't changed in centuries.

In a conversation years after we first met, Soroush candidly told me about his roots and the events in his early life that shaped his thinking. His father Farajollah was a grocer who sold sugar and tea and other basics in a small shop. His mother Batoul, who was named after one of the Prophet's daughters, was devoutly religious. Both had limited educations, although Soroush's father dabbled in poetry later in life. The family had no refrigerator, car, telephone, radio or television. Information was gleaned from the clergy, the neighborhood grapevine and the bazaar.

"My parents lived a very traditional life. They didn't try to modernize in any way. They didn't really want such things," Soroush reflected.

Soroush was born, perhaps appropriately, on Ashura. Ashura is the most emotional holiday for Shi'ite Muslims, similar to the Easter commemoration of Jesus' crucifixion by the Roman Empire. Ashura celebrates the martyrdom of Hussein almost seven centuries later at the hands of the Umayyad Dynasty. Although the religious sagas have significant differences, the legend of Hussein is as important in understanding Shi'ite Islam as the story of Jesus is in understanding Christianity.

Hussein was the prophet Mohammad's grandson. His death symbolized the first and greatest schism within the faith. It happened soon after the Prophet died, in A.D. 632, and was triggered by a political dispute over succession. The Prophet's family believed that leadership should go to Ali, the Prophet's cousin and son-in-law—and his first convert. Shi'ite literally means "follower of Ali."

But advisers and followers outside the family alleged that the Prophet had left no instructions and that the new leader should be chosen from the wider community. They formed the nucleus of the mainstream Sunni sect.

When Sunnis of the new Umayyad Dynasty then assumed leadership of the young Islamic world, Hussein and a band of fewer than a hundred, including women and children, decided to fight. They knew they'd be massacred. But they believed it was better to die fighting for justice than to live with injustice. In the battle of Karbala, an ancient city of Mesopotamia now in southern Iraq, they were all killed. Thirteen centuries later, Hussein's tomb in Karbala is one of the two greatest Shi'ite shrines.

Because of Hussein, revolt against tyranny became part of Shi'ite tradition. Protest and martyrdom became duties to God. And Hussein became the symbol of the human struggle against wrong.[5]

Just as Christians reenact Jesus' procession bearing the cross past the fourteen stops to Calvary before his crucifixion on Good Friday, so too do the Shia every year reenact Hussein's martyrdom at Karbala in an Islamic passion play during Ashura. Nowhere is the practice more honored than in Iran, the world's largest and preeminent Shi'ite country.*

But Soroush was also born just as Iran completed its first intense burst of modernization under the first Pahlavi shah, the self-educated but wily army colonel Reza Khan who, like Napoleon, had crowned himself king in 1926. Abruptly and ruthlessly, the new shah converted ancient Persia into modern Iran.

It was the most rapid period of change in the country's long history: Power shared for centuries with tribal leaders was tightly centralized in Tehran. A new industrialized economy centered on oil replaced agriculture, regional trade and carpets. And a new army, based on conscription and paid for with a new national tax, was built to secure power at home and in the region.

Inspired by Kemal Atatürk's overhaul of Turkish society after the collapse of the Ottoman Empire and attracted to Nazi Germany's efficiency and Aryan culture, Reza Shah virtually scrapped tradition: The Arabic lunar calendar used by Muslims elsewhere was abandoned in favor of the Persian solar calendar. Nomads were ordered to stop wandering. Women were told to shed the enveloping black chador, while both sexes were ordered to adopt Western dress. Pictures of the camel, a "backward" beast, and other symbols of the past were forbidden.

---

*Iran is the only country where Shi'ite Muslims are a large majority. Iraq (in the south around Karbala), Lebanon and Yemen have significant Shi'ite communities that range from a third to a half of their populations. Other smaller but notable Shi'ite communities are in Saudi Arabia, Kuwait, Bahrain, Pakistan, Afghanistan and Syria.

And everyone was told to take a last name—a process that turned out to be somewhat random and often confusing.

"Our family took a name from the job of my grandfather," Soroush told me. "*Dabbagh* means tanner. He worked in a tannery."

About the same time, a young cleric named Ruhollah took the name Mustafavi, which means "of Mustafa," after his father. Adding an *i* at the end of a Persian name denoted paternal ancestry—the equivalent of *O'* at the beginning of an Irish name, *Mac-* among Scots, *von* in German, *-son* among Swedes and *al* or *bin* in Arabic.

After Ruhollah Mustafavi became a cleric, he then followed the practice of his religious peers and added the name of his hometown. Since he was born in Khomein, he became Ruhollah Mustafavi Khomeini.

But Ayatollah Khomeini's older brother Morteza, also a cleric, took an entirely different route. He assumed the name Pasandideh, which roughly means "pleasing."

During his fifteen-year rule, Reza Shah was particularly contemptuous of religion: Islamic judges, taxes and laws were secularized, their replacements based on European models. Traditional parts of old Tehran were plowed to make way for paved boulevards and modern buildings. Islamic schools, the primary source of education in many corners of the country, were put under a government ministry and their curricula secularized and standardized, often on European models. Even the shah's choice of the dynasty's name was a jab at religion, for *Pahlavi* came from ancient, pre-Islamic times.

In a country with a civilization dating back thousands of years, the West generally became the model for change.[6]

The backlash among traditional families ran deep.

"My mother refused to take off her chador," Soroush told me, smiling as he recalled her ardor.

"When she and her sister wanted to go to the baths, because there was none at home, they had friends in the street signal them when there were no police. Then they ran swiftly to the bathhouse so they wouldn't be caught with their chadors. My mother was very staunch," he said.

His parents also never voted, a right first granted to men during the 1905–11 Constitutional Revolution at the end of the Qajar Dynasty and to women in 1963. Nor did they regularly read newspapers or hear news on the radio, both tightly controlled by the government.

"They were utterly against the regime because they thought it was against Islam. They wanted to do nothing to support it," Soroush reflected.

"And most people didn't listen to radio because they saw it as an instrument for the shah's propaganda."

Reza Shah was forced to abdicate after Britain and the Soviet Union, alarmed by his pro-Nazi sentiments, invaded Iran in 1941. His son Mohammad Reza Pahlavi, then just twenty-two, inherited the Peacock Throne. In fits and starts, the second and last king in the short-lived Pahlavi Dynasty pursued modernization with increasing direction from American businesses, banks, diplomats and military advisers.

Sleepy Tehran was transformed into a pulsing cosmopolitan city with international stature. The city sprouted high-rise Hilton, Hyatt and Sheraton hotels, Kentucky Fried Chicken franchises, bowling alleys and cinemas showing American movies. Big boulevards were renamed after Western fixtures, from Roosevelt Boulevard to Los Angeles Avenue and John F. Kennedy Square. The Great Bazaar, the largest and most legendary souk in the Middle East, faced competition from new shopping districts with Western fashions, appliances, furniture and food.

Iranian television ran an array of American programs, from *Peyton Place* to *Rawhide* and *Little House on the Prairie*. Tehran Radio had an English-language service, although American Armed Forces Radio also had its own local station. Nightclubs and casinos and the presence at any given time of thousands of foreign tourists, foreign contractors and foreign military advisers—the vast majority American—transformed Tehran's lifestyle.

Change began to look like a sellout in the eyes of the religious and traditional sectors of society that Soroush came from. Yet few Iranians dared do much more publicly than grumble. The consequences weren't worth it.

Ayatollah Khomeini was an exception. Often brazenly, the gauntly thin ascetic with the long white beard and bushy black eyebrows attacked both the pace and the pattern of modernization. His first challenge was published in a thin little book called *Secrets Exposed*. It railed against the Pahlavis in the kind of bombastic language that came to typify his rhetoric.

> Wherever you go and whomever you encounter, from the street-sweeper to the highest official, you will see nothing but disordered thought, con-

fused ideas, contradictory opinions, self-interest, lechery, immodesty, criminality, treachery and thousands of associated vices. . . . Given these circumstances, it should not be expected that the government would be regarded as just and legitimate in religious circles.

In short, these idiotic and treacherous rulers, these officials—high and low—these reprobates and smugglers must change in order for the country to change.[7]

For the ayatollah, the issue was Islam—and the Pahlavi betrayal of its traditions.

But Islam also provided the idiom of opposition. For three decades, the future Imam cleverly invoked its heroes and symbols in his campaign against the monarchy.

"Every day is Ashura and every place is Karbala," he often exhorted the faithful as he called on them to defy the regime, whatever the dangers.[8]

He also deliberately selected Ashura in 1963 for the boldest public attack ever waged by anyone on the second Pahlavi shah.

"We've come to the conclusion that this regime is fundamentally opposed to Islam and the existence of a religious class," he charged.

Calling the shah a "miserable wretch," he proclaimed,

Forty-five years of your life have passed. Isn't it time for you to think and reflect a little, to ponder about where all of this is leading you, to learn a lesson from the experience of your father? I hope to God that you didn't have in mind the religious scholars when you said, "The reactionaries are like an impure animal," because if you did it will be difficult for us to tolerate you much longer. . . . The nation will not allow you to continue this way.[9]

Two days later, the ayatollah was arrested. His imprisonment sparked demonstrations throughout Iran. It also created a new aura around the rebel ayatollah that forced other clergy with higher rank and greater scholarship—and different goals—to defer to him. Through his own political martyrdom, Ayatollah Khomeini redefined the national focus.[10]

Soroush was in high school when the cleric confronted the king. His family quickly became fans. When the ayatollah was released from prison ten months later, Soroush was among the thousands who traveled to the ayatollah's modest mud-brick home in Qom to welcome him home.

"It was dangerous activity and I wouldn't have gone on my own, but I had an uncle who was one of his followers and he took me, along with his sons. By that time Khomeini was already very popular among religious people because of his political activities," Soroush recalled.

"It was the first time I saw his face. He was very charismatic—and brave. You can't imagine the harshness and despotism of the time. He was the only one who spoke against the shah openly. I was impressed, although I wasn't ripe enough to fully understand his ideas. I was still too young."

A stint in the shah's notoriously tough prisons did nothing to silence the ayatollah. He picked up where he left off, only with new anger and tough new accusations. The shah responded with a tough new punishment. In 1964, Ayatollah Khomeini was banished from Iran altogether. He spent most of the next fourteen years in southern Iraq, just down the road from Karbala, where Hussein had been martyred.

As a teenager during these tumultuous times, Soroush lived on the cusp of tradition and modernization. He was the brightest of four children in a devout family. But his passion was for modern sciences and the world they represented.

"I first touched modernity through science," he told me.

After high school, Soroush became the first and only member of the family ever to go on to university. He did a degree in pharmacology, a practical skill, and then fulfilled compulsory service in the shah's army. His first jobs were briefly in a laboratory for food products, toiletries and sanitary materials in Bushehr, an arid city on the Persian Gulf, and then in a pharmaceutical lab in Tehran.

But Soroush was intent on seeing the world outside Iran.

"I always complained to my high school teachers that they didn't teach us enough modern ideas," he recalled, somewhat amused at his early stubbornness.

"So I tried to perfect my English to be able to study science abroad. I wanted to become familiar with the modern world."

In the 1960s and especially after the oil boom in the early 1970s, thousands of Iranian students flooded schools in Europe and the United States. Some were from wealthy families. Many went on government scholarships. In Soroush's case, a patron of his high school provided the means that his family couldn't.

In London, Soroush studied analytical chemistry and philosophy. But he quickly stepped beyond the conventional delineations of science to explore its deeper relationship with both political theory and God. He also wrote his first book, *The Restless Nature of the World.* It dealt with the constant flux of the universe and time as a fourth dimension.

As Soroush explored the modern sciences abroad, the movement against the monarchy gained momentum at home. It, too, blended tradition and modernity.

Indeed, for all the religious imagery attached to it, the upheaval in Tehran was arguably the most modern revolution ever in both goals and tactics. For the vast majority of Iranians, the issue was not whether to modernize but rather how and in what form.

The tactics of Iran's revolutionaries were also cutting-edge. Khomeini didn't need the equivalent of China's Long March or Russia's internal strife or France's bloody uprising to mobilize the masses. Khomeini came from tradition but he made use of every available modern instrument. From his base in Iraq, he used mimeographs and photocopiers and later audiotape and videotape cassettes to slip his message back into Iran.

His daughter later recalled how Khomeini sometimes didn't talk to the family when they were together because he was so caught up in the news on the radio or television.

"Even in the bathroom he has the radio with him," she once lamented.[11]

Khomeini's strategy succeeded. By the fall of 1978, the shah was so desperate that he made concessions to his archrivals in Iraq just to have Khomeini expelled farther afield to Europe. The ayatollah ended up in a Paris suburb, although he became far more famous in the process. He was also more accessible.

"I flew to Paris to see him. By this time I knew much more about him and he left a deep impression on me. When he came out from his room, I was stunned," Soroush told me.

"For ten minutes we talked about freedom and politics."

That was the first of several encounters the two men would eventually have. A mere four months after his arrival in Paris, Khomeini flew home on February 1, 1979, as a hero. Soroush soon followed. Khomeini later appointed him to the Committee of the Cultural Revolution.

"I used to go to him frequently. We had discussions, sometimes severe. As spokesman for the committee, I was outspoken and put forward suggestions," Soroush said.

"He was often more silent than talking. He used to listen to you very carefully and usually he answered very briefly. Meetings were usually short. But just being with him was always an exceptional thing."

Soroush then conceded, "But we never became so friendly that I could speak to him without reservation."

The outside world never understood the phenomenon of Khomeini. His stern, even growling visage seemed so repellent. But for millions of Iranians, the ayatollah genuinely had an aura that was critical in converting a divisive, disorganized and headless opposition movement into a successful revolutionary force. Khomeini combined vigorous nationalism with an impassioned eloquence, an absolutist's sense of righteousness and a mystic's superior airs. Even for many of those who rejected his Islamic message, Khomeini initially won respect for his unwavering commitment to Iranian independence and cultural dignity.

"If Khomeini created a hell," an upper-class Iranian professional educated in the United States once told me, "he created it with good intentions."

That aura was also the glue that held the new Islamic republic together during its first decade against extraordinary odds—and despite growing public discontent. Disillusionment was not limited to intellectuals, doctors, businessmen, artists and the upper middle class who resided in high-rise apartment blocks, modern homes or villas in the cool mountain foothills of north Tehran.

By the late 1980s, Soroush also had problems with Iran's new system.

"I didn't really change my ideas. I always wanted democracy and I thought our revolution was headed in that direction. I rushed home to Iran from London to have a role. In the early years, everything seemed bright and promising," he told me.

"But by and by, the direction of the revolution changed and it was no longer possible for me to go along with it."

Soroush began to see the Imam as only the instrument of a transition, not a personification of the revolution's ultimate goal.

"His personality was more impressive than his theory. His thoughts and views are a different story," Soroush said candidly.

He also began to see Islam not only as an idiom of opposition but also as an instrument for change. Islam wasn't the end goal, but it was the means through which Iran could reach the real mission of the revolution—modernization and empowerment. Soroush explained the role of Islam by telling me again about his mother.

"After the revolution, she started listening to the radio. For the first time, it had programs about religion. It was no longer the shah's propaganda," he reflected.

"She also voted eagerly after the revolution. If my father had been alive, he would have voted too. This revolution made people much more politicized. It took traditional people and people who'd never been involved in politics before and introduced them to modernization. The use of religion made them comfortable with it."

In a traditional society, the idiom and the instrument of reform had to be legitimate before change was acceptable.

"Islam was not only the best vehicle for modernization and democracy," Soroush told me. "It was perhaps the only natural vehicle."

CONVERSATIONS WITH SOROUSH—on campus, at the Research Institute for Human Sciences or after his Thursday night lectures—soon became a centerpiece of my visits to Iran. Asking him "What's new?" always elicited extraordinary answers because his philosophic musings didn't stop with Islam and democracy. That was only the warm-up.

When I went to see him again at the research institute in early 1995, he answered my question by telling me, in that innocent voice, that he was thinking "a bit" about the clergy. A more accurate description might have been to say that he was going after the clerics, or at least the more autocratic elements who then dominated the world's only modern theocracy. He did it, politely, by calling them fallible.

"The clergy, the intellectuals, the learned men who understand and interpret religion—their understanding is not above criticism. They're not prophets. They're not holy. They're not God," Soroush told me, slowly shaking his head.

"Some of them aren't very learned. Some of them aren't even pious. It's not always the case that they know religion very well or are the best commentators."

And because they're imperfect, he continued, the ayatollahs, hojatoleslams, sayyids, sheikhs and others of religious rank shouldn't have a monopoly on interpreting religion.

That was a heretical idea in a country where the Supreme Leader, or Velayat-e Faqih, has absolute authority derived from God. It was all the more sensitive because of the man who held it. The Imam's successor, Ayatollah Ali Khamenei, had much lower stature in the eyes of other clerics as well as the public, which made him particularly thin-skinned about criticism or challenges.

The idea of infallible authority is also a defining feature of Shi'ite

Islam, the faith's so-called second sect that accounts for up to 15 percent of the world's one billion Muslims. Shi'ite theologians are empowered to interpret religious law and duty for their followers. The rulings of senior Shi'ite clerics, in theory, are law. The hierarchy of the Shi'ite clergy is sometimes compared to its counterparts in the Catholic church.

In contrast, Sunni Muslims believe man's relationship with God is more personal, face to face, with less dependence on a priesthood. Their clergy serve largely as advisers to the faithful. Sunni clerics are sometimes compared to their Protestant peers.

The power of the clergy is the main reason that Iran's revolution, which originally combined a discordant array of nationalists, intellectuals, antimonarchists, Communists and devout Muslims, eventually came under the unifying spell of a religious leader. In a predominantly Shi'ite country where political opposition was largely outlawed or exiled, the clergy had special authority and legitimacy as an alternative.

But in 1995, Soroush began to challenge that power publicly. The idea of a Supreme Leader or religious guardian was an anachronism, he told me.

"I've had experience with totalitarian leadership," he explained. "That's why I've never been able to come to terms with the Faqih."

No one is perfect enough to have an absolute claim on understanding the truth, he continued. And no single understanding of Islam is automatically more correct or definitive than another.

"There should always be a plurality of interpretations because no understanding is the final or most complete one. Interpretation has to be renewed all the time. I'm not calling for anarchy in interpreting the text. And I'm not saying everybody has the right to interpret the Koran according to his or her own wishes. All I'm saying is that it's neither the state's right nor its duty to impose one particular understanding on the people," he continued.

"In Islam, it's the right of all people to believe in God and in the Koran. And it follows, then, that they all have an equal right to their own justifiable understanding of Islam. There's no official interpretation," he said, again using strong words in that soft voice.

"None," he said.

Soroush also dared to charge that the clergy actually stifled thinking about religion.

"In 1991, I gave my first controversial lecture in Isfahan," he recalled. "I compared the university with the seminary. My main point was that there's a red line in the seminary in the sense that you have to be careful not to trespass—or things will happen to you. There are unthinkables, untouchables. But in universities there are no red lines. Everything can be discussed.

"So I told them, 'Never think that the people talking to you in Qom are gods or prophets. They're talking to you only about their limited interpretations.' "

With a slightly mischievous smile, he added, "You can imagine the reaction. The head of the Qom seminary had some harsh things to say about me.

"But the students came to me later. They said about seventy percent of the students and the young clergy are with me, even though they are frightened and can't say so."

Soroush gave another lecture that year in the scenic Caspian coast city of Rasht. The students asked him to talk about why Iran's revolutionary spirit had cooled.

"I told them honestly. I said the seminaries are stagnant. I said you must not rely only on the clergy. You have to teach yourselves. I told them to go out and buttonhole the clergy, otherwise they won't teach you anything or improve their own knowledge," he explained.

"Then I also said the clergy has no feeling about the rights of the people. For them, it's the logic of power, not the logic of liberty," he said.

Smiling again, he noted, "Ayatollah Khamenei didn't much like this. It was the first time he criticized me publicly."

The regime's reaction was particularly vehement because Soroush's words resonated through a receptive audience.

By the mid-1990s, public resentment against the clergy had reached a new peak. Tehran taxi drivers often refused to give them rides. Stories were rampant in the capital about how some cabbies ran fingers across their throats to show contempt as they sped by mullahs waiting curbside. Irreverent jokes about the clergy, the local equivalent of classic ethnic slurs—such as "How many mullahs does it take to screw in a light-bulb?"—were common. On one trip, I even heard about a master of ceremonies at a Tehran wedding who did a long routine ridiculing the clergy—in the presence of several clerics.

Among those most opposed to the rule of the clerics were, ironically, clerics themselves. Despite Khomeini's overwhelming public support when he returned from exile, many in the clergy still didn't agree with either his ideas or a theocratic government, especially the Faqih. As the failure of that system increasingly threatened to taint Islam, discontent and dissidence also grew among clerics who weren't connected to Iran's government.

But Soroush didn't stop with challenging the ruling clergy's authority—a position already explosive enough to put him on an unofficial internal enemies list. He even challenged a critical symbol of the clergy's support: their money.

Muslim leaders have historically been supported financially by either the state (in most Sunni countries) or the people (in Shi'ite communities). Soroush advocated abolishing both traditions. The clergy should instead find other means of support so that they aren't "captives" of their pay-masters and so they don't feel obliged to propagate either official positions or popular preferences.

"This is a harsh and radical suggestion. Some people see this as putting petrol on the flames," he said, smiling coyly.

"But the clergy have to get money from elsewhere. Religion is only for authentic lovers of religion and those who will work for it, not for the dealers of religion. No one should be guaranteed a living, gain social status or claim political power on the basis of religion."

He paused again. "The clergy should work like everyone else through scholarship, teaching or other jobs," he said. "The clergy shouldn't feed on religion. They shouldn't sell religion."

Only independence, he said, can prevent the clergy—and Islam—from being compromised.

Soroush shied away from applying his controversial ideas to the tumultuous times of contemporary Iran.

With a knowing chuckle, he explained, "I'll be better served if I don't get entangled in such political affairs. Let other people draw the implications—and consequences."

The implications were profound. First and foremost, his growing body of work in books, magazine essays and lectures established the rights of individuals in their relationships both with government and with God. His ideas provided for the equality and empowerment of ordinary believers. They also opened the way for the majority—from the bottom up—rather than the clergy at the top to define the ideal Islamic state.

The ideal Islamic state, he pointedly added, is only legitimate when it comes into being because of popular will and consensus, not when it's imposed.

The consequences were profound as well. Of all his ideas, the one that created the most immediate trouble for Soroush was his conclusion about Islam as a political ideology. Simply put, he thinks it doesn't work.

"Religious ideology shouldn't be used to rule a modern state, because it tends toward totalitarianism," he told me.

"And no form of government, religious or otherwise, is capable of forcibly making a people religious."

A theocracy actually contradicts Islam's basic tenets, he added, because it vests power in an elite. The ideal Islamic republic is instead ruled by whoever is the best leader, whether secular or religious. And everyone has an equal right to run. The winners should be chosen by merit, not profession.

Again echoing a theme central to the Christian Reformation, Soroush argued that there should be a distinction between the roles, powers and responsibilities of mosque and state. That's a stunning shift for the only major monotheistic religion that provides rules to govern society.

He also argued against opposing secularism—or fearing it.

"Secularism is nothing more than behaving, looking and thinking in a scientific way," he said, in an almost dismissive way. "It has nothing to do with hostility to religion."

Secularism is the complement to religion, not its enemy, he added.

Yet like Luther, Soroush hasn't abandoned the core values of the faith, which he thinks can and should influence government decisions. And he doesn't preclude all clergy from a role in government. He instead argued against rigid thinking, fixed doctrine, elitism and questionable practices—all adopted over time.

"In an ideal religious society, no personality and no fatwa should be above criticism. Clerics must be as accountable as everyone else—and subject to removal from political office by the broader population," he said.

That idea, too, drives a dagger into the heart of the Islamic republic's system of leadership. It openly questions the authority of the Supreme Leader. It also implicitly questions the powers of top bodies unique to Iran's system—namely the Council of Guardians, a group heavily weighted with clergy, and the Assembly of Experts, a body restricted to clergy who elect and periodically reconfirm the Supreme Leader.

Islam shouldn't be used to vet the Islamic-ness of anyone else or to meddle in private lives or to control public thinking, Soroush added. It should instead be used to encourage growth and freedom.

With the first trace of excitement in his voice, he explained, "Islam is organic and dynamic and can easily be adapted to present conditions. And Islamic law is expandable. You can't imagine the extent of its flexibility.

"In an Islamic democracy, you can realize all its potential. You can have a very flexible society!"

THE CONTROVERSY OVER Soroush turned ugly in the mid-1990s, just months after we had that conversation. The reaction exposed the fears of Iran's conservatives about the impact of his ideas on their lives, positions, power and income.

First came the death threats. Some went to his office, others to his unlisted home phone. They were always anonymous. What distressed Soroush was that his family took most of the calls. Then came a series of physical assaults that left him bruised, battered and often in tattered clothes. Most were carried out by young vigilantes in murky gangs known as Ansar-e Hizbollah, or "Helpers of the Party of God." They were often referred to simply as Ansar, or "helpers."

As the campaign against him escalated, Soroush appealed to President Rafsanjani.

"I wrote and told him it doesn't become the country to have these kinds of things happen. I told him that I'm only a university teacher and member of the Academy of Sciences. I asked him what sort of hope I can give to students when they see their teacher under attack. And I told him that I only invite people to think," he told me.

"Then I reminded him of the saying from the Prophet that it's better to think for one hour than to pray for seventy years," he added.

"But I didn't get a reply."

A particularly vicious attack at Tehran University in late 1995 then elevated his plight to national attention.

"As I approached the lecture hall with my wife and several friends, I was surrounded by hooligans who insulted me and threatened to kill me. They tore off my shirt and grabbed my spectacles. Several friends who were trying to protect me were badly injured," Soroush recalled in a soft matter-of-fact tone.

Several dozen Ansar thugs pursued Soroush into the auditorium. Many of the two thousand students inside tried to provide a protective cordon for him. But raw clashes erupted as the vigilantes started throwing furniture. Soroush narrowly missed being hit in the face by a flying chair, which instead hit and seriously injured an arm he held up to block its path.

"Several students were hurt. I eventually managed to escape the hall, but only after I was hit in the head by a club," he said, shaking his head with quiet incredulity. He had escaped by fumbling his way in the dark until supporters helped him get off the campus grounds.

"This was a well-planned attack. We found out later that a minibus brought them to the lecture. It was done to silence me and to intimidate students not to invite me to speak," Soroush said.

The attack triggered an uproar on both sides of an increasingly polarized society. Students at the tree-lined and usually tranquil campus of the University of Tehran led a pro-Soroush demonstration—the first of its kind since the revolution. Conservatives in Parliament countered with a new law aimed in large part at undermining his support. It imposed severe penalties on anyone associating with "critics or enemies" of the Islamic republic.

The regime then began to really squeeze Soroush. Over the next year, he lost his three senior academic appointments, including a deanship. Other public appearances, including his Thursday lectures, were banned. He was forbidden to publish new articles. He was summoned for several long "interviews" by Iranian intelligence officials. His travel was restricted, then his passport confiscated. Even his garbage was picked through to keep track of ideas left behind on crumpled sheets from his yellow legal pads.

"When they summoned me to the [intelligence] ministry, I asked them, 'Why are you so afraid of me? I'm only a single man,' " Soroush recalled.

"They said, 'Yes, but the Imam was also a single man.' " Soroush rolled his eyes.

Kiyan, his last outlet and means of communicating ideas, was also denied access to printing paper. It was a trick the government occasionally used to close down publications that relied on government-subsidized newsprint. Soroush's supporters, including some well-known businessmen, stepped in to pay full price. At Tehran's annual book fair, another supporter anonymously contributed enough to make his previous books available at half price.

"There are freedoms in this country," Soroush told me later. "But you have to know how to get them. And sometimes the government has to give them to you not because of a willingness, but because of an inability to stop them."

The depth of the regime's anger and fear was evident at a 1995 press conference by Iran's long-serving foreign minister, Ali Akbar Velayati, a tall, elegant former pediatrician who was among the most visible Iranian officials.

Velayati complained to reporters that "the Dr. Soroush issue" hurt Iran's ability to conduct foreign policy. By dragging "scholarly issues" into public forums, he said, the philosopher "weakened" the foundations of the state and undermined "national harmony."

"Ruining national and religious beliefs isn't a service to the country, to the people or to Islam," he warned.[12]

For Soroush, that was the last straw. After years of trying to avoid direct confrontation with the regime that once employed him, he decided to strike back. His response was published in a Tehran paper and widely circulated in Iran and abroad.

"Is it logical to accuse me of these things when my speeches are stopped by beating me and tearing off my clothes? I'm a person whose only opportunity is to write and publish an article every two or three months in a specialized magazine with limited circulation," he wrote.

The letter used uncharacteristically emotive language:

Is it logical to say that a person who doesn't have access to radio or television stations, to newspapers, to mosques, to Friday prayer meetings or religious gatherings, that a person who is constantly pounded by the mass media with the ugliest attacks and accusations such as spying, incompetence, treachery, freemasonry, being an American agent, and being another Salman Rushdie . . . could weaken the state? . . . How is it that [officials'] efforts to strengthen the national and religious beliefs of the people are not getting anywhere and only this writer . . . has succeeded in casting a dark cloud? God knows that not even sorcerers have such powers.

The strange picture of Iranian society presented by the foreign minister is that of a termite-infested orphanage that could crumble with the slightest shove and whose children's minds are in disarray. And the picture he has painted of himself is that of a medieval priest wielding the

weapon of excommunication, while ignoring his responsibilities to preserve the cultural interests, integrity and reputation of this country.[13]

The campaign against him carried ominous broader implications,
Soroush warned.

A government and a country cannot claim virtue or honor if its academic community and artists are oppressed, intimidated and treated as
criminals for expressing their views; live in fear and insecurity; are
scared of exercising their intellectual and artistic talents; and see their
lives, work and reputation attacked by hooligans.

He ended the letter with a long poem. One of the last verses contained its own warning:

> To you, I seem
> Small and weak.
> But I can be an arrow
> Thrown at the eyes of enemies.

To ease tensions, Soroush called for an open debate with clerics from
the regime, all the way to Ayatollah Khamenei at the top.

"I said I have some unorthodox ideas and I don't conceal them. I said
I wanted to open the door of dialogue. But that infuriated Ayatollah
Khamenei. I was the first of his subjects who dared to talk to him this
way," Soroush later recalled. "And that wasn't tolerable."

Then Soroush showed rare frustration. "I don't know what has happened to our Islamic society that a leader is so holy that we can't ever
write to him or speak to him about ideas," he said.

But as the confrontation unfolded, Soroush was also aware that he
was part of a bigger problem.

"It's not just about me," he reflected. "The whole country's in a state
of turbulence. The regime is at its weakest point. It needs only a small
excuse to explode. People are unhappy for many reasons that have nothing to do with me. In fact, most of these people have never heard of me.

"This kind of condition can't be stable," he added. "It has to change,
for better or for worse."

Iran was, indeed, on the verge of imploding. The regime's response,
however, was to crack down even harder.

"The government closed newspapers, imprisoned critics, forcibly suppressed protests and condoned vigilante attacks against domestic opposition," Human Rights Watch reported in its 1995 annual survey. "Religious zealots from competing authorities interfered in people's everyday lives, enforcing ever-changing rules of conduct."[14]

For Soroush, the foremost advocate of change, the escalating tensions heightened the personal dangers. The problem was no longer sporadic harassment. Ansar thugs armed with knives and clubs started tailing and threatening him as he moved around Tehran. Intelligence officials at the misnamed Ministry of Information hauled him in again and again.

"They told me I was banned from speaking," he recalled. "I began to realize that they intended to imprison me or put me under house arrest."

Soroush appealed again to President Rafsanjani, this time in an open letter. "I'm mourning the death of a university in which learning is dead and the birth of barbarism is being celebrated," he wrote.

> The Ministry of Information, with threats and restrictions and frequent summons, has limited my activities and encroached upon my human rights and helped my opponents both in word and deed. How long will the intellectuals of this land have to endure the lawbreaking activities of these pressure groups and sit silently and tolerate unfitting behavior and threats? As a result of the impudent acts of these impudent people, I have lost my job security and my life is at risk. . . . This country has reached a point that a professor in order to attend his class has to prepare to die.[15]

Rafsanjani didn't respond, but Ansar did.

In its own open letter in a Tehran newspaper, the normally clandestine group charged that Soroush wasn't propagating philosophy but "secular and vulgar temptations" that undermined the Islamic state. Soroush's "deviant" ideas "negated all that is sacred" and created a "whirlpool of doubt and confusion," it said.

> Global arrogance and Zionism—a.k.a. the United States and Israel— have reached the conclusion that if they want to attack the foundations of the Islamic system of Iran they can find no sharper weapon than his ideas, ideas whose falseness has been proven time and time again in the history of the Muslim nation of Iran. . . . We aren't prepared to sell out the ideas of the revolution or the blood of our martyrs to secularism.[16]

Fearing for his life, Soroush decided his only recourse was to leave. In May 1996, he slipped out of Tehran.

Over the next year, Soroush spoke to Muslim students and Iranian groups on four continents, from Malaysia to Britain, Australia to Turkey and Egypt to Canada. During a month-long tour of the United States, he came to my house for tea. He'd just given a lecture at Georgetown University and was in a reflective mood, so I asked him if he had ever anticipated the impact his lectures and articles would have or the furor they would generate.

With a wry smile, he replied, "My wife once said to me, 'I never thought I'd lead this kind of life with you.' "

The crisis over reform didn't end with Soroush's departure, however. Indeed, by the mid-1990s, Soroush was no longer unique in issuing challenges to the regime. The theocracy faced a series of stinging demands for change from a cross section of society, ranging from the arts community to the military. One of the most striking came from Azizollah Amir Rahimi, a former general whose protest against the use of American military uniforms during the last shah's rule had landed him in jail.

"Rahimi's slightly eccentric and very stubborn," an Iranian journalist once told me.

With Ayatollah Khomeini's approval, Rahimi had been appointed to head Iran's military police after the 1979 revolution.

By the mid-1990s, however, he too was disillusioned. In a privately circulated letter, which made its way back to Iran on foreign radio broadcasts, he charged that the clerics were responsible for the misery in Iran.

"The nation is in poverty and the country is on the verge of explosion," he wrote.

Both Rahimi and his son were immediately detained. The regime tried to discredit him as a mental case and an opium addict.

There were many other challengers. Writers issued an open letter calling for an end to intimidation and censorship. Iran's theater and film community petitioned to remove "straitjacket regulations and supervision" over everything from plots to production. Intellectuals were emboldened to probe new ways to use Islam, ideas that spilled into the press and public debate. Iranians who once staunchly opposed the shah even began to talk publicly and longingly about the days of the monarchy—if not of the Pahlavis themselves.[17]

For growing numbers of Iranians, the regime had lost its claim to legitimacy. The revolution suffered from a sense of lost mission. For the first time, the regime's chief ideologues were being held to account. And a search was on for something different.

In many ways, the Islamic Republic was destined to face serious challenges. Its use of religion as a political idiom produced utopian expectations that no state—much less a developing country, even a major oil producer—could ever hope to achieve. Challenges finally erupted in the 1990s, when Iran had no wars to rally nationalism, no sapping crises with the outside world to divert public attention and no charismatic Imam to wield religious authority.

The internal turmoil was explained to me by Hadi Semati, an engaging young analyst at the Center for Scientific Research and Middle East Strategic Studies, a Tehran think tank. Like Hadian, he had done his doctoral work in political science in the United States.

"The debate today is basically between two visions: One side accepts the idea of a multifaceted, multidimensional religion that changes across time and space—and embraces pluralism," he explained, in an office crammed with books on politics and religion in both Persian and English.

"The other side says that Islam has only one essence and it can't be touched—therefore democracy is alien."

The debate had already changed the poles of Iran's political spectrum. In the 1980s, Iranian politics had been defined by radical religious hardliners on one end and realpolitik pragmatists on the other. In the 1990s, the issues had shifted, and so had the alignments. The new rival camps pitted conservatives against reformers.

But the vibrant reform movement didn't speak in unison either, Semati noted.

"Ah, there are so many voices," he added with a chuckle.

"This part of the debate is very rich and original, and it's not just about religion but also about technology and postmodernism. It's about how we can have a morally based state and society in a primarily secular world with a global interdependent economy.

"It's assumed that we'll have a religious state. The question, then, is how we reconcile modern politics, communications, technology and an avalanche of global culture. The goal is a 'domestified democracy,' meaning a democracy that is homegrown and compatible with our culture," Semati explained, as CNN news purred quietly on a small television in the corner.

"It's all the more important with the disintegration of Western civilization. We're setting the stage for the next century and the next intellectual, political and cultural movements," he said, reflecting the widespread belief that however deeply flawed Iran's theocracy was, its underlying premises were morally superior to the political abuses and social decadence in the West.

"We're doing it by tackling the most problematic issues of religion and its use in the modern world. The challenge is how to use technical advances without losing the religious and moral content so society won't disintegrate," he added. Or put another way, how to modernize without risking moral bankruptcy.

As part of this broader process, Soroush served as a stimulus for the Islamic reformation. His ideas had fueled a raging new debate and helped to create a climate where other reformers could test their own ideas and the public could demand greater participation.

"There are lots of clusters of reformers now," Semati said. "One group is concerned with reconciling democracy and the Islamic revolution. The second is more philosophical. It focuses on how to come up with a reformation within Islam. Others are looking at how to achieve political and economic development while safeguarding traditions and Islam.

"But all have the same message," he added. "All want to revitalize religion in some dynamic way."

As the debate gained momentum, the Iranian public also took a bold step in revitalizing and redefining its role. In May 1997, Iranians went to the polls in near-record numbers to elect a new president—and to reject the regime's designated successor to President Rafsanjani. They instead voted for dark-horse candidate Mohammad Khatami, who pledged to open up society and restore law and order.

Since his ouster from the Ministry of Culture, Khatami had also quietly become another advocate of Islamic reform. The movement for change was now within the regime.

IRAN'S UNICAMERAL PARLIAMENT meets in a cavernous chamber with deep royal-blue carpeting and an enormous crystal chandelier hanging from the high ceiling. Seven rows of red-upholstered seats run circularly around the room facing an elevated podium. Around the edge of the gallery for guests and press are twenty-seven large posters. Each is a portrait of one of the parliamentarians who died in the 1981 mass bombing, the bloodiest terrorist attack ever against the Islamic republic.

On a steamy August day in 1997, President Khatami gave his inaugural address before Parliament. Iranians had never heard anything like it.

"An Islamic government is one that considers itself to be the servant of the people, not their master. A government's authority is not realized by coercion or arbitrariness, but by legal acts, by respect for rights and by encouraging people's participation in decision making. People must believe that they have the right to determine their own destiny and that there are limits to government," he told the assembled lawmakers, most of whom had opposed his election.

Then he pointedly added, "We must try not to impose our personal preferences on our society at all costs. The government should even protect the rights of its opponents."[18]

Iran's new president also made an overture to his own opposition.

"Don't hesitate to speak the truth or talk of justice, for I am not above making mistakes," he said.

"Don't imagine that it's difficult for me to hear the truth. I don't wish you to imagine that I'm greater than you, for the one who finds it difficult to hear the truth and who finds it hard to implement justice will find it even harder to undertake fair and just tasks."

For a society that traditionally revered senior clerics as powerful and learned enough to interpret God's word, the sweeping public admission of fallibility was an unusual step.

Iran's fifth president was clearly a different kind of politician, as he proved over and over again during the next few months. He quickly built a reputation as accessible, candid, quick to smile and occasionally even humorous.

On his first day in office, he dined with fellow workers at the office cafeteria. On Clean Air Day, in February 1998, he made a point of taking public transport, both a communal taxi and a bus, accompanied by his chador-clad wife. A picture in the papers the next day showed him talking to a female passenger on the bus.

Four months later, he took off his clerical robes and turban and, wearing simple gray trousers and a white shirt, reported to a Tehran clinic and donated blood. State television that night showed the Iranian president stretched on his back as an intravenous needle in his forearm dripped blood into a glass vial.[19]

He even did a radio talk show.

"Go ahead, caller, President Khatami is on the line," the Tehran Radio announcer said.

With disarming charm, the Iranian leader spent the next hour answering questions on everything from serious foreign policy problems, such as the Iranian hostages then being held in neighboring Afghanistan, to social problems, such as the shortage of swimming pools in Tehran.

When eight-year-old Mojgan called from the northern town of Jajarm to complain that children had no park or pools to play in, the president replied, "You're right," and invited her and her family to visit the capital.[20]

In dealings with the public, press and other officials, President Khatami also discouraged the kind of cult of personality that had resulted in pictures of his predecessors plastered on the walls of public buildings, shops, airports, schools and private homes. He urged them not to use "flowery and exaggerated expressions" when addressing him— terms used in the past, such as "dear president, beloved by the Iranian nation." He didn't use the media as a personal outlet. His security entourages were small compared with those of several other officials. He even carried his own bags when he traveled.

Throughout his first year, President Khatami also often invoked Iran's underutilized constitution and pushed to change public vocabulary to embrace the rule of law.[21] At his first-anniversary rally, he admonished students who were shouting "death" to various issues and parties and countries.

"Please don't use such slogans," he told them. "I like to hear about life in these gatherings, not death."[22]

Within his first eighteen months in office, the new Iranian leader did more than anyone else since the revolution to change the theocracy's image, both at home and abroad.

In 1998, his debut at the opening session of the United Nations General Assembly marked a major turning point for Iran. Dressed in a diaphanous cloak of fine black mohair and the black turban that designates him as a descendant of the prophet Mohammad, President Khatami stepped before the green marble podium and proposed an unusual idea to the heads of state and foreign ministers from 185 nations.

"Allow me to speak here as a man from the East, the origin of brilliant civilizations and the birthplace of divine prophets: Abraham, Moses, Jesus and Mohammad—peace be upon them all," he began.

"Among the worthiest achievements of this century is the acceptance of dialogue and the rejection of force," he continued.

"If humanity at the threshold of a new millennium devotes all efforts to institutionalize dialogue, replacing hostility and confrontation with discourse and understanding, it would leave an invaluable legacy for future generations," he said.

A generation after the Islamic republic earned a reputation as one of the world's most dangerous states, the Iranian leader then proffered the hand of detente.

"I would like to propose that the United Nations as a first step designate 2001 as the 'Year of Dialogue Among Civilizations,' with the earnest hope that through dialogue, the realization of universal justice and liberty may be initiated," he said.

To the outside world, seized by fears that a new global division between Islam and the West would become a hallmark of the twenty-first century, President Khatami's brief speech signaled a commitment to conciliation rather than confrontation. For Iranians, the proposed dialogue carried the prospect of wider acceptance by an international community that had variously sanctioned, condemned or excluded the Islamic republic for two decades.

The speech still bore traces of resentment for past meddling by the outside world, notably the United States. The Iranian leader also gave notice that Tehran still intended to go its own way. But the rhetoric was gone. And so was the anger.

President Khatami's words were a conspicuous contrast to the revolution's early days, when founding father Ayatollah Ruhollah Khomeini railed constantly against dangerous foreign influences and Tehran aided and abetted groups targeting Western interests.

"We shall export our revolution to the whole world," the Imam had pledged. "Until the cry 'There is no God but God' resounds over the whole world, there will be struggle."[23]

Khatami's tone was also a far cry from the words of then President Khamenei, who had appeared before the world body in 1987 only to lambaste it as "a paper factory for issuing worthless and ineffective orders."[24] Tension with the outside world hadn't been limited to words. The day before, American helicopter gunships had opened fire on an Iranian naval vessel, the *Iran Ajr,* after photographing the crew dropping mines into the Persian Gulf's vital sealanes. More than a dozen American and Western hostages were also still being held by Iran's surrogates in Lebanon.

But in 1998, a new Iranian leader instead quoted from the Gospel according to St. Mark and talked of the world's commonality, past and future.

"All human beings come from one and the same origin and share a continuous and integrated history," he told the General Assembly. "Humanity, despite all its calamities and hardships, is heading towards emancipation and liberty. This is the unalterable human destiny."

President Khatami's debut at the United Nations fell just four months shy of the revolution's twentieth anniversary. And it capped his first year in office. The timing was important, because the speech also reflected a critical political juncture: Iran was starting to return to normalcy.

The transformation in tone was even more visible when President Khatami spoke to a small group of American reporters over breakfast the next day. Before his arrival in New York, Tehran had said he wouldn't be available to the foreign press, much less to any Americans. But at the last minute, a dozen American journalists were summoned to a twenty-eighth-floor suite at the United Nations Plaza, the towering glass hotel across the street from the world body where the Iranian delegation was staying.

President Khatami was relaxed and congenial from the moment he walked into the room to join us for breakfast.

"If I was given a wish, I would not be president of Iran and I would have twenty days to walk around New York, see its institutions and talk to people. But so far I've seen only the small rooms of this hotel and the halls of the United Nations," he began, smiling easily.

Over bagels, mushroom omelets and hash browns, Khatami talked candidly about the world and Iran's place in it. He expanded on his U.N. speech, in the process revealing both his study of history and the years he spent as head of Iran's library system, to which he was relegated after being purged from the Ministry of Culture in 1992.

"The misunderstandings between the West and Islam have historic roots—the Crusaders' wars on the Holy Land and after that the Turkish invasion of Europe and the West. These were not wars between Christianity and Islam, but conflicts between Christians and Muslims," he reflected, looking at us through big square glasses perched on his aquiline nose.

In contrast to other Iranian leaders, Khatami seemed comfortable with both himself and the Americans around him. Once the informal breakfast was over, we all adjourned to the next room, where television cameras and tape recorders were turned on, and he talked for another hour about a wide range of pressing issues, from low oil prices to the threat from neighboring Afghanistan.

Khatami even had kind words for the United States—or at least its people.

"In addition to industriousness, innovation, creativity and hard work, the power and strength that the United States has is not given by its politicians, but is the result of efforts by its people," he told us.

And he held out the possibility of an eventual thaw with a government that Iranian zealots liked to call the Great Satan.

"We need to create a pathway in the world of mistrust between the two countries," the Iranian leader offered. "If we can remove the misunderstandings between people, we can remove the misunderstandings between nations."

He wasn't talking about formal detente that very moment, clearly. The Iranian delegation had never responded to Secretary-General Kofi Annan's invitation to a lunch the previous day for visiting heads of state. The Iranians didn't say why. President Clinton did attend, however, and American officials later told me that they thought the delegation from Tehran was scared of an "accidental" encounter with the U.S. president.

But President Khatami did remove a huge barrier that had impeded relations between Iran and the West for a decade: the 1989 death verdict imposed by Ayatollah Khomeini on Salman Rushdie for his controversial book *The Satanic Verses*.

"We should think of the Salman Rushdie issue as completely finished," he told us.

Picking up again on his theme at the United Nations, he added, "We believe that what was shown during the Salman Rushdie case was a manifestation of the war of civilizations which was begun by the West against Muslims. From now onwards we want, rather than a war of civilizations, to push forward a dialogue of civilizations. We hope we have entered that era of dialogue."*

When an aide signaled that time was up, we thanked him and moved to go. But President Khatami wasn't finished.

"I want to end this meeting with a question. At the end of the twentieth century and the eve of the twenty-first century—and the third millennium—what is the legacy of humanity? What is the need of humanity today?" he interjected. The room went silent.

"In his famous book *The Republic*, Plato says 'What is justice?' The

---

*In a joint appearance two days later, the Iranian and British foreign ministers followed up with a formal announcement that both sides considered the decade-long drama over. And Salman Rushdie came out of hiding.

Koran says that the aim of the prophethood was defense of justice and equality. One can interpret the same meaning from the Bible and the Torah," the Iranian president continued, talking to the likes of Tom Brokaw, Christiane Amanpour, Dan Rather, the *New York Times* foreign editor and assorted diplomatic correspondents from major news magazines.

"But twenty-five hundred years after Plato, two thousand years after Jesus and fourteen hundred years after Mohammad, we still ask what is meant by justice. The very fact that humanity has not reached a united definition means we are *still* in a period of trial and error," he said, looking at us with deep concern.

"We need to have a dialogue among civilizations about the issue of justice. We must make greater efforts to have greater equality and justice for all humanity."

The new Iranian leader held similar conversations with United Nations officials. Secretary-General Kofi Annan called him "a man of his times who is determined . . . to work with his neighbors and the rest of the world. He's a man who believes in the rule of law and who also accepts that the only legitimate basis to power is the will of the people as expressed through the ballot box."[25]

President Khatami's rise to power reflected one of the most profound aspects of Iran's transformation: The clergy not only helped lead a revolution that transformed Iran. The revolution and the ideas of reformation also ended up transforming the clergy, sometimes in spite of itself. The clerics' very involvement amounted to a revolution in their traditions and beliefs.

More than any branch of Islam, Shi'ites historically were wary of political power. They viewed the state as imperfect, corruptible and a source of persecution.* But the revolution not only brought the clergy into the political system, it also made them accountable for how it was run.

Twenty years after the revolution, the transformation of the clergy

---

*Iran's official state religion is the Twelver Shi'ism, so-called because the early religious communities were led by twelve successive descendants of the prophet Mohammad through his son-in-law and cousin Ali, the first convert to Islam. A Shi'ite literally means a "follower of Ali." The mystical concepts of Shi'ism stem from the Twelfth Imam, who mysteriously disappeared in 874. Shi'ites believe he is hidden from view in a form of physical limbo known as "occultation" but will eventually return in a resurrection. While waiting for the Twelfth Imam to return, a leading Sh'ite cleric serves as his regent on earth. Ideologically, Shi'ites have never accepted temporal rule—until the Iranian revolution.

was far from over. Iranians were still struggling to sort out just what kind of role the mullahs should have. So were the mullahs.

A month after President Khatami's overture to the world community, Iran went to the polls. The vote was for the most obscure of Iran's many bodies—the Assembly of Experts. The eighty-six "virtuous and learned" clergy are roughly analogous to the Vatican's College of Cardinals. They're tasked to elect a new Supreme Leader upon the death of a Faqih and to periodically reconfirm him. The term is for eight years, although the assembly meets only for one week annually. It's never been known to challenge or otherwise oversee any of the Supreme Leader's decisions.[26]

Yet the election in October 1998 was in many ways as important as the presidential contest, for it amounted to a plebiscite on the theocracy.

The issue was not just who would be on the assembly. It was really about whether the clerics should have such a monopoly on power. It was also about whether the clerics should supervise or rule. And it was about where the theocracy, symbolized by the Supreme Leader, got its legitimacy. From God? Or from the people?

Like all Iranian elections, it was held on a Friday, the Muslim day of rest, to ensure maximum turnout. For weeks, the clergy had warned that failure to vote amounted to both sin and treason. Campaigning to get the vote out was far more intense than for seats in the assembly.

"For the Iranian nation, this is like the scene of a fully fledged battle against the enemy. The enemies are trying to discourage people, but the people are alert and will participate," Ayatollah Khamenei proclaimed shortly after he cast his own ballot.

It was a perfect day to get out, a gloriously warm autumn day with bright sunshine. I did a tour of the polling stations, starting at the Towheed Education Center, next to the Supreme Leader's home. Ayatollah Khamenei had voted there just a bit earlier.

Security was tight. I had to pass through two sets of police and my American passport got special scrutiny, the kind of treatment I used to endure regularly in the 1980s but never during the revolution's second decade.

As Lieutenant Javad Soleymanyan escorted me to the polling booth, the eager young cop urged me to be accurate in my reporting.

"The big turnout reflects the participation of the people," he said. "We hope the foreign media sends the right message, so the world will see how much the Supreme Leader is accepted and loved."

But in the light-green schoolroom only two voters were casting their ballots for sixteen seats allocated for the capital. The same was true at a dozen other polling stations, where voters tended to be outnumbered by poll workers, security and reporters.

At the Amir al-Momenin Mosque, Ali Kianiyan, a tall seventeen-year-old who planned to work in computers, said he'd voted because he needed the stamp from the polling station on his identity card to be admitted to college.

Amir Hossein, another teenager, said he'd voted to make a statement. He tucked a blank ballot into the large white box decorated with a green tulip on the top.

"A lot of my friends are doing the same thing. The government disqualifies candidates, so there's no variety. Then they try to trick us into voting by requiring us to have the stamp on our cards to do other things," he said with obvious disdain.

"Well, we're tricking them back."

The choices were indeed limited. In a major concession, the Council of Guardians had announced that women and laymen could run for the first time. Then the council promptly rejected the nine women and forty laymen who registered to run. They rejected most of the reformist clergy too. In the shameless manipulation of the electoral process that has come to typify most Iranian elections, more than half of the nearly four hundred candidates who signed up were disqualified—no specifics provided.

President Khatami acknowledged the issue. "Definitely there could have been more qualified people than were allowed, but nonetheless we still have a chance to choose our favored candidates," he said after casting his ballot where the Imam used to vote.

The pace of polling picked up a bit later in the day. To prod the numbers along, voting hours were extended by two hours, then another hour and then until the last person voted.

But the contrast to other events in the capital that day was telling. Azadi Stadium was packed for a soccer match between Iran and Iraq, even though a decade after the war between the two longstanding rivals ended there was still no formal peace and both sides charged that the other still held prisoners of war. Tehran parks bustled with picnicking families. In the evening, restaurants were crammed.

Of the dozens and dozens of people I asked, only a handful said they had voted.

"The conservative right had two choices," explained Sadeq Ziba-kalam, a Tehran University political scientist whom I stopped to see in between polling stations. He hadn't voted either.

"The first was to have a fair election and let many candidates partici-pate. That would have led to a huge turnout and would have been wonder-ful. But the right would have ended up with an assembly that could have created a lot of problems. It might have actually questioned the actions and decisions of the Supreme Leader. Some might even have been daring enough to say that the emperor has no clothes," he said, taking off glasses attached to a strap around his neck and resting them on his chest.

"Or they could try to produce a docile assembly through a controlled vote. To do that, they'd have to allow only candidates they're completely sure about and get rid of all independents. Then they'd get a low turnout. But this is clearly the wise option if you're in their shoes. It's the only way to stay in power."

Zibakalam said the poll was proving to be "a dismal failure" for the conservatives. He said that he didn't vote because it wouldn't make any difference, either in terms of who was on the assembly or what it would do.

"Obviously, most people feel that way too," he added.

At the same time, however, he said, Iranians didn't necessarily reject the idea of a Faqih.

"If there were a referendum tomorrow and people had to say whether or not they wanted a Faqih, maybe seventy percent would say yes. The concept is not at stake—yet. But its functions, powers and term in office are," he said.

"It's all progress that people are saying these things. It's part of politi-cal evolution. It's a good sign."

Indeed, across Tehran, Iranians seemed much more interested in talk-ing about what the election meant than in actually voting. Few of the people I interviewed, including voters, knew most of the candidates. But virtually everyone had an opinion about the role of the Supreme Leader, the Assembly of Experts and the clergy in general.

During the day I also stopped to see Ezzatollah Sahabi, a gutsy politi-cal iconoclast and editor of the weekly *Iran-e Farda,* or "Iran of Tomor-row." An older man with white sideburns who favored navy suits of muted pinstripes, Sahabi also didn't vote. Neither did anyone on his staff, he said.

"These last two elections have been very important in Iran. For the first time voters are really deciding things," he told me.

"In the presidential poll, Khatami got seventy percent and the people who had dominated government got only twelve percent. In this election, the ones who lost desperately want to show that they're as popular as Khatami. So they've devoted the past three months to a lot of propaganda to get the vote out. To ensure a core of voters, they obliged students, the military and others to vote.

"But voters want to show that they're not popular. A lot of people also want to say that the Leader should be supervised and that all people should have a role in supervising him, not just eighty-six clerics. Since that's not an option, they're communicating by not voting," he explained.

I told Sahabi that a prominent political scientist thought Iranians would still vote for a Faqih, if given a choice.

"I don't think most people want it, not as it is now. That's true even of the clergy in Qom. They don't accept Khamenei as the most learned cleric. They don't accept the position of a Supreme Leader," he replied.

"The Faqih may have seemed like a good idea at first, when the Imam was alive. But it's become the same as a dynasty. It's a dynasty with supernatural powers."

The next day, the government announced the official voter tally: Only 46 percent had turned out—just half of the 90 percent who'd voted in the presidential election.[27]

Conservatives defensively took a different tack.

"When some people say that the Leader's legitimacy depends on his popularity, they don't understand anything," offered Parliamentary Speaker Ali Nateq-Nouri, who'd been trounced by President Khatami a year earlier.

"Our regime gets its legitimacy from God."[28]

A generation after the revolution, the potential for reform and the wide diversity of Iran's political spectrum were probably best reflected among the Supreme Leader's own brothers. In a family of eight children, three of the four brothers had become clerics. Ayatollah Ali Khamenei, the second son, was also in the middle politically. His older brother was more to the right. But Hadi Khamenei, the Supreme Leader's younger brother by eight years, was a Qom-trained cleric on the radical left, a prominent newspaper editor critical of the conservatives, an ally and defender of Soroush—and a key adviser to President Khatami.

I called on Hadi Khamenei at the Presidential Advisers Building, a high-rise building of dark mirrored glass on Africa Square. A tall, lean man with an elegant leonine face accentuated with large aviator glasses, he was the first cleric I ever met without his turban. A long piece of cloth was draped on a corner coatrack, alongside his robe and above his shoes. Dressed in an open-neck shirt with rolled-up sleeves, he was strikingly relaxed.

"We were close as a family, but not in political views," Hadi Khamenei said, grinning in reflection.

I asked him about his recent lectures at universities and seminaries around the country. More than once he'd been attacked and beaten because of his controversial views. He'd received head injuries and been briefly hospitalized after Hizbollahis interrupted a speech he was giving at a Qom mosque. Local papers reported that the attackers broke mosque windows and tore up posters of the Iranian president as they shouted, "Death to Khatami."[29]

"There's a big debate going on now, and it's the most important issue facing society because it's so basic. It boils down to whether any official is above the law," he explained.

"My answer is no. The law should be above everything.

"But the political right, which considers itself to be the main support for the Supreme Leader, say that the Faqih is above the law, that he can change the law, that he can decree anything he feels is right," he said. "Naturally these supporters intend to use this power as well."

How? I asked.

"In everything," he replied. "If I gave you an example it would limit the potential impact of this power, because it really would be applicable to *everything*. It would be unlimited power."

And the danger is dictatorship? I asked.

"Yes," he replied, leaning his long frame back in his chair. "But those are your words, not mine.

"The wrong interpretation of the Faqih can cause a dictatorship," he said, this time in his own words.

To challenge the system, Hadi Khamenei had registered as a candidate for the 1998 Assembly of Experts election. As a cleric, he held the rank of *hojatoleslam,* or "authority on Islam," one position below an ayatollah. It was the same rank his brother had held when he was president and the same rank as President Khatami and most other clerics in government.

Not surprisingly, however, he was disqualified by the Council of Guardians.

"The council said that every candidate had to take an examination," Khamenei explained. "But I don't accept the council's right to examine me or any other candidate. So the council said that I couldn't run."

Khamenei shook his head. "The Council of Guardians also has too much power. They sometimes think they're above the law too," he said.

I told him that I'd often heard Iranians complain that the council seemed to make decisions more on the basis of personal political tastes than on qualifications, since its twelve members didn't have to explain their decisions. They weren't held accountable and there was no appeal mechanism.

"Again those are others' words," he said, nodding. "But I agree."

"The most important thing we're looking for today in Iran is the rule of law. And that means no one, whatever his position, is above it. Unfortunately for the rest of us, there are still people at the top who don't accept that basic right."

By 1998, THE ELECTION OF President Khatami had changed the climate enough that Soroush could return to Iran. Very quickly, he was in the thick of the reform movement again. The first thing he did was establish the new Institute for Wisdom and Research, where I stopped to find out what he was working on.

In his modest whitewashed office, a computer had replaced his yellow legal pad.

"I use the computer only with reluctance," he told me, with a chuckle.

He was already in the throes of planning a new scholarly journal. A bold new newspaper called *Jameh,* or "Society," set up by his followers had become the hottest paper in Tehran. A new magazine called *Right Path,* established by another group of former students and full of his ideas, had just put out its first issue. And *Kiyan* was flourishing again among intellectuals.

Perhaps more important, at least ten publications issued by the clergy devoted a great deal of space to his work—some critical, but the majority in support. His following was growing, in turn spawning a whole new generation of reformers.

"Soroush has redefined the elements of debate and issues that should be addressed by the clergy. His work is now having the biggest impact on the younger generation of clerics. But in fifteen years, they'll be senior clerics. So Soroush's full influence has yet to be felt," Hadian, the Tehran University political scientist, had told me a few days earlier.

"Islamic knowledge will not be the same in the future because of him."

Yet Soroush was also still having problems. He hadn't been allowed to return to the three universities where he had taught, which was depriving him of important income. His passport had been held for six months. And when the Muslim Students Society at Amir Kabir University had invited him to lecture, Hizbollahi thugs had once again gone after him.

"I fled. Otherwise I would have been hurt," he recalled. "The conservative right is still very powerful and they've prevented a lot of change."

Soroush had taken to varying his routes to work as well as his hours, for personal security.

Despite the public's demand for change, Iran's political transition had only begun. Reform was still an idea, although now on the table rather than under it.

Soroush was, nevertheless, plowing ahead.

What's new? I asked.

"My first article after a year away is about the right path. In everyday prayer, we recite ten times and entreat God to guide us to the right path," he replied, with an understated trace of excitement.

"Some say the only right path is Islam and the rest stray or are on a deviant path. But I argue that there are many right paths. I try to justify a pluralistic view of religions—the internal sects of Sunni, Shia and others and also the great religions like Christianity, Judaism and the rest.

"We think they go to hell and they think we go to hell," he added. "But I'm trying to say that Christians and members of other religions are well guided and good servants of God. All are equally rightful in what they believe.

"To some, this sounds like heresy," he said, with a knowing smile and a small shrug. "But this too has found listening ears in our society."

CHAPTER 3

VOICES OF THE
CULTURAL REVOLUTION

There is no fun in Islam.
                    —AYATOLLAH KHOMEINI[1]

The most stable and lasting system is the one which
creates the least limitations to freedom of expression.
In my view, freedom means freedom of thought and
security to express those thoughts without fear of
prosecution.
                    —PRESIDENT MOHAMMAD KHATAMI[2]

FOR DECADES, the most wretched corner of sprawling Tehran was the
country's main slaughterhouse. It was actually a compound of buildings
covering several blocks that spawned a seamy subculture of prostitution,
drugs and crime all around it. No one else was willing to live anywhere
nearby.

"The odor of blood and death drifted for blocks in all directions. To
live near it was to know what it's like to be stuck in hell," a cabbie told me
when I made my first visit to the neighborhood in the early 1990s.

By then, however, the slaughterhouse had been closed down and cleaned up. It'd recently reopened as the Bahman Cultural Center for the Performing Arts. Surrounded by gardens and decorated with wall-size murals in bright pastels, the whitewashed complex was the showcase of several new centers throughout Tehran created to provide drama, music, art, cinema and other forms of entertainment.

Ahmad Torabi, an energetic aide to Bahman's managing director, took me on a tour.

"The holding area where cattle and sheep were herded before slaughter is over here," Torabi said as we entered a long whitewashed building. "It's a theater now."

"*The Bear,* by Anton Chekhov, is playing at the moment. There's less of a problem with women's parts if we do plays from a long time ago. We hope to do *Cat on a Hot Tin Roof* by your Tennessee Williams in the fall, with Islamic *hejab* of course and maybe some slight adaptations to the script."

We slipped in the back and watched for a bit. The theater had a surreal quality. With large photographs of Ayatollahs Khomeini and Khamenei framing the stage, the one-act romantic farce opened with the lead actress, who played the part of an attractive young Russian widow of the Christian Orthodox faith, coming onstage and crossing herself.

Since *The Bear* was written in 1888, her garb was easily compatible with Islamic modesty. The plotline, however, had taken some tinkering. The romantic interplay between the widow and a neighboring landowner was all words, no action—meaning no touching. The final embrace had been cut altogether.

As I looked around the auditorium, I noted that only about a third of the seats were filled.

"We do a lot of plays from different countries and cultures. Recently, we've also done Chinese, Tajik and Armenian pieces," Torabi offered. "But music is generally more popular than theater."

Indeed it was. We went next to watch a rehearsal of the Bahman Philharmonic, with Noveen Afrouz at the piano, playing a Mozart piano concerto. The pristine acoustical hall was packed with young people who hadn't been able to get tickets for the sold-out recital.

"She's one of Iran's most famous pianists," Torabi explained. Afrouz, who wore a black-and-white polka dot headscarf, was clearly having a good time as she performed. The orchestra was all young people employed full-time by the center.

"This used to be the place where meat and bones from the animals were condensed into powder or meal for fertilizer," he added. "You can't recognize it now!"

In a nearby auditorium, a choral group was performing on a stage adorned with bouquets of gladiolus. The fifteen men wore black suits and white shirts—no ties, of course—while the sixteen women were gowned in green choir robes with yellow piping. Their first number was a hymn in serious praise of God, the second an anthem in glorious praise of Iran. The deeply tiered hall was packed with kids.

The appeal was obvious. In the chaotic southern suburbs, the cultural center had become an oasis. The grounds of the old slaughterhouse were rich with green grass, a rarity in Tehran. A soft Persian equivalent of Muzak was piped outdoors, offering a pleasing distraction from the honking traffic that buzzed on all sides. A playground provided slides and swings and bright yellow, red and pink play pieces. The exterior murals were also in warm colors. The most interesting wall featured a variety of kids with books, paints, pen and paper.

"They're the children of the butchers who once worked here," Torabi explained. "The people then were somewhat primitive in their knowledge. This shows how their children will now be cultured."

Rooms along the side offered classes in music, drama, handicrafts and sports. The classes included violin, piano, carpet weaving, silk flowers, wood handicrafts, computer language and gymnastics. Another set of rooms offered after-school and evening classes in various sciences, such as astronomy and physics. Adults were also welcome.

"The area where animals were slaughtered is an art gallery now. We feature local artists, but we're between shows at the moment," Torabi explained.

The most striking corner of Bahman—so-named because Bahman was the Persian month of revolutionary upheaval, when the shah departed and Ayatollah Khomeini returned—was the Charlie Chaplin Movie House. It was unmistakable. A fifteen-foot portrait of the Little Tramp, complete with bowler hat and lip mustache, was painted along the white exterior wall of the theater.

Why Charlie Chaplin? I asked Torabi.

"Ahhhh, because all Iranians know him. He's one of the film actors we love the most," he said. "The movie house can hold four hundred and fifty and it's often full."

Besides old films with Chaplin and his contemporaries, the theater showed an array of arty—albeit Islamically suitable—films from Iran, Europe, the United States and Asia.

After a decade of bitter xenophobia, Bahman symbolized the compromise struck between the Islamic regime and its public in the early 1990s. Iran still gave preeminent emphasis to its own culture and artistic accomplishments, but it slowly began to accept artistic expressions that didn't undermine Islamic sensitivities or Persian pride. In other words, the outside world was gradually being allowed back in.

Bahman also reflected one of the earliest attempts to prod the Islamic Republic into a postrevolutionary phase, to return the country to normalcy after a traumatic decade racked by political upheaval, war and Ayatollah Khomeini's death. Introducing fun in the Islamic republic was the brainchild of Tehran's then new mayor, Gholamhossein Karbaschi, who set out to rebuild society as he rebuilt the war-scarred capital. Karbaschi, a former cleric, was one of the earliest voices of reform within government.

Bahman, which even hosted Western culture, was a giant step. After politics, the revolution had initially had the greatest impact on Iran's culture. Purifying the arts of foreign influence had been as important to the Islamic republic's new identity as replacing the leadership. So most of the revolution's first decade—and the first republic—had been consumed with purging the recent past.

The revolution's original mission had been to isolate Iran from a threat that Ayatollah Khomeini had called "Westoxication." He'd borrowed the concept from Jalal Al-Ahmad, an influential thinker who coined the term *gharbzadegi*—or West-struckness—in 1963 in a book of the same name.[3]

"Culture forms the identity and being of a community. With a perverse culture, no matter how powerful a community may be economically, politically, industrially and militarily, that community is vain and empty," Khomeini had proclaimed.

"Iran has been hurt more by Westernized intellectuals than by any other group of men. Cultural reform and freeing our youth from dependency on Western culture precede all other reforms."[4]

The revolutionaries had been ruthless as they tried to create a new society centered on the devout Shi'ite Muslim, Iran's equivalent of the proletariat in Bolshevik Russia and the *citoyen* in Jacobin France. Thousands of artists had been chased into exile or forced into silence. State-controlled television and radio had been stripped down to religious programs, kiddie shows, sports and, during the war years, oft-repeated military documentaries. Foreign material had been banned in theaters and movie houses. Bookstore shelves had been cleared. Foreign fashion, in the form of miniskirts and ties, had been banned.

The cultural agenda had even shaped national security. Former Intelligence Minister Ali Fallahian once discounted American military maneuvers in the Persian Gulf as a threat to Iran. He'd toured the country to warn instead of a "cultural assault."

"Those behind this cultural offensive believe this method is far more effective than military might in countries that are run according to religious and philosophical doctrines," he had pronounced.[5]

In the end, however, Iran hadn't been able to cut itself off. The revolutionary culture was vulnerable, ironically, because of the revolution's own success. Khomeini had used tapes and videocassettes of his sermons, plus the telephone, to penetrate a border he'd physically been barred from crossing for fourteen years. His tactics had worked because Iranians were already savvy about modern technology; even an autocratic monarchy couldn't keep it out.

The revolutionaries had later found themselves in the same boat. They also hadn't been able to cut off the cross-border traffic or technical wizardry that let other ideas in the form of movies, music, television or literature trickle, seep and finally flood the public domain.

During the revolution's zealous first decade, a cultural underground had actually thrived. The outside world had been sneaked in on dhows that quietly crossed the Gulf from the Arabic emirates at night. Videos, tapes, books, magazines, CDs and other cultural contraband had been smuggled across the rugged Turkish and Pakistani borders. Iran Air crew members had brought banned material through customs after runs to Europe or Asia. And individual bribery had worked for everyone else at almost any entry point because of Iran's ever-deteriorating economy.

Sometimes the content had been crudely reproduced. One of my interpreters saw *Silence of the Lambs* and *I'll Take Manhattan* in Tehran before I did in the United States. As happened with most American and European movies, they'd been videotaped by someone in the audience during sneak previews in Los Angeles, home to the largest community of Iranians outside Iran, and shipped off to the Islamic Republic, where black marketeers did door-to-door business from the trunks of their cars.

Even the government had occasionally cheated. During the rough war years, more than a few Revolutionary Guards had told me of watching pirated copies of Sylvester Stallone's Rambo and Rocky series or any movie featuring Arnold Schwarzenegger. The troops loved American action films.

"They're supposed to rev us up," a young soldier told me in the mid-1980s. "And they usually do." Rambo was his favorite.

Scholars and government officials had also had access to the outside world. In 1988, I'd lunched with a small group of women researchers at the Institute for Policy and International Studies, the Foreign Ministry's think tank. Its library had been well stocked with issues of the *New York Times* and the *Christian Science Monitor,* plus the latest *Foreign Affairs, Middle East Journal* and several other periodicals. The racks had also offered recent publications from Russia, China, France, Britain and Germany, as well as a host of Third World countries.

"Oh, we definitely keep up," Mina, one of the female scholars, told me.

Over lunch, the ladies had wanted to know all about the 1988 Democratic and Republican Conventions, to be held a few weeks hence in Atlanta and New Orleans, and who was likely to replace Ronald Reagan. They had been, with unanimity, disparaging about Reagan.

"I think Art Buchwald knows more about Iran than Ronald Reagan does. I love Buchwald's columns. I loved the one best about an Iranian moderate that ran after Irangate," said Mina, laughing. She'd seen it in the *International Herald Tribune.* Any lingering hope that she'd had for Reagan had been lost after she read claims by former White House chief of staff Donald Regan that the president's schedule was determined by an astrologer.

"Could this really be true," she asked, "of an American president?"

Iran also hadn't been able to keep out the Persian services of the Voice of America and the BBC, neither of which the government jammed. For many Iranians, foreign radio broadcasts offered the primary source of news.

After the U.S.S. *Vincennes* shot down an Iran Air airbus en route to the United Arab Emirates in 1988, killing all 290 on board, I'd asked a businessman named Mehdi Gangi about public reaction.

"I was with a few friends," he recalled. "It was such a shock. We couldn't believe it from America. Every one of us thought maybe an Iranian missile did it and the government was just blaming the United States. We didn't accept that America shot it down until we heard it from the VOA and the BBC."

Despite the "Great Satan" rhetoric, Tehran's press also continued to publish American wire service stories and a daily array of news from the West, while the English-language papers ran European and American sports, features, health news, crosswords, comics such as "Nancy" and word games like "Jumble."

"Iranians have probably been far less cut off from the West than the West, with its free press, has been cut off from Iran," a long-serving European ambassador mused during an interview in the late 1980s.

By the early 1990s, Iran had recognized it could no longer keep the doors shut. Nor had it tried as hard to anymore. The regime's ability to survive Ayatollah Khomeini's passing as well as the war with Iraq and more than a decade of American economic sanctions had increased the sense of confidence that the revolution would not easily be undone. Iran's economic ties with a world rapidly globalizing after the demise of socialism had also made it more difficult.

Perhaps most important, however, the government of President Rafsanjani, which came to power in 1989, had recognized that public boredom was a bigger threat than the outside world. In one of his earliest acts, Rafsanjani had appointed Karbaschi mayor to revive Tehran.

Bahman and the string of new cultural centers where Iran mixed with the West in a controlled environment were part of the response. So, for a while, was the satellite dish. It transformed Iranian lifestyles as well as the skylines of most major cities almost overnight.

On a trip to Tehran in 1994, shortly after satellite dishes became the craze, I talked to a woman I'd known for years who used to brag about never watching Iran's Islamic television. This time, she confessed her infatuation with the huge array of programs available off her satellite dish. She was riveted to talk shows like *Oprah* and *Donahue.* She gossiped with friends over plotlines of American soap operas—*The Bold and the Beautiful* and *Santa Barbara*—as if the characters were real people. She and her husband spent evenings with the skimpily clad babes of *Baywatch,* the legal eagles of *L.A. Law* or the Carrington clan of *Dynasty.* And after she went to bed, her husband sometimes lingered for either the sports programs or late-night Turkish porn.

"You in America have better things to do. We don't," she told me.

For Iran's young, MTV and later its Asian equivalent out of Hong Kong were the rage. Kids planned forbidden parties around their favorite programs. Many adopted the hairstyles, fashions and slang of performers. A high school English teacher lamented the way dialogue from various shows took over in classes.

"English has been the second language in this country for many, many years, long before the revolution. And it didn't change when America became the Great Satan," the teacher said.

"But since satellites were introduced, the *kind* of English people speak has changed a lot! The vocabulary, the ideas, the attitudes, ooosh, it's much more common and so *familiar,*" she said disparagingly, since Persian language and customs tend to be quite formal.

The regime wasn't immune from the trend. Government officials, academics, newspaper offices and military headquarters were hooked into and on CNN or BBC news channels. I spent many surreal hours sitting in government offices being harangued by some official because of Western media coverage of Iran—at the same time CNN's Judy Woodruff, Bernard Shaw, Iranian-born and local favorite Christiane Amanpour or even Larry King appeared on a television screen in the background.

During President Rafsanjani's early years in office, the cultural climate generally changed in lots of other small but telling ways.

American publishers were allowed to have stalls for the first time at the annual book fair. At one book fair I attended in the early 1990s, the stalls of McGraw-Hill, Westview, MIT Press, American Veterinary Publishers and Little, Brown were packed with young students, middle-aged couples, local booksellers, academics and the curious.

I asked Behruz Narami at the McGraw-Hill stand if he was really an official rep.

"I'm a freelance agent for the McGraw-Hill branch in Britain," he said. "Selling American books in Iran is like selling Iranian oil to America. You can't do it directly, so you do it through foreign branches."*

I asked about the volume of book sales.

"Oh, we're very popular," Narami said. "McGraw-Hill's been a well-known name, long before the revolution and all the time since then. Many McGraw-Hill books are still used in universities. It's not hard to bring them from Singapore and Dubai dealers."

* At the time, despite economic sanctions, American oil companies were the largest purchasers of Iranian oil, mainly through intermediaries on the Rotterdam market. The Clinton administration subsequently tightened restrictions on importing Iranian petroleum products.

The book fair reflected the broader transition under way, as Rafsanjani attempted to shift Iran's focus from zealotry to pragmatism during the revolution's second republic.

In a separate section, the two militant Palestinian groups—Islamic Jihad and Hamas—also had stalls. Islamic Jihad offered gruesome posters of martyrs from its campaigns against Israeli troops in Lebanon or the West Bank. Arabic-language magazines were also for sale. The Hamas booth featured a documentary on the four hundred Palestinian deportees stranded for weeks between the Israeli and Lebanese borders. Israel wanted to get rid of them; Lebanon wouldn't take them. Videocassettes were available for sale, as was a pile of Hamas literature.

During the morning I spent wandering through the fair, I never saw a single Iranian stop by either stall for more than a minute or two, and usually only to briefly look at the posters and then meander on. No one bought anything. Exporting the revolution to their brethren didn't seem to much interest or inspire Iranians anymore.

The cultural opening of the early 1990s affected all the arts. Onstage, the City Theater in Tehran offered Persian versions of Shakespeare classics, such as *The Merchant of Venice,* as well as contemporary hits like Arthur Miller's *The Crucible.* The *Tehran Times* "Thought of the Day" box, once devoted to Koranic verses and Muslim thinkers, began quoting Keats, Voltaire and other great Western writers. At several local cinemas, a heavily edited version of *Dances with Wolves* played to sold-out theaters.

Western music, once banned, also crept back. The Tehran Symphony played Beethoven and Bach again. Even Muzak in public buildings and musical interludes on television went West. When I was in my hotel room I often turned on the Voice and Vision of Iran, the state-run television and radio stations, to monitor the news or see what else was being aired. One night I heard the unmistakable voice of Frank Sinatra crooning "Strangers in the Night." On the same 1994 trip, I went into the new Refah department store, a chain open around the clock, and heard a medley of Western tunes, including "Rudolph the Red-Nosed Reindeer," purring through the public address system. And in a particularly appropriate irony, the music played for any caller put on hold at the press section of the Ministry of Culture and Islamic Guidance was the theme song from *The Sting,* the movie starring Robert Redford and Paul Newman.

Of all the arts, music was a particularly sensitive issue in the Islamic republic. Iran's strict interpretation of Islam did not condone any influence that took a believer into a state out of his or her being, whether by alcohol, drugs or music. As a result, the Iranian media featured little music in the early years besides military marches and the new national anthem. Foreign music had been anathema.

"Western music dulls the mind because it involves pleasure and ecstasy, similar to drugs," Ayatollah Khomeini had warned in the revolution's early days.[6]

The problem of music—and how it was first addressed—had once been explained to me by Mohammad Hashemi,* the younger brother of then President Ali Akbar Hashemi Rafsanjani and a power in his own right as managing director of the Voice and Vision of Iran. We'd talked in the late 1980s, just a few months before Ayatollah Khomeini's death and just as the revolution had begun to moderate its militancy. Hashemi, whose cherubically round face and limited facial hair revealed the family's Mongol ancestry, controlled the two channels of television as well as Tehran Radio.

"There were some differences about the music we played," Hashemi had explained as he padded around his eleventh-floor office in gray-stockinged feet.

"This is an Islamic government organization, and since some people didn't like musicals or TV shows or series, they started to criticize us in several places—in the mosques and the newspapers and at Friday prayers.

"But of course," he'd continued, "we can't simply say, 'We're right, you're not; your understanding is not correct.' Usually in these sorts of differences you must have someone say who is correct. Our reference is Imam Khomeini. We write to him and ask him questions, since there's no reference in his books to this subject."

That, in fact, was exactly how many rulings, interpretations and fatwas were issued by ordinary clergy as well as the Imam. They were often merely answers to questions in what amounted to written conversations.

"In this case, he said most of the music was good and not against Islam," Hashemi had said.

"This kind of question isn't anything unusual in Islam. When you have to ask questions about daily personal life, you go to a mullah, just like when you go to a doctor for a cure. In this country, we go to the clergy

---

*As is common clerical tradition, Rafsanjani took the name of his hometown, Rafsanjan, after becoming a cleric. The "i" at the end denotes that he is a person of Rafsanjan, just as Khomeini's name denotes his origins in Khomein. The rest of Rafsanjani's family, however, kept the last name Hashemi, including his children.

on all social issues. With big questions, we go to the Imam. His word is the last word."

So with Khomeini's blessing, different kinds of music, including old foreign favorites, had once again played in Iran. Shortly before his death, even the Imam had mellowed—a bit.

The same problem had arisen over broadcasting foreign films and sports programs on wrestling and soccer.

"The Imam answered that he watched some of our programs and most were educational or useful and no impediment to Islam, but he said we have to be careful about nonreligious themes," Hashemi had explained, in a distinct American accent acquired when he had attended the University of California, Berkeley, and driven a local cab.

So, again, the shows had continued.

Like his brother, Hashemi was then among a growing faction—at the time described as Iranian "moderates"—who sought to make the Islamic Republic more compatible with contemporary times and more fully embraced by its people. As the climate further relaxed in the early 1990s, he launched new television channels and spiced up priggish programming. He added foreign shows like Agatha Christie's British mystery series *Poirot* and Pink Panther cartoons. Iranian television also broadcast the 1994 World Cup almost live. The delay of a few seconds was to allow crowd shots of women in Western dress to be cut.

The same year, the Voice and Vision of Iran even introduced its own version of morning television. *Good Morning Iran* mimicked the news-feature-weather format of its American counterpart. The first time I watched the show, it ran street interviews about new Iranian movies, snippets of upcoming children's programs, arty film of wildlife and a peek inside the latest shows at Tehran's art galleries.

But the regime still never strayed far from its mission. The main features on *Good Morning Iran* that day were heavy religious fare—a mullah lecturing on profiteering and an interview with a woman who had memorized the entire Koran.

Many of the other daytime and evening shows were also slim pickings. Two of the regular repeats were *A Decade of the Iranian Military* and *Fifty Years of Iranian Wrestling.*

For a weary and long-bored public, the changes at Iranian television and the other openings of the early 1990s were too little, too late. A columnist on the English-language *Iran News* wrote a tongue-in-cheek piece summing up public reaction.

"I managed to interview 80 percent of the Iranian people," the writer boasted of his fictitious poll. "And they all said the same thing: 'We'd be most grateful if the six channels were reduced to one. And then we'd be most grateful if that one channel stopped showing most of the things they show!' "[7]

Yet by the mid-1990s, the pattern and pace of change had moved way too far, way too fast for the new crop of conservatives who'd gained the political edge after the 1992 parliamentary elections. A confrontation between the voices of moderation and the conservatives, who had a vastly different vision of Iran's future, became inevitable.

An early skirmish erupted over the very technology that had helped bring the religious regime to power. That same technology now came to be viewed by conservatives as the revolution's nemesis.

The first flap was over VCRs. Conservatives in Parliament wanted to ban them completely. Pragmatists aligned with President Rafsanjani crafted a compromise that allowed Iranians to keep the video machines. But Parliament did vote to prohibit the vast majority of foreign videos. The government instead flooded the shops with mullah-approved local tapes.[8]

The VCR ruling, of course, did nothing to stem the cultural tidal wave. So Iran's conservatives then moved against satellite dishes.

In one of his last acts, the ranking Shi'ite cleric in the whole Muslim world handed down an edict condemning the big silver dishes that had sprouted atop homes, apartment buildings and office blocks. Grand Ayatollah Mohammad Ali Araqi had just turned one hundred years old when he issued a fatwa charging that satellites spread the "family-devastating diseases of the West."[9]

Picking up on his instructions, young Basij militants began barging into homes with satellite dishes and smashing or confiscating receivers. Both the public and the press reacted with outrage, leading Rafsanjani's government to try to rein them in. So the increasingly independent Parliament then simply introduced legislation to outlaw satellite dishes altogether.

"The government must defend Islamic cultural values, just as it has to defend the border," noted conservative Lotfollah Zarei Qanavati demanded in a tirade before Parliament. "Spreading corruption, robbing youths of moral values, decadent clothes and sexual problems are all deviations bred by satellite television."[10]

The bill called for confiscation of all dishes and fines of five to ten times their value for anyone who dared to keep them. The law easily passed the required three readings and went into effect in late 1995. When most owners simply moved their dishes inside courtyards or camouflaged them as air conditioners, Parliament called on the government to use military helicopters to fly over Iran's cities to track suspicious shapes atop apartment buildings and homes.

But Iranians are a determined lot and many were unwilling to surrender their first serious cultural freedoms. The Iranian press regularly carried hilarious stories of inventive satellite dish smugglers. My favorite story involved a police raid on a truck carrying tuna; inside the cargo police also found dozens of rather smelly satellite dishes.[11]

More to the point was a comment from Ibrahim Yazdi, the revolution's first foreign minister, who resigned after the American Embassy seizure and later became a dissident. "Nobody can close the sky," he told me.

For the rest of the 1990s, culture became the front line for a broader existential conflict over the extent of freedom that would be tolerated in the Islamic republic. Few issues were as contentious as the parameters of Islamic correctness.

The war over Iran's future played out in escalating clashes over both profound issues such as Islamic identity and the kind of mind-boggling minutiae targeted during the revolution's early years. Conservatives won several early rounds.

In one of the more absurd cases, an artist who converted her grandson's teddy bears into poster art for friends was denied permission by the Ministry of Culture and Islamic Guidance to mass-produce the work—on the grounds that animals don't wear clothes.

To counter the craze among Iranian girls for Barbie dolls, conservatives banned them. It didn't work. Every Iranian toy store I've ever been into has had shelves lined with Barbies—in miniskirts, shorts, slinky gowns and even swimsuits. So conservatives mandated production of an Iranian alternative. Islamically draped Sara took the place of Barbie; Dara was modeled on boyfriend Ken, although he was billed instead as her brother.

"Barbie is like a Trojan horse. Inside, it carries its Western cultural influences, such as makeup and indecent clothes. Once it enters our society, it dumps these influences on our children," explained Majid Qaderi, director of Iran's Institute for Intellectual Development of Children and the designer of the Islamic dolls.

"Barbie is an American woman who never wants to get pregnant and have babies. She never wants to look old and this contradicts our culture. Sara and Dara will reflect strict Iranian society."[12]

The government actually banned dancing dolls made in neighboring Azerbaijan and smuggled across the border. An entwined pair of male and female dolls, meant to resemble a Latino man and woman, danced the popular lambada to accompanying music. The Tehran press blasted the toys as "half naked," because the female doll had no *hejab,* and "depraved," because the pair touched, but they were actually outlawed because they were dancing.[13]

In the theater, a Tehran production of Tennessee Williams' *The Glass Menagerie* was challenged in 1995 when students wrote local papers to protest that a man and woman touched and lit cigarettes onstage, the latter a public offense because it was the Muslim fasting month of Ramadan.

"The female and male entered into very vulgar physical contact," the students said in a letter to the conservative newspaper *Jomhuri Islami,* or "Islamic Republic." "We still haven't recovered from the shock when an actor and an actress embraced very tightly and uttered a line to the effect that 'We have to censor the kissing,' " the students complained.[14]

The play was canceled.

For a production of Chekhov's *Uncle Vanya,* censors from the Ministry of Culture and Islamic Guidance ended up permitting live piano music, a drinking scene and an Islamic version of a Victorian snood bedecked with ribbons to denote curls to cover the actresses' hair, but only after an enormous back-and-forth in Tehran's media and long delays as censors deliberated.

"I don't know when they'll give us their decision. They come to rehearsals, they watch, then they go away. Then they come again, they watch and go away," director Pari Saberi told me when I visited the theater. "We may be rehearsing forever."

Beethoven and Mozart concerts also led to protests in the media. A conservative paper ran a long poem entitled "For Whom Do the Violin Bows Move?"—a parody of Hemingway's *For Whom the Bell Tolls.* It suggested that the music choices catered to "the worm of monarchical culture"—specifically women "with pushed-back scarves" whose Islamic dress was not properly modest and men with "protruding bellies" who had grown fat off the black market—and not the "downtrodden" in whose name the revolution had been carried out.[15]

Publications that went too far out on a limb suddenly found they couldn't get access to state-subsidized paper—the only way virtually all newspapers and magazines could afford to publish, because they charged readers only a few cents. Because of paper shortages, independent and serious journals increasingly had to tell contributors that they couldn't pay for articles. Some even had to tell authors that any prospect of getting into print depended on writers' helping to pay the costs of publication. New financial pressures led several weeklies to become monthlies and monthlies to become bimonthlies. Book authors, playwrights and screenwriters awaiting approval from the Ministry of Culture and Islamic Guidance found that their manuscripts lingered longer and longer in the censor's office. Some went into quasi-permanent limbo.

Parliament also drafted a bill to formally purge all Western words from Farsi, banning them in everything from public addresses and books to advertisements, the latter not an easy task in a country with vast amounts of imports from the West.

No one was exempt. "Officials, together with the legal, executive and representative organs of the state, will not use Western words any more in their speeches, interviews or written statements," the bill stipulated.[16]

Most ominous, however, were the physical and professional attacks on writers. The most egregious case was the 1994 arrest of Ali Akbar Saidi Sirjani—a leading dissident writer, a historian and a best-selling novelist.

The formal charges were drug abuse and espionage. But few took the allegations seriously, even key government officials. When I pressed a long-serving civil servant at the Ministry of Culture and Islamic Guidance about whether he really, *really* thought the regime would be able to convince either Iranians or the outside world that Sirjani was a spy, he looked at me for a long time. Then he shrugged. Almost everyone I interviewed assumed the real offense stemmed from passages in many of Sirjani's history books about Iran's pre-Islamic tradition of respect for human rights.

Eight months after his arrest, the regime quietly announced that Sirjani had died in prison of a heart attack. It seemed an unlikely sequence of events. The family said the author, in his sixties, had no history of heart problems or drug use.

I went back to my contact at the Ministry of Culture and Islamic Guidance and asked again if he really, *really* believed the government's story. This time he didn't even bother to answer.

But the showdown over culture in the mid-1990s was hardly a one-way fight. In a marked departure from its conduct during the first republic, when it exhibited a cowed public silence, the arts community didn't surrender. This time, new voices emerged—with a response.

One of the earliest rounds of the counteroffensive came in the form of an open letter entitled "We Are Writers." It represented ten months of work by eight of Tehran's literati who argued among themselves, sometimes ferociously, over its content. After days of anxious telephone calls, faxes and secret meetings, 134 writers, novelists, poets, journalists, scholars and literary translators—including many who had once rallied around the regime—signed it.

The tone was almost apologetic and the language tame. But the three-page letter nonetheless ranked as the boldest cultural protest since the revolution. It politely requested—from whom it never specified, the government never mentioned—three things:

- First, an end to censorship. "Our main goal and priority is to remove the obstacles to freedom of thought, expression and publication," it said.
- Second, freedom for writers to associate. "What is going on is a democratic process toward the formation of an independent, professional association for writers," it explained.
- Third, noninterference in writers' private lives. "Invading the private life of a writer as a method of gathering evidence to criticize her/his written work is a flagrant violation of her/his human rights and infringement of her/his privacy," added the letter innocuously addressed "To Whom It May Concern."

"We Are Writers" was never published at home, of course, although it was sent to forty Iranian publications as well as the Ministry of Culture and Islamic Guidance. It was set for the pages of *Takapou,* one of a handful of new magazines testing official taboos. *Takapou* is Persian for "search." Censors ordered the letter cut at the last minute, according to Mansour Koushan, the *Takapou* editor and one of the letter's eight drafters.

"We Are Writers" was fully aired only outside Iran—by the BBC, the Voice of America and a few Western publications. Arthur Miller, ironically one of the few Western playwrights whose works had been performed in Iran, read it at an annual PEN conference. Czech President

Vaclav Havel, a playwright who had led the opposition movement against Communism, publicly praised the signers for their political bravery.

But many in Iran knew about "We Are Writers," in no small part because conservatives publicly went after the signers. Conservative papers blasted the writers as "café-haunting guerrillas," Freemasons and atheists, the latter particularly problematic in the Islamic Republic. And during Friday prayers at Tehran University, where clerics sermonized their version of government policy, Ayatollah Ahmad Jannati issued an open threat.

"You want to write lies, to make accusations, to mar others' reputations and to weaken the foundation of our young people's beliefs. But our people and our officials aren't going to let you do that," he warned.

"Let me tell you that if you don't observe the limits and if you keep doing what you're doing, then the Hizbollah people will definitely come to sense their duty."[17]

But the voices of reform and moderation clearly won some ground in this particular battle. Other parties were also emboldened to speak out.

"We believe the writers' problem should be looked into by the country's cultural officials in a healthy atmosphere and away from vilification, accusation and slander," countered *Gozaresh Hafteh,* an independent publication meaning "Weekly Report."

"Let us never forget that demonstrating patience, tolerance and forbearance before others' views and words is the most cardinal step toward a true democracy."

On state-owned television, a prominent member of Parliament also criticized the way young censors with little experience were empowered to pass judgment on the work of seasoned writers. He implied publicly what Iranian writers charged privately: that censorship was often arbitrary to the point of being whimsical and that it usually had as much to do with a writer's suspected politics as with his or her artistic product.

The writers themselves also sensed a nuanced gain.

"Something is certainly happening," reflected Changiz Pahlevan, a charming and slightly paunchy man who was one of Iran's best-known political writers and a signatory of the open letter. He'd come under earlier attack by conservatives who'd charged he was an atheist, even though he'd openly and often talked about a role for religion in society.

Why now? I asked him shortly after the letter was released.

"Most of all because there's a deep-rooted desire for change," he said.

"Attitudes are shifting both in society and government. There are even some high-ranking clergy who are open-minded and respect the differences of opinion."

He paused for a moment. "I actually think the desire for cultural change is deeper than the desire for political change," he added. "This is part of a critical moment for Iran."

Other signatories said "We Are Writers" indicated that a cultural monologue was becoming a dialogue.

"Eight or ten years ago it wouldn't have been possible to get together and put out a letter like this," explained Reza Baraheni, an avant-garde poet with a distinctive white goatee. "Some people in government now look at these things with a cooler head than in past years. We can say these things because we know there's an audience."

Baraheni, another of the letter's eight drafters, had been jailed both by the shah and during the revolution's early days—in the same prison. In 1981, the revolutionaries had held him in solitary and made him go through a mock firing-squad execution. Released after three months, he lost his position at Tehran University in 1982, forcing him to teach creative writing and literary theory in his cramped, book-lined basement.

I visited him at his north Tehran home shortly after "We Are Writers" came out. Despite his experience, he and others argued that the revolution ending twenty-five centuries of monarchy was not counterproductive for Iran's literary community.

"The revolution—which I distinguish from the government—opened new ways of looking at things and gave writers access to more people," Baraheni explained. "Remember, censorship didn't begin after the revolution. The shah's government ordered all printing shops to publish only books approved by the writing bureau of the Ministry of Culture. The bureau was a euphemism for censorship."

The political upheaval particularly opened the way for a revolution in Persian literature. For over a millennium, poetry had had priority in a land that revered the lyrics of mystics such as Hafez, Ferdowsi, Rumi and Attar, who wrote at the height of Persian and Islamic glory in the thirteenth and fourteenth centuries.

"Today three other narrative forms—history, fiction and movies—have become more significant than reading poetry, the historically representative form of literature here," Baraheni added.

"So too have themes changed because of the revolution, the

eight-year war with Iraq and the overall empowerment and literacy of a greater number of people."

That knowledge didn't make the fallout from "We Are Writers" any easier. Many signers received direct or indirect threats about their jobs or prospects of future publication. Baraheni and three others were summoned by intelligence officials and interrogated.

"I was told to sit on a chair facing the wall. After a long time, someone came in and told me not to look back and to listen carefully. I was told I was *persona non grata,* no longer welcome in Iran," Baraheni recalled. "I was told this was my last warning."

Within a month, 10 of the 134 had withdrawn their names. Others were nervous.

One of the signers was philosophical. "More of us may back down. I may even have to do or say something to keep my job," he told me. "But knowledge of the letter and what it represents is now out there, and for all this government's power, it can't retract an idea."

That idea, in fact, did inspire others. Within months, more than two hundred film directors and actors issued another petition appealing for an end to stiff state controls of Iran's movie industry. It called for "cancellation or serious reduction in the straitjacket regulations and complicated methods of supervision" of film production. This one did make it into the Iranian press.[18] The response was a ban on the export of any film portraying a "negative image of Iran."

Claiming a monopoly on truth, the Government of God had decided to actively quash all challenges, whatever the form.

Fearful of losing any further ground, conservatives within the clergy, Parliament, the judiciary and the Council of Guardians escalated the cultural offensive. From late 1994 through mid-1997, Iran witnessed the most repressive campaign since the 1979 upheaval. The conflict began to look more like an internal crusade or inquisition.

The trend paralleled the internal political struggle. President Rafsanjani, a masterful politico, became a lame duck after his 1993 reelection. The momentum behind greater cultural and artistic expression faced the same fate as his ambitious plans for political and economic reform: Parliament's conservative bloc balked. The internal balance of power increasingly shifted in favor of Ayatollah Khamenei, the weak former president whose tenuous position as Supreme Leader was consolidated courtesy of conservative political pressures and Hizbollah thuggery.

The transfer of power was reflected in the skirmish over control of Iranian television and in the ouster of President Rafsanjani's brother as its managing director. He was not alone. Conservatives increasingly targeted individuals pushing for cultural freedom. This was the period during which Abdul Karim Soroush, Iran's leading philosopher, came under physical and verbal attack.

In 1996, a new television series entitled *Hoviyat,* or "Identity," targeted other intellectuals through a mix of crude innuendo and outright slander. Baraheni was one of them. The program charged that he was a "decadent person" and that his literature was "immoral."

For most of the writers, the worst charge was that of being a stooge to Western ideas. In a typical *Hoviyat* show, the screen would fill with an American hundred-dollar bill and the printed face of Benjamin Franklin would fade into a picture of the Iranian writer under attack. Voices of the hosts—all men noted for their melodramatic incantations during funerals and Ashura commemorations—would wail with obvious disgust as they read something written by the latest victim. Then they'd offer their own conspiratorial spin about what the passage really meant.[19]

Most writers felt the impact, directly or indirectly. In 1996, Baraheni was again summoned by intelligence officials.

"This time I was told that nothing of mine could be published until further notice," he later recalled.

He opted to flee Iran altogether. He ended up with refugee status in Canada, teaching at the University of Toronto.

Many left behind found that their work went into limbo. In 1996, virtually none of the fifteen hundred fiction manuscripts and screenplays submitted to the Ministry of Culture and Islamic Guidance won approval for publication or production.[20]

The ministry instead issued new censorship rules: No close-ups of women in movies. For both cinema and stage performances, no makeup and no women running—lest their movements reveal the shape of their bodies. And for plays, movies, television and literature, no antagonist could carry the name of one of the most sacred figures in Islamic history—Mohammad, Ali, Hassan or Hussein.[21]

Writers and publishers who dared to defy conservative commands paid a price. In a typical incident, a Tehran bookstore was firebombed for publishing a book condemned by conservative clerics as "un-Islamic." The attack led the mullahs to publicly praise the arsonists "for doing what the government should have done." When a newspaper published by other clergy countered that those kinds of comments encouraged anarchy, its offices were mobbed by demonstrators chanting, "Death to the enemies of Islam."

Several dozen Hizbollahi militants, including women, also attacked two Tehran movie theaters that showed the popular new comedy *Present from India.* The film was about a merchant who took a bride from India. What sparked the violence was the joyous wedding scenes, including a four-minute segment showing little girls dancing. The problem was that the film was set at the same time as the 1980–88 war raged between Iran and Iraq, and the militants viewed this as disrespectful to the hundreds of thousands of families who had lost husbands, sons, fathers, uncles, cousins, and even grandfathers during the conflict.

The thugs chanted slogans against the film as they smashed glass doors and video games inside the waiting area. The attack ignited a panic—and then a stampede in which several moviegoers were trampled underfoot and a pregnant woman was pushed down the stairs. The protest amounted to a warning, the local press reported, about the government's "negligence" in issuing permits for the movie to be made and then screened.[22]

In the end, the Ministry of Culture and Islamic Guidance censored the four-minute segment—and made the director recut the film. Both theaters, however, opted against showing it again.

The highly visible and volatile struggle for the revolution's future had a sweeping impact on Iranian society. As in the revolution's early days, most Iranians retreated. This time, however, they weren't cowed by conservative pressure. This time, many Iranians simply moved cultural events into their homes.

An evening I spent at a middle-class home in hilly north Tehran was typical. About twenty of us sat on the floor against long cushions woven in rich reds and browns. We chatted while supping on a refreshingly light yogurt soup with dill and cucumbers. A three-year-old with a ponytail pranced among the bowls of potato chips and pistachios until most were gone. Her mother, the hostess, was an elegant woman dressed in turquoise balloon trousers and a turquoise, pink and white floral shirt—with jewelry to match.

As we sat cozily on the floor, a man in the corner began to tap on a santur, a Persian instrument that was a cross between a xylophone and a zither. It was melodious, if slightly tinny to an unaccustomed ear.

"He was very famous before the revolution," one of the guests said of the musician. "He used to play in many of the clubs. Now he gets some work in private homes, but not very much."

Soon the hostess's brother-in-law began to sing along to the music, his eyes closed and his body swaying slowly side to side. He worked in biology and genetics, his wife said, but his first love had always been the poetry of Hafez that he'd put to music.

As the beat picked up, many of the men began to click their fingers and several urged the hostess to dance. She took to the center of the floor and began to move rhythmically and rather erotically. Light from the chandelier above her exposed the outline of her hips and thighs under her clothing, which, somehow, I sensed that she knew. The guest next to me asked if I'd seen this type of dancing before. I made the mistake of saying yes, that I had lived in Beirut for several years.

"This is nothing like the way the Arabs dance," interjected the guest, clearly appalled. "This kind of dance is done *only* in Iran!"

Later in the evening, another guest brought out the manuscript of his latest book. It was among those that had been awaiting approval for more than a year. For the next half hour, he read us a section of his fictional tale of love and sin, jealousy and envy. We all sat back on our cushions and quietly conjured up images of the encounters he described. The deeper he got into the story, the more it sounded like a Puritan plotline out of Nathaniel Hawthorne rather than a lusty Persian update of *Arabian Nights*. It was, nonetheless, compelling.

He stopped long before the end, to unanimous disapproval.

When we pressed him to tell us what happened in the story, he added mischievously, "You'll have to wait until it's published."

Throughout the evening, liquor flowed freely. "Vodka or brandy?" the host had offered me.

I asked where he'd managed to get liquor, thinking of the homemade stills I'd seen on visits to Saudi Arabia.

For several years, he replied, he'd had a regular source of quality moonshine. But he didn't want to divulge the details.

Other guests told me that Armenians, who were legally allowed to make wine for the Christian sacrament, were a common source. A few pharmacies, I'd been told on earlier trips, used their equipment on the Islamic weekend to produce local liquor. The richest Tehranis, the host said, relied on the genuine labels smuggled in through the borders and sold at exorbitant prices even by black-market standards.

Liquor, however, was not the Islamic republic's biggest substance issue. As Iranians found themselves stuck at home, opium use became increasingly rampant. The practice predated the revolution by centuries, even among the kings and the clergy. Reza Shah Pahlavi, founder of Iran's last dynasty, smoked a little opium, usually standing up before he went to work, a United Nations drug expert told me. Opium was eventually outlawed during his rule, but its use continued among wealthy and middle-class adults. Although alcohol was forbidden in Islam for seventeen centuries, Iran's clergy didn't issue fatwas against drugs until after the revolution.

After 1979, however, locally grown opium was cheaper and more accessible than alcohol, despite the dangers. Tehran newspapers regularly reported dozens of drug busts and executions for drug convictions.

Growing numbers of Iranians, however, didn't seem to care.

"It dulls the pain of boredom," explained a middle-aged businessman.

AMONG IRANIAN POLITICIANS, Ataollah Mohajerani often dared to be different. Very different.

In 1997, the engaging forty-four-year-old former academic, diplomat and politician stood before Parliament and described Iran's Ministry of Culture and Islamic Guidance as the "laughingstock" of government. The statement was daring because Mohajerani had just been appointed to head it.

"I condemn the burning of bookshops, the beating of university lecturers and the attacks on magazine offices. And if I go to the Ministry of Culture and Islamic Guidance, I will oppose almost all the current methods," he boldly told Parliament.

"This is because I believe we must value our artists, writers and filmmakers, as they deserve our respect. We must create an atmosphere of peace and tranquillity in all centers of culture where all citizens can express their ideas and where the seeds of creativity can blossom."

It was a go-for-broke speech. Mohajerani had been elected to Iran's first revolutionary Parliament in 1980, yet virtually no one thought he'd be confirmed by the crop of conservatives who had the majority a generation later. Iranian pundits predicted he'd be the scapegoat to signal President Khatami that he better watch his step.

But Mohajerani instead admonished the conservatives.

"Islam is not a dark alley," he told Parliament. "Everyone can walk freely in the path of Islam. Everyone who has accepted the Islamic republic and its constitution must be subject to tolerance."[23]

To the astonishment of many both in and out of government, Mohajerani was confirmed—with a healthy margin. President Khatami's old ministry once again became the agent for openings in society, rather than the means to hold it back. And Mohajerani became the spokesman and flag bearer for the new leadership's boldest initiatives—pluralism of ideas at home and a dialogue of civilizations with the outside world.

"Concepts such as freedom, democracy and the establishment of social institutions—going back hundreds of years in Western societies—in no way contradict the Islamic faith," the new culture minister said shortly after taking office.

The new government elected in 1997 signaled that it intended to end the years of cultural claustrophobia and restrictions.

Eight months later, in the spring of 1998, I went to see Mohajerani, who still looked boyishly youthful despite the first traces of white around the chin of his dark, stubbly beard. He had just returned from a trip to Paris and he broke the ice by recounting, with animated enthusiasm, his stops at the Louvre, Chartres Cathedral and the Victor Hugo Museum.

I reminded him about something else he'd said during his confirmation hearings.

"If a person worries about everything but freedom, he's neglecting the major issue—freedom. Freedom is the major issue and other matters are minor," he'd told Parliament.

So I asked him what he'd been doing since he came to the ministry to improve freedom in Iran.

"We've had a good beginning. The first day I came to the ministry, I lifted the ban on two movies banned under the previous minister. They were screened immediately. It was a message to the cinema industry people that the tough measures exercised in the past won't be there anymore," Mohajerani said.

"I also permitted publication of many books previously banned. In the press, a new era has begun. Many, many publications have joined the press community since we came to office. And in music, there've been a lot of concerts. Almost all the promises I made have already materialized," he added.

Did the new environment also mean that Iran was prepared to tolerate films and books and music from the West, in the spirit of President Khatami's call for a dialogue of civilizations? I asked.

"Oh, Western movies are running on our screens. Our point is to strengthen our own national movie industry, not necessarily to cut off movies from the West," Mohajerani replied. "And many Western books are quickly translated and published here now."

Indeed, although Hemingway, Faulkner and Steinbeck novels had been around since Khatami's stint at the culture ministry, I'd begun to notice new English and Persian editions of John Grisham and Danielle Steel novels in Tehran bookstores too. And one of the ten best-sellers in 1998 was a translated edition of *Men Are from Mars, Women Are from Venus,* the self-help gender guide by American John Gray.

Iranian television had also loosened up. By then, it was producing its own sitcom, in which the characters Mariam and Ramin bore a striking resemblance to Alice and Ralph Kramden. The slapstick plots were right out of *The Honeymooners.*

The Islamic republic also produced its own game shows, although *Challenge* was clearly inspired by *Jeopardy,* and *Grand Prize* looked uncannily like *Wheel of Fortune.*

Western music was also no longer reserved just for concert halls. Tehran garbage trucks played Beethoven symphonies as they made their rounds.[24] Most telling of all the changes on Iranian television was a music video featuring Eric Clapton.

Sometimes pointed, sometimes startling were the "Thought of the Day" column in the *Tehran Times,* which had once again expanded to include contemporary American cultural icons. Three consecutive issues in October 1998 were typical. In a country where every act and every printed word has more than one meaning, the choices were particularly intriguing.

"Prejudice is a burden that confuses the past, threatens the future and renders the present inaccessible" came from American poet Maya Angelou.[25]

"One can never consent to creep when one feels an impulse to soar," cited blind and deaf innovator Helen Keller.[26]

"Humor, you can't exist without it. You have to be able to laugh at yourself. Otherwise, you suffer," quoted actor Kirk Douglas.[27]

In light of the new cultural diversity, I asked Mohajerani about a shift in the underlying message of the revolution. I asked particularly about the debate spawned by Soroush—whether the Islamic republic accepted only a single "right path" in religion, in political goals, in cultural values or whether Iran was prepared to acknowledge multiple right paths. In other words, pluralism.

"The very idea of debate on this issue is something new in our society. When you speak of a right path or right paths, it's interesting. It shows that people are looking at issues from different angles," he replied.

"A civil society or a lively society is one where these sorts of discussions should take place."

Did that mean there was room in Iran for full freedom in the Western sense? I asked.

"Obviously we don't share the same definition of freedom as in the West. Freedom has different definitions. The main difference is that in the West, it's freedom 'from' something, which means that obstacles must be removed in the way of individuals. But in religious terms, it is freedom 'for,' which means that freedom must be in service of the perfection and prosperity of human beings," Mohajerani replied.

I pressed him for an example.

"Well, in the United States, you recognize the right of homosexuals to live together. Your president in his election campaign announced that he'd allow homosexuals in the army and considered this to be a concession," he said.

"But the religious community totally rejects this phenomenon. If you consider that a restriction on freedom, then the religious community imposes this restriction."

A few weeks earlier, the annual United Nations human rights survey had reported that Iran had recently witnessed "incontestable" progress on human rights, including freedom of speech. But it was also critical of the Islamic republic, particularly of the executions and stonings. So I asked Mohajerani if he ever foresaw a time when—because of President Khatami's emphasis on greater individual freedom and restoring the rule of law—the Islamic republic would get a positive report card.

"It's possible," he mused. "But the point is that the rapporteurs of human rights must be familiar with our religious instruction and beliefs. Since they're not, they may consider certain things we believe in to be violations of human rights.

"For instance," he continued, "if you deliberately kill someone, you have to be executed for it. As a legal and religious punishment, this sen-

Billboard art of Ayatollah Khomeini overlooking his elaborate tomb on the outskirts of Tehran

President Mohammad Khatami, reformist president elected in 1997

Poster of Iran's two Supreme Leaders, Ayatollah Khomeini and Ayatollah Khamenei

Philosopher Abdul Karim
Soroush, the "Martin Luther of
Islam"

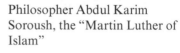

Tehran demonstration in
support of the government,
1998. Headbands proclaim
willingness to be martyrs.

Billboard art depicting the
seventh-century Shi'ite
martyrdom, now commemorated
during Ashura

Charlie Chaplin Movie House at Bahman
Cultural Center, where East and West
occasionally meet

Akbar Abdi, the leading comedic actor in
Iran's film industry

Culture Minister Ataollah Mohajerani and his wife, Presidential Adviser Jamileh
Kadivar. Both became targets of conservative politicians' campaign against
reform.

Mahboobeh Abbas-
Gholizadeh, editor of
Farzaneh magazine for
female intellectuals

Marzieh Sadighi and Golam Reza Shirazian,
husband and wife Members of Parliament

Vice President Massoumeh
Ebtekar, former hostage-
takers' spokeswoman

Jalal Shahpasand and Jila Abdolrasooly at a family-planning course, a prerequisite for a marriage license in Iran

Ayatollah Mustafa Mohaqeqdamad, reformer on women's rights and family issues, at Iran's Academy of Sciences

Dr. Fereidoun Forouhary at a Tehran vasectomy clinic. After doubling its population, Iran is winning awards for family planning.

Azadi (Freedom) Square in Tehran. A monument to the monarchy became a symbol of the revolution.

Martyrs' Cemetery in Isfahan, for victims of Iran's eight-year war with Iraq

Lily Sadeghi at bust of Hafez, Iran's most revered poet

Homa birds at Persepolis,
ancient capital of Persia's
early kings

Putting Islam on the Internet: Ayatollah Ali Korani
at Qom computer center

Nasser Hadian, Tehran
University political scientist
and analyst

Student leaders Ali Tavakoli, of the Office to Foster Islamic Unity, and Heshmatollah Tabarzadi, of the Union of Muslim University Students and Graduates

Pizza parlors are a favorite hangout for restless Iranian youth.

Anti-American wall poster on a building in downtown Tehran

tence has to be handed out. We can't say no, please don't do that, because the human rights people might be upset."

But even for those who accepted capital punishment, stoning a person to death seemed a particularly cruel and archaic means of execution compared with other modern methods, I said.

"I agree," he replied, nodding slowly. "We have to sit down with the human rights people and find some solutions, especially with the new environment created in Iran after the election. This issue is open to discussion to find different ways."

I noted, however, that President Khatami's attempts at reform and dialogue, the central elements of the "new environment," were often stymied. His campaign pledge to restore the rule of law especially faced major obstacles.

"Nobody in government defends extremism and hard-line groups," Mohajerani replied, a wincing smile of acknowledgment crossing his face.

"Even these hard-line groups, when they do something wrong, they immediately announce that they weren't behind the wrongdoing. This is a very important achievement. We need time to make these groups understand that their violent actions won't be useful or have positive results."

Then why hadn't the government physically intervened to stop them? I asked. Was it capable of stopping them?

"Yes, of course," he said, again clearly pained. "The government is doing its best to stop them."

The conservative campaign against reform, in fact, hadn't ended with President Khatami's election. In many ways, the war over Iran's future had only escalated. The stakes had suddenly become bigger and the political alternatives starker, in large part because the new president had announced plans to push Iran's democratic experiment one giant step farther: He called local elections.

It was the first step since the revolution in distributing power beyond the capital—and the clergy. Local polls had originally been mandated by the constitution a generation earlier, but the fractious corps of politicians in Tehran had resisted ceding even a tiny bit of power. One thing or another—the war with Iraq, Ayatollah Khomeini's death and a new Supreme Leader, internal wrangling and other elections and a troubled economy—had provided excuses to stall.

For twenty years, Iranians had voted for only three kinds of officials: the president, Parliament and the Assembly of Experts—a total of fewer than 350 people. Overnight, local elections—pointedly set for the same month as the revolution's twentieth anniversary, in February 1999—would introduce some 190,000 officials to run the villages, towns and cities of Iran.

"You can't imagine the importance of these elections," Nasser Hadian, the Tehran University political scientist, had explained to me. "This will be the critical step to institutionalize democracy—which was why those in power before Khatami were so reluctant to have them. They didn't want to give up their privileges. Once they transferred power, they knew they couldn't get it back."

So in 1998 and 1999, the arena of internal battle became the officials, intellectuals and ideas most closely associated with President Khatami. For every attempt to cross the front line defining freedom in Iran, conservatives retaliated with a heavier barrage to hold it back.

The first strike was against President Khatami's closest allies. And the first target was Tehran's reformist mayor, Gholamhossein Karbaschi. The mayor also just happened to have been a key player in the president's winning presidential campaign. A former cleric, Karbaschi had been imprisoned for three years during the shah's regime. After the revolution, he worked for Ayatollah Khomeini. He later shed his turban and robes for a suit and a secular job as mayor of Isfahan and then Tehran.

In terms of reform, no other politician had a more proven or impressive record than Karbaschi. Since being appointed to the Tehran job by President Rafsanjani in 1989, he'd developed a Robin Hood image for taxing the rich *bazaaris*—the backbone of support for the conservative clergy—to pay for parks, housing, landscaped freeways, playgrounds and public entertainment facilities like the Bahman Cultural Center in the capital's poor southern suburbs. As publisher of *Hamshahri* newspaper and a member of the national Farabi Cinema Foundation, Karbaschi had also been instrumental in establishing greater freedom of expression in the arts.

When Parliament started complaining about possible corruption, the conservative judiciary ordered Karbaschi's arrest in April 1998. His trial, the first ever to be run on Iranian television, riveted the country throughout the following summer.

"It was all internal politics. It was like an inquisition," Hadian explained.

"Everyone knew the case was created to make a point. Karbaschi may not have been totally clean, but he was no more corrupt than many other people in this country who are still in office. At least people got something in exchange—a public, televised trial. You can't say that about most of the others."

After a prolonged trial, Karbaschi was convicted. He was sentenced to five years in prison, a twenty-year ban from politics, sixty lashes and a half-million-dollar fine. Several of his top aides were also tried, convicted and imprisoned, despite their protests that they'd been tortured.

Karbaschi's sentence was later reduced to two years and the lashes were eliminated. But with local elections around the corner, the conviction nonetheless sent a chilling message about how much change would be tolerated.

Abdullah Nouri was next. Nouri was the powerful interior minister who had responsibility for critical jobs like running all elections and administering Iran's twenty-six provinces. He served as one of President Khatami's two major voices of reform; Mohajerani was the other. He'd actually had the job before under President Rafsanjani, but he'd been squeezed out with Khatami in 1992. Nouri also just happened to be Karbaschi's chief supporter and in charge of his defense fund.

In a petition, thirty-one conservative members of Parliament demanded Nouri's impeachment. The vague charges included "creation of tension in society," "laxism" for allowing demonstrations in support of a dissident cleric and "provocative interviews" about the Karbaschi trial.

"Continuation of Nouri's service is detrimental to the tranquillity and stability in the country," the petition warned.[28]

What actually peeved conservatives was Nouri's decisions to relax enforcement of tough Islamic strictures on public behavior and to grant permits for political gatherings, notably to student groups critical of conservative policies. He'd also moved aside several conservatives within his ministry. Most important, his role in running the local elections would almost certainly have a major impact on the openness of the process and the type of people allowed to run.

President Khatami tried to stop the impeachment. He publicly called Nouri "a blessing" and appealed to Parliament not to act rashly. Nouri also appeared before a packed parliamentary hall to defend his actions—and issue a warning.

"Be sure that the government is so powerful that it will not be weakened by issues like this," he told a session that was broadcast live on Tehran Radio. "Whoever the interior minister may be, he must continue the path of political development," he said, using the code words for reform.[29]

Nevertheless, in June 1998, he was impeached. He'd been in office only ten months.

President Khatami retaliated by naming Nouri to a new and specially created vice presidency for development and social affairs. The seven vice presidencies in Iran are appointed jobs that don't need parliamentary approval. But the saga was far from over.

A few weeks later, Mohajerani and Nouri were physically attacked. On a steamy Friday in September 1998, some eighty Hizbollahis bushwhacked the culture minister as he emerged from Friday Prayers at Tehran University. Shouting "Death to liberals," they beat Mohajerani in the body and face and left his clothing in shreds. The Hizbollahis then went after Nouri, roughing up the cleric and knocking off his turban, as he finished prayers on the campus grounds.[30]

The second set of strikes were fired against Iran's new media, the dozens of publications licensed by Mohajerani after President Khatami's election. The fate of one gutsy little paper, which went further than all others, was a microcosm of what many faced.

Jameh—or "Society," so named for the new government's pledge to build a civil society—was launched in February 1998. It ran at least a scoop a day, as well as dozens of stories no other news outlet dared to run.

It even covered the misadventures of Ansar-e Hizbollah.

It also broke the story of the Revolutionary Guard commander's behind-closed-doors speech calling for the "beheading" of Iran's reformers, and followed it with an editorial condemning his "martyrdom-seeking" remarks as vestiges of a "bygone era" and advising him "to speak with a civil and lawful tone" as stipulated in the constitution.

And not only did *Jameh* write about Soroush's lectures and books, but the diminutive philosopher actually began giving his Thursday evening talks at the publisher's home.

The paper even interviewed American officials and, sparking huge controversy, a former Iranian official after his release from fifteen years in prison for being an American spy—Iran's longest-serving political prisoner.

"*Jameh* has two functions. We're trying to build up the level of democratic discourse. And we're a good test case to see how much freedom the government can tolerate," Mashallah Shamsolvaizin, the paper's bearded and soulful editor, explained when I stopped by the editorial office. *Jameh*'s forty-five young male and female reporters worked in the cramped quarters of a converted house.

"We know Iran's democracy today is a minefield," Shamsolvaizin added, with a chuckle. "We like to think of ourselves as the mine finders."

Overnight *Jameh*—sixteen pages of unconventional news, commentary, acerbic satire, political cartoons and a heavy dose of culture—quickly became the most popular daily in Iran. Kiosk dealers could barely keep it on the stands, even though it was published twice a day, and three times on a good news day. Young people and many less than enthusiastic about the regime bought *Jameh* because it ran very little official news. Women, the middle class and intellectuals liked it because half the paper was devoted to cultural issues.

But it also quickly got into trouble.

Four months after *Jameh* was launched, a revolutionary court found the publisher guilty of "defamatory and untruthful articles . . . contrary to public moral order."[31] The primary offense was the article about the Revolutionary Guards commander who wanted to behead reformers. A month later, *Jameh* was banned altogether.

Mohajerani tried to defend the paper and others that dared to be different.

"We may not agree with the stance of a particular publication, but our personal opinion shouldn't prevent the paper from publishing," he said at Iran's annual press convention. "Fortunately, in the current atmosphere, different voices accepted within the constitution of the Islamic Republic are being reflected by the press."[32]

He'd also visited *Jameh*'s offices—a step widely seen as a stamp of approval.

But his appeal was ignored by Ayatollah Mohammad Yazdi, the head of Iran's judiciary and a leading conservative. "The Islamic people of Iran will not tolerate insults and attacks against their beliefs and the Shi'ite clergy," Yazdi shot back.[33]

Not to be diverted, the same staff merely relaunched the same paper, but under a new name. *Tous* had the same cutting-edge editorial policy. The new paper even made headlines in other publications by running an interview with former French President Valéry Giscard d'Estaing, who claimed that Ayatollah Khomeini had asked for—and received—political asylum when he went to France in 1978, shortly before the revolution.

It also openly took on the conservatives, most notably in a scathing editorial about the attacks on Mohajerani and Nouri at Friday prayers.

"The people who are doing these things are the same as terrorists. And those who don't act or say anything, it's to benefit their personal power, not to benefit revolutionary ideology," *Tous* editorialized.[34]

At Friday prayers, Yazdi again shot back. "The newspapers and magazines today, in the name of freedom, are committing all sorts of wrongs. The publication of a banned newspaper is particularly outside the law. I expect the culture minister to act before someone has to step in and act on his behalf," he warned in a sermon on the press.[35]

Almost predictably, *Tous* survived only a few weeks. When Mohajerani didn't close it down, the conservative judiciary banned it—again for "publishing lies and disrupting public order."[36]

Defiantly, the editor and publisher tried to relaunch the paper a third time. But both were soon detained and placed in solitary confinement. Their arrests in the fall of 1998 marked the onset of a conservative siege of the new independent press.

"It's like having a loaded gun pointed at you. The only thing you don't know is when it's going to be fired," Hamid Jalaipour, the paper's robust and usually quite jovial publisher, told me when I tracked him down at his mother's house. After a month in prison, he'd eventually been released, but the charges had been left hanging. He remained in danger of being picked up again at any moment.

Like many journalists under scrutiny, Jalaipour was an odd target. His revolutionary credentials were impeccable. He had been an activist against the shah's regime. After the revolution, he'd worked for the Interior Ministry for a decade. He'd then worked for the Foreign Ministry for eight years, and he was technically still on its payroll. He'd also lost two brothers in the war with Iraq and a third in an attack by the Mujahadeen. But he and others on the *Jameh-Tous* staff came to symbolize another set of new voices in Iran—and the broader effort to push the Islamic republic into a postrevolutionary period.

"I as a revolutionary man don't believe today in revolution, but in evolution. And yes, you can go ahead and write that—and use my name," he said, as a big smile gave way to a laugh. "I'm already in so much trouble anyway."

"I also don't believe the clergy alone should run Iran," he continued.

"The clergy can be part of political activity, but participation should be based on merit. After struggling for so many years, I've grown from having an ideological viewpoint to believing in pluralism."

The impact of *Jameh-Tous* extended far beyond its readership. The mere presence of the paper—and its overwhelming popularity— transformed the journalistic climate. More and more publications began to run nonregime news. Satire became a standard in most papers. Several publications launched columns that reported on other papers' scoops or juicy gossip heard on the Tehran grapevine. Even the stodgiest old papers and the official Islamic Republic News Agency began to lighten up.

But more and more papers came under fire as well. Over the next few months, more than a dozen publications received warnings or were closed. Virtually all were put out by people who'd long worked within the system and who had good revolutionary credentials.

Among the other targets was *Zan,* or "Woman," a new paper published by Faezeh Hashemi, the daughter of former President Rafsanjani, who was still a member of Parliament herself. She'd won the second-highest vote tally in the multiseat Tehran constituency in the 1996 elections.

Hashemi also challenged revolutionary convention—running editorials against stoning, exposés on the return of prostitution, satires about the tradition of paying blood money required to compensate for a murder or manslaughter and news stories about the high rate of suicides among the young. *Zan* even dared to report in early 1999 that the former empress, Farah Diba, had sent a New Year's message to Iranians. It didn't dare report what the message said—just that she had sent it.

Within days of the story about the former empress, *Zan* was also banned. Another voice was silenced.

After *Tous* was shut down, the campaign against reform escalated. That's when the killings began.

The third wave of strikes was launched in November 1998, when husband-and-wife activists in a small secular party were found stabbed to death in their home. Since the house was not burglarized, the motive behind the gruesome murders was widely assumed to be political.

A month later, two dissident writers were murdered. The pattern was identical: Each went missing. Each was found dead a few days later—on a roadside and under a bridge. Each had been strangled. Personal effects— wallets, money, rings—weren't touched. Each had recently again been interrogated by intelligence officials because of their attempts to revive the writers' association.

Both had also signed the "We Are Writers" letter.

A third writer was also found dead under mysterious circumstances, although reports disagreed over whether he suffered a heart attack. It didn't matter. The climate was so electric that if a writer was late for an appointment or unsighted for a few hours, it set off alarm bells.

"The major objective was to send a message to the writers and others trying to organize the civil society promised by President Khatami," Hadian explained.

"The message was 'Go home and be quiet. If you continue on this course, this will be your fate.' They wanted to make the price of reforms too high."

With just two months to go before the local elections, the murders also had a chilling impact on the public.

"The other goal was to discourage people from voting for reformers," Hadian said. "They wanted to make reform synonymous with instability."

In an unusual move, the Ministry of Culture and Islamic Guidance issued a scathing attack, implicitly directed at others in government.

"Behind this saga, we see plots and antirevolutionary subversion. Their purpose is nothing but to discourage people, weaken the regime and strike a blow at the new atmosphere in the Islamic Republic," the ministry said.[37]

To quell a bad case of public nervousness, President Khatami ordered three cabinet ministers to launch a special investigation. It seemed unlikely to come to anything concrete or surprising. The murky forces that carried out any of the myriad misadventures inside Iran had always been well protected; they sometimes seemed to have carte blanche.

Then Iran's intelligence community disclosed its discovery of a secret network—made up of its own operatives. In January 1999, less than a month after the last murder, a terse statement said several had been arrested and indicted for the recent "heinous killings" and "wide-ranging mischief." No names of the rogue elements were provided. No ranks disclosed. No numbers in the death squad—or squads. And no specifics about what other acts fell under the curious catchall category of "mischief."

"It's most unfortunate that there are a number of irresponsible, misguided and unruly personnel of this ministry—undoubtedly manipulated by clandestine agents and serving foreign interests—who have committed these criminal acts," said the statement issued by the Ministry of Information, the official name of the supersecret intelligence bureau.

The investigating committee then pledged "to pursue clues to identify the entire gang linked to the murders. A number of others have been fully identified and are presently under surveillance."[38]

Fessing up to any form of official roguery was new in Iran—for either the monarchy or the theocracy. But coming clean on something with the magnitude of death squads, even though their existence had always been widely assumed, stunned Iranians.

Then the intelligence minister resigned. In Iran's unusual power structure, key security positions—such as the intelligence chief and the Revolutionary Guard commander—were appointed by the Supreme Leader rather than by the president.

"It was like another revolution!" Hadian said, with an excitement that reflected his own sense of disbelief. "Announcing it publicly, accepting the guilt, introducing the idea of accountability as a right of the people—these were all new, very, *very* new.

"Just as important, the people who were behind this, they found they can't compete with freedom. They wanted to frighten people into believing. But their tactics couldn't compete with the free market of ideas. This is a *very* important victory," he added.

The revelations, however, again didn't end the war. Conservatives launched yet a fourth strike.

This time, with local elections approaching, conservatives went after several of the reformist candidates running for the thousands of village, town and city councils. Unlike the national elections, the municipal elections did not involve the Council of Guardians in vetting candidates, in part because of sheer volume. Instead, a parliamentary oversight committee, also heavily weighted with conservatives, was empowered to review the list of candidates. And it did disqualify dozens of people who registered to run, mainly on grounds of "unrevolutionary" behavior or credentials.

But four candidates for Tehran's city council were at the heart of the war between conservatives and reformers. They all came from President Khatami's camp.

Abdullah Nouri, twice an interior minister and still a vice president, was disqualified on grounds related to his earlier impeachment. Saeed Hajarian, the president's senior adviser who'd recently resigned to open a newspaper, was cited for failing to provide a written pledge proving his allegiance to the Supreme Leader. Ibrahim Asgharzadeh, the former spokesman for the student hostage takers in 1979 who'd three months earlier invited the hostages to come back as a step toward rapprochement with the United States, was disqualified because he had a judicial record with a revolutionary court.

The fourth was Jamileh Kadivar, the press adviser to President Khatami and an appealing young woman of warmth and authority, who was disqualified for not having submitted her resignation from the presidency in time. On that charge, I had some knowledge. I happened to have called on Kadivar the morning she submitted her resignation in early November 1998, three months before the election and well before the final deadline.

We had first met when she was a graduate student at Tehran University in the early 1990s and I attended one of her political science classes to talk to students. In the small world that includes even Iran, the class was given by my friend Hadian. After President Khatami's election in 1997, Kadivar was named a presidential adviser.

The appointment made her half of Iran's leading power couple. Mohajerani was her husband.

On the day she submitted her resignation, we'd talked about Iran's future over mango juice and cookies in her high-rise office overlooking Tehran. We discussed her resignation, her decision to run and her meteoric rise through the ranks since that political science class. She said she'd be sorry to leave the president's office, but she felt Iran had reached an important turning point.

"The local elections," she reflected, "are critical in determining the prospects for an Islamic democracy."

This time, however, President Khatami and his cabinet refused to cave to conservatives. Since the parliamentary committee didn't have the infallibility of the Council of Guardians, the government challenged its decisions on all four candidates as well as several others. It was largely a game of bluff, since there were no precedents. Indeed, one of the reasons the reformers decided to fight back was that this election would set those precedents.

Whether or not the four were qualified to stand went back and forth right up to and on election day: They were. They weren't. They were. They weren't. When election day came, on February 26, 1999, the four names were already on the ballot. As people voted, it was a *fait accompli*.

To no one's surprise, four of the top five winners were Nouri, Hajarian, Kadivar and Asgharzadeh, in that order. The fourth in the top five was Fatemeh Jalaipour, sister of the publisher of *Jameh* and *Tous*. The sixth was Mohammad Atrianfar, editor of former Mayor Karbaschi's paper *Hamshahri*. All fifteen winners for Tehran's city council—as well as for the vast majority of councils throughout Iran—were supporters of President Khatami.

The conservatives still didn't give up. For the next two months, until the new city councils met for the first time, the parliamentary committee argued that the four disputed candidates as well as others hadn't really won, because, of course, they hadn't been qualified to run in the first place. Again, it was back and forth right up to and on inauguration day.

But on April 29, 1999, President Khatami formally ended a long history of heavily centralized rule in Iran by personally inaugurating Tehran's city council. In a small wood-paneled hall next to the capital's municipal center, he heralded the historic moment.

"We are witnessing one of the most visible manifestations of people's control over their own destiny. The people have taken a decisive step toward freedom and national pride," he said. He called on the councils to "play a leading role in establishing a civil society and allowing the population to play a role in decisions affecting their destiny."

In an indirect jab at Parliament, he called for the councilors to be the "intermediaries" between authorities and the people. And in an even more unusual public comment on the internal political divide, Khatami also denounced the "monopolistic forces that seek to model society according to their interpretation of religion and law and to impose their point of view."

And then he pledged to persevere. "I stand firmly by all of the promises I made to the people," he vowed.[39]

In its first action that day, the council voted Nouri, the impeached former interior minister, to be its chairman.

Just as the new councils across Iran were being seated, however, conservatives struck again.

First, Mayor Karbaschi, who was out on bail while he appealed, was ordered to report to notorious Evin Prison. It was a major blow. Even conservative members of Parliament had told me that they didn't expect him to end up serving time.

Second, conservatives on the Special Court for the Clergy, which operated outside the control of government, charged a leading reformer with "disseminating lies and disturbing public opinion." Mohsen Kadivar, a popular young cleric and seminary professor, had offended the traditional clergy by writing several articles about why Iranian politics should be more autonomous from religion. He'd dared to compare practices in the Islamic republic with repressive controls on freedom of expression under the shah. He'd also questioned the powers and righteousness of the theocracy.

"From both a legal and religious point of view, it's quite permissible to criticize the Supreme Leader or the ruling establishment," he wrote.[40]

The charismatic cleric also just happened to be the brother of Jamileh Kadivar, the new city councilwoman, and the brother-in-law of Culture Minister Mohajerani.

In his first appearance before the special court, Kadivar boldly rejected its right to try him on the grounds that it was unconstitutional. He instead demanded a public court.

"Investigation into political and press offenses must be carried out in the presence of a jury and by a qualified court of the judiciary," he told the court.[41]

Kadivar's case over the extent of freedom in Iran became an instant cause célèbre. Posters of the young cleric from a noted Shiraz religious family were plastered all over Tehran. Students held a candlelight vigil in the hills near Evin Prison, where Kadivar was being held without bail. Chanting "freedom of thought, forever, forever," they released doves as a symbol of liberty. More than two hundred journalists also signed a petition condemning Kadivar's arrest as unconstitutional and calling it an "offense" against Iran's writers and intellectuals.

One press commentator even compared him to Galileo before the Inquisition.[42]

In a reflection of changing times, his sister lashed out at the clerical court in front of television cameras.

"They're worse than the military courts of the shah's regime," she charged.

The trial was swift. So was the conviction. Kadivar was found guilty and sentenced to eighteen months.

The third move was against Mohajerani himself. In a transparent and rather clumsy move on the eve of the city council inauguration, conservatives in Parliament called for his impeachment. The charges were vague accusations such as "failing to uphold Islamic and revolutionary values," "insulting religious sanctities" and allowing "liberal" policies on the press, book publishing and the arts.

Perhaps more to the point, the petition by thirty-one members of Parliament also criticized the minister of culture and Islamic guidance for allowing the revival of the banned union of prominent writers and intellectuals, the same organization at the heart of the "We Are Writers" petition.[43] The emergence of public organizations threatened traditional centers of power like the Parliament, just as the city councils did.

"This poisonous cultural atmosphere created by the minister's tolerance has allowed writers to write against the system and Islam," said Mohammad Hassan Jamshidi, one of the thirty-one to sign the petition.[44]

Portraying the impeachment as a last-ditch effort to eliminate the danger posed by "liberals," conservatives also collected thousands of signatures from traditional religious institutions and areas.

"This is a totally political move," Mohajerani said about the petition. He tried to dismiss the charges against him.

"The time for banning publication of opposition views has passed. The chick can't be put back in the egg," he told a news conference on the eve of the vote. And he expressed pride that so many papers had been licensed in his first eighteen months that daily circulation throughout Iran had more than doubled.[45]

"The policies in the field of culture won't change. We have only just begun setting the stage for greater tolerance," he vowed.[46]

At a time when even young pupils had access to the Internet, trying to cut Iranians off from the outside world was counterproductive, he warned.

"We shouldn't be embarrassed by the opposition's views. Rather we should let them be raised—and we would better spend our time trying to find suitable answers to them."[47]

Yet even his staunchest supporters thought the culture minister faced the fight of his professional life. The *Iran News* reported that the odds were stacked against him.[48] Faezeh Hashemi, the reformer, newspaper editor and member of Parliament, predicted that he'd be ousted.[49]

On May 1, 1999, Mohajerani strode into the paneled parliamentary chamber and once again refused to appease or to apologize for his policies. In another fiery and defiant speech, he told a hushed Parliament, "Tolerance does not mean the weakening of values. Ideas must be responded to with ideas."[50]

For more than an hour, he entranced Parliament with sweeping knowledge of both Persian and Arabic verse, citing Koranic injunctions from memory in support of intellectual freedoms and showing a wide command of Western arts and literature to prove they didn't threaten Islam.

The Iranian media reported a nation equally riveted by the proceedings, which were broadcast live on Tehran Radio. Taxi drivers, intellectuals, housewives, students and bazaar merchants tuned in. The staff of a reform newspaper reportedly burst into tears and cheers during the speech.

At the end, the culture minister tried to put his position in perspective. "Do you think that if I go away, the problem of culture in this country will be resolved?" he said. "If that's the case, then the Supreme Leader and the president can send me away."[51]

In the end, the vote was 135 to 121. Mohajerani survived.

An editorial in the *Iran Daily* probably reflected the views of the majority of Iranians. "This was a fresh breath of air for the cultural, press and artistic atmosphere in the country," it editorialized.[52]

The vote, however, didn't end the tension.

"The minister's vote of confidence doesn't mean that the ministry's handling of cultural issues has been proper," the conservative journal *Abrar* commented after the vote. And it warned of a "turbulent" cultural situation to come.[53]

"Mohajerani must try now to lead the ministry back onto the right path in order to ease the troubled minds of our members of Parliament," the paper said. The key term, of course, was "right path," as in "one way."

But for the first time the conservatives appeared to be fighting a rear-guard action.

"Behind this vote was another story," Hadian said. "The conservatives are losing their ability to rally a majority. Some members of Parliament have begun to see the writing on the wall.

"With elections for Parliament in 2000," he added, "some have begun to realize they must adjust to the times if they want to have any hope of surviving politically."

Although Parliament's conservatives had put Mohajerani on notice that they were still watching, the climate had clearly changed.

Four days after Mohajerani won his vote of confidence, a majority in Parliament—146 of the 270 members—signed a petition calling for Ayatollah Khamenei to grant an amnesty to former Mayor Karbaschi.

The staff of *Jameh* and *Tous* launched a new paper called *Neshat*—or "Happiness."

And the culture minister announced that he hoped to soon ease the ban on satellite dishes, at least partially. Four years after Parliament out-lawed them, artists, academics, journalists and government officials were going to be eligible to have them at home.

"I can watch foreign television at work, but I'm forbidden to do so when I go home," Mohajerani explained.

"It's time to stop being afraid of the outside world."[54]

AKBAR ABDI IS Iran's greatest comedic actor. A playful, pudgy man with fat cheeks and a thick walrus mustache that turns down instead of up at the sides, Abdi is best known for his breakthrough role in a break-through film called *The Snowman.*

The movie broke so much ground, in fact, that it was pretty much banned indefinitely by the Ministry of Culture and Islamic Guidance in 1995. The black-comedy plotline involved an Iranian who went to Turkey in a desperate bid to get a visa to the United States. He repeatedly got scammed, leading him into ever deeper intrigues and compromising antics. But that wasn't the most controversial part of the film. What really offended censors was that Abdi played a woman.

"I was the Tootsie or Mrs. Doubtfire of Iran," he said with a mischie-vous smile when I visited him in 1998 on another movie set in Tehran.

As one of the character's ruses, Abdi did exactly what Dustin Hoff-man did as Tootsie and Robin Williams did as Mrs. Doubtfire: He disguised himself as a woman to get what he couldn't get as a man. The main scam in *The Snowman* had Abdi dressed as a woman paying money to a man he thinks is an American to marry him—since marriage to an American is one of the few surefire ways for an Iranian to qualify for a visa.

But to conservative censors, the plot was also a surefire way to get slapped with an official ban for being "un-Islamic," even though *The Snowman* was supported by the official Islamic Propagation Organization and even though the character ended up falling in love with an Iranian woman and returning home.

"It was a wonderful part. A man trying to be a woman is one of three roles every actor wants to play. The other two are an addict and a crazy person," Abdi said, puffing on a Marlboro Light during a filming break. He'd just finished entertaining the cast and crew with a funny Turkish song and a little jig. They were all still chuckling in the background.

The Snowman did finally open in Iran, however. After President

Khatami's 1997 election, one of the new culture minister's first acts was to lift the ban on the Abdi film. It instantly became a box-office hit. I saw the film several months after it was released; it was still playing in Tehran cinemas. For his role, Abdi told me proudly that he'd been nominated for a best actor Tandee, Iran's equivalent of the Oscar. The film also grossed more than any other movie that year—by far.[55]

Abdi claimed that he wasn't bitter about the delay.

"I wasn't worried, because the film probably was a little bit ahead of its time," he reflected. "Even three years later, it still had problems."

Big problems, in fact. On the day *The Snowman* was to premiere in Isfahan, militant Hizbollahi thugs attacked the local theater. They destroyed posters of the film. They threatened people lined up for the show, including females and children. And then they attacked anyone who didn't flee.

The cinema succumbed—and shut down. *The Snowman* opened in November 1997 in twenty-two other Iranian cities, but not in Isfahan.

Just to make sure that the theater didn't try again, militants returned for several days and held "God Is Great" victory prayers on the street outside. No one even tried to stop them. Nor did police and city officials in Isfahan step in, despite the fact the Hizbollahis repeatedly broke several laws.

In a sign of the times, the showdown was defused only after the leading local ayatollah intervened—on behalf of the movie. Ayatollah Jaleleddin Taheri used his Friday prayer sermon to scold Isfahan officials for their failure to act—either to ensure law and order or to allow an unbanned movie to be shown.

"If the police and intelligence forces and the governor's office are unable to deal with them," the seventy-year-old cleric warned, "then let them tell me and I'll put them in their place."[56]

Taheri's word was final. So *The Snowman* finally opened in Isfahan too, several weeks after its premiere elsewhere. Again, it was an instant hit.

I asked Abdi if humor was more sensitive in an Islamic theocracy—or if there was even such a thing as Islamic humor.

"It's better not to use terms like that," he replied. "After all, what is human humor? It's the same for Christians too."

Then with a twinkle in his eye, he boomed, "Oh, I'm afraid the ceiling will collapse because I'm telling such lies!"

The film's producer and several crew members who'd gathered around to listen laughed again.

"What I mean is that a human should be a human and know God. But he shouldn't be afraid if he says this kind of thing is true: We're all humans with similar values," he added, in a more serious tone.

I asked Abdi if he was religious, and if being religious was important to an actor hoping to make it in the Islamic Republic.

"I can't say I'm very religious, but I believe in God. I believe in God very much," he said.

"At the beginning of my life, I believed because of my mother. Since I loved her very much, I wanted to follow her way. As a child, I prayed and fasted because I wanted her to love me. It's the same at the other end of life. Sometimes when people grow older they think they should get closer to God. They think if they no longer commit the sins they did when they were young, then they'll get closer to God," Abdi added.

"I'm not like that. Now I really believe in God."

The thirty-eight-year-old actor, however, hardly fit the outside world's image of a devout Iranian believer. He had shaken my hand when we were introduced. During the filming break, he sat across from me in a heavy military uniform for his part as a famous nineteenth-century shah. The bulky black jacket with gold trim and epaulets was wide open, fully exposing his white T-shirt underneath.

I asked Abdi whom he most admired as an actor or director.

"God," he said, pausing. Then he smiled. He clearly thought my questions were taking the religious stuff too far.

"No," he said, smiling and waving his hand sideways in the air as if to erase his words.

"It's probably Buster Keaton. For him, humanity is important. He cares about the other side of the coin. Sometimes when I've seen his films or biography I've actually broken into tears because I see a similarity between us. He was a very lonely person. And usually comedians know sadness better than others."

Before he resumed filming in the opulent Mirror Room of Golestan Palace—golestan means "rose garden," and is so named because of the splendid flower beds all around it—I asked Abdi if there was any other daring role he wanted to play.

"I think playing a bisexual would be very interesting," he mused.

In light of my conversation with Mohajerani about the arts portraying homosexuality, I asked Abdi if he really thought that kind of role could ever be written into an Iranian movie script.

"Who would've thought a man could play the role of Tootsie in Iran?" he replied. "So maybe even that's possible here.

"Maybe . . ." he repeated, for emphasis.

". . . Someday," he added. Then he turned and went back to the set, cracking jokes in Persian to amuse the crew.

A few actors do have star quality in Iran. Ihsan, the wiry little taxi driver who'd taken me to Golestan Palace, had lingered on the edge of the set during my interviews. He came up close when I talked with Abdi, almost hovering over me at the end, so I introduced him.

"It was like meeting Clint Eastwood or Charles Bronson," he gushed later. "We don't get opportunities like this."

Yet making a film in Iran is not a major production, at least compared with the way most American or European movies are made. Both the cast and crew of Abdi's movie were tiny—six actors and actresses and a staff of thirty camera, sound, light and set technicians. As in most Iranian films, the director was also the lone screenwriter. The set had no trailers for the stars or caterers for lunch. The cast and crew had all taken public transportation, or driven themselves and parked in the small lot outside the palace. Lunch was strictly brown-bag.

Equipment was also sparse. The lone camera was a German-made Arriflex BL4S.

"This kind of camera probably hasn't been used anywhere in the West for fifteen years or more," Habib Allahyari, the film's tall dapper producer, told me as I inspected it.

"After eight years of war and two decades of sanctions, we make quality films good enough for the whole world with this old equipment. Give us your facilities and we'll give you ours—and then we'll compare films," he added, though with envy rather than anger.

For all the pride Iranians have in their films, the industry gets few perks. The crew had to suspend shooting for a couple of hours until repairmen quit making banging, clanging noises as they worked on the old downtown palace, built just a few years after Tehran became the capital. The shahs were coronated in the ornate first-floor ballroom before the court aristocracy and diplomatic corps. Anyone can visit now, though few besides foreign tourists bothered a generation after the last shah's departure.

Iranian movies also tend to be low-budget, to say the least. Abdi's new movie involved a sixty-day shoot and was one of the costlier recent productions, Allahyari said. The budget was about $185,000, and it was that high only because the producer counted on a big audience. The last movie Abdi starred in grossed a billion tomans, or about $1.2 million at the exchange rate of the time.

Yet Iran's vibrant and original cinema may be the richest cultural byproduct of the revolution—often in spite of the revolutionaries themselves.

In the 1990s, Iranian films were good enough to become standards at the world's major film festivals. And they fared well, taking major prizes at Cannes and other festivals from Switzerland to Singapore, Canada to South Korea, Italy to India to Israel, Japan to Germany, Australia to Argentina, Belgium to Brazil, Spain to China. They won for best picture, best foreign film, best director, best script, best actor, best documentary, best short film and best jury. *The Taste of Cherries,* the story of a man talked out of suicide by the taste of cherries, won the Cannes Palm d'Or in 1997.

Iranian films even did well in America. The New York Film Critics Circle named *The White Balloon,* a poignant tale of a little girl and her brother who lose their money on the Iranian New Year and their encounters with people who try to help them retrieve it, as the best foreign film in 1996. It also won the Cannes Caméra d'Or for best first feature film in 1995.

Of the seven-year-old girl who plays the lead role, the *Hollywood Reporter* raved, "She displays a range of emotions that would stymie Meryl Streep."[57]

Life in the Mist won the Horizon award for short films at the Aspen Filmfest in 1999. It was a powerfully simple story of a young Kurdish boy who made the family's only cash income by carrying goods on his mule along the rough Iran–Iraq border. With the death of the mule, he was forced to carry the goods himself, in turn triggering other challenges and adventures.

In 1999, Lincoln Center in New York, the American Film Institute in Washington and the Chicago Art Institute all held retrospectives honoring director Dariush Mehrjui, arguably the father of modern Iranian film, who's been ranked by both domestic and foreign critics as the most important of Iran's new generation of directors.[58]

In Hollywood, *Children of Heaven* was one of the five films nominated for a foreign Oscar in 1999. The heartrending tale centers on a nine-year-old boy named Ali who accidentally lost his seven-year-old sister Zahra's only shoes, a tattered pair with pink bows. To hide the loss from their poor and occasionally employed father, Ali and Zahra swapped the only pair of shoes between them, racing to meet after her school shift ended and before his began. Sharing a single pair repeatedly got both children in trouble. To solve their problems, Ali entered a long distance race—in which, of course, shoes were a prize. The catch was that it was third prize. The subtle ending did not include Ali's winning the shoes.

The competition for best foreign film that year was arguably the toughest in Oscar history. Iran's *Children of Heaven* was up against Italy's *Life Is Beautiful* and Brazil's *Central Station*—both of which were so impressive that their foreign stars were also nominated for best-actor and best-actress Oscars. *Children of Heaven* lost to *Life Is Beautiful,* which also took the best-actor Oscar.

Despite the rich variety of plots, Iranian films tend to share several striking features: Characters aren't crafted from superlatives—the prettiest, wealthiest, most powerful, bravest or strongest, nor the most evil, ugliest, dumbest or most cowardly. They're instead quite ordinary folk: small shopkeepers, poor families, children or housewives. The settings are not sets but real homes and back alleys, villages and schoolyards, downtown shops and public streets.

The stories also don't center on earthbound asteroids, spy escapades, sinking ocean liners or historic epics. Little is glamorous.

The common thread in many Iranian films is instead a deceptively simple story line culled from small events, encounters or challenges that subtly offer the grist for bigger themes. The heroics involve getting through the calamities of daily life, rarely unscathed. Many amount to modern fables that leave viewers with hauntingly deep feelings.

In Hollywood, *Daily Variety* said of *The White Balloon,* "By turns suspenseful and amusing, the deceptively slight tale is a charmer with lots of local color. [Director] Jafar Panahi parlays the most basic raw ingredients into a modest slice of life with near-universal appeal. . . . Long opening shot through lively populated streets conveys an unmistakable sense of place. Bittersweet ending strikes the right tone."[59]

As in all aspects of Iranian public life, in cinema the filmmakers have faced severe restrictions. Censors must first approve projects and then okay the final cut. The government controls raw film stock. Women must always be portrayed wearing a chador or full *hejab* head-and-body covering—even in the privacy of the home, where in reality Iranians of both genders can wear whatever they want. Actresses also can't be shot in prolonged close-ups, which would exploit female beauty. No female over the age of nine can be touched. Sex and gratuitous violence are strictly banned.

Yet in content, Iranian films have increasingly probed sensitive subjects and even circumvented the forbidden.

"There are even ways to allude to sex," an Iranian director told me, on condition that I never identify him in any way. "In one film I saw recently, a man plays with his ring, pulling it up and down over and over on his finger as he says he was working on his project all night. Everyone knew what was meant.

"We've really become quite inventive in communicating with our audiences. It makes going to Iranian movies a lot of fun. Everyone looks for secret meanings in every little gesture," the director said.

"In some of mine," he added with a chuckle, "people found things that weren't intended."

Like the members of Iran's outspoken press, filmmakers have grown quite bold in their criticism. Characters challenge the status quo. Plots focus attention on the shortcomings of the Islamic system. Dialogue redefines the boundaries of what can be talked about in public. And few subjects are off-limits.

The White Balloon took subtle jabs at an array of social ills, including poverty, racial bias and child exploitation.

Mehrjui, the father of modern Iranian film, wrote and directed a quartet of films—*Banoo* (1992), *Sara* (1994), *Pari* (1995) and *Leila* (1997)—about the personal and professional plights of women. Each involved a revelation or rebellion; each ended with the women's defying convention or chucking their husbands and heading out on their own.

Mehrjui's *Hamoon* (1990), which ranked in a 1997 poll of film critics and the public as the best movie in Iranian history, was a dark comedy about modern Iranian life that dared to poke at everything from fixations with Islamic religious figures and Iran's troubled economy to gender inequality.

The Makhmalbafs, father-and-daughter directors, personified the transition within Iranian film. Mohsen Makhmalbaf spent five years in prison during the monarchy for attacking a policeman, a crime he committed at the age of seventeen. After the revolution, he was first known for his religious and ardently revolutionary films. But he rather quickly progressed to secular stories that made him one of Iran's most famous and oft-awarded directors.

By the 1990s, Makhmalbaf was making movies that coyly challenged revolutionary truths. His fifth film was blatantly antiwar. The next two were banned. His seventh film, *A Time to Love,* was a particularly controversial tale about a married woman who falls for a younger man. But the subject of a forbidden love affair was not what caused the ban, several Iranian writers told me. The problem was that it had three endings. The controversy was the message: Perception varies. So does truth. There is no single or right path.

In 1998, Makhmalbaf's daughter Samira made her international film debut with *The Apple,* the true story of a poor, illiterate man who had kept his twelve-year-old twin girls locked inside their tiny home from infancy until neighbors reported him to local officials. He later explained that he feared the girls' purity would be spoiled by strange men's gazes. The plot revolved around the gradual exposure of the girls—almost mute, totally unschooled and physically and mentally disabled—to the outside world. Although at times tragic, *The Apple* was also laced with gentle humor as the twins for the first time tasted ice cream, used a comb, played with a hand mirror and coveted a neighbor boy's shiny apple.

The simple tale was laden with allegory. With only one real male role in the father, Makhmalbaf admitted she was addressing the situation of women.

"I wanted the film to make this point: All it takes to imprison many, many women is one man," she said shortly after the film opened in New York in 1999.[60]

"What I noticed about those two girls is that the more they came into contact with society, the more complete they became as human beings. For me that became a metaphor for all women," she told the New York press. "Women in Iran are like springs. When you push them a lot, when they're under pressure, they're closed. But if they want to be free, and if they try, they burst out with a lot of energy."[61]

At a broader level, the surreal tale of the twins also aimed at the heart of Iran's political debate about the degree of liberty the paternal clergy would allow their flock.

The film was all the more novel because its stars were the real sequestered twins—and their father and blind mother. The younger Makhmalbaf convinced authorities to allow the girls, who'd been taken away from their parents, to return home on a monitored basis as she made a movie about their introduction to society. *The Apple* was *cinéma vérité*.

Samira Makhmalbaf's own story was also interesting. An attractive young woman with long braids and a part down the middle of her black hair, she was only seventeen—the same age her father had been when he challenged the injustices of the shah's regime—when she heard about the twins on an evening news program and immediately decided to make a movie that took a hard jab at the theocracy. The film was shot in eleven days, usually with only a single take of each scene. She was eighteen when it showed at Cannes and at the New York Film Festival to critical acclaim.

In a telling comment, one critic at Cannes asked her, "What kind of country is Iran? Is it a place where twelve-year-old girls are incarcerated, or where eighteen-year-old girls make movies?"[62]

Although she didn't say it, the answer, of course, was both.

By the late 1990s, few films dealt directly with themes that glorified the revolution anymore. And the few produced for propaganda purposes didn't do well.

Sandstorm, a movie about the failed 1980 mission to rescue the American hostages in Tehran, was among the last. Released in 1997, the film cost almost $2 million, more than ten times the average Iranian movie budget. It was visually authentic, right down to American helicopters, military uniforms and weapons. It had all the elements of an adventure epic—spy escapades, military daredevilry and international intrigue. It featured one of Iran's top stars as Colonel Charles Beckwith, the commander of Operation Desert One. And the pre-release hype for the movie was right out of Hollywood.

Yet *Sandstorm* bombed. On opening day, only half the seats at the premiere performance were full.[63]

"There's no nostalgia about those days anymore," explained a Tehran political scientist who'd taken to the streets both to oust the shah and to welcome Khomeini back from exile.

"Besides, I don't have the money these days to waste on movies. And if I did, I'd rather find something either more entertaining or more relevant to my life now."

But a generation after the revolution, Iranian films were probably most striking because the vast majority had little or no reference to Islam, except maybe a passing mention of a Muslim holiday or a scene that

showed a mosque because it happened to be near something else important to the plot.

The depth and sophistication of Iran's secular cinema have been all
the more surprising because the only form of storytelling in Persia for
millennia was either religious or poetic. The only public performances for
centuries were the annual Islamic passion plays reenacting the martyrdom of Hussein during Ashura.

A millennium after it was written, the most famous legend is still the
Shahnameh, an epic of sixty thousand couplets written in the tenth century chronicling Persia's history. It took Ferdowsi, the first great Persian
poet, thirty years to write. Poetry was so treasured at the time that the
reigning monarch, Sultan Mahmoud Ghaznavi, was reputed to have four
hundred poets attached to the court.[64]

Although Ferdowsi died penniless after the sultan shortchanged him,
his *Shahnameh* is still recounted in Iranian families. It's available in most
Iranian bookstores, often with fancy gold-leaf illustrations. Every Iranian I've ever asked about the best books on Iran has directed me to the
poetic *Shahnameh,* despite the fact that it's a thousand years old.

Theater also didn't really exist in Iran until well into the twentieth
century. The first Iranian movie was screened in 1930, but serious cinema
didn't begin until after World War II.[65] And both forms of dramatic arts
were largely imitations, in content and style, of foreign productions.

"We had a cinema industry but the quality was very poor. Most films
shown here were either Western or Indian—or Iranian imitations of
Western or Indian movies," said Mojtaba Raie, a smallish man with
tortoise-shell glasses and a full head of graying curls who was directing
Abdi in his new movie about a nineteenth-century shah entitled *The Vic-
torious Warrior.*

"In all the years before the revolution, less than a half-dozen films
were good enough to be noticed abroad. It wasn't the government that
wanted the industry to make bad films, it was just the situation of society.
That changed after the revolution, when the whole culture of this country
also changed," he said, as palace workmen finished up their banging
repairs and the film crew worked on the tricky job of lighting a room with
walls made entirely of inlaid mirrors.

"The revolution brought some things that look strange to some people, such as *hejab,*" he continued. "But it also made us focus on ourselves
and our values. We learned that to make good films we should look at our

society, not try to make films about themes in other societies—except in Farsi.

"Of course we have limitations," he conceded. Raie has had his share of film scripts turned down or delayed. Like many in the industry, he complained that censors too often judged projects based on their own personal tastes, not Islamic or government standards. And tastes changed as censors changed, making what was once acceptable forbidden and vice versa.

"Some limitations aren't all bad. They've forced us to be more original," he said.

"*Hejab,* for example, means we can't show kissing or touching to say the characters love each other. We have to find an artistic way to show it— through behavior toward each other or through the forgiveness they show each other. I personally think this is a much more interesting way to show love than through a kiss. I'd never think to show a love affair in a bedroom scene now, even if I could."

I asked Raie the formula for mixing modern cinema and Islam. I mentioned the second annual Tandee ceremony that had been held that week at Tehran's House of Cinema. The head of the film section at the Ministry of Culture and Islamic Guidance had opened the festivities by invoking religion.

"Artistic talent is a blessing that God has bestowed on certain individuals," he'd said. "The purpose of holding such a festival is so that we won't take such talent for granted."[66]

But Raie scoffed at my question. "Oh, I don't believe there's any such thing as Islamic cinema," he said.

"Each director sees events through his own eyes and then makes a movie that captures that vision. If he's looking only for Islam, then he'd make a religious movie."

It was a critical point. To the outside world, the revolution and the theocracy born out of it were one and the same. But most sectors of Iranian society, including filmmakers, made a distinction: The political upheaval aimed at ending autocratic rule and redistributing power was one thing. The subsequent Islamic government that eventually replaced the monarchy—and then imposed its own restrictions—was quite another.

In other words, whether or not they liked the theocratic government and its policies, many artists, writers and filmmakers still felt the revolution itself had had a positive side for Iranian culture. It had opened the way for artists to explore new forms of expression, beyond what the royal court ordered, supported or condoned. It had fostered originality. And it had created a climate that focused on both universal and local issues, but from an Iranian perspective and in an Iranian genre.

The rebirth of Iran's movie industry after the revolution is widely dated to a film called *The Cow*. It was actually shot a decade before the revolution. Released in 1969, it was the second work of Dariush Mehrjui, then a new young director. The plot revolved around a poor village that dissolved into chaos after the loss of its lone cow.

At the time, *The Cow* won prizes at film festivals in Venice and Chicago. Thirty years later, the *New York Times* still called it "dazzling" and raved about its "spare, allusive . . . starkly beautiful black-and-white photography and an extraordinary lead performance."[67] But the monarchy in 1969 had banned it, as it did again later with two other Mehrjui films. The portrayal of poverty in *The Cow* had disturbed the shah—and embarrassed him six years after his own White Revolution had introduced reforms designed to address the enormous gap between rich and poor. *The Cow* signaled his failure.

Film critics in Iran—as well as the United States, Europe and Asia—now rank *The Cow* as the first of the so-called "New Wave" of Iranian films. So, ironically, did Ayatollah Khomeini.

"Khomeini actually encouraged the arty movie," Mehrjui explained when I went to see him at his north Tehran home in 1998. Dressed in a blue shirt hanging loose over sweatpants, his dark hair disheveled, Mehrjui was roguishly handsome and very much the arty director.

"After the revolution, the whole industry was in jeopardy. Many cinema houses during the revolution had been attacked or burned down for being centers of corruption. Plus, image is prohibited in Islam," he said.

Indeed, the Islamic restriction on portraying images actually prevented Saudi Arabia from getting television until the 1970s. Iran already had it, so banning the visual arts was not an option after the revolution. Besides, Khomeini had made several videocassettes and granted dozens of television interviews before the revolution. Both had been critical in elevating him from the obscurity of exile to leadership of the revolution's widely disparate political factions.

After the revolution, Iran's visual media did become sensitive about images of religious figures. One of the most popular series on Iranian television, *Imam Ali,* was about the first Shi'ite Muslim. It was all shot without showing any drawing or image of either Ali or the prophet Mohammad. They were portrayed in shadows or with a single hand or foot to denote their presence.

The theocracy's early movies were also religious.

"At first, only propaganda films were being made and no one went to see them," Mehrjui said. "Then comes this remark from Khomeini about *The Cow,* which he saw on TV. Afterward, he said, 'Don't say cinema is bad. We're not against cinema per se. We're only against films that are meant to corrupt people.'

"This became a big headline in the paper and opened the way for other kinds of films that had human feelings. It couldn't have happened without Khomeini," he added.

Ironically, Iran's isolation also helped. The ban on most foreign films in public theaters created a captive market at a time cinema in other countries was increasingly dominated by American movies.

"The whole world of cinema during the past twenty years has been engulfed and devoured by commercial cinema. More and more, the grand tradition of making films as art, especially in Europe, Latin America and India, has died out because of the domination of American cinema," Mehrjui said.

"Iran is the only country that still has a tremendous enthusiasm for deep, existential, artistic films that are truthful about life—because our doors are locked to American and other commercial films. So our cinema is not only alive," he added, "it's flourishing."

Yet Khomeini's blessing of *The Cow* didn't mean Mehrjui's subsequent films had any guarantees.

"I've always faced obstacles and all kinds of terrors," Mehrjui said, as he peeled a small succulent tangerine from a plate of fruit on the long dining room table where we sat.

Just like the monarchy, the theocracy also banned two of his films. *Banoo,* or *The Lady,* was held back for more than seven years.

Banoo had a simple story line: The lady was Mariam, a wealthy woman abandoned by her husband who decided to take in a poor family. She shopped and cooked for the family. She tended to their illnesses. She allowed them to bring in relatives. She did nothing when they began, quite blatantly, to steal her family heirlooms. The family's betrayal of trust, in the end, left her with little.

"*Banoo* was banned for showing the poor stealing and for portraying them in a less than favorable way. Actually, it wasn't officially banned—the ministry just said let's wait and see, and so it went into limbo for seven years. Disrespect for the poor was the official reason," Mehrjui explained.

"But there are other terrors too. There's the terror of having to be politically correct—not to criticize anyone or propagate any cause," he added. "There's the terror of finding capital to make the movie. There's also the terror of the market, worsened by the problem of theater space."

Iran's cities have had a chronic shortage of theaters in which to show films dating back to attacks on movie houses during the shah's ouster. Afterward, many others were converted into religious facilities. Only about half of Iran's movie houses still operated after the revolution. Nationwide, Iran had only 270 theaters, with a total of a hundred thousand seats, for a population well over 60 million.[68]

"Oddly enough, the top ten percent of our best films, the ones that are shown abroad the most, rarely get a chance to be shown for any period of time here," Mehrjui explained.

"And there are all kinds of crooked regulations and pressures on theaters and distributors to show a specific film. So the good ones end up in a small cinema—and for a short time."

The election of President Khatami had improved Mehrjui's situation. Mohajerani lifted the ban on *Banoo* in 1998—seven years after it was made—to much local fanfare and acclaim. The *Tehran Times* hailed it as "another turning point" in Mehrjui's career.[69]

Yet as Iran tentatively began relaxing its strict regulations and censorship, the very freedoms most filmmakers wanted also posed new dangers. What would happen if other doors were opened in the process? The chance to further develop an indigenous industry meant some tough decisions—issues that in many ways made the film industry a microcosm of Iran a generation after the revolution.

Mehrjui personified the conundrum.

Raised a devout Muslim, Mehrjui believed in the integrity and purity of film to the point that he switched his major at the University of California, Los Angeles, from cinema to philosophy because he thought the film professors were Hollywood hangers-on and has-beens with limited artistic vision. That antipathy didn't mean he rejected the West or its modern culture. He talked warmly about the way J. D. Salinger and Saul Bellow had shaped his thinking. Among his quartet of films about women, *Pari* had been inspired by Salinger's *Franny and Zooey,* while

Sara had been influenced by Ibsen's *A Doll's House.* And *Banoo* had been partially shaped by Buñuel's *Viridiana.*

Mehrjui also kept up with American film. As we talked at the dining room table, his wife, a Harvard-educated architect, was watching a pirated copy of *Jackie Brown,* starring Samuel L. Jackson, in the living room.

"He's already seen it a couple of times," she said of her husband.

Yet the cultural openings in Iran after Khatami's election were letting in the very things Mehrjui and Iran's other filmmakers most feared. American movies were no longer available only on the black market. They were also back in Iran's limited number of theaters and running on television.

"If we had total freedom, our cinemas would be flooded again by American films because the public is so thirsty for what they haven't seen in twenty years—Supersound and special effects," Mehrjui said, his hand combing through his rumpled hair.

"They'd go out of their minds. And the consequences for our own industry would be very bad," he added.

"We could end up back where we were before the revolution."

It was not an idle worry. During the first of my two trips in 1998, friends excitedly told me about watching *E.T., RoboCop* and the very dated *All the President's Men,* the story of the *Washington Post* investigation that led to President Nixon's resignation. Iranian television, run by conservatives, showed pirated copies of *The Towering Inferno* and *The Good, the Bad and the Ugly.* Tehran University announced a Robert De Niro Film Festival, including the gruesomely violent *Cape Fear.*[70]

During my second trip, *Little Buddha, The Last Emperor, Mr. Bean, The Usual Suspects, The Game, Seven* and *Titanic* were among the American movies that had been screened recently. *Seven,* starring Brad Pitt, struck me as an unusual choice, again given its focus on violence.

To understand the impact of American movies on Iran's film industry, I went to see Amir Esfandiari, director of international affairs at Tehran's Farabi Cinema Foundation, the major funder, distributor and promoter of films in Iran. Esfandiari had graduated from Northeastern University in Boston and had lived for fifteen years in San Francisco before returning home in the mid-1990s.

Seven was approved for public showing, he explained, because the film didn't actually *have* violence in it.

"It was just *about* violence," he said. It probably also helped that

Seven was about sin—each sin ultimately incurred the appropriate punishment."

Scenes from *Titanic* had even made it onto television, Esfandiari pointed out. Of course, the main scene selected—and replayed more than once—showed the passengers praying as the ship sank.

I told Esfandiari that I'd recently seen two formerly forbidden movies—*The Snowman* and *Banoo*—and that I liked both very much.

"Oh yes," he replied. "*The Snowman* is the top-grossing film in Iran in a long time. It's still very popular."

I asked if the movie had made Abdi the biggest star in Iran.

"Among Iranian actors, he's up there," Esfandiari said, nodding. "But to be honest, the biggest star in Iran at the moment is probably Leonardo DiCaprio."

CHAPTER 4

MEN ARE FROM TEHRAN, WOMEN ARE FROM ISFAHAN

> The traditional outlook, based on the erroneous no-
> tion of superiority of men over women, does injustice
> to men, women and humanity as a whole. We should
> recognize that both men and women are valuable
> components of humanity that equally possess the
> potential for intellectual, social, cultural and political
> development.
> —PRESIDENT MOHAMMAD KHATAMI[1]

ON A COOL SPRING EVENING in 1998, I went to a basketball game
in Tehran. Iranians are generally not tall people, so scoring was modest,
to say the least.

The Sahand players, dressed in black Nike gear, had enormous grit—
and the most fans. Loud rhythmic chants from family, friends and supporters in the orange bleachers echoed through the gym every time
Sahand got the ball.

"You're lions. You're lions. You're lions," they shouted in lilting Persian refrains.

133

But the Sahand Lions never really had a chance. They looked as if they were playing a neighborhood pickup game next to Pakvash, the league-leading team, dressed in snappy white-and-aqua uniforms. Pakvash had far greater size and strength. The final tally was a definitive 45–23.

Both teams had twice as many turnovers as baskets. The game also featured almost no fouling. Only one Pakvash player was ejected—for having long nails that scratched the Sahand center. Otherwise, it was a quite civilized event. Tea was served courtside and the refs and game officials shared a large box of Iranian sweets on the officiating table.

The game was unusual in other ways too. The arena had no scoreboard. An official tallied baskets on two pieces of paper with carbon in between so each team would have a copy. Fans had to keep their own count.

On the wall instead was a quote from Ayatollah Khomeini. "Athletes should have morals on the sports field too," it admonished in big letters.

And attire was notably informal. The ref wore a sweatshirt with two spotted Dalmatians on the front and Disney's Lady and the Tramp on the back. One coach was dressed in a Calvin Klein T-shirt, the other in a gray Chicago Bulls jersey.

"Hey, Michael Jordan is popular everywhere," Pakvash coach Manijeh Norozian told me.

The game was most unusual, however, because the players, coaches and fans were all the same gender—female. The one exception was the three-month-old son of Sahand captain Sima Adeli, a forward who used half-time to sit in the bleachers and nurse her baby.

In 1998, basketball was a big sport among women in the Islamic republic. Tehran alone had five leagues, with eighty-four teams.

"And it's growing *very* fast," said Nina Saleh, manager of the Hejab Club, the women's sports arena where the game was held, and a former captain of the national team. "We don't have enough facilities to keep up with the demand."

Indeed, despite cumbersome clothing, limited space and harassment by religious zealots, Iranian females have flocked to sport since the early 1990s. Only ten thousand women engaged in intramural sports on the eve of the 1979 revolution. Two decades later, some 2 million participated in soccer, basketball, swimming, tennis, handball, skiing, aerobics, fencing, judo, shooting, volleyball, rowing, horseback riding, gymnastics, golf, Ping-Pong, karate and tae kwan do. Women even engaged in water-skiing, despite being forced to wear a slightly ridiculous, not to mention dangerous, coat and scarf—both waterproof.[2]

And commitment was intense. After the game, I talked to Elaheh Adeli, Sahand's diminutive star and the sister of the team captain. She told me how she practiced regularly at the women's club, as much as teaching at a girl's school allowed. But several mornings a week, she also threw a baggy coat over her sweats, pulled tight head cover over her short bobbed hair and ran to a local lot to practice. The scrappy Sahand guard then engaged in what, for an Iranian woman, was a blatantly defiant and potentially dangerous act.

"I play basketball with my husband and his pals," she confessed to me, with an impish grin.

The day after the basketball game, I went to visit Simin Ekrami, a denim-clad sculptor with a mop of curly dark hair and bare feet. Since the mid-1980s, Ekrami has worked artistic magic with chunks of wood, clay and plaster of paris. But lately she had quietly begun working on sculptures once unthinkable in the Islamic republic—what she calls "uncovered and anatomically correct" figures of women.

Everyone else called them nudes.

"These are *études* for monumental works," she told me as we walked through a house and courtyard garden filled with rounded, sensual torsos perched on pedestals, tables and floors.

They hadn't been shown in public galleries, of course. A vast percentage of new Iranian art, especially pieces with themes that were less than Islamically correct, was displayed in private showings by invitation only. The only piece of art I'd ever seen without *hejab* in the Islamic republic was a larger-than-life portrait of Empress Farah Diba, the last Pahlavi queen, which still hung in a former palace. The government's decision to show her cleavage, neck and bare arms was clearly a political statement.

Otherwise, the theocrats were relentless in forcing art to conform to Islamic modesty. After the revolution, the government even issued an ultimatum to the Museum of Contemporary Art about a large bronze statue of a female at the entrance: Either take it down or make it comply. The statue was preserved by adding crude fiberglass *hejab* to her hair and legs.

Other art wasn't so fortunate. In an Iranian art book, the ballerinas in Edgar Degas's famous *Dancers Practicing at the Barre* were airbrushed out completely, leaving an empty room and practice barre. The tutus didn't meet the standards of *hejab*.[3]

For most of her career, Ekrami had complied with the unspoken rules. She crafted large stone sculptures commissioned by Tehran's mayor for local parks and the airport. She also worked on logos—one for the post office and another of geometric boxes and squares for an urban organization.

"But there came a time when I couldn't resist working on anatomical figures," she explained. "For a sculptor, what could be more interesting? And who knows a woman's body better than a woman?

"I'm really proud of them," she added, surveying her new pieces. "And if anyone comes to ask me to cover them, I won't do it."

In the 1990s, a revolution erupted within Iran's revolution. Its pace has been slower. It has rarely spoken with a single voice. And it still faced obstacles so formidable that, in comparison, ending 2,500 years of monarchy looked almost easy. But the passions that have emerged from disparate corners of Iranian society to inspire a vibrant women's movement are just as deep as the emotions of 1979.

The impact has been visible in every aspect of Iranian life. In politics, an unprecedented two hundred women ran for the 270-seat Parliament in 1996. And fourteen won—more than the total of women in the U.S. Senate at the time. In 1997, four women registered to run for the presidency—at the same time a poll by *Zanan* magazine revealed that 72 percent of the public approved of the idea of a woman as president. A year later, nine women tried to stand for the Assembly of Experts. In both elections, all the women were rejected by the Council of Guardians that vets candidates—but because of lack of qualifications, not gender. By then, even the clerics would no longer dare declare sex an issue.

Before a stadium full of women during Women's Week, Ayatollah Ali Khamenei, the conservative Supreme Leader, declared in 1997, "A blind imitation of Western women is noxious. The feminist movement in the West has only brought sexual promiscuity." Yet even he commanded "greater participation of women in social and political affairs" and urged traditional families to allow their daughters to seek higher education.[4]

As the revolution celebrated its twentieth anniversary, almost a third of government employees were female—a major achievement when Iran was compared with the religious Arab monarchies across the Persian Gulf. In Saudi Arabia, so few females were employed in government ministries that many buildings had no women's lavatories. At a Riyadh office, I once had to wait while a men's room was cleaned up and then three men stood guard outside while I used it. In contrast, various Iranian ministries employed 342 female director-generals.[5] And five thousand women ran in Iran's first local elections in 1999. More than three hundred won, several taking among the highest vote counts.

Professionally, growing numbers of Iranian women had also become lawyers, doctors, professors, newspaper and magazine editors, engineers, business executives, economists, coaches and television newscasters. By 1999, Iran had 140 female publishers, enough to hold an exhibition of books and magazines published by women.[6] In the arts, they'd become painters, authors, designers, photographers and movie producers, directors and stars—and winners of international awards in all three.

In education, Iran was cited in 1998 as one of the ten countries that had made the most progress in closing the gap between boys and girls in the education system.[7] More than 95 percent of Iranian girls were by then in elementary school. Over 40 percent of university students were women—compared with 28 percent in 1978. And more than a third of university faculties were female.[8] In 1998, Zahra Rahnavard, a writer and the wife of a former prime minister, became the first female university chancellor—at Al-Zahra University, Iran's equivalent of Wellesley or Mount Holyoke.

Just as important was the general sense of power shared among Iran's women. Millions had begun to define the way Islam was applied and to put their own imprint on widely diverse aspects of Iranian life. Since 1994, female pressure had changed laws on employment, divorce, child custody, alimony and maternity leave. The overwhelming turnout and unity of the female vote had been one of two factors behind the 1997 victory of President Mohammad Khatami in the biggest election upset since the revolution.

Women increasingly—and boldly—were speaking out.

"Unfortunately, our society has inherited certain erroneous assumptions that are accepted in the name of religion," reflected Zahra Shojaie, a woman who was director of the High Council of the Cultural Revolution under President Rafsanjani and later became President Khatami's adviser on women's affairs.

"Some people regard a good woman to be chaste and submissive, one who doesn't seek personal and professional growth. This is totally wrong. Nowhere in the Holy Koran has it been said that women should be bound to the home."[9]

Most Iranians agree that whatever happens to the revolution's political agenda or economic goals, its deepest impact will be on Iran's social order. If this is true, then the revolution's legacy may be most enduring among women.

That's not, of course, what the clerics intended. Their original goal was more akin to gender apartheid.

After the revolution, the theocrats dismissed virtually all women who had risen to positions of importance during the monarchy—including 22 members of Parliament, 330 in local councils, 5 mayors and thousands of educators, civil servants and diplomats. The new constitution also removed critical inroads made over the previous half century.

The new Islamic republic's intentions were best reflected when the minimum age for marriage was lowered to nine, the official age of puberty.

The ideal revolutionary woman was supposed to be well trained in tradition, limited to supplicant roles as housewife and mother, willing to cede control of most aspects of life to fathers, husbands or brothers and, needless to say, pious. To put them in their place, women were ordered to cover every part of the anatomy save face and hands. To ensure they wouldn't still tempt men, everything from schoolrooms to ski slopes and public buses was strictly segregated.

In the early days, the rules were fervently enforced. Bad *hejab,* meaning exposed hair or skin and makeup, was punished with seventy lashes or from ten days to two months in jail. Female adulterers were stoned to death. Roadblocks at night checked to make sure female passengers were relatives of male drivers. Homes suspected of hosting parties with unmarried couples or youths were raided. Females caught in either situation were subject to virginity tests.

As a foreign woman, I often had surprising access to senior government officials interested in relaying messages to the outside world. But I sometimes had real hassles during my own run-ins with the morals police.

One episode in 1987, at the former Hilton Hotel, renamed the Independence after the revolution, was in stark contrast to my first trip to Iran in 1973, when I stayed at the hotel and had a drink at its bar. The hotel was, at best, sloppy about telephone messages and paging and I was waiting for several calls about appointments. So when Farhang Rejaie, a Tehran University political scientist, arrived for an interview, I asked him to come to my room where we could talk in the sitting area. We'd been chatting for several minutes when the phone rang.

"We know there's a man with you," the anonymous male voice said.

"Unless you both come out immediately, we'll be forced to come in. We're across the hall."

Slightly rattled, Rejaie and I immediately headed for the lobby, where we found a table near the window. A couple of minutes later, the hotel assistant manager interrupted us.

"I must ask you to move," he said. "The men, you know, are playing sports."

The place we'd selected overlooked the Hilton tennis court and pool and, as a woman, I wasn't supposed to look at skimpily clad men—the same reason women were banned from soccer and wrestling matches.

So Rejaie and I moved again, this time deeper into the lobby. In the end, however, we never finished our conversation. Soon after we sat down, I saw a woman who looked a bit like Darth Vader sweep through the lobby, her chador billowing and exposing only her eyes, nose and mouth. She looked my way and had a few words with a waiter who served tea and cakes. He draped a white cloth over his left arm, placed a pink card on a plate and then walked over to present it to me.

"The Islamic society kindly seeks your considerate observance of its customs in promotion of mutual respect," the pink card read—in English. "To further our good relations, we respectfully request your observance of Islamic dress during your stay with us."

The reverse side had a picture of appropriate attire, in case there was any doubt. Apparently my headscarf had slipped, revealing a bit of hair. As the *komiteh* woman observed from the other side of the lobby, I pulled up my *hejab,* and she left. So did a very shaken Rejaie.

Individually, the encounters were irritating petty harassment. But it was easy to see why the government's strategy to intimidate into compliance led so many women initially to simply stay home. The coercion wore women down. After my three encounters in just an hour, I gave up and went back to work the phones from my room.

During the revolution's combative first decade, the pettiness of enforcement often bordered on the ridiculous. In my favorite Tehran bookstore, I once found copies of William F. Buckley's novel *Saving the Queen,* kind of an odd book to find in Iran, given the author and the title. The cover was even odder. A black Magic Marker had been used to draw over the fictional queen's arms and hair. The same thing initially happened to pictures of women in the few foreign magazines allowed into Iran.

At a pharmacy along the Caspian Sea, I once found the shapeless drawings of women on products such as Mentholatum Deep Heat and Vitalis Vita-E crudely covered with several tiny white stickers. Only the face, toes and hands showed.

"The morals police come around sporadically to take a look at what we sell," said Babak Khamzadeh, the owner's teenage son, who worked the shop on weekends.

"Any picture of a lady can be trouble. The first time we'll get a warning. The second time we face a penalty and confiscation of the product," he told me.

The attitude often reminded me of a piece of exquisite handblown glass from the tenth century that I had seen in an Isfahan museum. I had asked the museum guide about the unusual slanted lip at the top of what looked like a small vase or thin bottle.

"In aristocratic families," he explained, "men gave those to their wives to collect teardrops, so the women could prove how much they'd missed their husbands."

Ten centuries later, Persian tradition and Islamic customs were still a powerful combination—and probably one reason the clerics never contemplated a counterchallenge by Iranian women. But just as the authoritarian monarchy had not been immune from the global demand for empowerment, so the tough theocracy was not isolated from the global movement for equal participation by both genders.

Circumstances helped. The war with Iraq diverted manpower to the front for eight costly years. Women were needed, both in the workplace and to support the war effort. Exploding population growth put enormous demands on the government to rapidly expand its bureaucracy, as well as schools, health facilities and other social services, which it couldn't do without using women. A worsening economy also forced wives to work; it wasn't uncommon to find a husband and wife holding down three jobs between them.[10]

"Ironically, the clerics contributed unwittingly but decisively to the injection of women into the public sphere. The revolution has given women a keener sense of their rights, created among them a sense of community and turned them into an informal constituency or pressure group," said Haleh Esfandiari, a scholar from one of Iran's oldest families who commutes between Tehran and Washington, D.C., and who has always been my guide on women's issues.

Iranian women also proved to be irrepressible. And even the clerics, in the end, had to begin ceding ground.

"In Iran today, women are regarded with awe because of the combative attitude they adopted toward the state's attempts to interfere in their private and public lives," added Esfandiari, whose book *Reconstructed Lives* chronicled the resurgence.

"The regime has been forced tacitly to acknowledge that it can't exclude women from public life and that its ability to dictate how women will behave in the private sphere is strictly limited."

Most concessions have been subtle and slow. But occasionally, symbols of change are striking.

At the opening ceremony of the 1996 summer Olympics in Atlanta, the Iranian contingent was led by Lida Fariman, dressed in a scarf and coat, both a brilliant white and a stark contrast to the dour and dark colors worn by women at home. She was the first woman since the revolution to compete in the summer games. A target shooter, Fariman was also the first Iranian woman ever to carry the flag ahead of her fellow Iranian athletes onto the Olympic field.

Despite an official request to stay away "to safeguard women's dignity," some five thousand women crashed the gates of Tehran's Azadi Stadium in 1998 to welcome home Iran's soccer team from the Asian Games, where a victory over Australia had secured a berth in the World Cup. Authorities ended up letting them stay, and later opened up soccer, volleyball and tennis matches to female spectators, albeit in gender-segregated sections. A female sportswriter was even allowed to cover soccer.

By the decade's end, Iran's police academy had been opened to women. The first graduates were assigned, not surprisingly, to a "vice and social depravity squad" in towns along the Caspian.[11] The Islamic republic also appointed its first female judges—a major breakthrough, since historically the judiciary is the one field that Islam outlaws for women.[12] Newspapers dared to run articles suggesting not only equality but also physical superiority.

"Does Menopause Provide Evolutionary Advantage?" pondered a *Tehran Times* headline in 1998.[13]

And one of the best-selling books in Iran was *Men Are from Mars, Women Are from Venus.*

In some areas, women were merely recouping gains lost after the monarchy collapsed. Yet the revolution's feminist movement has been quite distinct from activism under the shahs. The majority of women haven't been trying to end Islamic rule. They've instead worked from within Islam to correct its path.

The difference was explained to me by Mahboobeh Abbas-Gholizadeh, the articulate editor of *Farzaneh* magazine and the prototype revolutionary. At age nineteen, Abbas-Gholizadeh had taken to the streets to campaign against the shah. As a college student in Egypt, she had been deported for protesting the shah's exile in Cairo. She had returned to Iran and studied religious law in the theological city of Qom.

But a generation later, she was a divorced mother of two daughters who climbed mountains on weekends, smoked Marlboros—and wrote editorials challenging the same revolution.

"It hasn't done enough for women," she told me, over a cup of tea in an office decorated with posters and weary plants.

Tired of waiting, Abbas-Gholizadeh is among a growing group of women trying to reinterpret Koranic verse and adapt Islamic traditions known as *hadith*. Since male power brokers have failed to help, Iran's females are looking for ways to do it for themselves.

"What I say about women's rights is based on what I studied of religious law and logic. And I can tell you from knowing the Koran and *hadith* that whatever the clerics are doing is *not* what's written in the Koran. It's only their interpretation—their male and sometimes chauvinist interpretation," she explained in a tone of self-assured authority.

Interpreting Islam is based on four elements: the Koran, the *hadith*, wisdom and consensus, the last introducing an element of compromise, she added. Men have dominated interpretation for centuries because they had a monopoly on consensus and education. Since women were excluded from the process, the perspective historically reflected male interests.

"In fact, the Koran says that men and women are equal before God. And those who are better are better because they're good Muslims, not because they're men or women," she said. "We've put together a list of verses from the Koran. Many can be interpreted as promoting equality."

Among the verses the new breed of Iranian feminists cite:

On financial rights: *"Men shall have the benefit of what they earn and women shall have the benefit of what they earn."* Chapter 4, verse 32.

On gender respect and parity: *"The Believers, men and women, are protectors, one of another: they enjoin what is just and forbid what is evil."* Chapter 9, verse 71.

And on rights in divorce: *"If you fear a breach between the two, then appoint a judge from his side and a judge from her people."* Chapter 4, verse 35.[14]

Farzaneh, which is half in Farsi, half in English, explored Iran's new theology of feminism. Modeled on the Canadian *Journal of Women and the Law* and the University of Chicago's *Journal of Women in Culture and Society,* the quarterly ran articles such as "Human Rights of Women in Islam," "A History of Silence and Debates Today" and "Gender and Thought." A regular *Farzaneh* feature called "Quarterly Discourse" probed the feminist agenda, in pieces with telling titles such as "How to Proceed" and "The Long Way Ahead."

"It's not enough to shout about women's problems. We should find a solution," Abbas-Gholizadeh said, reaching for another cigarette across the tinted-glass conference table.

The Islamic Republic's new activists were as distinct as the political environment. The most outspoken women were no longer the Westernized or upper-class elites who had high profiles during the monarchy. Many were instead from traditional families, rural areas and even clerical circles. Many of the two hundred female candidates in the 1996 parliamentary election came from provincial areas and were never before involved in politics. Even more of the five thousand women who ran for city councils in 1999 were from rural areas and traditional families.

"When you see women in small provinces competing with their male counterparts and winning, that's really very significant. They're part of a whole new generation of women since the revolution who want a better balance between religion, modernism and tradition," Abbas-Gholizadeh explained.

"We want our rights but in an environment compatible with our beliefs. That means we don't believe we have to live in a Western system in order to share power. But we're also not going to trust men in our own system to grant us our due.

"In other words," she said, with a twinkle in her eye, "the women's movement that has emerged from within the revolution is both its enemy and its friend."

Given the dangers to dissidents, especially during a half-dozen murders of prominent writers and thinkers in 1998 and 1999, women like Abbas-Gholizadeh have been almost brazen in challenging male centers of power. The *Farzaneh* editor had no qualms about criticizing the various branches of government, including officials she otherwise supported, as well as both sides of Iran's widening political divide.

"I voted for Khatami, but that doesn't mean I have to follow every word he says. I have a duty to put pressure on him to pay attention to this issue," she said. "So now I'm writing articles warning the president that he'll lose popularity unless he pays more attention to gender issues. We have expectations, you know."

Abbas-Gholizadeh's list of concrete demands covered everything from signing international treaties on human rights and child abuse to amending Iran's so-called "family laws" and allowing women to hold more public debates on the problems they face. When we met, she was particularly riled that the government had succumbed to pressure from conservatives to block a panel discussion about gender discrimination at a national book fair.

"The conservatives are much worse, of course. They believe there's already far too much 'equality.' And frankly, I'm sorry to say that in the struggle for power between conservatives and moderates, the rights of women have generally been delayed or ignored," Abbas-Gholizadeh said.

But she reserved special criticism for other Islamic feminists who'd gained power, then not performed.

"Some of the progressive women now involved in government think too much about their positions and the political game and not enough about other women who need them the most," she added.

In an office staffed completely with women, the *Farzaneh* editor still wore the tight black hood known as a *maghnaye,* which is slightly reminiscent of a nun's habit in the way it circles the face, and a chador. Among themselves, women can remove Islamic cover. So I asked why she opted to keep on the extra layer of clothing.

"You in the West dwell too much on *hejab.* And the conservatives here use it too much to pressure us," she said, scolding me a little. Abbas-Gholizadeh had clearly had many discussions about *hejab* over the years.

"The issue for us is *not* dress. I fully acknowledge that a woman can be a good Muslim without *hejab.* And I know some women here don't like it. For me, it's a personal choice. It's something spiritual and a way of saying that my body is precious. Maybe you should look on it as a social uniform, like Chinese dress in Mao's time," she said.

"Frankly, the chador," she added, a smile again crossing her face, "is no longer an appropriate symbol of what women are doing in Iran."

MASSOUMEH EBTEKAR WAS the first woman made famous by the revolution—at least in the eyes of the outside world.

Known simply as "Sister Mary," she made her political debut in 1979 as the angry spokesperson for the students who seized the U.S. Embassy.

She was only nineteen at the time. Her memorable young face—the lids drooping slightly above long eyelashes and the cheeks so fresh and color-less without makeup that they seemed almost raw—became a fixture on the nightly news.

Ebtekar was a model of revolutionary militancy. Speaking in English, she'd recount American crimes against the Iranian people or threaten to put the hostages on trial if the deposed shah wasn't returned to Iran. Ironically, the accent was distinctly American, learned during a childhood at Philadelphia's Highland Park Elementary School while her father worked on his doctorate in engineering. The exposure obvi-ously hadn't softened her politics. She lashed out against the hostages with a frightening air of authority, even though she had no official stand-ing. She was only a freshman at Tehran's Polytechnic University at the time.

Once pressed by an ABC News correspondent about whether she could envision using a gun to kill the hostages, Ebtekar bluntly replied, "Yes, when I've seen an American gun being lifted up and killing my brothers and sisters in the streets, of course."[15]

Inside the sprawling embassy compound, Ebtekar was the only woman many of the male hostages ever saw. They secretly dubbed her Sis-ter Philadelphia, Screaming Mary and Mary the Terrorist.[16]

Sergeant William Quarles, a Marine security guard, recalled his first encounter with her.

"She talked my ear off about the revolution, about the ayatollah, about politics, about the shah, and about SAVAK, the shah's secret police—she went on and on. I said to myself, 'They're trying to pump my head full of ideology. They're trying to brainwash me,'" he said shortly after his release.[17]

Years later, many hostages still remembered Sister Mary with bitterness.

"I recall her as someone who should have known better. Having lived in the United States for six years, having seen who we are as a people, and then to say the things she said about the hostages, particularly her con-stant declaration that we should be put on trial—I really deplored her attitude and treatment of us," Bruce Laingen, the ranking American among the hostages, told me.

Mike Metrinko, the embassy's spirited political officer, remembered the final television interviews Ebtekar did with the hostages the day before they were freed.

"She wanted us to say how well we were treated," he recalled. "She reminded me of Tokyo Rose."

After the 444-day ordeal ended, Ebtekar was rewarded with a job as editor of *Kayhan International,* an English-language paper. She was only twenty-one. At the time, the parent Kayhan Publishing Company was headed by a then little-known cleric named Mohammad Khatami. But Ebtekar soon opted to return to school to study medical technology. She eventually earned a doctorate in immunology and joined the faculty of a Tehran university. She also married and had two children. For the outside world, she basically faded into the world of academe and motherhood.

As a sideline, however, Ebtekar also became an Iranian feminist. And once again, she was ardent and outspoken. She founded the Center for Women's Studies and Research. She and a colleague launched *Farzaneh,* the intellectual journal on women's issues. She represented Iran at the United Nations summits on women in Nairobi and Beijing. She ran symposia on the role of women in Iran, the Mideast, the Islamic bloc and the world. She designed a university curriculum for women's studies. And she wrote extensively on women's rights.

She even explored the role of women in other faiths, including the Virgin Mary. In a 1994 article in *Farzaneh* entitled "The Chosen Woman," Ebtekar concluded that the Virgin Mary's attributes of faith, purity and social commitment made her "a flawless personality that deserves to be considered as a model for the bewildered human race" in the twenty-first century.[18]

I once asked Ebtekar why she chose the Virgin Mary—or Mariam, as she's called in the Koran. It certainly indicated that her brushes with Western culture weren't all negative.

"I often thought about the fact the Holy Koran gives a very significant role to the Virgin Mary. A whole chapter's devoted to her. She's referred to as a model for children, for everybody, for the world. That includes men. She had a superior level of understanding, a spirituality," she replied.

"For me, it was inspiring, it was charming the way that the Holy Koran speaks about the Virgin Mary. The account shows that she withstood all the difficulties and emerged successful."

Over the years, Ebtekar had become a different kind of model. Sister Mary became simply a sister.

She also typified an emerging group known as "regime women," or those who believed that equality was best achieved through an Islamic government. Thousands sought new status by working for it, directly or indirectly.

The feminist role eventually won the attention of Ebtekar's former boss. And when he emerged from the political backwater to win the presidency in 1997, Mohammad Khatami fulfilled his pledge to bring more women into the political process by turning to Ebtekar. He appointed her vice president for the environment.* The revolution's first famous female thus became Iran's highest-ranking woman—and among the top female job holders in the Muslim world.

As vice president, Ebtekar took on her new cause with the same ferocity she had displayed during the embassy takeover. I saw her give a speech at a Tehran conference in 1998, when she was again railing angrily, this time about pollution in Iran's major cities and the dangers facing the Caspian Sea as the world scrambled to develop its vast energy resources.

"At least eighty-five percent of caviar comes from the Caspian and it's now threatened by pollution and industrialization along the coast," she warned an audience of oil executives and analysts, including several from the United States.

"There's been a fifty percent cut in the caviar catch over the last ten years. This only stands to get worse!"

The aging of the revolution's youngest militants reminded me a bit of American radicals in the 1960s—the likes of Tom Hayden and Bobby Rush—who became big politicos in the 1990s.[19] But Ebtekar fared even better. In 1999, the respected Davos Economic Forum of world leaders, held annually in Switzerland, selected her as one of the hundred leaders for the twenty-first century.

What happened to Ebtekar in the intervening generation reflected what happened to many revolutionaries. As the causes to oppose disappeared—the shah, the United States in Iran, Iraqi aggression—their focus shifted to the issues that got them involved in the revolution in the first place. In her case, the cause was empowerment, specifically of women.

I called on Ebtekar at her downtown office a few months after her appointment and asked what her new role indicated about Iran's feminist movement. By 1998, she was almost forty years old, a full-figured mother, her eyelids drooping a little bit more, but she was still intense and energetic.

" 'Feminism' is not a word we use in Iran," she insisted, holding up

*Iran has a handful of vice presidents, most of whom are assigned specific issues. All are appointed by the president.

her hands as if to physically resist the idea. "It has Western meanings that include sexual liberation. But if you mean equal rights and equal status and dignity as a human being, then we've advanced greatly since the revolution."

So did her appointment indicate even greater strides?

"Change is inevitable. It's part of life. It's part of what God has created," she said. "Our religious perspective about life, about society, about politics, it carries a dynamism that is able to meet evolving circumstances and times."

For a vice president, Ebtekar had an office that was modest in size and decor, largely bookcases. We sat across from each other in big chairs, my laptop on my lap. Ebtekar doesn't smile easily or often, but she was quite chatty and hospitable. She also no longer wore the *maghnaye* hood that the most devout women wear to cover their hair, draping the loose chador over it. Instead, she wore an autumnal scarf of rust, deep gold, green and white. Some of her female aides had on even brighter ones—a blue paisley, a soft pink print and a bright shade of green. It made them all look far less severe. And it made me think of Vatican II, when the Catholic Church allowed nuns to modify and even shed their habits.

I asked Ebtekar what it was like to be Iran's top female official, and how she was treated by the half-dozen other vice presidents, all male.

"I haven't sensed any negative feeling in terms of being a woman sitting on the cabinet not able to get my ideas through. On the contrary, they've been very understanding, very supportive. I've heard many, not only in the cabinet, say, 'Now that we have a woman on the team, we have to help her. We have to make sure that she succeeds,' " she told me.

As proof of the collegiality, she noted that when the rest of the cabinet prayed at meetings, she prayed with them in the same room.

"There's no religious basis for separation of men and women in prayer or inequality in any other aspect of life," she added. "I'm sure that negative attitudes still exist. But it doesn't come out that easily anymore because the general understanding is that the woman *should* be in society."

Ebtekar also pointed out that she had the legal authority to close down factories and other facilities that didn't abide by environmental regulations—even places attached to other branches of government and plants virtually all run by men.

Rules in the Islamic Republic have been riddled with contradictions from the beginning. But the women's movement, especially the rise of women through the ranks, underscored some of the absurdities.

An Iranian woman's testimony in court carried only half the weight of a man's. But she could sit as an equal among the vice presidents.

A woman couldn't leave the country without her husband's written and notarized permission. But she could close down industries—which employed hundreds of men—for polluting.

In mosques as well as in all prayer rooms in public buildings, factories, businesses and even airports, men and women were segregated to pray. But at cabinet meetings, they could do it together.

Among ordinary women, the contradictions were even more bizarre. Females can't shake hands with or touch a male to whom they're not related and women must ride in the back of buses. But they can be squashed in between men—shoulder, buttock and thigh pressing against one another—in public taxis.

Females can't date men in public. But they can sit together in darkened movie houses or theaters.

Female and male students must sit in separate sections of university classrooms. But they can walk and talk together off campus.

Women can't be used in advertising or portrayed in any form to promote products and they can't sing alone in public. But they can act on stage and screen—with men.

On gender issues, Iran was clearly still a work in progress, with the emphasis on "work."

I told Ebtekar that her appointment hardly reflected unanimous support for a woman in such a high position. In fact, the job was striking because it didn't have to be confirmed by Parliament. Twenty years after the revolution, not a single woman had held a cabinet post that had to be approved by the conservative-dominated *majlis*. Her appointment really seemed to be only symbolic progress, especially when compared with the fact the last shah had two women in his cabinet way back in the 1970s.

"It's a gradual trend," she conceded. "As a first step, President Khatami has done the best he could. He had women candidates for the ministries and he was very sincere about considering them.

"Maybe the concern was that ministerial positions need a lot of executive experience. And maybe, when weighing the capabilities and experience of male and female candidates, he decided it was too early to appoint a woman as a minister. The important point was just giving women an opportunity to be chosen. Since he was serious about providing a decision-making role in cabinet, he decided instead to choose a woman among his vice presidents.

"But it's *not,*" she vehemently interjected, "only a political gesture."

The sensitivity of appointing a woman to the cabinet was reflected in the fate of the shah's first female cabinet minister. Farrokhru Parsa, a widely respected minister of education, had been executed shortly after the revolution. The charge was leading girls into prostitution.

Almost twenty years later, Ebtekar's appointment indicated the reformist government's intent to bring women back into senior positions—and on issues other than women's affairs.

"Throughout the country, women are moving from the services to more professional work in both the private and public sectors," she told me. "Statistics show about a twenty percent increase over the past two or three years."

The medical schools where she still taught a class were an example, she explained. In 1998, about 25 percent of the faculty were women, while some 45 percent of medical students were female.

Almost as an aside, I made the mistake of wondering aloud how Ayatollah Khomeini would have felt about the changes.

"Oh no," Ebtekar stopped me, again vehemently. "Despite opposition among both politicians and religious circles, Khomeini was very serious about integrating women in social, political, educational and economic activities. He took every opportunity to make clear that he didn't want women to go back into isolation."

Like many regime women, Ebtekar credited the Imam first and foremost for helping the cause of women.

"When conservative clerics advocated putting up walls between male and female students in university classrooms, Khomeini insisted the sexes could study together," she said.

"He wanted women not to comply necessarily with Western standards, but he said that there was no obstacle for women's advancement in Islam. His strategy opened the way for religious families to send their girls to school in rural areas, in tribal areas. And today, a generation later, there's an emerging elite of expert Iranian women who've had a university education," she added.

What Ebtekar didn't say was that the Imam also had a long record of promoting gender apartheid. During the monarchy, he personally launched a nationwide protest when the shah enfranchised women as part of the White Revolution in 1963. Khomeini condemned giving women the vote as promoting immorality and lewdness.

"We are against this prostitution. We object to such wrongdoings. . . . Is progress achieved by sending women to the *majlis?*" he'd said in a speech from Qom. "Sending women to these centers is nothing but corruption."[20]

After he replaced the shah, Khomeini's admonition that women not work "naked" in government ministries was instantly interpreted as an order to impose the chador.[21] He and his lieutenants then reversed many of the most important gains made by Iranian women over the previous half century.[22]

Yet Khomeini did play a role in fostering a distinctly Islamic and Iranian version of feminism. The truth is that he needed women—first to make his revolution and then to sustain it. Stuck in exile, the Imam appealed to Iranian women to rise up and march against the shah. And they did. By the hundreds of thousands, they took to the streets of Iran's major cities. The picture of city squares and major boulevards packed with traditional women in their black chadors is one of the lasting images of the revolution.

After his return, the Imam appealed for women to support an Islamic republic in a national referendum to define the new form of government.[23] Again, they did, providing a badly needed endorsement that cemented the control of the religious theocrats over the secular technocrats who'd run the transition. And during the traumatic eight year war, he called on them to urge husbands and sons to volunteer to fight Iraq, to make do with tightly rationed food and fuel and even to leave home to work.[24]

In the process, tens of thousands, perhaps even hundreds of thousands of women who'd never before participated began to be empowered. Ayatollah Khomeini's savvy sense of realpolitik also resulted in pragmatic steps. He recognized that the female franchise couldn't be rescinded. He also declared that children of troops killed in the war should remain in the custody of their mothers—rather than being put in the charge of the nearest male relative, as Islamic law decrees.

Because of actions during the final decade of his life, the ayatollah is now portrayed in Iran as a proponent of women's rights. The official line is reflected in a slim volume entitled *Pithy Aphorisms: Wise Sayings and Counsels,* a collection of the Imam's pronouncements. I picked up a paperback copy at the mosque next to the ayatollah's Tehran residence after his death. It was published, the introduction explained, to provide a

"fresh review" of his thoughts and to "ease the longing pains of separation . . . for those who follow in his path."

A special section on women did indeed make the ayatollah out to be a
leading advocate of their rights.

He praised their part in ending the monarchy. "Iranian women have a
larger part than men in this movement and this revolution," he said. "Our
men are indebted to the bravery of you lionhearted women."

He also acknowledged an evolution in the role of women generally. "I
observe a wondrous change in the community of women, far beyond that
of men," he said. "In our age, women have proved that in a fight they
march by the side of men or ahead of them."

And he implied gender equality. "In an Islamic order, women enjoy
the same rights as men—rights to education, work, ownership, to vote in
elections and to be voted in," he said. "Women are free, just like men, to
decide their own destinies and activities."

The evolution of the Imam's views on women was reflected within his
own family. The Imam married his wife Batoul, the daughter of an ayatollah, when she was only thirteen; he was nearly thirty. During nearly
sixty years of marriage, Batoul was not seen in public or photographed.
She didn't even fly with the ayatollah from Paris on his triumphant return
to Iran in 1979. Hers was a cloistered life of running the house, preparing
his simple vegetarian meals and raising four children. In keeping with
Islamic tradition, she didn't attend his burial.

But the Imam's daughter, Zahra Mustafavi, went to university and
became an activist, often speaking on women's issues. She worked alongside her husband at a Tehran research institute. She was fairly accessible
to the local and foreign press. I interviewed her a couple of times in the
1980s. She was articulate, poised and engaging. Once she gave me a peek
inside the family when she described how the ayatollah dealt with fights
among his children.

"When I was ten, Ahmad was six. We'd been fist-fighting and I went
to Father and said that either I stayed or Ahmad stayed, but not both of
us," she recalled, with a chuckle.

"Then my father told me that I should be responsible, that just
because my brother was a boy didn't mean he was better or smarter or
stronger. He talked to me in such a way that I ended up feeling sorry for
my brother."

The next generation of females went even further. All of the ayatollah's granddaughters studied for advanced degrees and in the 1990s were out working. One became a doctor.

I better understood Ayatollah Khomeini's vision of feminism when I went to see the "Exhibition on the Prestige and Dignity of Women" at Tehran's concrete-modern Museum of Contemporary Art in 1993. The show was part of celebrations marking the fourteenth anniversary of the Imam's return to Iran. In films and photographs, it was a tribute to the talents of Iranian women. An Islamic fashion show was thrown in for flavor.

The pictures featured women performing in the theater and riding tractors in the field, collating data on computers and testing eyes for glaucoma, performing surgery and leading a camel caravan, doing research in a library and experiments in a chemistry lab. Among the most impressive photographs were those that showed handicapped women, one drawing a picture with her teeth, another hooking a rug with her toes, a third dialing a phone with her foot. All three worked for a living.

At the same time, the fashion show featured frocks that were the Islamic version of Victorian dress. But they had real color, not just the blacks, browns and grays of early-revolution garb. And the waistline was back—at least a rather loose drawstring version of a waistline.

"With this style, you can move better!" a sign declared.

Yet in their zeal to conceal, the costumes remained cumbersome and insensitive to weather and function—not to mention the joy of personal expression.

To me, the message was that women could be trusted with brain surgery but not to deal with advances from men. Women had the freedom to choose among the professions but not what clothes to wear. Since I was a Western woman, my experience in Iran is probably skewed, but the majority of women I've met over the years didn't like at least some of the tough restrictions or the identity imposed on women.

Yet I've also talked with dozens of regime women who honestly prefer the physical safety of Islamic dress, the legal protection of Islamic dictates and the cultural legitimacy of Islamic social customs.

Massoumeh Goolgeri called it "opportunity without exploitation."

I met Goolgeri, a plainly wholesome woman with a stainless-steel Seiko watch showing from underneath her black chador, at Zahra's Society in Qom. Like Tehran's cemetery, the society was named after the prophet Mohammad's daughter. The four-story, yellow-brick building was, like all of Qom, bland and undistinguished. But it represented a bit of history in the Muslim world. Goolgeri also claimed it symbolized the gains women had made in an Islamic theocracy.

Zahra's Society is a seminary for women who aspire to be ayatollahs.

Iran's version of feminism has spawned an interesting twist, especially in the context of debates within Christianity and Judaism about female clergy: A revolution ultimately defined in religious terms also raised the profile of women in religious professions.

"Before the revolution, women could be educated or we could be religious. You had to choose," said Goolgeri, one of the society's instructors.

"As a religious woman from a traditional family, I had no voice or role in the system. And realistically, I had no hope of bettering my life. I would have had to take off my clothes and dress as the shah's sister dressed to go to university or enter many hotels. Do you call that freedom?"

"But now we can be both educated and religious," Goolgeri added as we sat on a rug sipping tea. Many of the society's classrooms had no chairs. After depositing shoes at the doorway, students and faculty alike sat on the carpeted floor. It was a traditional setting.

Sitting with us was a young acolyte of fresh, scrubbed beauty who was enthralled by this bit of history. She was barely out of her teens and had no memory of the monarchy. The girl scribbled furiously in a large notebook as her instructor talked.

Zahra's Society was purely a product of the revolution. During the monarchy, female students in Qom had adjunct status in classes taught by men at male seminaries. After his return to Iran, Ayatollah Khomeini commanded that women should have their own religious institutions— and be encouraged to teach as well as to learn. The Imam's instructions were still visible on colorful placards hung throughout the otherwise austere seminary.

"During the revolution, women were on the front lines," one banner pronounced.

Declared another, "You brave ladies ensured the victory for Islam shoulder-to-shoulder with the men."

When I visited in 1993, Zahra's Society had a student enrollment of four hundred Iranians and seven hundred foreigners from four continents. Among them were students from unlikely places such as the United States and Russia, small nations such as Bosnia and Third World countries like India and the Philippines. Since then, similar facilities have been set up in other parts of the Islamic Republic.

"The revolution didn't impose religion on me. It opened up opportunities," said Goolgeri, who was also a mother of four. "*Hejab* doesn't limit me. It frees me to be a person judged not by beauty but by actions and thoughts. My life has been much improved, and I think my three daughters will have real opportunities."

"Now that more women are on the path to becoming an ayatollah," she added, "the revolution is introducing real equality."

MARZIEH SADIGHI WAS thirteen when she married Golam Reza Shirazian. He was nineteen.

"It was a love match," she told me almost three decades later, as her husband nodded in assent. "He was the son of family friends."

The two have been inseparable, professionally as well as personally, ever since. She did her master's degree at Auburn University while he did his doctorate. Both became engineers; both specialized in transportation.

When they returned to Iran, both worked on city planning in Mashhad. Both then became senior officials in Tehran. Together they established a transportation company. Together they cofounded the University of Ebnesina, a private university specializing in the sciences. And together they had four children.

"We've both enjoyed and benefitted from doing things together," she reflected when I visited them on the Ebnesina campus. "We've always agreed on most things."

In 1996, both decided to run for Parliament, both as conservatives. Both won.

But then they began to break the mold. It started when Sadighi got more votes than her husband. Since then she has proven to be her own woman.

"Sometimes we have real quarrels over the pros and cons of proposed laws," she told me with a chuckle in 1998.

"We don't decide how to vote together, not at all! We make up our minds and then vote—sometimes differently," she added, as an invisible hand beneath her black chador pulled it tighter under her chin, leaving a pair of oversized glasses as her one distinguishing feature.

Shirazian, who had snowy white hair and a matching beard, added quickly, "When she votes for a bill and I don't, friends often say to me, 'Can you go home tonight?' "

As conservatives, the two members of Parliament have a definitive role in determining the scope of women's progress in Iran. Islam is, first and foremost, a religion of laws. To change the way the religion has been both understood and practiced for thirteen centuries requires one of two steps: first, reform within the religion itself based on new interpretations, the kind of work done by Soroush and other intellectuals or clergy; second, crafting of laws by Muslim states that redefine, redirect or even supersede Islamic law as traditionally understood.

Laws are also the reason the theocrats have always had a hard time charting a course on women. They could undo only so much.

For six decades before the revolution, women had slowly won a succession of rights, beginning with the first public school for girls in 1918 and reaching a high point with the vote in 1963—both despite the clergy's opposition.[25] Once educated and elected, women campaigned for legal changes in centuries-old Persian and Shi'ite customs. The Family Protection Laws of 1967 and 1973 required a husband to go to court to divorce rather than simply proclaim "I divorce thee" three times, as stipulated by Muslim law. A wife could initiate divorce for the first time and her permission was required for a husband to take a second wife. Child custody was left to new family-protection courts rather than automatically granted to the father. The age of marriage was raised in 1967 from thirteen to fifteen and in 1975 to eighteen.

Inequities weren't eliminated. The monarchy's criminal code imposed no punishment on a man who murdered his wife after finding her in bed with another man. The Passport Law required women to have notarized permission from her husband to leave the country. And Islamic inheritance laws still applied: A son inherited twice the amount of a daughter. A widow without children received only one-fourth of a husband's estate; with children, she received only one-eighth.[26]

But women were on a roll. Iran's pattern of progress was so widely recognized that Tehran was selected to host a conference of the United Nations Commission on the Status of Women.

Then came the revolution. Once again, men could abandon wives by simple declaration, while wives had no judicial recourse for divorce. The penal code reverted to ancient Islamic traditions, including stoning to death for adultery. Children of divorce always went to the father; widowed mothers could lose their children to the nearest male relative.

And men could enter into "temporary" contract marriages, as allowed in Shi'ite Islam.[27]

But the theocrats never rescinded the two basic rights they historically opposed: education and the vote. Indeed, the voting age for both sexes was lowered from eighteen to fifteen. And that right alone made a comeback virtually inevitable.

The pendulum started to swing back in the late 1980s with a confluence of events: The eight-year war with Iraq ended. Hashemi Rafsanjani was elected president. Ayatollah Khomeini died. And the revolution moved into its second phase.

So a weary public began pressing for the changes that had been expected after the monarchy ended but had been put on hold by the war. Women particularly wanted their due. And new models emerged, many from clerical families. Rafsanjani's own daughters became trailblazers. One headed the Olympic Committee, published a newspaper, was elected to Parliament—and streaked her hair and wore jeans under her chador. The other headed a high-tech hospital, worked for the Foreign Ministry—and donned designer clothes under her chador.[28]

In the mid-1990s, the feminist agenda reached Parliament. Pressure mounted not only to act but to enact.

"I'm proud of what our Parliament has done for women. Some of the new laws are quite practical in dealing with specific problems," said Sadighi, as she outlined recent legislation.

"Take *mehr*, the money women have in a marriage. Before, women could be left in poverty after a divorce, because the value of their *mehr* amounted to nothing after many years. A woman who got married forty years ago might have had twelve thousand rials, a lot of money at the time. Today that'd barely pay for a taxi home from the court."

The centuries-old Persian custom of *mehr* is what a man pledges to his wife-to-be. A woman can claim it at any time during a marriage to use as she pleases or take it with her in a divorce. But Iran's currency plummeted after the revolution, dropping from seventy rials to the dollar in 1979 to eight thousand to the dollar in 1999. Along the way, thousands of women were left destitute because a once-hefty *mehr* was a pittance by the time their husbands left them.

So a mid-1990s law mandated that *mehr* be adjusted for inflation when paid out by a husband to his wife. Banks were ordered to provide constantly updated tables so women couldn't be duped.

"That protects a woman financially. It also makes it more expensive for a man to abandon his wife," Sadighi said, as her husband again nodded. "It'll make him think twice."

Other new laws covered employment of women.

"We had to face the reality that many women not only *want* to work, they *have* to work. But they also want to be there for their families. So the *majlis* passed a law that allows women to work half-time for half-salary if they have a baby or an ill family member—without the danger of losing their jobs. Other women can also work three-quarter time, leaving work a couple of hours early to take care of young children," she added.

Another new law opened the way for women to retire early—and still get a partial pension. "In the past, she had to work the whole time to get anything," Shirazian explained. "And because of a woman's many obligations, that wasn't fair."

Ultimately, the extent of freedom in the Islamic republic will be determined by the way the female population is treated. But ultimately, any Parliament in the Islamic republic is also likely to go only so far, which will never be far enough for vast numbers of Iranian women.

The limits were reflected in two particularly controversial laws proposed in 1998. One was a response, ironically, to President Clinton's affair with Monica Lewinsky. Like the media everywhere else, Iranian papers covered the unraveling drama—albeit without details of the sexual acts. But several did publish photos of Lewinsky, Genifer Flowers and Kathleen Willey, three of the president's alleged paramours. The backlash played out in angry debates on the floor of Iran's *majlis,* as well as in both houses of the United States Congress.

Embarrassed by the tabloid-like coverage, ninety members of Iran's Parliament jointly introduced new legislation that banned "any exploitative and humiliating portraits of men and women, any insult against the female sex, advertising a luxurious lifestyle and articles that provoke antagonism between the sexes."

The Khatami government opposed the measure and quietly tried to see it watered down—or defeated. But the bill passed the required three readings.

"In addition to creating problems for his society, Mr. Clinton is creating problems for our society too," Ataollah Mohajerani, the minister of culture and Islamic guidance, lamented after the bill had passed its first reading.

Under pressure, the ministry banned *Fakur,* or "Thinker," from public newsstands for continuing to publish pictures of the three women. The magazine was later fined and temporarily suspended.[29]

Sadighi didn't vote on the first of three readings of the bill. She was in Mecca on pilgrimage. But she didn't support it, she told me.

"The law says that a publisher can't use a woman's body just to sell a publication—for example, a picture of a bride with a lot of makeup when there is nothing about her or about a wedding in the publication," she explained.

"The idea is to present women based on their capabilities and knowledge, not their beauty or bodies—an idea I support," Sadighi explained.

"But we have enough regulations already to deal with this issue. If you have something to say about a female, like Queen Elizabeth, that's fine. But we don't want to exclude women completely. I wouldn't have voted for it."

In the end, however, it passed.

The other legislation segregated medical services for the separate sexes, a kind of health apartheid. Women could go only to female doctors and have tests administered by female technicians. Men could go only to male physicians.

Sadighi supported the concept, but was concerned about the specifics—and whether Iran had enough female doctors, specialists, nurses and medical technicians to provide equal care for women.

On the other hand, she added, "it'll provide important employment opportunities for women."

The second law passed too. Later, however, the Council of Guardians, which vets all legislation for compliance with Islam, rejected it—on a technicality. It said the law created new services without providing funds to pay for them.[30] So it went back to Parliament for reworking.

"These are difficult decisions, because we are mixing politics with religion and real life," Sadighi offered. "We have to be careful not to damage religion and not to damage politics.

"So we're still very much in a testing phase."

CHAPTER 5

LOVE, MARRIAGE AND SEX
IN THE ISLAMIC REPUBLIC

We don't teach rhythm because it's not sure enough.
—DR. MOHSEN NAGHAVI

SHAHID NAMJOU CLINIC IS a modest building of pristine, white-washed rooms in downtown Tehran where neighborhood families get their babies inoculated, their broken bones set and their fevers measured. *Shahid* means "martyr" and Mr. Namjou was either among the few hundred killed during the revolution or, more probably, among the tens of thousands who died during the grisly eight-year war with Iraq—no one at the clinic seemed to know which precisely. During the revolution's first decade, martyrs were a common theme, as Tehran renamed streets, squares and schools that once honored the monarchy and its allies, both local and foreign. In their early zeal to purge the past, the revolutionaries dedicated even small government facilities such as clinics to Iranians who had died for the cause.

On a spring morning, as a cool rain tapped against the windows, I met Jalal Shahpasand at Martyr Namjou's clinic. The tall, husky restaurateur with a groomed mustache was clearly in love. The object of his affection was Jila Abdolrasooly, a young woman with classically sharp Persian features whose raven hair was showing from under a bright royal-blue scarf. She sat next to him, closely.

"My family knew Jila's family, so they introduced us. Then we started seeing each other," Jalal explained as he glanced at her with a smile. Matchmaking still prevails in Iranian society, even among the small minority who end up marrying for love.

A year after they met, Jalal continued, he decided he was ready. So one night after dinner at Jila's house, after family chaperones had finally gone off to watch television, he had escorted her to a settee, then picked up her hand and whispered, "Will you marry me?"

Jila, smiling, had nodded her assent.

"We had to be traditional because some of the family expected it," Jalal recalled. "And actually it was quite romantic."

I sat with the betrothed couple in the white-tiled clinic classroom as they waited for the one thing more important in Iran than a marriage license—a certificate proving they'd passed the nation's family-planning course. No one gets married in Iran without it.

Just as the martyrdom of Namjou symbolized the revolution's early years, the birth control class at the clinic named after him reflected what happened as the Islamic republic aged: Sober practicality had begun to replace frenzied emotions as the basis of policy. The government was becoming proactive about the future, not just reactive to the past.

The no-nonsense lecture on human biology and reproduction—in a society where Islamic modesty requires women to be covered from head to toe and prohibits men, at least in theory, from wearing tight trousers—also accentuated the colorful contradictions that make Iran an interesting, even intriguing place. There were no euphemisms in this classroom.

Abol Fazl Mohajeri, a fatherly figure with a thick fringe of white hair around his head and dressed in a white lab coat, talked bluntly to the half-dozen couples seated on wooden chairs painted, some time ago, bright green.

"Welcome, welcome," he began, a big smile on his face. "Tell me, what's the goal of getting married?"

"To have an independent life," replied Jila, who at twenty-nine ranked as an older bride in Iran. Hers was a common refrain. Many Iranians, male and female and whatever their age, stay at home until they wed.

"Fulfilling the prophet Mohammad's message," offered a teenage girl named Tahereh, who'd met the mate her parents had selected only a week earlier.

"Yes," said Mohajeri, adding what the others wouldn't say. "But it's also about having regular sex.

"And as I'm sure you know," he continued, ignoring the wave of blushing among both brides- and grooms-to-be, "we face an increasing population—and the problems that go with it. This is true all over the world, but most of all in developing countries."

In fact, Iran ranked as one of the world's worst offenders during the revolution's first decade. Clerics in the young revolutionary government had urged Iranian women to breed an Islamic generation. Millions of mothers had more than complied.

When Ayatollah Khomeini returned from exile in 1979, Iran had a population of 34 million. By 1986, a mere seven years later, the population had soared to well over 50 million.[1] The theocracy's decision to lower the marriage age for females from fifteen to nine, the official age of puberty, had contributed mightily. By 1986, the average Iranian woman was bearing seven children.

The logic had once been explained by a ranking cleric. "We'd just had a revolution that faced threats from both internal and external enemies," Ayatollah Nasser Makaram-Shirazi had said. "We wanted to increase the number of people who believed in the revolution in order to preserve it."[2]

By the late 1980s, however, the ruling clerics realized that the country's soaring numbers were actually more likely to undo the revolution than to save it.

"It was really a simple matter of arithmetic, not religion," a pharmacist had explained to me. "The year before the revolution, Iran's income from oil was about twenty billion dollars, which had to provide for thirty-four million people. And that was during peacetime.

"By 1986, Iran had added another twenty million people, yet income from oil was down to only sixteen billion to eighteen billion. We were also into the sixth year of a very costly war with Iraq. The government finally began to understand that there weren't enough pieces of the pie, literally, for all the people we were breeding."

The hard realities produced an economic epiphany among the clergy. In 1989, the year of Khomeini's death and the onset of the second republic, the government officially put family planning on its agenda.

The decision was a microcosm of the single most important turning point in Iran's revolution: The ruling clergy's original goal had been to create an ideologically pure state based on religious tenets. But never in thirteen centuries of Islam had the clergy ruled a state, much less coped with a complex economy. And as practical problems mounted, the government learned the hard way that to sustain the revolution, Iran itself had to survive. That meant figuring out how to keep a modern state afloat.

The bottom line: In the world's only modern theocracy, the needs and realities of the state suddenly superseded the dictates of Islam or the traditional practices of Muslims. And as ideology was tempered by reality, the birth control program came to symbolize the revolution's turn toward pragmatism. The government of God plummeted, with a thud, back to earth.

The premarital family-planning course, launched in 1994, represented a more seasoned government's attempt to slow down and eventually reverse the trend.[3]

At Martyr Namjou clinic, Mohajeri outlined the new thinking for the young couples: "As you begin your own families, you should consider the problems of economics, education and social life that come with large families," he said, launching into a lesson on the limitations of Iran's budget, the environment and a woman's time.

"So what," he continued without skipping a beat, "do you know about contraception?" Since the females had done most of the talking so far, he gestured this time to the men.

"Women have pills, men can use . . . things," Jalal replied, quietly.

In a robust voice, Mohajeri shot back, "Ah, let's not be afraid to name these devices. That's why we're here. They're called condoms and this is how they work."

Talking as he proceeded to pull a flesh-colored condom over the model of an erect phallus, Mohajeri noted, "And women don't have one thing and men another. Couples should make the decision together, not leave it for just one partner to decide."

Assisted by maps of the male and female anatomies on the wall, he then offered demonstrations of other birth control devices—including IUDs, pills and even Norplant—for the couples to consider.

Normally a more detailed film shows some of what Mohajeri and a nurse demonstrated. But Ashura was approaching and music and other things associated with entertainment are technically taboo during Muharram, the month in which the ten days of Ashura commemorate Hussein's seventh-century suffering. Unfortunately for this particular class, the late-twentieth-century film on sexuality had lots of background music, so it was on hiatus.

Other aspects of the class mixed incongruous elements from past and present—ancient culture and women's lib, traditional marriage patterns and modern genetics.

"What do you want from God?" Mohajeri asked the couples at one point.

"Healthy children," replied Jila.

"Yes, that's right," the instructor said with hearty approval. "It's not important whether the baby's a boy or a girl, as long as it's healthy."

As in other parts of Asia and the Middle East, a male child was traditionally deemed to be more valuable, or at least more essential to a family's income and legacy. Families were often not considered complete without at least one. Ironically, a government widely perceived by the outside world to be repressive toward women actively preached their equality—in family-planning classes anyway.

The same message is plastered on billboards along Tehran's boulevards and back streets: "Daughters or sons, two children are enough."

During a break, Jalal told me that he considered the class "quite good. It's better than I thought. I actually learned a lot," he added, implying that at thirty-nine he was more savvy than the average Iranian groom.

The reaction of the young couple whose marriage had been arranged may be more relevant to Iran's future. Tahereh Seyedi, a pudgy teenager whose round face was tightly enveloped in a black chador, came to the class with Javad Goudarzi, a twenty-eight-year-old fiberglass worker with a bushy mustache. Because this was only the couple's second encounter, Tahereh's father and Javad's sister had come with them. The two young females, who hadn't met before, sat in a row directly behind the men.

The younger couple's marriage had been arranged when a mutual friend introduced their parents. After the parents had agreed to a potential match, Javad was allowed to call on Tahereh and chat—once. A week later, Tahereh had received a marriage proposal from Javad relayed from his parents to her aunt to her. Her acceptance went back along the same route. The next time they met was to come to the clinic, with chaperones.

I asked the entourage what they thought of the class.

"When I got married there was no course like this and as a result I have six kids," replied Tahereh's father Daoud, a forty-four-year-old gro-cer. Between the two of them, he noted, Tahereh and Javad had a dozen siblings.

Might he have used birth control if he'd known about it? I asked.

"Oh, a hundred percent sure I would've used it. Two kids are enough," he said. Then he excused himself to go talk to the doctor.

I asked the young couple how many children they wanted.

"No more than two," Tahereh said firmly, taking the lead.

And would they use birth control?

"Oh yes," she said, as Javad looked on. "But I don't think there are any good ones for women without side effects. A woman shouldn't take the pill for too long and the IUD is not a hundred percent sure."

The implications for men were obvious, and a rather intense and can-did discussion then ensued between Tahereh and Javad that gradually attracted others. The nurse finally intervened to sort through the myths and facts of family-planning techniques. The debate was still going on when I eventually had to leave.

Part of the problem was that birth control in an Islamic society has its own cultural requirements—and limitations—as I later learned at Iran's Ministry of Health.

"Some forms of contraception, such as Norplant, still allow bleeding, and Muslim women can't pray when they're bleeding. So some people don't like it," explained Safieh Shahriari, an engaging gynecologist in her thirties who served as Iran's senior expert on family planning.

"Well, actually," she corrected herself, "if the bleeding's heavy, they shouldn't pray. But if it's light, they should bathe and then they can pray. But it's often difficult for religious people to go to the baths every day before prayer."

Even at the end of the twentieth century, the idea of birth control was clearly a huge leap for traditional families and the devoutly religious. Overcoming that kind of gap between tradition and technology was one reason that Iran's first family-planning program, introduced in the early 1970s by the monarchy, had had limited impact.[4]

The Islamic republic had been more successful in reaching a wider audience because it'd won approval from the clergy, many of whom had called just a few years earlier for the birth of an Islamic generation. Tehran was rife was stories of mullahs delving into the sayings and actions of the prophet Mohammad to determine his views on the subject of family size thirteen centuries earlier—when world population stood at less than 300 million.[5]

The policy reversal hadn't been easy. The cabinet's first vote on birth control, in 1988, passed by a lone vote. Debate had been so intense that the prime minister had balked at publicly announcing the decision.[6]

Winning a religious seal of approval began with a hastily arranged fatwa from a prominent cleric. Over the years, I've often asked which ayatollah had been brave enough to issue the first fatwa on family planning and just what exactly it had said. Although the edict was widely cited, no one I met seemed to remember the source or have a copy. The consensus was that it called family planning a good thing and appealed to Iranian families to limit their offspring. But the vague fact that one existed somewhere out there seemed to be enough.

Later, to deal with specific techniques, Ayatollah Khamenei, Iran's Supreme Leader, issued "religious advice" in the form of answers to questions, a common way of obtaining rulings on sensitive matters. The Ministry of Health eagerly provided me with a photocopy in English. It read:

> 1. Is contraceptive use by women allowed to prevent pregnancy or not?
>   *In the name of God, with a husband's permission it is allowed.*
> 2. On condition that the necessary authority is obtained, what will be your advice for the following:
>   Oral contraceptives and other related drugs?
>   *In the name of God, it is allowed.*
>   Intra-uterine device?
>   *In the name of God, if there was no forbidden touch and look, it is allowed.*
>   Female sterilization?
>   *In the name of God, if it is performed wisely and consciously and there was no forbidden touch or look, it is allowed.*
>   Hysterectomy?
>   *In the name of God, with a husband's permission, it is allowed.*

After the Supreme Leader issued his judgments, the clergy generally seemed to sign on to family planning in fairly short order. All forms of birth control, most of which were difficult to get during the revolution's early years, began to be issued free. Questions weren't even asked about a recipient's marital status.

The mullahs also took an active role in relaying the message. During Iran's annual Population Week, pegged to the United Nations Population Day in July, mosques and centers of religious study all over Iran began focusing on the importance of small families and the steps needed to keep them that way.

"We ask religious leaders to tell people when they're praying about the effectiveness of population control in dealing with social and economic development," Dr. Shahriari told me.

"Since the program started," she added pointedly, "other Islamic countries have often been surprised at how the religious leaders actually support us."

I MET ABBAS FARSI, a diminutive truck driver with a rail-thin mustache and the first strands of silver in his hair, underneath the most famous water tower in Tehran. It was also the most unusual advertising space. In giant white letters painted on blue, the tower promoted the No-Scalpel Vasectomy Clinic located right beneath it.

Farsi had come to the clinic in 1998 because he and his wife had just had their second child.

"That's enough," he told me firmly. "We want to give the two we have a good education. And frankly, we can't afford any more."

Farsi's decision to have the procedure—and his willingness to talk about it—reflected the public's acceptance of family planning in less than a decade. Reversing course had been, in the end, fairly easy.

"My wife's been taking the pill for almost two years and we were worried about side effects," he explained. "So I talked to several people who've been through this and they were positive. The fact that there's now a way to reverse it made the decision easy."

Farsi hoped to have the ten-minute procedure, plus the thirty-minute session of personal counseling that included a video demonstrating the whole process, before heading to work. Like other forms of birth control, it was free. By 1998, the program had become quite popular in Iran.

When the neighborhood clinic first offered vasectomies in 1993, a green line was painted from the front door to the vasectomy counseling area in the back so embarrassed men wouldn't have to ask directions. But Iranians no longer seemed self-conscious about the subject. Without the slightest hesitation, every man I stopped was willing to answer questions, sometimes of a fairly personal nature, or have his picture taken under the No-Scalpel Vasectomy Clinic sign. One even asked for a copy.

Among them was Mohsen Rezaie, a lightly bearded twenty-nine-year-old bus company employee and father of two. "Vasectomy is much better than withdrawal," he told me candidly after finishing the standard two-month checkup.

Had he any fears before the procedure or any reservations afterward? I asked.

"Sure, I'd heard rumors about the possible effect," he said. "But there were no problems. I think it's improved rather than hurt relations with my wife." Withdrawal had been the couple's only precaution before the vasectomy.

"We both feel much better about sex, because we're not afraid of another pregnancy. I've recommended it to my friends," he volunteered.

Were any considering it?

"Two have already had it," he replied with a smile.

Word of mouth has been critical to the campaign, for credibility as well as hard information. At least 40 percent of all vasectomies in Iran have been referrals from family or friends who had the procedure, according to Fereidoun Forouhary, the clinic's ebullient senior surgeon.

As proof, he pulled out a photo album of well-known patients who'd brought in referrals. One picture showed an elegantly robed cleric who, Dr. Forouhary noted proudly, had escorted a couple of friends or colleagues to the clinic almost every week since he'd had the procedure.

The clergy had specifically endorsed vasectomies, just as they had endorsed birth control for women. The Ministry of Health had already given me a copy of Ayatollah Khamenei's "religious advice" on male sterilization, but Dr. Forouhary insisted that I look at the copy he kept under the glass on his desk.

"When wisdom dictates that you do not need more children," Iran's Supreme Leader had proclaimed, "a vasectomy is permissible."

Unlike his religious advice about female sterilization, however, Khamenei's guidance this time did not suggest that permission from the wife was either necessary or advisable. But winning over Iranian men had still taken more than a fatwa.

"In the beginning we had many problems. This is a religious country, and when people don't know about new things they have a hard time accepting them," Dr. Forouhary conceded. "A couple of things made a difference.

"We started with the standard outpatient surgery, but response was slow. So after about two hundred and forty cases, we had a Chinese doctor come train us in the no-scalpel technique using a laser. After that the numbers skyrocketed."

Between 1993 and 1998, the south Tehran clinic alone performed 14,790 vasectomies. By 1998, it was averaging about 350 a month. Government clinics nationwide performed more than 280,000 vasectomies over the same period, a figure that did not include private clinics.

In contrast, he said, Pakistan had performed only 6,000 vasectomies from 1992 to 1998 in a population more than twice as large.

Counseling also made a big difference in changing attitudes, the cheery, white-haired surgeon continued. The clinic staff tried hard to avoid pushing the procedure, to avoid the kind of backlash against coercive tactics experienced in India.

"If a man has just one child, for example, we go through the other options in the event he might decide later that he wants another," Forouhary explained.

Speaking candidly, he added, "We also counsel men on the number-one concern, which is performance. We explain that the testicle has no relation to sexual emotions, which come from the brain. When you look at a sexual thing or hear about sexual matters, that's when you have an erection. So what a vasectomy does will have no bearing on sexual performance."

With a little chuckle, Forouhary noted that another step improving public response had been advertising on the water tower.

"Almost immediately, the numbers doubled," he said.

Iranians love their statistics. And they collect them on an astonishing array of subjects, including several aspects of vasectomies.

"The motives for a vasectomy fall into four categories," Dr. Forouhary said, pulling out a stack of recent charts. "Forty-three percent say they have enough children, one in four do it for economic reasons, about a third say it's a combination of the first two and eight percent do it for fear of genetic disease."

He also had graphs on the ages of the men, the ages of their wives, the number of children already in the family, the number of unwanted pregnancies, family income levels and jobs, reasons they selected sterilization, source of information on the procedure, the average time span between a man's vasectomy and his wife's menopause (to indicate how many births might have taken place) and the type of birth control used before the procedure. One out of three couples had previously depended on withdrawal.

The impact of Iran's family-planning program may be partly due to imaginative, even unique touches that revealed as much about the Islamic Republic as about its success in population control.

"We decided it would help couples to give each man the two tiny pieces of waste we cut out," Dr. Forouhary told me.

"Then we ask him to show the pieces to his wife, who'll be very happy and love him even more because he's done this for her health. It's important psychologically," he said.

Gesturing enthusiastically, he added, "It liberates sex life."

Waste? I asked, a little unclear. The energetic doctor then explained the entire procedure in an anatomical detail that I didn't fully need to understand the point. In simplified form, the "waste" is the little pieces cut after being pulled through a tiny puncture.

Discussions about sex had clearly come off the list of taboos in the Islamic republic—despite the fact men and women who weren't related still couldn't touch each other, not even to shake hands, to avoid inappropriate contact or arousal. And the subject wasn't limited to premarital classes or vasectomy clinics. By 1998, family-planning programs had reached virtually every sector of society.

"We now have health rooms in every factory where we train workers in population and distribute contraceptives. They're all free," said Dr. Shahriari, the gynecologist from the Ministry of Health. A lot of attention went into factories, because workers had the lowest participation in family planning—only about one in ten was using birth control techniques by 1998.

During Population Week, schoolchildren worked on population projects developed jointly by the Ministries of Education and Health. Besides an intense advertising campaign, Iran also offered incentives for media coverage in the form of quasi-holidays. The government provided the largely Tehran-based press free trips to Isfahan and Shiraz, the historic centers of Iranian art and architecture and poetry, to cover family-planning activities.

"It's a little encouragement," said Dr. Shahriari, with a slightly conspiratorial smile.

The program was also no longer limited to Iran's major cities. To reach remote mountain villages, rural tribal areas and nomads, the Islamic republic had assembled mobile teams. They'd started in the early 1990s as small groups of health workers consulting on contraceptives. But by 1998, Iran had eighty large teams, each made up of thirty specialists, including anesthesiologists, nurses, lab technicians and surgeons capable of performing vasectomies or tubal ligations.

"Some go by helicopter. Many go by four-wheel drive. And others,"

Dr. Shahriari added, "still have to go by donkey. But we can get almost everywhere now."

IN THE ISLAMIC WORLD, *badr* is a word with a lot of historic symbolism. It literally means "full moon" in Arabic. But it was also the name given to the prophet Mohammad's sword and to his first military victory in A.D. 623, when he set out to spread the glories of the new faith across the Arabian Peninsula. Islamic troops then swept west across north Africa and into southern Spain, and east into Persia, central and south Asia and finally China. The word carries so much symbolism that when modern-day Arabs launched the 1973 Mideast War, the campaign's code name was Badr.

Iran's success with family planning was due in large part to a pilot project run out of the Badr Clinic in south Tehran. The corps of faithful this time, however, was female. And the goal of this campaign was to win converts to the glories of family planning. Of all Iran's family-planning programs, this one may well have had the most far-reaching impact—and not only on limiting family size. It also had a profound impact on the role of women.

I visited the Badr Clinic in 1992, when the project was still in an embryonic stage. Mohsen Naghavi, a tall, slender physician with a reddish tint to his mustache and yellow worry beads in his hand, explained the idea.

"The head of the World Health Organization in Geneva said in one of his speeches that no country can solve the population problem without the help of the majority of the people. We based our programs on that philosophy," he said.

As in the early days of Islam, he told me, winning the first converts had been the hardest part.

"The staff at the clinic would look at women waiting in line to consult with nurses or doctors to see who might do. We'd look at who was talking, who seemed intelligent, who might be helping others. Then the staff studied their records to see who might have grown-up children and, so, more time," Dr. Naghavi said. "When we found the right combinations, we'd invite them to be volunteers."

In the first year, after talking to thousands, the staff found three hundred women who agreed to go to the Badr Clinic weekly for classes on family health care. After the training, the volunteers were dispatched to go door-to-door in their communities to proclaim the new faith. Their tactics varied, depending on the audience.

"If neighbors were starting a new life, a volunteer would tell them about nutrition, cancer screening and general family care. For a family with four children, she'd tell them about the benefits of population control and various contraceptives," the doctor said.

Among poor families, a volunteer might talk about food availability—and how importing basic necessities would mean higher costs or reliance on foreign powers.

Among devout families, a volunteer could emphasize the benefits to the faith. "She might point out that it's better to have one healthy, educated Muslim than it is to have a hundred uneducated, unhealthy Muslims," Dr. Naghavi explained as his hand flipped rhythmically through the worry beads.

Among hard-line revolutionaries or heavily politicized families, a volunteer might talk about defending the Islamic republic.

"She might explain that Iran is in a zone that is geostrategic and we have to pay a lot of money to keep a large military. We need our money for security, not babies," he added.

"This shows how much we've changed. In the revolution's early days, the government told women to have babies for defense. Now we understand that defense is based on technology, not people."

In promoting family planning, Iran excluded only one form of contraception. "We teach all the major methods except for rhythm," said Dr. Naghavi. "We don't teach rhythm because it's not sure enough."

With two female doctors I then visited a class of volunteers who'd come to Badr for a weekly update and to compare notes. Most were at least in their thirties. Some wore the black chadors of the most devout. But several also had on headscarves and baggy *roopoosh* coats. They were all willing to talk quite freely about their work: The initial hurdles in promoting a sensitive subject. The problems of persuading men to limit offspring. Their own early reluctance to use contraceptives. The impact of birth control on overall family health. And not least of all, how the program affected them. For many, it had transformed their lives.

"This offers us a chance to participate in society. It gets us out of our houses and helps us improve our personalities. We're now deciding things for ourselves," said Sakineh Nouri, a middle-aged volunteer in a dark *roopoosh*.

A woman named Soghra who was reluctant to give me her last name added, "The more children a mother gives birth to, the less energy and time she has for other things, including herself. And women have a right to better themselves too."

The most telling story, however, came from a quiet woman named Robabeh Asad, who was about to turn fifty. She had waited until several others had finished.

"I've learned that we have choices. I had to marry at the age of nine. But I'll never let that happen to my daughter. I'm telling her to become a person first. She's going to finish high school. To make sure," she said, pointing to a teenager in the back of the room, "she now comes to this class too."

Afterward, I expressed surprise that family planning was actually feasible in the most religious areas of poor south Tehran.

"The poorer they are, the more they want to change their lives and, so, the more spirit they have," Dr. Naghavi replied.

With a fair amount of skepticism, I then pressed him on how much change the theocracy could realistically expect. He'd just told me that Iran's population had reached 58 million in 1992.

The beads still flipping, he became reflective. "It took fifteen years in the United States to convince people not to eat oily foods and fats and you're still working on it," he said. "How do you expect us to solve this problem in a short time?"

I remembered those words when I went back to look at Iran's campaign in 1998. By then, the program no longer had to blindly recruit volunteers from among strangers in waiting rooms. More and more women converts had signed on. After their own training, many volunteers had then trained their own neighbors and friends.

"Across the country, we now have about thirty-five thousand volunteers," Dr. Shahriari told me when I stopped at the Ministry of Health.

Numbers told the story. Nationwide, the number of children born to the average woman had dropped from 7 in 1986, the peak year, to 2.7 children in 1998. The figures represented such a staggering turnaround that skeptical foreign demographers were helping Iran expand the database and sampling techniques to verify the trend. Nonetheless, Iran's campaign won worldwide praise. Population groups cited it as a model for both the Third World and the Islamic bloc.

"We're suggesting that Muslim countries send people to observe the program in Iran," Nafis Saik, chief of the U.N. Population Fund, said in 1995. "It's soundly planned and it responds to people's needs."[7]

Despite political tensions between the U.S. and Iranian capitals, Population Action International in the United States also bestowed its highest commendation on Iran's program in the mid-1990s. And in 1999, the United Nations gave its highest population award, presented by Secretary-General Kofi Annan at a ceremony in New York, to the health minister who had designed Iran's innovative program.

The program still had serious glitches. Despite pervasive family-planning options, one in three pregnancies was still unwanted by one or both partners, a government survey in the late 1990s showed. And among unwanted pregnancies, 35 percent of the couples used oral contraceptives, indicating they were misused or not fully understood.

The initial success also didn't eliminate the long-term dangers. Even if the government meets its long-term objectives, Iran's population is still projected to reach 90 million in less than twenty-five years.

ON A BRISK AUTUMN EVENING in 1998, I attended the marriage of Mariam Salamian to Amir Farjad. Actually, I just went to the lavish reception. Most weddings in Iran are private affairs. The only people at the ceremony, usually at the bride's home, are those who are *mahram,* which means so close in the immediate family that they couldn't marry either the bride or the groom. Because they are *mahram,* males and females—siblings, parents and grandparents—can all be in the same room.*

Afterward, the receptions are often larger celebrations bringing together the wider family and friends who are not *mahram.* That means the sexes, including the bride and groom, must be in different rooms. Or, as at this wedding, they were in different ballrooms on separate floors of the Homa Hotel, the former Sheraton, renamed after the revolution for the national bird.

In appearance, the newlyweds could have been at any Western wedding. Unlike the people in neighboring Central Asian republics, where Muslim couples often still don traditional ethnic clothes, most Iranians wear Western dress—a holdover from changes during the Pahlavi era.

Mariam, a raven-haired beauty with high cheekbones and wispy bangs, was dressed in a sleeveless white designer gown with a beaded bodice and a full skirt. A tiara tucked into her elaborately upswept hair

*Males and females who are *mahram* are also the only ones who can touch each other in public, whether shaking hands or embracing.

held the veil. Amir, in a smart tux, looked a little like Fabian, the teen heartthrob of the 1960s. His hair was in a pompadour that threatened to fall onto his forehead.

"The bride and groom have much in common," the groom's father, Mehdi Farjad, told me as he waited for the first of five hundred guests to arrive. Mariam was twenty-two, Amir twenty-four, he said. They both had professional ambitions. She was planning to go to university to study psychology. He had just graduated in computer sciences. They came from the same economic class and the same part of Tehran. Both of their parents were *bazaaris,* or merchants.

They were also cousins.

"My sister is her grandmother," said Farjad of his new daughter-in-law. That made the couple close second cousins—very close: only one generation removed. The groom's grandfather, a cleric who was also the bride's great-grandfather, officiated at the ceremony.

The marriage had been arranged a year earlier between the families. To varying degrees, Islamic strictures and Persian traditions still prevail in most households on the eve of the twenty-first century.

"They've been together a lot since then—always at her mother's house, of course," Farjad assured me. "They know each other so well now and they are not just satisfied with each other, they love each other too." When they arrived in a wreath-bedecked car, the cooing couple did indeed seem enamored of each other.

But I asked Farjad if he wasn't concerned about the potential for genetic problems in the couple's offspring or the longer-term dangers of inbreeding.

"Oh no," he said confidently, shaking a full head of white hair. "They've been genetically tested. It's a government regulation. And they have a certificate to prove that they're okay."

Marrying within the extended family is a long-accepted practice in Iran, in the wider Islamic bloc and in other parts of the developing world where tribes, clans and ethnic groups are still important units of society. Historically, it was a way of knowing the background of a spouse and ensuring an ongoing role in the family. It discouraged separation or divorce. It also helps keep resources or financial assets within the family.

The practice may be even more important in Iran since the revolution. No statistics are available, but the Islamic republic's stringent limits on social life, particularly during its first decade, almost surely reinforced the practice of looking within the extended family for a spouse. Males and females have few other ways of meeting each other, at least legally. On the revolution's twentieth anniversary, love was certainly the cause of marriage for only a distinct minority.

But with the kind of pragmatism that produced the birth control program, Iran has gone a giant step further in dealing with the practice—and well beyond the premarital blood tests for sexually transmitted diseases required before the revolution.

In 1994, Iran introduced a nationwide program of education, screening, counseling and genetic medical tests for couples who marry within families. It's unprecedented in the developing world. Although other states officially discourage intrafamily marriages, little is done to prevent it or the potential medical consequences, particularly in the Arab world.

I saw a small part of the program at martyr Namjou's clinic, where discussion of intrafamily marriage was an integral part of the family-planning class. The instructor bluntly addressed the subject of having the right partner—and the right distance on the family tree.

"Marrying a cousin can be very dangerous because of genetic problems. It can lead to serious and incurable diseases in the children," he warned, going into detail about the possibilities that clearly made some couples squeamish.

"But if a couple insists on getting married," he told them, "they must go to a specialist for lab tests before they have children. And we're here to help with that."

The process begins when Iranian couples go for prenuptial blood work. They're questioned at the clinic and later in the family-planning class about any family ties to the intended spouse. If the prospective bride and groom are relatives, they're interviewed on the history of disabilities in the family and other intrafamily marriages. High-risk couples are sent on to genetic specialists for medical tests.

"We have several examinations to give them to make sure there aren't any problems," Dr. Shahriari, the gynecologist at the family health department, told me later. "We feel this is a *very* important issue."

Marriage in Iran includes other unusual practices. The most controversial is the uniquely Shi'ite custom of temporary marriage, or *siqeh.* The idea was originally an offshoot of polygamy introduced to deal with both sex and economic need. Sunni Muslims have always rejected the practice and it was rare under the Pahlavi dynasty. But the theocracy revived it.

At a Friday Prayers sermon in 1990, then President Hashemi Rafsanjani championed *siqeh*. "We imagine it's good if we suppress ourselves, endure frustrations and be patient in our sexual desires. But this is incorrect. It's wrong," he told thousands at Tehran University and millions more listening on radio.

"God has created certain needs in human beings, and he does not want them left unanswered. . . . Short-term marriage has been sanctioned to guarantee the health of the family and permanent marriage. It's there to satisfy temporary needs that exist in all societies."[8]

Siqeh represents one of the greatest contradictions in the Islamic Republic. The government mandates seventy-four lashes for a woman not properly covered and stoning to death as punishment for adultery by either sex. But it allows a man and woman to engage in a temporary sexual relationship for anywhere from an hour to several decades.

A hairdresser once lectured me angrily on the subject. "It's nothing more than legalized prostitution," she raged. "It's for sex-crazed men or old women in their forties and fifties who need a man." Middle- and upper-class Iranian women often derisively referred to it as the "law of desire."

Yet some Iranians viewed it as both pragmatic and more honest in dealing with basic human sexuality than Western promiscuity.

Among them was Jamileh Kadivar, one of the youngest senior advisers to President Khatami, who later went on to win election to Tehran's city council.

"Temporary marriage in our religion generally has provided a solution to problems that exist in many societies. In the West, when boys and girls have sexual relations, there are no rules. But in Islam, they follow special laws," she told me when I called on her at the Presidential Advisers Building, a black-glass high-rise near Africa Square where her ninth-floor office overlooked the sprawling capital.

The practice does have pragmatic components, its supporters claim. It's one means of providing economic security for women, notably the poor or the thousands of widows from the 1980–88 war with Iraq that produced some million dead or wounded. It also offers an alternative to young people who don't have the economic means for a permanent relationship.

But *siqeh* is inherently lopsided.

"The limitations are mostly for the woman," Kadivar conceded.

In a temporary marriage, the man may or may not already be married. Indeed, a man can have an unlimited number of temporary wives, plus up to four permanent wives. But a woman in a permanent marriage can't take a temporary husband. And after the temporary marriage is over, a woman can take a second temporary husband only after three menstrual cycles to show she isn't pregnant.

And there are other inequities: A man can break the temporary marriage contract, but a woman can't. The marriage is automatically annulled on the expiration date. If the husband should die before the expiration date, the wife does not inherit, although a child from the union does.

The practice also features some bizarre twists: Virgins must get written permission from their fathers to engage in temporary marriage, although nonvirgins needn't bother. The marriage is also supposed to be formally registered, like a permanent marriage, even though many couples simply take an oral vow.

I asked Kadivar if she didn't think this was all rather unfair.

"We believe in the equality of men and women, but not in their similarity. And frankly, the problem is that men are usually weaker than women in sexual matters," she said. "Don't you accept that?"

Did she mean that women are stronger than men? I asked.

A smile crossed her face. "Of course," she said.

What circumstances justified the need or desire for a temporary marriage? I asked.

"This is a practice not just about a sexual relationship," she said. "If a couple wants to get to know each other in a way that will lead to a permanent marriage in the future, then they can have such a temporary marriage.

"Or if a man is going on a trip and he can't take his family with him, perhaps he'll have a problem. But when he has permission to have a temporary marriage, then he can avoid the problem. Our religion is based on making society healthy. So this arrangement is for the benefit of society too."

But would she tolerate a temporary marriage by her husband? I asked.

Kadivar was married to Ataollah Mohajerani, the Minister of Culture and Islamic Guidance, and I knew their marriage had been a love match. They'd known each other since he had been her religious studies professor. After he was elected to Parliament, he had called her parents and asked for her hand—an offer she had fully anticipated.

"Some people have a sixth sense," Kadivar had once told me. "I had a seventh sense about this."

They were wed in 1983 and had since had three children. But she'd also told me that as a cabinet minister he was traveling the country a lot—without the family.

"Oh no, I would never let him have a temporary wife," she said, laughing.

Although she accepted *siqeh* in principle, Kadivar didn't accept it in her own life. It was a common reaction when I broached the subject with both men and women.

"The majority of people in Iran don't engage in this practice," she said. "Even most men aren't interested."

Indeed, perhaps the most profound impact of Iran's diverse programs on love, marriage and sex may well have been in slowly but surely redefining acceptable social behavior—often in defiance of long-standing customs.

Traditional practices had become open targets for the press, as I heard when I visited *Zan,* the first women's daily newspaper in Iran, shortly after it began publication in 1998. *Zan,* appropriately, means "woman." An engaging young political reporter named Farimah Sharifi Rad, who was dressed in a baggy beige *roopoosh* and a big black scarf, showed me around *Zan*'s offices in a large former home in north Tehran.

What, I asked Rad, were the hottest issues of the moment for her paper?

"One of them is a new law being debated in Parliament now about the age of marriage," she replied.

"The marriage age now for girls is nine and for boys it's fifteen, which are the ages of puberty under Islamic law. Article 1041 in the civil law code says that no one is allowed to urge people under this age to get married—unless they have permission of both fathers. The debate is about this condition. Most people want it removed," she said.

I told her that didn't seem like much progress to me.

"But in small villages, towns and even some places in Tehran, girls suffer from this law because their fathers actually give this permission," she said.

Why on earth would any father marry off a daughter younger than nine years old? I asked.

"Some fathers think that marriage is so important for girls that if it happens sooner she'll get a better husband, or that their daughters will adapt better to marital life at a younger age," she replied, shaking her head. Rad had married four years earlier at the age of twenty-four. It was a love match to an engineer whom she had met while training in mountain climbing.

And debate over the law had in turn sparked a wider public discussion, she said. The majority of women now wanted the age of maturity raised—and many had begun to say so.

"What is the age limit in the United States?" she asked.

I had to scramble to remember that it varies by state, but I told her I thought the youngest age in any state was sixteen.

"It's not true of all women, but the majority would probably prefer something around fifteen," she said.

What chance was there that it would change? I asked.

"For now, none," she replied. "But public attitudes are changing."

IN APPEARANCE, Mustafa Mohaqeqdamad is very much the traditional ayatollah. His full beard, a fashion requisite for the clergy, is graying. His turban is black, reflecting his status as a descendant of the prophet Mohammad. When we met, on a cool fall evening in 1998, he also wore the classic robe called an *aba* that drapes over a cleric's shoulders and somehow never seems to slip off. When clerics move down the street, their *abas* often billow and sway behind them rather elegantly. His was brown and it was draped over a floor-length gray clerical tunic.

Mohaqeqdamad, however, is anything but traditional. On issues of the family, he has been revolutionizing the revolution.

In the late 1980s, he began pushing the envelope, not to mention his reluctant colleagues, on some of the most sensitive subjects facing modern Islam—women's rights, polygamy, divorce and child custody. By the late 1990s, many of his fatwas were of greater immediate interest to ordinary Iranians than the intricacies and intrigue of Islamic politics. Some could yet end up having a wider impact, far beyond Iran.

"You know, on the subject of marriage, Islam was actually enlightened for its time," he mused when I visited him at the Academy of Sciences, where he headed the Department of Islamic Studies.

"Before Islam, the Arabs were free about marriage. A man could have a hundred wives if he really wanted. But the Koran said a man could have a maximum of only four."

Multiple marriages were first condoned in the wake of the Prophet's campaign to spread the new faith in the seventh century, he explained. The goal had been to ensure that war widows were not left indigent.

"Today we look at this issue differently. For example, the Koran has a verse that says that if a man can't treat the second, third or fourth wives with justice and exactly the same as the first wife, then a man should not marry again," he said.

"So I ask, who is the Koran addressing? Who can determine whether a man can treat wives with justice? The Koran is certainly *not* addressing the husband. And what does justice mean? Having money? Having the power of sexuality? Who can determine these things?" Mohaqeqdamad continued, his robust voice filling the academy's library.

"My answer is that only society can judge. And society's representative is the state. So I argue that the state should have courts where anyone who wants to get married for a second time must go to explain why—and whether he has the money and the time and so forth. And the court should then investigate the case. It should look at the situation of the children and how the women feel about this. All these factors must be weighed evenly," he said.

Mohaqeqdamad clearly didn't believe in polygamy. But since the practice is mentioned in the sacred texts left behind by the Prophet, no cleric can outlaw it completely. The ayatollah's goal was instead to restrict multiple marriages to situations of need, as he believed Islam originally intended. Today, he said, that might mean a poor family where the wife is a permanent invalid and unable to take care of the children and the husband can't cope alone.

But he also sought to inject a role for the government. In a modern world filled with issues unforeseen by the faith's founders, Mohaqeqdamad argued, the state should be able to intervene for the broader good of a modern Islamic society, even if it flew in the face of religious and cultural traditions.

A year before he died, Ayatollah Khomeini had taken a similar position. He'd issued a fatwa in 1988 ruling that the Islamic state was superior to Islam. If necessary, he said, even the seven pillars of Islam—including fasting, praying and the Hajj pilgrimage—could be suspended in the interest of the state.

The Imam called government "tantamount to a total vice regency from God." It was also among "the most important divine injunctions" and had "priority" over many other divine orders, he decreed.

"The ruler can close down a mosque if need be or can even demolish a mosque that is the source of harm if its harm cannot be eliminated except by demolition," the fatwa declared.[9]

But translating that generality to the most sensitive social traditions in the Islamic world was a huge leap. The formal process, Mohaqeqdamad explained, is known as *ijtihad*. It empowers the clergy to adapt Islam and its laws to new problems.

"The word is derived from *jihad,* which means "trying." *Jihad* isn't just fighting, as many think. At the beginning of Islam, when the Prophet and his followers were trying to expand Islam, they were struggling with the enemy. So gradually this word was used in the context of fighting. But that's only one definition," he said.

"The meaning can be more basic. For example, if you want to see me, you should *jihad* to see me. Determining the rules of God from the original holy text and other sources is *ijtihad.*

"And the person who does this, after at least fifteen years of study, is a *mujtihid*—another word derived from *jihad.* A *mujtihid* knows what to do about the way of God when circumstances change. And I am a *mujtihid,*" he said, beaming.

Mohaqeqdamad is both an unusual and an unusually qualified *mujtihid.* He is the grandson of Grand Ayatollah Haeri, a famous scholar who once taught Ayatollah Khomeini at Qom's legendary seminary. Mohaqeqdamad also spent twenty years studying, teaching and rising through the clerical ranks at Qom.

But his career then took an unusual twist. He went off to Catholic University of Louvain in Belgium for seven years to write a thesis on the protection of civilians during wartime under Islamic and international law. He has since traveled widely, including to the United States—where he lectured at Stanford and Temple Universities in the 1990s. His interpretations now have a wide following, not only in Iran.

Mohaqeqdamad's impact has probably been greatest on the ultimate source of male domination in Iranian families—divorce. Once again, he dared to take on one of Islam's longest and strongest traditions.

"The Koran says that divorce is in the hands of the husband only and every man can divorce at any moment he wants—without cause or motivation. But a woman can't divorce her husband. This had been the civil code of Iran—before the revolution and after," he said, as we sipped tea and ate sugar cookies.

"But based on a verse in the Koran, I have a new interpretation. If there's a difference between the husband and wife, the Koran says the family of the wife should send an arbiter and the family of the husband sends another arbiter and they search for the cause of the difference and the facts of the situation," he continued.

"So I ask again: Who is the Koran addressing? Who is witnessing this struggle? Who is 'you'? It's not the husband or wife.

"Of course," he answered himself, "the Koran is addressing society— and the representative of society is again the government. So the government should take this message from God and designate a court where a man who wants to divorce his wife must go and the court will then investigate the reasons with both the husband and the wife. So my fatwa is that no man can divorce his wife by simply saying so. Only the state can decide it."

With obvious pride, he then added, "You won't hear anything like it from anyone else, so it's my fatwa, and you can quote it."

Iranian marriages are unusually legalistic. Most are based on a contract and both sides can stipulate additional terms, although husbands traditionally have had the last word because of their right to spontaneous divorce.

But as chief of Iran's judicial review board for twelve years, Mohaqeqdamad introduced a new idea: Wives should also have the right to initiate voluntary divorce.

"I put this into law: Every woman now has the right to have this in her contract of marriage," he explained. "If marriage is a bilateral act, then divorce certainly can't be a unilateral act."

Designed to give women options not provided by Islamic tradition, the new standard marriage contract allocated half the property obtained during a marriage to the wife in the event of divorce. The contract with flowery decoration but blunt language also outlined twelve grounds on which a wife can initiate divorce—if a husband is mad, if he provides her no money, if he does something immoral in the eyes of Islam, if he can't produce a child after five years and so forth.[10]

The new thinking was soon translated into a new law. Iran's Parliament subsequently passed legislation with four groundbreaking stipulations: First, divorce to be legal can be granted only by a court. Second, when a husband seeks a divorce without the consent of his wife, she is entitled to half of his property in compensation for her work in the home and child rearing. Third, a woman assistant judge should help investigate the circumstances of the divorce petition and assist the court in making the final decision. Fourth, women in the workforce can't lose jobs for family reasons; they also must have generous options for part-time work or early retirement with pension.[11]

For Islam, the law in turn had far wider implications—with their own revolutionary impact.

Shortly after the law passed, I'd gone to witness one of the new divorces. The drab little court decorated with a faded city planner's map looked more like a classroom. Mohammad Naseh, a judge with a white beard and dressed in a worn brown herringbone suit and an army jacket, presided from an old wooden desk. Akram Pourang, the female assistant judge, garbed in a chador, sat at a second desk across from him.

Both had been judges during the monarchy. She had been stripped of her title after the revolution, then brought back as an investigator and special adviser by the new law in 1993. The son of a mullah, he had survived the change in regimes.

The first case they heard could have been from anywhere. The 1979 marriage had begun to sour within a year. Sedigheh, dressed in a chador and looking particularly miserable, felt wronged by her husband's negligence and greed. Davoud, a tall bank employee dressed in a blue sweater vest, felt betrayed when she went home to her mother.*

The first reconciliation produced a son, but this only complicated a dysfunctional marriage that was on and off for fourteen years.

What made the case interesting was that she was the one suing for divorce. He didn't want it.

"He gave me no money for food or the house. He told me to use my income as a teacher to pay for everything. I had to move home with my mother to survive!" she explained to Pourang, the female assistant judge. Judge Naseh spent much of the time answering a phone on his desk that frequently interrupted the morning proceedings.

As Sedigheh talked, Davoud became angry and stood up to protest.

"Sit down and be quiet," Pourang commanded. "Your turn is next."

They'd tried a second reconciliation because of the child, but money was still a problem. Again she went back home to mother.

"Her story isn't true," Davoud protested. "She left me and that's why I didn't pay her expenses. If she wants anything from me, then she'll have to live with me to get it."

The bickering couple sat on wooden chairs against the wall as a rotat-

---

*Both asked me to withhold their surnames.

ing stream of relatives and friends told tales of marital misery. In the end, Sedigheh got her divorce—although she had to forfeit her *mehr* and any prospect of alimony to get it.

The new law basically restored terms introduced during the monarchy in the same kind of family courts instituted during the monarchy. Yet the case of Sedigheh and Davoud symbolized why the change this time around had greater resonance. It marked a milestone in Islam.

First, the new law implicitly recognized that the modern state, not Islamic tradition, determined marital status. A divorce, to be legal and binding, had to be processed through government channels, not simply asserted according to Islamic laws, or Sharia. It also accepted that laws governing society should be adapted to the times.

Second, it decreed that women have important rights within a marriage and that a man isn't the only one to determine marital status—a big step on the long road to gender equality within Islam. Traditionally, Muslim women were under the guardianship of a man, be it father, husband, brother, uncle or son. Women were basically treated as minors. The law reinstated them as adults and, potentially, as independent citizens.

Third, it allowed a woman to be a judge, albeit in a secondary role. Women were part of the decision-making process, deemed wise enough to interpret the law for themselves and to shape court edicts.

As Pourang interviewed witnesses, Judge Naseh leaned across his desk. "I may have the title. But I don't make a ruling unless we agree. She's as important to me as Kissinger was to Nixon," he said. She also appeared to be doing most of the work.

Fourth and finally, it accepted that women should have special opportunities and in some cases wider parameters than men in employment.

Like their counterparts in most countries, Iranian women still have a long way to go—and in many areas probably longer. Despite new laws, enforcement is often limited or nonexistent. Tradition prevails, particularly outside the major cities.

"There's still no equality yet for women in family law or criminal law. Some of these changes are only good steps to what we had in the past, not to the future. Before the revolution, women could be judges," Mehranguiz Kar, a noted female lawyer and feminist, told me when I visited her Tehran office, which is decorated around a large scale of justice held by a blindfolded woman.

Yet by the revolution's twentieth anniversary, each of the new rights had potentially sweeping implications far beyond the divorce court.

The new thinking had also gradually begun to change even the most daunting family problem faced by Iranian women: child custody. According to Islamic tradition, a divorced mother is allowed to keep a female child until the age of seven and a boy child only until age two. After that, full custody reverts to the father. A mother has virtually no visitation rights unless they are granted by the husband.

I heard a lot about the child-custody law during a visit in the spring of 1998, because of the death of eight-year-old Arian Golshani. Tehran was abuzz with outrage, which in itself was an interesting development, since in earlier years similar cases might not even have gained public attention, much less triggered public demonstrations.

After her seventh birthday, Arian had gone to her father, despite the fact he was a drug addict with a criminal record and a documented pattern of abusing the child.[12] She was dead within eighteen months. Her death had been particularly long and tortuous. Her skull was fractured. Both arms were broken. Burn marks covered her body. And she weighed only around thirty-five pounds.

Because she was forbidden from seeing her children, Arian's mother found out about her daughter's death from an article in the newspaper.

Iranian law makes it difficult to find a man guilty of murdering his own child. Arian's father was, indeed, acquitted of the murder, although he was sentenced to two years in prison for hurting his child. But the case nevertheless made Iranian history. During the trial, the courtroom was packed with female protesters. And the local press closely covered the case—from the perspective of its injustice, an issue at the very heart of Shi'ite Islam.

More important, the case led the overwhelmingly male-dominated Parliament to act. A new law in 1998 stipulated that a child could no longer be awarded to an unfit father. It also defined the qualifications needed for custody in a way that usually disqualified men.[13]

"This is a case that bothered all Iranians," Mohaqeqdamad told me. "It showed that this is another issue that should be in the hands of a court. All family law should be decided in court, not just by tradition."

The ayatollah's work had, not surprisingly, made him a champion among women—an achievement that seemed to please him.

To air his position on polygamy, Mohaqeqdamad opted against a publication catering to his clerical peers and instead went directly to the audience most affected. "I declared it in the magazine *Zan-e Ruz,* 'Today's Woman,' " he said proudly.

As he talked, it occurred to me that his views were a product of his own family experience as well as his scholarship.

"You must love your wife a lot," I said.

"Oh yes, a lot," he said, undeterred by the intrusion into his personal life.

I asked if his marriage had been arranged.

"It's an old custom in Iran that the mothers go to a family and choose for the boys. Islamic law says that every man should see his wife and speak to her and see her body before the marriage. But against Islamic law is culture and custom and tradition. And clerical families have a custom of the groom and his bride not seeing each other," he explained.

I asked if he had been nervous on his wedding day.

"I was more than a little scared," Mohaqeqdamad said, laughing at the recollection. "I was only nineteen and my wife was fourteen."

The experience had an impact. His three daughters were all several years older than their mother had been when they married.

Had he arranged their marriages? I asked.

"Yes, but a little differently," he said, chuckling. "When the boys' mothers came to us and said they were interested in having their sons marry one of our daughters, I told them I couldn't accept before they visited each other. I was afraid my daughters would say they didn't like who we accepted. You know, this was very dangerous for me," he said, still amused.

After their marriages, all three girls had also gone on to be professionals. One was a lawyer, another was an engineer and a third was a high school teacher.

I asked Mohaqeqdamad if he envisioned further changes in the laws defining family life in Iran.

"Oh yes, we're still in the process of making Islam fully modern," he said. "Things will be very different for my children's children."

CHAPTER 6

THE ISLAMIC LANDSCAPE

TEHRAN

Iran is not blessed with one of the world's loveliest capitals.

—Lonely Planet guide

"IRAN IS NOT just Tehran," presidential adviser Jamileh Kadivar once told me. "Iran really is the beauty of Isfahan, the passion of Shiraz and the history of Persepolis."

"Iran is not just Tehran," my friend Lily Sadeghi once told me. "Iran is also about the greenery of the Caspian and the nomads of Fars and the fire temples of Yazd."

"Iran is not just Tehran," Ministry of Culture and Islamic Guidance press official Hosein Nosrat once told me. "Iran is the mountains of the north, the deserts of the south and the waters of the Persian Gulf to the west."

All of that is true. Indeed, for a country with so much rich history, Iran's capital is in many ways the least typical Iranian city. It is, by local standards, virtually new.

In medieval times, when Iran's other cities were already cosmopolitan crossroads between East and West and Iranians were major players in the world of science and the arts, Tehran was an unknown backwater. It was described in the thirteenth century as "a village of half-savages who lived in underground dwellings and earned their livelihood from highway robbery."[1] It didn't become the capital until the eve of the nineteenth century—some two and one-half millennia after the birth of Persian civilization.

And yet by the end of the twentieth century, Tehran was very much Iran. It had become the hub of commerce, culture, communications and, of course, government. It was the headquarters of one of the world's most prosperous oil industries and, during the monarchy, its sixth-largest army. It hosted world leaders, from Roosevelt, Churchill and Stalin at the first Allied summit in 1943 and President Carter in 1978 to the fifty-plus kings, sultans, emirs and presidents of the Islamic bloc in 1997.

Tehran also accounted for a fifth of Iran's 62 million people—more than 12 million, up from only some 300,000 in 1930. By the century's end, the capital was well on its way to becoming one of the new "hypercities" of the twenty-first century, teeming with people it can't hold. Even with the Islamic republic's impressive family-planning program, the growth rate could still make Tehran one of the world's five or six most populous cities by 2025.[2]

Visitors flying in can sense the size of the capital even before they land. Intense clusters of twinkling lights go on and on and on and on, making you wonder if the vast urban sprawl actually has limits—and if the plane really intends to land at all.

Tehran's rapid rise from obscurity also illustrates Persia's scramble to merge with modernity, from a name change to its physical appearance. With the exception of a few mosques, the Iranian capital was never either very oriental or very Islamic. It lacked the landmarks of Cairo or Istanbul, the intrigue of Beirut or Casablanca, the oldness of Damascus or Baghdad, the glory of Samarkand or Petra and, even after the Islamic revolution, the religious relevance of Mecca or Jerusalem.

Modernized Tehran has instead been characterized by drab block-functional architecture, gaudy neon lights and cars—lots and lots and lots of carbon-belching, perpetually honking, crazily driven cars.

In a practical sense, cars are even more of a problem than Tehran's human population. Traffic became an issue when soaring petrowealth in the 1970s led almost overnight to a tenfold increase in the number of cars, roughly 75 percent of which were in the capital. By the 1979 revolution, a million cars were crowded onto the capital's narrow labyrinthine streets and tree-lined boulevards. Tehran's car population had tripled, at least, again by the century's end.

"And why not drive?" a Swedish diplomat once mused enviously. "They pay only around twelve cents a gallon for petrol. It's about the cheapest price in the world."

Congestion became so bad in the mid-1990s that a major Iranian newspaper calculated that Tehranis wasted an accumulative 1.2 billion hours annually trapped in traffic jams.[3] And pollution produced by automobile exhausts hung low over the city like thick cigarette clouds, which actually made living in Tehran life-threatening. Only Delhi, Beijing and Calcutta had worse smog.[4]

Tehran's geography—it is perched at the foot of the towering Alborz Mountains with little wind to disperse the smog—didn't help. As the revolution prepared for its twentieth anniversary, pollution primarily from cars and trucks had become so thick that all schools and universities were closed down by the government for several days. Old people and anyone with respiratory or heart ailments were told to leave the capital altogether.[5]

Just how Tehranis deal with traffic—or perhaps don't deal with it—is now a defining characteristic of capital life. The Lonely Planet travel guide for Iran warned in 1992 that Tehran's traffic was "lawlessly aggressive," even "homicidal."[6] Since then, it's gotten much worse.

"Officially, we have an average of a hundred and one accidents a day," an official from the Ministry of Roads and Transport once told me. "Proportionately, that's ten times higher than the average in the world's other major cities.

"But unofficially, we probably average closer to five hundred accidents a day. Most people just don't report them."

Tehran's traffic is, simply, the world's worst. It redefines chaos. The evidence is overwhelming: Virtually no car over a few weeks old is without dents, serious scratches or unmatched paint patches. They're almost badges of honor. It's little wonder why. Tehran has unique rules of the road. Over the years, my friend Lily Sadeghi and I have catalogued them:

- To turn right, get in the far-left lane.
- Sirens mean it's time to race the approaching ambulance or fire truck.
- After missing an exit on a busy highway, back up.

- All lanes are for passing—forward or backward.
- Red lights mean go.
- Three lanes mean four cars or, during rush hour, five.
- In heavy traffic, take over a lane of oncoming traffic or, during rush hour, two lanes. In that spirit, two-way streets often become one-way—just as a one-way street is usually two-way.
- And speed is limitless.

Pleading with taxi drivers to slow down is fruitless. It can even be dangerous.

"No problem, no problem," a veteran cabbie once told me, turning around to look at me as his car sped blindly ahead. "I don't have many accidents."

Lily, who is docile and tolerant to a fault, turns into a maniac when she slips behind the wheel.

"I have to drive like them to survive," she once told me. "If I drove like you do in America, I'd never get anywhere. I'd still be in my driveway."

To get around the logjams that often require hours to move short distances, more and more Tehranis have turned to motorcycles. The problem is that a single motorbike often carries as many as are crammed into a car. It's not at all unusual to see Dad in front, Mom in a flapping chador behind and a tot or two, even an infant. And if a street is too busy to allow them to pass, motorbikes have been known to veer onto the sidewalk, sweeping past pedestrians and occasionally knocking them over.

The government has tried virtually everything to discourage driving and to regulate traffic, including banning all private cars in the city center from dawn to dusk. The move was a boon to Tehran's zippy orange taxis but a bust for workers in a city with no subway and limited bus service. Over the years, officials have repeatedly proposed increases in gasoline prices, only to find Parliament reluctant to approve such a publicly unpopular move.

Tehran's traffic and its byproducts, which have made the capital literally unlivable at times, are in many ways a microcosm of the revolution's broader political and economic challenges—and the response to them.

"Everyone hates the problem," lamented the official from the Ministry of Culture and Islamic Guidance about Tehran's gnarled traffic. "But most people hate the solutions even more."

———

TEHRAN IS NOT, however, without its beautiful sights and interesting corners. Indeed, for all its woes, the city is rich with parks, thousands of acres where Tehranis stroll, play, exercise, gossip, picnic, paddle boats, view animals, smell roses, play Ping-Pong, watch waterfalls, feed ducks, eat ethnic and even, quietly, date.

Mellat Park is one of my favorites. *Mellat* means "nation" and the stairway leading up to a man-made lake is lined with large bronze busts of the nation's greatest poets, scientists and philosophers: Ibn Sina, an eleventh-century philosopher and physician whose medical texts were taught in Europe until the seventeenth century. Hafez, Sa'di and Ferdowsi, the great medieval poets whose works are still admired today. Razi, the ninth-century scientist and inventor of medicinal alcohol.

Park life is also a barometer of the public mood in Iran. I've often gone to Mellat to sample political opinions. Changes in social mores are also usually first visible in the parks. In the late 1990s, young people flocked here on Fridays, the Muslim sabbath, to rent canopied boats, walk among the gardens of primroses, violets, chrysanthemums and marigolds or sit on benches and flirt.

Over the years I've had many interesting encounters in Mellat. Among them was one with an elderly man who'd tutored the father of General Norman Schwarzkopf, who led Operation Desert Storm against Iraq, in Persian for three years when the family lived in Iran.

"Obviously, long before the revolution," the old man noted. "He was quite a figure here. I've always wanted to communicate with his boy. Do you think you could take a letter back to him for me?"

I demurred. For several years, the government asked foreigners if they were carrying letters for others when they left the country. Luggage was thoroughly searched. Taking a letter to an American general didn't strike me as such a hot idea. The old man was understanding.

"I didn't think so," he replied. "But I had to ask. I ask everyone who's going to America, but in fifteen years I've never found a taker."

I suggested that he try the mail. I've always been surprised by the efficiency of Iran's mail, even to addressees that the government might question. I'd sent postcards to former hostages more than once and they'd all arrived in short order. But the old man looked at me skeptically.

"It's different for Iranians," he said.

Mellat was also the first public place where women engaged in open-air exercise. In 1998, I joined a class already in progress one morning just after 6:00 a.m. I heard the workout music and the women chanting along with the instructor even before I found them. Then, on the back side of a hill, I came upon some three dozen women ranging in age from their early thirties to their late fifties running in place, doing jumping jacks, kicking forward and kicking back, stretching, touching toes, all in a lively rhythmic routine—and all despite the cumbersome limits of their baggy *roopooshes* and scarves. They were also wearing cotton gloves. But they were clearly having fun.

"All this clothing is a bit of a hassle, but we've gotten used to it," Malih Latifi, the dark-haired, diminutive and fit instructor, told me after class.

"Besides, it's worth it. This is the only time we work strictly for ourselves. The rest of the time we're doing things for husbands, our children or the house. Four mornings a week we come out here and commune with nature and one another, and once a week we go into the mountains to hike for two or three hours."

I asked if the gloves were part of their Islamic attire.

"No," she said, laughing at me. "We wear them because we touch the ground and it's dirty. This is *not* Saudi Arabia. We don't cover everything!"

Latifi had started the class as a volunteer thirteen years earlier after developing an exercise routine out of books. It had quickly proven popular. The authorities had tried to stop the women on the grounds that aerobics were too sexual and suggestive. But the women had stood firm. Protégées from her classes then started their own exercise programs at other parks. Although the workouts were supposedly strictly for women, I saw a couple of men slightly shielded by bushes or trees jumping, kicking, bending, touching the ground and stretching along with Latifi's instructions.

They weren't alone. Exercise is quite popular in Iran, and throughout the park men in sweats were jogging and middle-aged couples or pairs of women were taking brisk walks as morning light broke over the capital.

"This is a busy place," my friend Lily said, as we navigated to avoid a string of joggers.

I've also spent many Fridays, the Muslim sabbath, when Tehran shuts down, wandering the hilly towpaths lined with delicate acacias and towering pines in Ferdowsi Park. I usually stop for a while at the foot of Ferdowsi's waterfalls and watch the little kids watching the elegant white swans glide across the big pond. It's quite calming.

Ferdowsi is at the northern peak of Tehran in the foothills of the

Alborz Mountains, where the air is still sweet. Like a lot of landmarks, it has been renamed. It was originally called Jamshidi Park, after Jamshid, Iran's first and probably mythological king. But in 1997, it was renamed for Iran's Homeric poet, shifting the focus from the monarchy to nationalist history.

Ferdowsi stretches for miles and miles and is the kind of place where families have reunions and even business groups meet for picnics. I once went to Ferdowsi for the annual reunion of the Islamic Association of U.S. and Canadian Graduates. Despite Iran's official animosity toward the Great Satan, thousands of Iranians have been educated in the United States since the revolution. On a warm Friday afternoon in May 1995, I joined a group of some 150 men, women and children who had turned out to play volleyball and eat hamburgers. Except for a break at noon for prayers, when men assembled in a separate area to pray toward Mecca, the picnic could have been at any American park.

"Our membership is about seventy percent academics and about thirty percent government officials," explained Mohammad Badr, a Missouri-educated business administration professor with a salt-and-pepper beard and heavy tortoise-shell glasses. Badr also served as executive director of the group of North American grads.

"Two of our members are now ministers in President Rafsanjani's cabinet—Najafi at Education is an M.I.T. grad and Kalantari at Agriculture comes from Iowa State. Of course, you could also count Nourbakhsh, who's head of the Central Bank. He's a UCal at Davis grad. And then there are two members who are deputies at the Oil Ministry and about a half-dozen other deputies spread through other ministries."

In one of the Islamic republic's early governments, so many of the revolutionary officials had been educated in California that even Iranians talked about the "Berkeley mafia" that ran the political show.

Some had brought back American spouses. At this picnic, families included wives who came from Arizona, Hawaii, California and Tennessee. A decade after the revolution, some 250 American women married to Iranians were still living in Iran—enough to have an informal American Wives Club. A couple even worked for the government editing English-language publications. By 1995, however, their numbers had dwindled significantly.

But visiting Tehran's parks is not just about being Islamically correct in public. Like everything else in Iran, the parks also reflect an evolution in the revolution.

Shatranj, Tehran's newest park, proved the point. After the revolution, the government banned chess—an ironic move, since Iranians like to claim the age-old game originated in Persia. (I also have Indian friends who claim it originated in India.) I've never found an Iranian official to authoritatively explain why it was a taboo. Some friends claim it's because the kings and queens and knights are elements of a monarchy. Others claim it's because the game sometimes involved betting.

Either way, the ban was effectively lifted when Tehran's innovative new mayor opened Shatranj in 1991. Walking around the park is like wandering through a human-size chess game. Its paths are paved with black and white stone tiles. Giant pieces are placed nearby for anyone who wants to play a human-size game. Along the paths, thirty yellow benches with permanent boards are set up for regulation play. And in the event of unseasonable weather, two castle-like halls—one for men, the other for women—each have eight tables indoors.

As a chess lover, I've had a good game or two with total strangers at Shatranj, which is Persian for "chess."

Another sign of changing times was at Nowroozabad Park, where horse racing resumed in the mid-1990s—complete with legal betting at two trailers on the edge of the track. Not only was the whole operation government-sanctioned, on the day I went to watch, President Rafsanjani's son had two horses competing and Speaker of Parliament Ali Akbar Nateq-Nouri, an accomplished equestrian, was among the three thousand in the stands.

"The history of the tamed horse in Persia dates back five thousand years and polo was started in Persia more than two thousand years ago. The horse is part of the Persian family and racing is part of our tradition," explained Morteza Faraji, the enthusiastic director of Iran's Equestrian and Equine Breeding Organization.

"And there's nothing un-Islamic about either racing or betting. The Koran mentions horses in several passages. God's oath is 'on the hoof of the horse.' The horse is a V.I.P. animal," he continued.

"Betting is also allowed in the *hadith,* Islamic traditions, for shooting, riding and even swimming. To encourage sports, betting was advised by the Prophet, first just between riders and owners and then it spread."

Although women were for years banned from the two most popular Iranian sports—soccer and wrestling, largely because of the skimpy male attire—women were allowed to watch racing. Track seating at the Nowroozabad course was segregated by gender, but at least a third of the fans watching the races of Arab steeds, Kurdish horses and Caspian ponies were female. Dozens of them were also lined up at the betting windows.

"Oh, there are lots of women who ride in Iran. We have women show jumpers in competitions and some of the most famous horse breeders are women," Faraji added. "We just don't have women jockeys yet."

DESPITE ITS OWN LACK of history, Tehran is home to some of the world's most unusual museums. Of course, it has the standard collection and the archaeological museum is particularly fine. The floor devoted to pottery, bronzes, animal sculptures and jewelry, dating back to the fifth millennium B.C., makes other great exhibits from the first century A.D. look like comparatively new junk.

But four other unconventional museums really tell the story of Tehran and the revolution—what brought it on and what happened to it afterward.

At the top of the list is the capital's foremost landmark. Azadi Tower is as synonymous with Tehran as the Opera House is with Sydney, the Eiffel Tower with Paris and the Statue of Liberty with New York. An enormous muscular structure blending modernity and Mideast architecture, the monument consists of an elevated tower rising powerfully from four legs that look almost like massive wings pushing it into the sky. Arabesque windows at the top of the tower, more than 150 feet up, offer a lofty view across the capital—at least when it is not obscured by smog.

The tower was originally called the Shahyad, or "commemoration of the shah," and it was built by the Pahlavi Dynasty to commemorate the 2,500 years of the Persian Empire. It was, appropriately, constructed of 2,500 white stone pieces of diverse sizes and shapes. And it does inspire awe.

"The shah didn't do much for us. But he did put up the only really memorable building in Tehran," a cabbie once told me as we circled the monument en route to the nearby airport.

The museum chronicling Iran's history is in the tower's basement. I first toured it in 1973, and for all the sensual grandeur of the tower, the inside was a disappointment. Four dozen or so prehistoric, pre-Islamic and prerevolutionary artifacts were only a symbolic collection. Displayed dramatically against black marble walls, the gold and enamel objects, painted pottery and miniatures were selected to mark particular milestones in Persian history. It provided an art timeline but little else. A conveyor belt then transported visitors through other rooms with hokey scenes from Iranian and world history, including one with young naked bodies profiled against a background of the sea to portray "the creation."

The white monument dominating Tehran's skyline is more significant for how it came to be than for its contents. As a record of the past, the tower symbolized the shah's folly. Indeed, the ultimate irony is that the tribute to the monarchy was completed in 1971—just as the era of kings was nearing an end. The tower also embodied both the progress and the problems that ended the era.

It reflected the progress because it was built as Tehran became a boomtown. The same petrowealth that produced the monument, after oil revenues soared in the sixties then quadrupled in the early 1970s, turned the capital into a magnet. Buses from all corners of the country ferried passengers in search of jobs, housing, education and urban frills and thrills. That first big spurt of growth made Tehran one of the fastest-growing cities in the world.*

It reflected the problems because the changing face and pace of life were unregulated. An already poorly planned capital rapidly became a sprawling city of mushrooming and chaotic growth. Thousands of villagers who came to the big city still ended up living village lifestyles.[7]

"You can't believe how fast this city changed. I went abroad to university, and when I came back I didn't recognize it. I got lost more than once," a political scientist in Tehran once told me.

"People thought coming to Tehran guaranteed a better life. But in a lot of cases it only got worse."

Mohammad Reza Shah Pahlavi responded with fancy development schemes for everything from literacy to low-cost high-rise apartment blocks. He also indulged in big-ticket purchases, ranging from plans for nuclear power plants and computerized industries to a fleet of Boeing 747 jets for Iran Air. Across the board, the oil boom spurred the greatest economic leap in Iranian history. Income soared from $200 to $1,000 per capita in real terms during the monarchy's final fifteen years.[8]

Growth throughout the 1970s, however, was widely uneven. Many of the shah's pet projects provided prestige. But several were controversial and few offered lasting solutions. The gap was visible near Shahyad Square, where large groups of village migrants waited for employers

---

*The postrevolution baby boom fueled the second growth spurt.

seeking day laborers. Along Tehran's southern fringe, warrens of squatters' huts sprang up in a city that hadn't been able to cope with the influx.

In the end, progress actually spurred discontent. Heady expectations produced by new prosperity, urbanization, education and industrialization weren't met fast enough. Then the regime hit serious economic bumps in 1977. The shah tried to put a brake on speeding inflation and an economy in serious overdrive. But his anti-inflation program instead increased unemployment. On top of deep political grievances, public anger mounted over the government's failure to convert national wealth into greater individual benefits.

"In the decade before the revolution, almost everyone benefitted from oil wealth in some way. But for many either it wasn't enough or it led to greater expectations, political as well as economic," the political scientist said.

"People began to feel they should have some say in how national wealth was allocated. In other words, some say in the system."

The pattern fit past revolutions. In the English, American, French and Russian upheavals, Crane Brinton wrote in his classic *The Anatomy of Revolution,* the underlying tension did not pit "feudal nobility against bourgeoisie in 1640, 1776 and 1789, or bourgeoisie against proletariat in 1917." Instead, he wrote, "These were all societies on the whole on the upgrade economically before the revolution came. The revolutionary movements seemed to originate in the discontents of not unprosperous people who feel restraint, cramp, annoyance rather than downright crushing oppression. Certainly these revolutions were not started by down-and-outers, by starving, miserable people."[9]

Revolutionary passions were instead felt by those who had enough to live on and yet still "contemplated bitterly" privileges they felt they were due, Brinton wrote.

"Revolution seems more likely," he concluded, "when social classes are fairly close together than when they are far apart."

The same was true in Iran. Again, the powerful white monument served as a symbol. As discontent exploded in 1978, the shah's tower became a staging ground for protesting the shah's rule. More than a million Iranians turned out at a pivotal demonstration in December to demand the shah's ouster and Ayatollah Khomeini's return.[10] Despite rhetoric that the revolution was carried out on behalf of "the down-trodden," vast numbers of the ideologues, clerics and activists who showed up at the monument—as at all other protests—came from the middle class.

"These were not peasants who had grandiose dreams," the political scientist explained. "These people turned out because they knew enough to recognize what they didn't have. And they knew enough to realize what was possible."

A month after that last demonstration, the shah was forced to leave. Two weeks later, Ayatollah Khomeini came home.

The new Islamic government acknowledged the role Tehran's leading landmark had played in challenging the monarchy it originally honored. The white monument was promptly renamed Azadi, or "Freedom," Square. And during the revolution's first two decades, every anniversary was celebrated around its tower.

Two other unorthodox museums are, coincidentally, both located on Taleghani Street in downtown Tehran, on the same block as the old U.S. Embassy. Both were created after the revolution. Both are modest, unassuming facilities in storefront buildings easy to miss. And they have a common theme: They're dedicated to the Islamic Republic's confrontations with the outside world.

The Martyrs' Museum commemorates Iraq's 1980 invasion of Iran and the costly eight-year conflict that followed. It's a macabre place. The first floor is lined with glass cases. Each case tells the story of one or more martyrs, often in their own words. Their heroics are illustrated with bloodied clothing, torn letters, shrapnel-sprayed Korans and other battle-damaged belongings found on their bodies. Each display also includes a red plastic tulip, the symbol of martyrdom in Iran.

On the day I visited in late 1998, I was met at the entry by an enthusiastic young guide named Javad who first congratulated me for visiting the museum.

"We don't get many foreigners," he said, as if he didn't understand why the place wasn't one of Tehran's leading attractions. He then insisted on taking me to his favorite displays.

One of the most famous exhibits is a "petition to God" signed by fifteen soldiers appealing for permission to sacrifice themselves to preserve Islamic Iran in the spirit of Hussein, the original seventh-century Shi'ite martyr.

"We pledge ourselves to become martyrs," read the petition written in an awkward young scrawl. "We will fight until we die to defend our country." Underneath, each had signed his name.

"Within a year, they were all martyred," Javad told me, as if their fate was an honor rather than a tragedy.

Another window featured the poignant last letter of a soldier to his mother.

"Mother of mine, my martyrdom will complete your contribution to the revolution," wrote twenty-two-year-old Hormuz Khamel. He died soon thereafter in a battle with Iraqi forces at Dehloran.

The most famous display was dedicated to Mohammad Hossein Fahmideh, a teenage martyr often cited by Ayatollah Khomeini for his bravery.

"The Imam mentioned him in many speeches because this young boy fastened a grenade to his belly and put himself under a tank, like a kamikaze. This was not an order he got, but something he decided by himself to do," Javad explained.

"This is a model of the Russian tank that killed him," he said, pointing to a miniature plastic tank positioned next to a full-size model of a grenade that dwarfed it. "He did it to save the revolution. The Imam considered his commitment a model for us all."

Fahmideh had been only thirteen years old.

The museum's goal was to emphasize how much the war had benefitted the revolution, despite its horrendous cost in human life. Its impact was quite the opposite.

After the tour, I was invited to have tea with Hassan Jafaari, a small man with a dark beard who served as the museum's public relations officer. He was also a veteran, having served both as a Basij volunteer and in the regular army. But he had since traded in his uniform for a gray suit and an open-necked shirt. No tie, of course.

I asked Jafaari what role the war had played in those troubled early years, when political fragmentation, economic pressures and international isolation repeatedly threatened to undermine revolutionary fervor.

"It's true, the war led to great unification among the people," said Jafaari. "The war was really important in keeping the revolution alive."

Since not many tourists passed through the museum, I asked Jafaari who did come to visit—and why.

"We bring all the schoolchildren here to make them aware of how much was sacrificed. Those of us who remember the war don't ever want to go through it again. It was the most difficult time this country faced in more than a hundred years. Probably more," he said. "But the majority of this country is very young, so even ten years later a lot of people have little or no memory of what happened.

"But we do more than that," he added. "By keeping the war alive, we help keep the spirit of the revolution alive too."

The third museum—and the one most symbolic of the revolution's early days—is actually little more than a large shop across from the Martyrs' Museum on the corner of the old American Embassy compound. It's dedicated to Iran's encounter with the United States. It's popularly known as the Den of Spies Center.

There's actually not much to see except a lot of words. The exhibits all center on the classified papers and memorabilia taken during the 1979–81 seizure of the embassy, when fifty-two American hostages were held for 444 days. The shelves are filled with copies of forty volumes labeled "Documents from the U.S. Den of Espionage."

Each volume chronicled United States policy and an array of CIA covert operations in the Persian Gulf region. The Students Following the Imam's Line—the group of young zealots who seized the embassy, not all of them students—had meticulously pieced the classified documents together from embassy shredders. Visitors can browse through or buy any of the thick volumes for less than a dollar, less than the cost of the paper used to produce them.

"There are eight more volumes to come, but there's a paper shortage," explained a young clerk dressed in jeans.

I asked which were the most interesting volumes.

"I haven't actually finished any of them," he admitted, with a shrug. "I've started them more than once when business was slow, but they're a little boring."

The clerk was also not a member of the Students Following the Imam's Line or its offshoots. He didn't know any of the youths who'd stormed the compound and swiftly seized it. Indeed, in the year he'd been working there, he couldn't recall any of the original captors ever coming to visit.

"They're just like everyone else involved in the revolution. They're looking after their own interests," he mused. "Life is more practical now."

I asked the clerk if he even remembered the embassy takeover.

"No," he said. "I don't remember the revolution either."

So why did he work at the Den of Spies Center?

"It's a job," he replied. Besides the forty-two hours a week he put in at the old U.S. Embassy, he also worked twenty-four hours a week as a telephone technician.

I asked him who visited the unconventional museum. Despite the heavy downtown traffic outside, the only other visitors that afternoon were an elderly woman and her daughter. One of the major limitations of the documents and other memorabilia is that they're all in English.

"You can see from the guest book," he said, pointing to a stand with a large ledger for visitors to sign. "Most people who come in are foreigners like yourself. Or, occasionally, Iranians come looking for other kinds of books."

The two women were browsing in a small section of books on poetry, fiction and current affairs that had been added to the inventory in recent years to help the Den of Spies Center pay its operating costs. Books on Japan were particularly popular, the clerk said.

"Iranians don't really have much interest in the American spy documents anymore," he added. "It was a novelty once. But that whole episode is ancient history now. What would they do with them anyway?"

The fourth museum is the most unusual in Tehran, not only because it's in an eerie subterranean vault in the basement of the Central Bank or because its thick, tightly guarded doors open only twice a week for a total of just five hours. It's unusual instead because it houses one of the two most dazzling collections of jewels in the world.[11]

Displayed behind forty glass showcases, the pieces are marvels of vanity and opulence. They range from a pure-gold chastity belt to the Pahlavi crown—crafted of more than fifteen pounds of diamonds, sapphires and pearls, topped with a white feather. They include intricate gem-encrusted egg cups as well as an astounding gem-encrusted globe with 51,363 big stones and weighing in at seventy-five pounds. The globe's oceans are all emeralds. Two in the Pacific Ocean are over 200 carats. Names are in diamonds. And land masses are crafted from sapphires and rubies. The largest ruby, at 75 carats, is in Texas.

"It's not only beautiful. It's also accurate in longitude and latitude," explained Mohammad Qajar, an aging guide whose grandfather was the last Qajar shah. The feudal Qajar Dynasty ruled Persia from 1794 until 1925, making it the penultimate family to rule Iran. The globe had been ordered by Nasser ad-Din Shah, the guide's great-great-grandfather.

"The idea was to take the loose stones in the treasury, which were kept in leather bags, and put them into something that might not, well, disappear," he added. "There's nothing like it in the world."

The other piece of monumental value—historically, artistically and monetarily—is the Peacock Throne. It stands at the entrance to the exhibit and actually looks more like the base of a double bed with a back-board. Guidebooks describe it as a square divan on gold legs inlaid with thousands of precious stones forming flowers, leaves and birds.

The beauty of the crown jewels, which formed the basis of Iran's wealth in the pre-oil days, also once inspired both poetry and wars. The Afghan attack plundering Iran in the early eighteenth century, as the Safavid Dynasty was crumbling, launched the most famous conflicts. Nader Afshar, a noncommissioned officer in Iran's army, seized the moment—and power. He finished off the Safavids; then, after declaring himself king in 1736, he chucked out the Afghans as well as the Russians and Turks who were also making inroads into Persia. He then led a military expedition to India to retrieve the dispersed jewels—and came back with even more than Iran had lost, including the Peacock Throne and the 182-carat Sea of Light diamond, which to this day is still the largest uncut diamond in the world. It, too, is on display in the museum vault.

But restoring the nation's wealth and the country's imperial borders did not compensate for Nader Shah's despotic ways. His assassination, in 1747, created instability that allowed outsiders to again plunder Iran's royal treasury. Most of it vanished. Several pieces ended up in the Tower of London, the world's other great repository of jewels. Only about one-tenth of the jeweled treasures remain in Iran. But they still constitute a priceless collection.

For all the history and beauty in the unusual museum, however, the dark vault with its halogen spotlights was far from busy on the day I visited in 1994.

"It's mainly tourists who come here now," Qajar conceded somewhat wistfully, nodding at the group of Japanese who kept getting too close to the glass showcases and setting off an obnoxiously shrill alarm.

The museum was a painful place for many Iranians suffering severe economic duress. Between early 1993 and my visit at the end of 1994, the rial's value had been halved against the dollar. Inflation was running at least 40 percent, with the price of some basics increasing 200 percent over that period. So despite Iranians' fascination with their history and culture—and a wealth of museums to prove it—growing numbers no longer had much time for either.

"These pieces are all so fantastically beautiful. But it makes me so sad to see them, because that's what they represent, a fantasy," said my young female interpreter.

"I had a pendant that was handed down from my mother and her mother and a long way back. It wasn't anything like these, of course, but it was the most precious thing in my family. I had to sell it to buy things I needed to survive."

Once upon a time, the dazzling *objets d'art,* tiaras, pendants, necklaces, earrings, turban adornments and other baubles played a vital part in the Iranian economy. The shahs used the jewels as collateral against government borrowing. But even the flashiest expressions of the monarchies' self-indulgence could do little to alleviate the economic woes of the Islamic Republic.

TWENTY YEARS AFTER the Islamic revolution, Tehran was still a mixture of cultures—sort of.

At 5:30 a.m. on a November morning so dark it seemed like the middle of the night, I went to the bar mitzvah of Amid Sahiholamal, a small but intense thirteen-year-old who was dressed in a dark, oversized suit and dark, oversized glasses almost identical to the pair worn by his twin sister Arezoo. Despite the male dress code in Iran, he also wore a red tie.

The bar mitzvah was so early because many years ago the rabbi at Abrishami Synagogue had declared that the best time to pray was before sunrise. The rabbi had long since departed for Brooklyn, but the practice continued.

Iranian Jews also usually hold the ceremony on the day after a thirteenth birthday. In Amid's case, it happened to fall on a weekday, when many friends and family had to be finished by 8:00 a.m. to go to work. That included Hoshay Eliassian, an elderly Jew who, in the absence of a rabbi, had been designated the person most qualified to conduct religious rites. Unfortunately, he also had a day job at the Ministry of Agriculture.

The ceremony began after Amid and Arezoo had together adorned the altar with vases of red and white gladioli. With his father, a vendor of baby furniture, at his side, Amid then covered his shoulders with a white tallis, the shawl worn while praying that signifies one's willingness to perform all the commandments. He tied to his forehead a small black box containing a piece of white animal hide that in tiny lettering proclaimed his love of God with all his heart, all his mind and all his soul. As a family friend darted around the room recording every word on a video camera, Amid then proudly read from the Torah in Hebrew.

The coming-of-age ceremony had an informal air. Family friends who'd been caught in Tehran traffic or who hadn't gotten up early enough dribbled in throughout the service. Children arriving to attend school on the floor below peeked in or sneaked in the back to watch. At one point, a phone in the corner of the room rang and rang; everyone tried to ignore it. At the end, women segregated in their own smaller section on the left ululated loudly to congratulate the child for reading so well from the holy book. The men declared, "God is great." The cantor sang. The kids clapped. And the congregation munched on cookies passed down the aisle and candy thrown in the air.

At a sumptuous breakfast feast after the ceremony, Amid was animated and quite chatty as he moved among the adults accepting their good wishes. I asked him about his future.

"I want to be a pilot when I grow up," he told me.

Since flying options in Iran are pretty much limited to the state-owned national airlines and Iran's air force, I asked Amid if he'd be willing to work for the government.

"Sure," he said, somewhat perplexed that it might be an issue.

Iran's Jews, who predate the arrival of Islam from the Arabian Peninsula by almost a millennium, are one of the oldest communities in the Jewish diaspora. They've traditionally had a different kind of status—and relationship with the government—than their counterparts in the neighboring Arab world.

Jews were in Iran from the early days of Persian civilization. As recounted in the Bible, Cyrus the Great conquered neighboring Babylon, today's Iraq, in the sixth century B.C. and decreed that the Jewish slaves be freed. He then mandated reconstruction of the Jews' destroyed first temple. He even helped recruit labor and raise funds for it. The Old Testament book of Ezra records:

> Thus saith Cyrus, king of Persia, The Lord God of heaven hath given me all the kingdoms of the earth; and he hath charged me to build him a house at Jerusalem, which is in Judah.
>
> Who is there among you of all his people? His God be with him, and let him go up to Jerusalem, which is in Judah, and build the house of the Lord God of Israel. . . .
>
> And whoever remaineth in any place where he sojourneth, let the men of his place help him with silver, and with gold, and with goods, and with beasts, besides the freewill offering for the house of God that is in Jerusalem.

Cyrus's motives were not all altruistic. He saw in the Jews of Palestine a buffer between the Persians and the rival Egyptians, the leading Arab power.[12] But not all Jews moved to Israel after their liberation. Many opted to live in Persia. So many Jews settled in what is today called Isfahan that it was known as Yahudiyeh or Dar al-Yahud, Farsi and Arabic titles both roughly meaning "haven of Jews."

Jews had other ties to Iran. Esther, the Biblical Jewish queen who saved her people from persecution in the fifth century B.C., and Mordecai were reputedly buried in the western city of Hamadan. Daniel, the Old Testament prophet venerated by both Jews and Muslims, was buried in southwestern Iran.

Over the next 2,500 years, Jews became integral parts of Iran's financial and business sectors, the legal and medical professions and the arts. Jews were even major players in Iran's world-renowned carpet industry. Tehran's legendary bazaar has had many Jewish merchants, while Jews also worked in the oil industry after it was launched in the twentieth century.

"You know, it's not as if Jews and Muslims are opposites," said Yafa Parnianpour, the gregarious fifty-year-old Jewish housewife with a husky voice and streaked blond hair who had invited me to the bar mitzvah.

"We share the same God. We don't eat pork. Many of our other dietary laws and hygiene practices are very similar. The *hejab* really had its origins in Judaism. We always wore scarves for services before the revolution," she continued.

"I imagine the daily life of a Jew here is not all that different from being a Jew in a Christian country. You know," she added with a wink, "the Virgin Mary wore *hejab* too."

Iranian Jews have gone through periods of harassment, notably during the Qajar Dynasty. But they fared better under the two Pahlavi kings. In the twentieth century, Jews also generally became more fully integrated into Iranian society. The ghettos began to disappear.

"Most of my life, relations between Jews and Muslim have been pretty normal. My family has always lived primarily among Muslims. My friends from childhood were mostly Muslims," Parnianpour said. "And we all think of ourselves as Iranians."

In fact, during the ceremony, Parnianpour had been able to explain only the parts of the service conducted in Farsi.

"I've been to enough of these that I should know what's being said, but I never learned Hebrew," she explained.

In Iran, the two cultures also share many social practices, such as arranged marriages. Both before and after the revolution, I'd often seen the final courting ritual when, under maternal supervision, prospective Jewish brides and grooms were introduced to each other over tea in the lobby of one of Tehran's hotels. If both were satisfied with the prospective partner, the marriage would be approved.

Like her Muslim contemporaries, Yafa had had an arranged marriage, several years before the revolution. It had been arranged through a mutual friend who, in her case, happened to be an Assyrian Christian.

"He asked my husband, who sold textiles for men's suits, why he hadn't married, and my husband told him he was a particularly religious man who needed a certain kind of wife. The friend told him he knew a Jewish family in his neighborhood with an unmarried daughter," Yafa said, a smile breaking out on her face as she recalled the story.

"So my husband passed by our house and saw me in the distance. Then, after he got an introduction to the family, he came and asked my father for my hand." Although a decade separated them, Yafa said, the marriage had been a good one.

"My Muslim friends went through the same thing. It's an Iranian tradition. The only difference is the wedding ceremony," she added.

Tehran's synagogues also blended the cultures. Yafa had earlier taken me to Yousef Abad Synagogue on a street of the same name. Its walls were richly decorated with distinctly Persian tiles in deep shades of azure, navy, yellow and royal blue; its floors were covered with Persian carpets. It was widely considered the most beautiful synagogue in Iran and, some claim, in all twenty-two Muslim Mideast countries.

At its strongest, in the first half of the twentieth century, Iran's Jewish community boasted 150,000 members, making it one of the largest in the world. Major migrations began after the 1948 creation of Israel. By the 1979 revolution, 80,000 were still in Iran. Two decades later, only some 30,000 remained. Yet despite the Islamic revolution and the virulent anti-Israel rhetoric—"Death to Israel" has been a rallying mantra—Iran still had more Jews at the century's end than any other Muslim or Mideast country except Israel.[13]

The revolution, in fact, never opposed Judaism. Shortly after his return from exile in 1979, Ayatollah Khomeini met with leaders of the Jewish community and other minorities and issued a fatwa ordering that they be treated well. Christians and Jews, he stressed, were "people of the book" and shared a single monotheistic religious tradition. In the case of

Jews, he also pronounced that they should be distinguished from Israeli Zionists.

The Islamic republic's new constitution in 1980 then stipulated that Jews—and three other religious minorities—should have their own representation in the new unicameral Parliament, or Majlis. The proportion is one seat for every 150,000, the same as for Muslims. So, in the unlikely event that their numbers increased significantly, Jews could even have more than one.[14] The Jewish parliamentarian took his oath of office on a Hebrew Bible. Jewish customs and laws—on divorce, for example—were also accepted by the new Islamic courts. And Jews were conscripted into the army. Several even became heroes during the Iran–Iraq war, a fact noted at the Martyrs' Museum in a special display for minorities.

On an erratic and sometimes unpredictable basis, Iran's Jews have also been included in other aspects of Iranian officialdom. Iran's delegation to the 1995 U.N. Conference on Women in Beijing included the head of the Jewish Women's Organization of Tehran. At the summit, Farangis Hassidim, the administrator of Tehran's Jewish Hospital, spoke about Jewish women in Iran.

Although diminished in number, Iran's Jews remained a vibrant and active community, some with strong attachment to a country genuinely considered their homeland. Manouchehr Eliasi, the Jewish member of Iran's Parliament and a physician at the Jewish Hospital, traced his ancestry in Iran back 2,500 years. (Eliasi shouldn't be confused with Eliassian, who officiated at the bar mitzvah.)

Queried in 1998 about why Jews stayed in Iran, Eliasi burst into tears and replied, "We love our country. This is my birthplace. I love its smell."[15]

The revolution had a somewhat ironic impact on Iran's Jews. Many I met over the years recounted how they had become more devout under Islamic rule than they had been under the shah.

"The regime became more religious and so did we," Eliassian told me after he finished officiating at Amid's bar mitzvah. "Before the revolution, attendance at synagogues was sometimes sparse. Mainly the old followed Jewish practices. Jews were like everyone else in a secular society.

"But now," he continued, "the synagogues are full. People practice Jewish customs. There is more awareness and pride. I think we are actually a stronger community."

Several women at the bar mitzvah told me stories of their strengthened religiosity. Some who had gone to public schools as children said they enrolled their own children in Jewish schools after the revolution. Others reverted to kosher diets. Many who had been brought up in a secular environment had joined Jewish groups after 1979 and become closer to Jewish friends. More Jewish homes added mezuzahs, which contain a tiny prayer scroll, to their doors.

Iran's Jews also managed to maintain a sometimes surprising variety of institutions after the revolution, including a handful of synagogues in Tehran and two dozen more in other cities. To accommodate some 15,000 Jews, the capital offered five Jewish schools, eighteen different kosher butcher shops, a Jewish nursing home and a 110-bed Jewish hospital considered so superior that 95 percent of its clients were Muslims, including top clergy.

In some respects, Jews even had greater freedoms—as long as they didn't proselytize—than Muslims. They could produce wine and partake of it at weddings, bar mitzvahs and, quietly, at home. Whether or not they were related, men and women could not only sit in the same room, they could also dance together at wedding receptions. Boys and girls, tots through teenagers, could mix freely at meetings of Jewish youth groups. Jews generally didn't come under the kind of intrusive scrutiny from morals squads that Muslims did, as long as their activities were out of the public eye.

Yet two and a half millennia after their arrival, the story of Jews in Iran seemed as if it was entering the final chapter.

Most of the seventy or so people at Amid's bar mitzvah were older friends of the family. The young were leaving as fast as opportunities or visas allowed. The trend was underscored by the absence of Amid's brother, the oldest of the Sahiholamals' five children. He had trained abroad as a rabbi—and moved to Brooklyn.

Despite Ayatollah Khomeini's fatwa, the early days had been tough for Jews—and tough to get over. A Jewish businessman charged with support for Israel, corruption and association with the crown was a victim of summary justice during the revolution's early excesses. For years, the government kept all passports, and Jews particularly had trouble getting permission to travel outside Iran at all, much less the multiple-exit permits issued to other citizens. The government often held back permission for one or more members of a Jewish family to travel abroad at the same time.[16] A trip to Israel could lead to confiscation of a Jew's passport. And

Jews were unable to even call or send mail directly to relatives in Israel. Both had to be done through intermediaries in Europe or the United States.

New forms of discrimination were also introduced after the revolution. Jewish schools had to have Muslim principals. Children in Jewish schools could no longer be taught in Hebrew. Kids also had to attend school on Saturday, the Jewish Sabbath. All applicants for public-sector jobs were screened for their Islamic credentials. Senior slots in government automatically went to Muslims. Jews complained of long delays in publishing a book, making a movie and having civil suits go to trial. *Tamouz,* the only Jewish newspaper, was banned in the early 1990s for complaining about the confiscation of Jewish school buildings.

Things improved a bit after President Khatami's election in 1997, mainly as part of the broader relaxation in Iranian society. In a letter to the Jewish Society, he called for improved relations among all Iran's religious communities.

"I hope that with the help of God and the friendliness and cooperation of all followers of the godly religions, we will be more successful in achieving the high goals of the Islamic Republic of Iran," he wrote.[17]

Yet, at best, Iran's Jews were still relegated to the status of *dhimmi,* a term meaning "protected religions" that came from the early days of Islam and usually referred to separate and not equal Christian and Jewish minorities.

The inequity was enshrined in the ancient Mideast custom of "blood money," compensation paid by the family of anyone who killed someone—by accident or design—to the family of the victim. Blood money was a traditional way to preempt revenge killings and family feuds. It was a full-fledged part of Iran's judicial system. But after the revolution, a new law stipulated that blood money for a Jewish woman was only half the amount due for the death of a Muslim man. The life of a slain Jewish man was worth only an eighth of the worth of a Muslim man. (The same proportions applied to other minorities.)

Whatever their attachment to Iran, most Jews expressed weariness or resignation about their future. Many felt vulnerable to the whims of Iran's revolutionary politics. The panic many felt immediately after the revolution was revived in 1999, when thirteen Jews were charged with spying for Israel and the United States. The Foreign Ministry claimed the arrests had nothing to do with religion, but the case was widely interpreted as an attempt by conservatives, who dominated the intelligence agency and judicial branch, to block the potential for rapprochement between Tehran and Washington.

"Washington's support for these spies shows that the United States remains the enemy of the Iranian people. This should be a lesson for those in Iran who support a resumption of relations with the United States," reported *Jomhuri Islami,* Iran's most conservative newspaper.[18]

Many Jews recognized they were pawns in a bigger game, but it didn't help. Twenty years after the revolution, few felt much incentive to stay—and even fewer to have their kids stay.

At the kosher butcher near Asbrishami Synagogue, everyone who came in to buy the special cuts of lamb or beef either wanted or planned to leave.

"I'd stay if my family were here but my kids have already gone and I miss them. They won't come back and I don't want to die away from them," said an older woman standing under a picture of a stern Ayatollah Khomeini. To avoid questions about their allegiance to Iran, many businesses run by religious minorities put large pictures of the Imam in prominent places.

A middle-aged man said only financial problems kept him in Iran. "I'd go but the exchange rate for foreign currency is so high that I can't afford to get out and start over. Even if I sold the property that's been in my family for generations, I wouldn't have enough," he said.

Another woman with her teenage daughter said she had no big complaints about the Islamic system. "They leave me alone, even the Hizbollahis," she said. "But you sense that important people just wished we weren't here."

"It's less the attitude than the lack of opportunity," chimed in a younger man.

The future of the shop itself told the story. Two of three massive refrigerators, the old-fashioned kind of white porcelain with glass doors, were empty. The third had a lone slab of beef and a single lamb carcass hanging inside. Once a bustling business that closed only on the Jewish sabbath, it was open only three days a week by 1999.

"My father has run this shop for more than three decades, but business is really down. Jews are leaving and the economy gets worse and worse. Meat is one of the first things people cut back on. It's true of Jews as much as Muslims," said Koorosh Baradarian, the twenty-something son of the owner who helped on days the shop was open.

"The need for my father's business is dying out, so I've gone back to study engineering at Tehran University. But I'm not sure if I'll be able to get a job once I graduate," he added.

The same dilemma had already led his brother to leave. Baradarian pulled out his brother's new business card. "Eliass Kosher Butcher, 8829 West Pico Blvd., Los Angeles 90035," it read.

"When my father retires, we'll close this shop," Baradarian told me. "Then I'll probably leave too. And that'll be the end of the family line in Iran."

IRAN'S BIGGEST CONTRIBUTION to world religion actually predates Islam by a millennium—and the Islamic revolution by more than three thousand years. Yet the ultimate irony for the world's only modern theocracy is that the one faith Iran gave birth to was by the end of the twentieth century the smallest of its recognized religions.

I found one of the last traces of it literally in smoldering ashes when I stopped at an innocuous building off Mirza Kouchakhan Alley in central Tehran. The burning embers flickered tentatively atop a large black urn in a small inner chamber far from any windows—and the danger that rain or a wind gust might snuff it out. A tall white-haired man with a stoop and a bad tremor sat nearby to stoke the embers, just in case.

"This fire's been going for almost a hundred years," the old man told me proudly. "We brought the original flame from the longest-burning fire in the world."

The flame came from Yazd, a central Iranian city and the historic center of Zoroastrianism, where a single fire has been lit for more than fifteen centuries—since A.D. 470. Iran's Zoroastrians worship light as the symbol of a good and omnipotent God. So fires, the symbol of light, are kept perpetually going in places of worship that are, not surprisingly, known as fire temples. A fire is roughly the equivalent of a Christian altar or a Jewish bima.

Zoroastrians, a name more difficult to look at than to say, are followers of Zoroaster,[19] a "divine helper" who lived some six centuries before Christ. He emerged in that critical period between 800 B.C. and A.D. 650 when religious creativity worldwide took giant leaps, spurred by the emergence of Israel's many prophets, China's Confucius and Lao-tzu, the Buddha in India, Jesus in Palestine and the prophet Mohammad in Arabia.[20]

Although largely unknown now, Persia's Zoroaster was as influential as the other prophets, holy men and philosophers in shaping the religious legacies that live on today. Zoroastrianism was among the earliest faiths to believe in one god; its role in shaping Judeo-Christian thought is widely acknowledged by Biblical scholars. Its ideas about the devil, hell, a future savior and the worldly struggle between good and evil ending with a day of judgment, the resurrection of the dead and an afterlife had a great impact on all monotheistic faiths, even Buddhism.

Zoroastrians also shared common practices with other cultures of their time, as I learned when I called on Rostam Chahsadi, the Zoroastrians' frail high priest, one afternoon when he was receiving followers and visitors at his office.

"The idea of fire temples did not start with Zoroaster," Chahsadi told me, beckoning for me to sit on a chair next to him at his desk. At eighty-seven, he had almost completely lost his hearing. Two thick hearing aids didn't help much, so I had to speak directly into his ear.

"The first civilized nations all built fire temples—in China, Egypt, India, Greece and Rome," he continued. "The practice began in the days before matches, so wherever people lived they built a structure for their fire, and then they took from the fire to make food. The first school was built at a fire temple, then came the library and a ministry of justice."

The practice of fire worship started during the reign of Jamshid, the first Persian king, sometime between 1500 B.C. and 1200 B.C., the old man noted. When Zoroaster appeared, hundreds of years later, the fire temples were still in use.

"Zoroaster taught that the omnipresent God can't be seen. But people at the time worshipped gods they saw, so they asked Zoroaster to prove to them the existence of such a god," Chahsadi said.

"Zoroaster said God is like the light, like all light. And he wasn't the only one to explain God in terms of light. The same thing was said by Moses when God appeared in the flame of the burning bush. Long after Zoroaster, Christians said God is the light of love, justice and kindness. And more than a thousand years after Zoroaster, Islam taught that God is the light of the heavens and the earth.

"So in all four monotheistic religions," the high priest said proudly, "prophets symbolized God in the form of light. Monotheism has roots in Zoroastrianism, and all monotheistic religions share ideas with Zoroastrianism."

Zoroastrians were also the first to have prayers for the five divisions of the day; most Muslim sects also pray five times daily. Confession of sins in thought, word and deed is also integral to belief, just as it is in Catholicism.[21]

At its height, Zoroastrianism became the Persian empire's first state religion. The faith proved to be a great unifier and eventually had adherents spread from the Mediterranean to south Asia. From the third century to the seventh century A.D., however, it began to ebb, challenged first by the spread of Christianity from the West and then Buddhism from the East and, finally, Islam from the south.

As the twentieth century ended, however, Zoroastrians still considered themselves to be the original and purest Persians.

"We're the *true* Aryans," said a middle-aged man who sat in on my conversation with the Zoroastrian high priest. "We're not the ones who are dependent on the Arabs for language or ideas about God."

But Zoroastrians then numbered less than 300,000 worldwide—and accounted for less than 0.1 percent of the population in Iran.* The sense of Zoroastrian commonality with other religions was also fading. Both the faith and the faithful stood out as distinctly different in Islamic Iran.

In contrast to the forbidding blackness or dark colors of Islamic modesty, Zoroastrian women wore white headscarves in the fire temple. In public, their dress was bright, embroidered layers of clothing. In contrast to beards or the three-day face stubble of Muslim males in Iran, Zoroastrian men were clean-shaven. Male elders of the faith wore all white, usually Nehru-style jackets and the kind of boxy white caps now most associated with Hindus.

The Zoroastrian calendar is also unique. Like the Western, or Gregorian, calendar, it is solar—not lunar, like the Muslim calendar. But Zoroastrians divide the year into twelve months of thirty days, plus five additional days. The calendar has no weeks, although the first, eighth, fifteenth and twenty-third are holy days. Each of the thirty days is named after—and presided over—by figures that are roughly equivalent to angels or archangels. Like the Persian calendar, which predates Islam, the year begins with the vernal equinox on March 21.

Zoroastrian rites were unique too. During my visit to the fire temple, I sat in on a service commemorating the death of a couple thirty years earlier. Two large sepia-toned pictures of the deceased couple rested on easels in front of the congregation. Clean-shaven men and women in

*Government figures in the late 1990s reported that Muslims constituted 98.5 percent of the population, while all the Christian sects accounted for only 0.7 percent of the population, Jews 0.3 percent and Zoroastrians 0.1 percent.

white scarves were on separate sides of the room. Up front, two Zoroastrian priests sat behind a large wooden desk. On the wall behind the priests was a huge oil portrait, at least ten feet high, portraying Zoroaster. He, too, was clad in a white robe and white cap. Lest anyone challenge Zoroastrian loyalty to Iran, however, small photos of Ayatollahs Khomeini and Khamenei were propped atop loudspeakers flanking Zoroaster's portrait.

The ceremony consisted largely of a long series of melodious chants by Cyrus Hormuzi, the lead priest, whose resonant voice filled the big hall. It was clearly arduous work. Every few minutes, Hormuzi plucked tissues from a Kleenex box on the desk to mop his heavily perspiring brow. By the end of the service, a pile of soggy tissues lay on the desk near two large vases of white gladioli and two small white candles. Hormuzi later told me that the chants came from the Gathas, seventeen of Zoroaster's hymns that record his teachings, and the Avesta, the Zoroastrian holy book.

Participation by the faithful during the service was largely limited to standing a couple of times and pointing fingers skyward, toward the light, in response to Hormuzi's rather pleasing voice.

"It's a form of praying, like Christians' putting their hands together to pray or crossing themselves and Muslims' praying toward Mecca," an older woman sitting nearby explained to me.

Several large platters heaped with dates, figs, dried apricots and pistachios were laid out on tables in front of the desk. Zoroastrians are tight-knit, in part because intermarriage with Muslims or adherents of other faiths is strictly forbidden. So rites usually end with a social function, even after the commemoration of a death that happened three decades earlier.

For most of the past 2,500 years, Zoroastrians also had a particularly distinct practice in dealing with the dead. They don't believe in burial. Because air and earth are both sacred, they avoid cremation and burial. Instead they traditionally left bodies on "towers of silence" for the vultures and the sun. Tehran still has one, and several "towers of silence" are visible on the peaks of mountains between Yazd and Kerman. But the practice of exposing corpses ended in Iran in the mid-twentieth century.

On the eve of the twenty-first century, Zoroastrians were taking other steps to modernize one of the world's oldest faiths.

"Now we want to change from wood to gas to keep the fires going,"

Chahsadi told me. "We use gas and electricity in our homes, so there's no reason we shouldn't use it in our temples too."

To understand what role Zoroastrians played in Iran's Islamic political culture, I went to see Parviz Ravani. In 1999, Ravani was serving his second—and he said final—term as the Zoroastrian member of Parliament. I called on him in an office starkly bare except for a desk and the omnipresent photographs of Ayatollahs Khomeini and Khamenei.

Ravani was surprisingly candid. "The minorities have only five parliamentary seats to the two hundred sixty-five the Muslims have, so we can't really do anything in terms of significant legislation. And believe me, there are things we'd like to change," he said.

At the top of the list were laws that discriminated against minorities by encouraging conversion to Islam.

"For example, if my child becomes a Muslim, then all my property will go to that child upon my death. None of my other children who didn't convert will stand to get anything. That extends even to my nephew. If he becomes a Muslim, then all my property would go to him, not my own children," Ravani added.

"That's a problem not just for Zoroastrians but also for Christians and Jews and any other religion too."

Like the female members of Parliament—who actually outnumbered them—the five minority politicians tended to sit together during legislative sessions, Ravani said. But they acted individually out of concern that Muslim politicians might suspect any joint strategy was a plot against them.

"We're free to say what we want in Parliament. No one says, 'What are you doing?' or 'You can't say that.' Most of the time we each talk about our people's problems. I talk six or seven times a year, which probably makes me the most active of the five minority members," he said.

Overall, he added, Zoroastrians and the other minorities could be worse off—even much worse off—considering the neighborhood.

"Minorities live better in Iran than in other countries in this region. We do our religious things freely," he added, noting that he made wine at home, as did many of his friends. "We're much more comfortable and much safer than Muslims in India or Christians in Saudi Arabia," he said.

Zoroastrians, Jews, Assyrian Christians and Armenians (the only minority with two seats) are also more fortunate than other minorities in Iran, including Sikhs, Catholics and especially the Baha'is, who don't have special political representation. Their electoral choices are limited to Muslim candidates.[22]

Like members of the other recognized minorities, many Zoroastrians told me that they fared better after the election of President Khatami, who was born and brought up in Yazd. His father, a powerful cleric, had worked closely with the local Zoroastrians.

"Khatami has lived among us and knows us well," Ravani said. "He knows we want coexistence."

Yet after almost three thousand years, the Zoroastrians were also leaving Iran.

Ravani's wife and two children lived in Toronto, where she was studying pediatrics in a Canadian university. And the brother of Rostam Chahsadi, the Zoroastrian high priest in Iran and technically in the world, was also a prominent priest—in Los Angeles. Neither case was unusual. As the twentieth century ended, California could claim more Zoroastrians than Iran.

SHIRAZ

> Its inhabitants are, amongst all Persians, the most subtle, the most ingenious, the most vivacious, even as their speech is to this day the purest and most melodious.
>
> —EDWARD Browne,
> *A Year Amongst the Persians,* 1893

Iran was born around Shiraz. More than 3,500 years ago waves of Aryans, a nomadic Indo-European people who much later would inspire the country's modern name, moved from chilly northern climes to the grand oasis near the Mountain of Mercy. Ever since then, the area around Shiraz has inspired the country's deepest passions—about the raptures of the soul and the mysteries of the spirit, about lyrical poetry and about the roses that abound almost year-round in its vast gardens and along its boulevards.

In the medieval world, Shiraz was one of Asia's most important and innovative cities. It was known for learning and art, painting and literature. Inspired by his hometown, an architect from Shiraz later provided the design for the Taj Mahal in India. By the eighteenth century, Shiraz was Iran's national capital.

By the revolution's twentieth anniversary, however, Shiraz was, alas, no longer a pretty city. It had become tired, worn down. It didn't have an innovative mayor like Gholamhossein Karbaschi, who beautified Isfahan and then revived Tehran. The decline in tourism and in Iran's general economic health had turned Shiraz into just another rather tacky Mideast city of yellow clay-brick buildings and small storefronts with cheap aluminum signs.

Yet two things redeem Shiraz: the history that permeates the area and the people who live there. Shirazis are, as British diplomat Edward Browne pronounced a century earlier, the loveliest in Iran. And the southern city's place in Iran's history will always make it an important site.

Visiting Shiraz should really begin in nearby Persepolis, the ceremonial capital of the Persian Empire dating back to the sixth century B.C. Persepolis is the surviving symbol of Iran's early greatness and what made it one of the world's first superpowers. It also offers further insight into why the Pahlavi Dynasty ultimately failed.

I made the fifty-minute drive there, somewhat precariously, in a 1977 Chevy Nova, one of the last vestiges of the American presence. It had been somewhat crudely repainted—its original shiny brown, because by law cars in Iran can be repainted only the same color, a provision designed to help control theft. Just who would want to steal a 1977 Nova—which had an odometer, according to the wizened driver, that had turned over too many times to remember—was open to question. It was one of a similar fleet used primarily as taxis in Shiraz.

"In this economy, you work until you die," explained the driver, who had recently turned seventy. "The same is true of your equipment."

Persepolis is more interesting for the sense of antiquity than for the ruins themselves. Darius I, who reigned from 521 to 486 B.C., first ordered construction of a ceremonial capital across the vast plateau at the foot of the crusty brown Mountain of Mercy. Over the next two centuries, subsequent kings each added a palace. Here, every spring, the diverse peoples of the Persian realm, which stretched from the banks of the Nile in North Africa and the Danube in Europe to the steppes of south Asia, came to pay homage to the king of kings, the *shahanshah,* during the holiday of Now Ruz. To this day Now Ruz, which celebrates the vernal equinox on or about March 21 and the beginning of the Iranian new year, is the most important national holiday. It supersedes even the revolution's anniversary, Mohammad's birthday and the Shi'ite commemoration of Ashura. Iranians are, always, Iranians first.

The complex of palaces at Persepolis was originally called the Throne of Jamshid, after Persia's first king. The Greeks account for the name change. They called the city Persepolis, or "capital of Persia," which they adapted from the ancient Farsa, or Parsa, meaning Pars' town. (The surrounding province is still called Fars, and Iran's national language is Farsi.) Ironically, the Greek name that has stuck with Persepolis over the millennia dates only from the time after the city was sacked and burned in 331 B.C. by Alexander the Great to symbolize his defeat of Persia and the end of its imperial power.

But even in the city's destruction Alexander had to concede Persian greatness, for he first ordered Persepolis's enormous library translated into Greek.

The approach to Persepolis is still grand. Atop the 111 stone stairs climbed centuries ago by gift-bearing envoys and princes, literally an exercise in humility, are gigantic stone columns that once reached more than sixty feet skyward and that hint at the extraordinary magnitude of the buildings, particularly for the times. Walls of reliefs chronicle the annual pilgrimage to Persepolis of Egyptians, Babylonians, Armenians, Syrians, Afghans, Ethiopians, Indians, Libyans and many others with tributes of gold, silver, ivory and jewels, rich fabrics, swords and an array of animals, including camels, lion cubs, buffalo, sheep, bulls and even a giraffe. Other reliefs depict the Immortals, the 10,000-man palace guard at the heart of Persia's military might. The Immortals were so named because whenever one fell, another immediately replaced him.

Almost everything else that once stood here, however, is left to the imagination. The ruins are just that—ruins. There is no sense of the wealth that required Alexander to order 30,000 horses, camels and donkeys to carry the goods in Persepolis's royal treasury back to Greece. Today, Persepolis is a rather sleepy place.

On a late November day, with a hot sun still blazing, two backpacking Dutch students wearing identical black "Alcatraz psycho ward" T-shirts, a small group of intent Japanese tourists and a sophomore class from the University of Shiraz were the only people wandering across the artificially elevated plateau. Traffic was so slack that the man running the Fuji film stand had wandered off without worrying about closing his kiosk.

I stopped the college students, all boys, as they finished the tour. Since most had been born the year the revolution ended 2,500 years of monarchy, I asked if there wasn't something almost heretical about visiting the site honoring Iran's first kings.

"Not at all," volunteered Hossein, a lanky and slightly sunburned youth with fuzz on his chin and L.A. Gear sneakers on his feet. The others all crowded around to chat with a foreigner.

"Persepolis is a symbol of Iranian civilization and history. We're proud of our ancestors. And the monarchy wasn't so bad for Iran. There was a time when Iran was a superpower and that was during a monarchy."

Did that mean they'd be interested in a monarchy again someday? I asked.

In unison came a chorus of emphatic no's, some with expressions of disbelief that the question had even been asked.

"We want a government where there's freedom, more freedom than now, but which also operates according to Islamic law," Hossein explained. "We want a system that doesn't urge or command us to do anything."

So what had they learned on their field trip? I asked.

"This is a good place to learn about the kings," Hossein replied, "and why the dynasties disappeared."

Indeed, for the contemporary Iranian, Persepolis may be best remembered as the place that reflected the last king's folly. In 1971, Mohammad Reza Shah Pahlavi hosted the world's most magnificent party in Persepolis to commemorate 2,500 years of Persian civilization. Under massive yellow-and-white tents, presidents and princes from sixty-nine countries drank *première classe* French wine out of Baccarat crystal and feasted on caviar and roast quail catered by Maxim's in Paris. At a cost of at least $200 million, the celebration was billed as the "greatest gathering of heads of state in history."[23]

The Persepolis fete, however, came at a time of drought in the provinces of Baluchistan and Sistan, as well as in Fars, where the celebration was held. As the foreigners reveled on drink forbidden by Islam, Iranians were not only excluded from the festivities, some were starving.

The party at Persepolis also served to bring Ayatollah Khomeini to public attention again from his exile in neighboring Iraq. The ayatollah was scathing about the shah's hubris, extravagance and lack of concern about his own people.

"Islam," he declared, "is fundamentally opposed to the whole notion of monarchy. Anyone who studies the manner in which the Prophet established the government of Islam will realize that Islam came in order to destroy these palaces of tyranny. Monarchy is one of the most shameful and disgraceful reactionary manifestations. Are millions of the people's wealth to be spent on these absurd celebrations? Are the people of Iran to have a festival for those whose behavior has been a scandal throughout history and who are a cause of crime and oppression, of abomination and corruption in the present age? . . . The crimes of the kings of Iran have blackened the pages of history."[24]

The attack marked an escalation in Ayatollah Khomeini's campaign, as his focus expanded from the villainy of a single individual to the evils of an entire system of government. The ayatollah also used the Persepolis fete to promise that he would return from exile to liberate Iranians from corrupt dynastic rule—a pledge that drew implicit parallels with the prophet Mohammad's return from exile in Medina to Mecca, where he created the first Islamic government.[25]

Persepolis thus symbolized both the monarchy's beginnings and its end.

After wandering among the relics for a couple of hours, I stopped briefly in the shade of one of the few remaining porticos and struck up a conversation with Mohammad Mohammadpour, an aging grounds-keeper with a white stubbly beard. I asked him how Iranians felt about Persepolis twenty years after the revolution.

"Sad," he said. "Sad about what we are now, compared with the greatness of what we once were."

The revolution might have gotten rid of a bad king, he added. But it hadn't helped restore Iran's power, international stature or wealth. When we spoke, Mohammadpour was being paid 500,000 rials a month, less than $100 at the exchange rate at the time—a rate that soon declined even further.

"Before the revolution, I was paid enough to buy two and a half gold coins," he said, referring to a popular way Iranians both save and hedge against inflation. "Now I can only buy one coin of gold. So today I'm worth only forty percent of what I was before the revolution.

"At this rate," he pronounced," it'll be a long time, a very long time, before we're a real power again."

THE SOUL OF IRAN can be found in a quiet rose garden in northeast Shiraz. The garden is the burial site of Hafez,* perhaps the world's greatest lyric poet in the fourteenth century and a thinker still widely venerated more than six centuries later.

*Hafez's full name was Shams ad-Din Mohammad Hafez.

"Hafez was the poet of life," Soroush once told me. "He was the voice of his time and also the typical Shirazi."

Hafez has turned out, however, to be a voice of this time as well. Hundreds and hundreds of Iranians now make pilgrimages daily to the tomb of Hafez, a pen name that means "he who knows the Koran by heart." Most come to consult him—literally.

After a hot day in the sun at Persepolis, I went to Hafez's garden as the sun set. The fragrance of flowers created a magical smell in the clear evening air. Against the bustle of the city, the garden offered a sense of contemplative calmness.

Hafez lies in the center of the park in an alabaster sarcophagus beneath a large cupola resembling a dervish's hat that is lined with mosaic tiles of aqua and navy and other rich shades of blue. Towering stone columns support it. Spotlights on the side shine up to illuminate its exquisitely intricate ceiling. The tomb itself is inscribed with lines from Hafez's most famous *ghazals,* a form of poetry with six to fifteen verses linked together by inspiration and symbolism rather than a logical sequence of ideas. One of them describes what Iranians should do when they visit the garden to commune with the poet:

"Sit near my tomb and bring wine and music. Feeling thy presence, I shall come out of my sepulchre," Hafez wrote shortly before his death in 1389.

I watched as eight female students, a young couple with a baby, three middle-aged men and a dozen or so others stood around or near the tomb to obey Hafez's instructions, each at his or her own pace. As music played softly in the background, each began the ritual by quietly reciting a phrase from the Koran.

Each then silently asked a question of an important personal nature—about love, family, health, work or home. Finally, each let a copy of Hafez's classic work open randomly to a page of verse. The answer to the question was in the poem. Some read the verse softly to others; some read it over and over to themselves. Afterward, several stepped up to the tomb, tapped the corner and quietly again said a few words.

As dusk turned into a starry night, I went to the little bookshop at the garden's edge to buy a copy of *The Divan of Hafez,* the poet's most popular work. Two young soldiers still in uniform were also buying a book; they had forgotten theirs. Both were university graduates, one in agriculture and the other in political science, doing their mandatory national service.

I asked what had brought them to Hafez's garden.

"We've come every couple of days since we were stationed here two months ago," said Mustafa Rahimirad, the political scientist, a lanky twenty-three-year-old wearing gold frame glasses held around his neck by a black strap. "We usually stay an hour or two."

What was the attraction? I asked.

"If you have a problem and you don't know what to do, Hafez will guide you. Whatever you ask, he will answer," Rahimirad replied. "We also like it here because the atmosphere is different from any other place in Iran. I can't explain. It's mystical."

I told him he made Hafez sound like a prophet.

"When you reach the position as a mystic that you know what God is, then you become part of God," he said.

Because the book would be a major expenditure on a soldier's pay, I offered to let the young men be the first to use my new copy. So we wandered back to the tomb, where Rahimirad said the short prayer and spoke silently to Hafez. Then he closed his eyes and let the book fall open to a verse. He landed on page 338 and read softly.

He then went over and tapped the corner of the tomb.

Later, I asked Rahimirad if Hafez had really answered his secret question.

"Of course." He smiled.

Twenty years after the revolution, Iranians were turning to sources other than the clergy for inspiration and answers. Hafez was among the most popular, in part because of his attitude toward the clergy.

"Because of his own deep suspicions, Hafez was very outspoken against the clergy in his time. That's why he so appeals to the heart of Iranians today," Soroush once told me.

After the soldiers left, I joined eight young women, all students at the University of Shiraz, as they took turns reading Hafez's poems aloud to one another. They seemed to swoon with satisfaction after each finished a verse. The dead poet was clearly a pop idol.

"We've been coming here every weekend for two years, since we started university," said Elham Khayrandish, a fresh-faced eighteen-year-old majoring in art and clothes design.

Again, I asked what the attraction was.

"I got to know Hafez when I was a child, because my mother studied literature," she explained. "Then I got to know him on my own when I was fifteen and began to write poems myself. I had him as my teacher. He taught me how to become a lover of God and to be a mystic."

Iranians are divided about the subjects of Hafez's poetry. He writes of women and love and wine and magical rapture. Some Iranians believe in the literalness of his verse—that the subjects are all about physical human pleasures.

> Oh cup-bearer, set my glass afire
> With the light of wine! Oh minstrel, sing:
> The world fulfilleth my heart's desire!
> Reflected within the goblet's ring
> I see the glow of my Love's red cheek,
> And scant of wit, ye who failed to seek
> The pleasures that wine alone can bring![26]

Others believe he is a Sufi mystic writing only of spiritual love in allegory. His work varies widely in tone, making either interpretation feasible, as in this case:

> Oh wind of morning, rise and tell
> My love who like a white gazelle
> Forever loiters proud and free,
> That she shall no more torture me.
> Because of her, this summer day,
> Across the desert sand I stray
> To find, when day at last is done,
> The Vale men call Oblivion.[27]

Although Islam has always been a religion of laws and logic, it also has a rich mysticism that has evolved over the centuries, primarily through the Sufis. The word "Sufi" comes from the Arabic term for wool, or *suf,* and the early mystics' practice of donning rough, white woolen robes to reflect their piety and rejection of the material world.

But the rough asceticism later evolved into an emphasis on deeper passions and ecstasy in the love for the divine. The Sufi mission expanded from a single quest for life's broader meaning to include real sensual enjoyment through spirituality. The idea stems from the Sufi belief that God is inherent in creation, not transcendent to it.[28]

Sufism reached a peak in the medieval world of the twelfth century when it gave birth to several formal Sufi brotherhoods centered on pious saints. Among them were the wandering dervishes, who roamed the world in spiritual pursuits. But the basic goal of all the orders was the same: to achieve union with God through detachment from the material world and by performing rituals involving meditation, self-hypnosis, fasting, dancing or the use of drums. Hafez wrote,

> Let Sufis wheel in mystic dance
> And shout for ecstasy;
> We, too, have our exuberance,
> We, too, ecstatics be.[29]

Using wine as an allegory, Hafez also wrote of the Sufi passion for God:

> The rose has flushed red, the bud has burst,
> And drunk with joy is the nightingale.
> Hail, Sufis! Lovers of wine, all hail!
> For wine is proclaimed to a world athirst.[30]

Sufi practices have survived the centuries in quiet corners of the Islamic world, especially among intellectuals and clerics. In the 1990s, as Iran's revolution was increasingly bogged down by the complexities of the real world, Sufi ideas and poets were again making something of a popular comeback.

In no place was the trend more visible than in Shiraz, the birthplace of Hafez and Sa'di, another medieval mystic poet who traveled the world for thirty years as a dervish on an open-ended spiritual adventure. At the end of the twentieth century, Sufism still permeated the city landscape, perhaps most visibly in a chain of eight new fast-food joints called Sufi Burger.

The fascination with sensual spirituality also helped explain why such an ugly city was still, beneath the surface, so interesting. Hafez wrote of Shiraz,

> Right through Shiraz the path goes
> Of perfection;
> Anyone in Shiraz knows
> Its direction.[31]

I asked Khayrandish, the art student, how important the medieval poet was to modern Iran.

"If you want to know anything about Iran and the religion of its people, you should go to Hafez. He gave Iran its soul," she said, with youthful awe.

"His words are eternally relevant. They always have something new for the old and they provide a sense of the old for the new. They are a code to live by. Whatever their religion, whatever their state of belief, all Iranians listen to the words of Hafez."

FOR CENTURIES, Shiraz was also famous for the grape that produced an exquisite wine. Its merits are recorded as far back as the twelfth century by Omar Khayyam, the astronomer, poet and author of *The Rubaiyat,* who wrote that it inspired his work.[32] Shiraz vines were so respected in modern times that they were transported for duplication to major vineyards as far afield as France and California, Australia and South Africa.

But that ended with the monarchy and with the Islamic republic's ban on alcohol. On the revolution's twentieth anniversary, wines from the Shiraz grape were produced to acclaim and profit all over the world—but not in Shiraz.

Before leaving Shiraz, I decided to see what had happened to the world-renowned Kholar Winery. Everyone I stopped to ask directions told me it was down near the post office on the main street, which after the revolution had been renamed Vali-e Asr, a reference to the Shi'ites' missing twelfth imam. But no one was able to tell me exactly where it was. So finally I went into the post office and asked. Sure enough, the post office had been the winery.

Postal officials were unwilling to tell me its story. But a middle-aged woman named Raffat, who wore a striking black velvet *hejab* and was waiting in line to make a long-distance call, told me that the factory for wine and beer and vodka had been occupied and burned down at the very beginning of the revolution. Then the property had been confiscated and the post office complex built in its place.

"It was really such a pity," she added. "Our black and golden grapes produced the best wine in the region. It was exported all over the world."

I asked if Shiraz still produced grapes for eating.

"Oh of course, but they're still consumed for wine too," she said. "Before the revolution, we had only one refinery. Now we have one in every home."

ISFAHAN

What is admirable in so large a city with so many inhabitants is the abundance and opulence which reigns. . . . Most of its surroundings are incomparably beautiful and fertile.

—French Knight Jean Chardin,
while living in Isfahan, 1673–77[33]

ISFAHAN IS a city of both splendor and sadness. It's a city of deep religious belief and yet soaring artistic beauty. To outsiders, it's a city of contradictions. But for Iranians, Isfahan is the most truly Persian city.

Its splendor lies in the Islamic monuments that are the largest and most magnificent collection of palaces and mosques anywhere in modern Iran—and that rival anything in the Islamic world. During the day, the rich blue tiles used in bulbously sensual domes, arabesque vaults and towering minarets glimmer off the surrounding desert as if to prove that humankind can create grandeur even in the bleakest environment. At night, the city has an ethereal sheen as the blue tiles reflect light from the moon and streetlamps. No one who wants to know Iran, past or present, should miss Isfahan. It's such a treat to the senses.

Isfahan's heyday was under Shah Abbas I in the sixteenth and seventeenth centuries. The greatest king of the Safavid Dynasty made Isfahan the capital of Persia—and something of a pleasure pit. He threw notoriously wild parties at the Palace of the Forty Columns, the most unusual royal site in Isfahan. The complex, ironically, is not a palace, nor does it have forty columns. It's instead an open pavilion where Abbas the Great received guests in front of a long, reflecting pool lined with rosebushes. And the pavilion really only has twenty pillars—which reflect in the pool and produce the look of forty. The pillars have since become so integral to Iranian life and lore that the term "forty" is interchangeable with "many."

"If a family has six children, you're likely to hear them say they have forty," an Isfahani tour guide told me. "It means the same thing."

But the heart of Isfahan has always been in the vast central plaza built by Shah Abbas I as a polo grounds and playing field for the Safavids. French chevalier Jean Chardin described the bawdy nightlife on Shah Square almost four hundred years ago, "One saw on the square charlatans, puppet-shows, thimble-riggers, verse and prose story-tellers, preachers and even tents full of prostitutes."[34]

Twice as large as Moscow's Red Square, Isfahan's plaza still ranks as one of the world's largest. All forms of nightlife disappeared, of course, after the revolution, when the plaza was renamed Imam Square after Ayatollah Khomeini. The main outlets of city life, however, are still concentrated there.

At one end is the vaulted bazaar—an artisan's mecca, because Isfahan is the artistic and craft center of Iran. At the other end is Imam Mosque, a massive complex covered inside and out with the blue tiles that are Isfahan's trademark. It dwarfs visitors. The seventeenth-century mosque, still widely recognized as one of the most stunning buildings in the world, has acoustics so perfect that stomping on the black paving stones beneath the dome generates a ripple of seven equal echos.

On the west side of the square is the Palace of Ali Qapu, which means "sublime gate" and was the Safavids' seat of government. The seven-story building was known as Iran's first skyscraper, because it afforded a view of the city and beyond. On the east side is the Mosque of Sheikh Lutfollah, a small architectural masterpiece built to honor a cleric described by Iran tour books as the "Islamic Billy Graham of his time."[35]

Twenty years after the revolution unseated the last king, the polo field goalposts were still visible. But otherwise, the plaza symbolized how times had changed—and how much. For all its current beauty and sensual past, Isfahan was gripped by a brand of Islamic zealotry arguably more dogmatic than in the theological center at Qom. Despite the easing of social restrictions elsewhere, the Isfahan grapevine still buzzed with stories about Hizbollahi vigilantes roughing people up and morals police regularly stopping young couples or groups of young males and females on the street to make sure they were married or related.

The Lonely Planet guidebook on Iran published in 1992 noted: "In view of the town's unrivaled visual legacy, it's surprising for the foreign visitor how little Iranians like this town and its people. . . . These days the town is better known as a citadel of inflexible *Hizbollahi* thinking, filled with rude and unhelpful bureaucrats, scheming and tight-fisted private citizens and dishonest merchants. . . . Another popular saying to the effect that Isfahan would be perfect were there no Isfahanis in it has a great deal of currency to this day."[36]

Fervor was deep even among fairly Westernized Isfahanis, as I found when I met Hossein Payghambary, the thirtyish proprietor of the Nomad Carpet Shop, a store catering to tourists on Imam Square. The reasons, he told me, had as much to do with the outside world as with the revolution.

"Islamic traditions have always been strong," he said, as he tried to sell me a small tribal rug at an exorbitant price.

"Isfahan became the capital under the Safavids, who were the first to embrace Shi'ism. That was when religion became important to our identity—our separate identity—and our ability to resist being consumed by foreign powers."

Once one of the world's largest cities and a vital trading center, Isfahan has a long history of foreign occupation or intervention. It's been occupied over the centuries by Arabs, Turks, Tamerlane's Mongols, Afghans and, in the twentieth century, Russians. The Safavids originally embraced Shi'ism to make Iran distinct from the neighboring Ottoman Empire, which was ruled by Sunni Muslims. Shi'ite Islam was among the most important sources of cultural cohesion and political separateness to prevent outsiders, even other Muslims, from absorbing Isfahanis. Shi'ism quickly became synonymous with nationalism. Three centuries later, that deep religious commitment also explained why Isfahan had been among the most turbulent cities during the 1978–79 revolution.

Payghambary, who had a De Niro–esque mole on his right cheek, embodied the seeming contradictions of Isfahan. His English was flawless and he had traveled extensively abroad. He conversed easily with Australian and European tourists who stopped by his shop. He sent out Christmas cards each year; I received one a couple of months after we met. And he wore a red-and-black checked shirt and cotton khakis that could have come out of an L. L. Bean catalogue.

Yet he had fought in the war with Iraq as both a Basij volunteer and a Revolutionary Guard. And all of his life, he told me, he had read the Koran and prayed daily "with meaning."

"I guess you could call me a Hizbollahi," he said, obviously viewing the affiliation as a title of distinction.

For Payghambary, the revolution was far from winding down. His political allegiance to the Supreme Leader was "total and unquestioning," he said.

"There's a sentence in the Koran that says to follow God, and then to follow the messenger of God, and then the messenger of the messenger. The Supreme Leader is the messenger of the messenger, and anyone who opposes him has no knowledge of Islam," he said.

Payghambary's biggest concern was instead about the dangers of changing Iran too fast—or changing it at all.

"The Supreme Leader wants the country to move, but he doesn't want people to move around naked on the streets," he said, in reference to a very slight recent relaxation in the Islamic dress code. "The practices of Islam must not change."

I asked what that meant in terms of daily life.

"We don't want others to decide what women should wear or what we do at night. We don't want to eat McDonald's or Kentucky Fried Chicken or Wimpy burgers," he replied.

"We want good chicken kabob with saffron rice."

But Isfahanis have paid a high price for their religious fervor, including the highest number of martyrs during the eight-year war with Iraq. A decade after the war ended, signposts throughout the city still boasted of Isfahan's part in the bloodiest modern Mideast conflict.

The biggest billboard on the airport road showed a sea of military helmets on the ground above the slogan "Martyrs get to see first what God created."

Graffiti on a main-street fence proclaimed, "Martyrdom is prosperity for us" in letters at least four feet high.

A war that other Iranians had worked hard to forget lived on in Isfahan.

The sad side of this beautiful city was visible at the Rose Garden of Martyrs, a sprawling, densely packed cemetery in the heart of Isfahan. The city's war dead—or at least those who could be identified—were buried there. The graveyard had an eerie, personal feeling about it, because a large picture of each soldier was encased in a glass frame above his grave. The sight of row after row after row of pictures of boys and men, young and old, running on for several blocks really humanized the war—and its toll.

Among the early casualties was Reza Hesamzadeh, a Basij volunteer. He had been eleven years old when Iraq invaded in 1980 and only thirteen when he died in 1982. The intervening years had sun-bleached his photo, but he still looked like the schoolchild he had been when he died.

"Khomeini, you are the spirit of God. You are the light of my heart," proclaimed a message inscribed on his tombstone. "What the enemy fears is your revolution." Two pots of faded pink plastic flowers rested on the corner of his grave.

"I remember Reza's death," said Hassan Enayati, the cemetery's seventy-year-old groundskeeper who had buried all the martyrs and stayed on after the war to care for their graves. "He was the first in the family to die.

"The family had four sons and all four were Basiji. Three of them were killed. But Reza is the only one buried here," the groundskeeper explained. "He was the only one who was recognizable."

Iran treated its war dead differently from others who had died. They were buried in separate cemeteries or sections. Gravestones of war victims were each distinguished by the photos and an etching of a dove, a symbol of martyrs' automatic entry into paradise. The bodies of soldiers also were not washed. They were buried as they died.

"They're like Hussein," Enayati explained, as he rubbed the gray stubble on his face. "He was the first martyr and his body wasn't able to be washed. Everyone who died in this war was following in his path, so they are buried the same way."

All told, Isfahan lost some 11,000 of the more than 123,000 volunteers and regular troops who died during eight years of conflict. Their names were all recorded in stacks of enormous leather-bound ledgers piled on the shelves of Enayati's tiny office.

"One day alone we had six hundred and sixty dead. On another day we buried two hundred and sixty. They were all Basij," Enayati said. The Basij did many of the costliest jobs in the war, like serving as human minesweepers and stopping the tanks and armored personnel carriers of Iraq's better-equipped and better-trained army. They also accounted for most of the dead.

I asked Enayati how Isfahanis felt about Iraq a decade after the war ended. I asked because that week the Iraqi soccer team had played in Tehran before a packed crowd. The team, which had stayed at my hotel, had been treated well.

"Iran has also had a soccer match with the United States. Soccer is different from politics and ideology," he explained.

"Isfahanis still believe we should have gone to war," he added. "And if Iraq or anyone else invades us, we'd do it again. This revolution is still something to fight for."

QOM

Visitors to Qom should be reverent.
—Lonely Planet guide[37]

Qom is for and about one thing: religion. The main focus of the city is religious training in its famous seminary. The overwhelming visual image is the sea of black and white turbans that seem to be worn by most of Qom's men. The city's main export, not surprisingly, is mullahs.

Visitors first get a hint that Qom is about the spiritual rather than the temporal existence as they leave nearby Tehran and hit the toll road to the center of Shi'ite theology. After paying the tollbooth attendant, there's a separate slot for a religious charity. Depositing a few rials is a good deed that supposedly guarantees a safe journey. Drivers doubting the need to pay up have only to look at the totaled car, complete with paint-bloodied dummy hanging out the window, that has been pointedly placed on an elevated stand near the booths.

The hour-plus drive to Qom is the second hint. The bleak desert scrub and scaly brown hills look like the backside of a rhinoceros—and that's the interesting part. The terrain then straightens out and opens to smelly salt flats closer to the city outskirts. Only God could love this kind of countryside.

Qom itself is only marginally better. It's a drab colorless city of dusty streets, tired sun-bleached buildings and uninteresting architecture, except of course for the blue-tiled mosques and religious institutions. Driving from cosmopolitan Tehran to ascetic Qom is like going back in time.

Yet even Qom is going through a transition. In some ways, the changes to a long-established way of life have been more fundamental here than in any other part of the Islamic republic. The past and the future are reflected in two of the city's religious landmarks.

One is a traditional home of mud and straw on a small side street. The Islamic part of Iran's multifaceted revolution had its roots here because Ayatollah Khomeini launched his campaign against the Pahlavi Dynasty from this house. It's now open to the public, so I stopped by on the eve of the revolution's twentieth anniversary to see what had happened to it. A guard at a small post outside the front door made me surrender a camera with the stern warning, "No pictures, none at all. This is a place of reverence."

I asked the guard if many people still visited the Imam's modest home.

"Oh yes, two hundred, three hundred, sometimes five hundred a day," he replied. That morning, however, I seemed to be the only one around.

Decades after Khomeini first moved to this little house, little had changed. Beyond the entry was a small courtyard with a tiny tiled pond surrounded by rather forlorn rosebushes. An empty clothesline still hung above them.

Inside, the house had a raw feeling about it. Some of the lights were merely bulbs dangling on cords from the ceiling. For a city that claims to make Iran's finest silk carpets, the red wool rugs were well worn and cheap. And like many traditional homes, it had virtually no furniture except for a couple of bookshelves and a chair draped with black cloth and raised atop a platform that Khomeini used when he received his followers or gave talks. It struck me as a kind of clerical throne.

A senior cleric named Ayatollah Khatam Yazdi sat on the floor in the Imam's old study drinking tea poured from a cup into a saucer, a common practice when tea is too hot. Yazdi had been a colleague of the Imam's, so I asked him if he'd be willing to tell me his memories of the period when Ayatollah Khomeini had lived in this place.

"I don't have time!" he said, dismissing me with a wave of his hand. He then went back to drinking tea from the saucer.

Hojatoleslam Ghazanfari, the cleric in charge of the Khomeini home, was more hospitable. When I asked him the same question, he was more than willing to chat. So we sat cross-legged on the floor near the ayatollah's chair, both of us in our stocking feet, since shoes had to be left at the door.

"From the walls and doors, you can still get memories and stories of what happened here," he told me as we sipped salty cups of tea brewed from the salty local water.

"Many visitors from Europe, the Gulf, south Asia, the Arab world, other Muslim countries and even America have come to hear them," he said. Most, he added, came away surprised by the simple dwelling.

"There was a rumor that Khomeini lived in a palace and that it was bombproof. But this house is made only of mud and straw, not even brick. The Imam's life was really very simple. Except when he received people, he, too, usually sat on the floor," Ghazanfari explained.

Khomeini's austere lifestyle turned out to be an asset, especially when he launched an attack on the last Pahlavi monarch's desperate attempt at reform in the early 1960s. The shah dubbed the six-point package his White Revolution. It centered on land reform, but it also granted women the vote, privatized state-owned factories and introduced a literacy campaign and profit sharing for industrial workers. The reforms did lead to changes, most notably new schools, roads, factories and bridges. In the end, however, the impact of critical measures such as land redistribution were often limited.[38]

The White Revolution instead ended up propelling the ayatollah to the forefront of Iran's opposition. From his little house in Qom, Ayatollah Khomeini issued a fatwa calling the reforms "a serious threat" to Islam and urging all believers to boycott the 1963 Now Ruz New Year celebrations.

"In order to warn the Muslim community of the imminent dangers facing this country of the Koran, I declare the New Year to be a period not of festivities but of mourning," he warned. "Oh Allah, I have performed my first duty, and if you allow me to live longer and permit me I shall shoulder other tasks in the future."[39]

The ayatollah's attack began to redefine the format of Iran's opposition, long dominated by secular figures. It began to have an Islamic veneer too.

The shah took note when he struck back. To silence the clergy, he had more than sixty detained. Hundreds of theology students who were normally exempt from national service were ordered to report to the army. Government funding to certain clergy was cut off, while security was tightened around Qom. In a nationwide speech, the shah charged that the clerics were "black revolutionaries."[40]

Ayatollah Khomeini then threw down the gauntlet. During Ashura celebrations, he made his famous declaration that the monarchy was "fundamentally opposed to Islam itself and the existence of a religious class." He warned the shah that "the nation will not allow you to continue this way."[41]

Two days later the ayatollah was arrested, sparking demonstrations throughout the country.

Ten months in prison did nothing to cow the Imam. He came out angrier and more daring, lashing out boldly at the regime the very day he arrived back at his Qom residence to an audience of thousands. Within weeks he confronted the shah again, this time over increasing American influence. He was particularly incensed over a new law granting all United States military personnel and their dependents immunity from prosecution for crimes committed in Iran. The new law passed by the rubber-stamp Parliament coincided, not accidentally, with a $200 million loan from the United States that the shah wanted to modernize Iran's military.

"Our dignity has been trampled underfoot. The dignity of Iran has been destroyed," Khomeini said in a speech to followers in front of his Qom residence. The measure, he charged, reduced the Iranian people to a level lower than that of an American dog. If someone runs over a dog belonging to an American, he will be prosecuted. Even if the shah himself were to run over a dog belonging to an American, he would be prosecuted. But if an American cook runs over the shah, the head of state, no one will have the right to interfere with him. . . . Let the American president know that in the eyes of the Iranian people he is the most repulsive member of the human race today because of the injustice he has imposed on our Muslim nation. Today the Koran has become his enemy.[47]

On November 4, 1964, the shah's secret police came to Khomeini's home for the last time.

"They came over the wall, not through the door," Ghazanfari recalled, as if it had happened the day before. "But the Imam was down the street, so they beat an old man who was staying here to find out where the Imam had gone. Khomeini heard the shouting and returned and asked why they were hurting an old man.

"The security people didn't recognize him and said they were looking for Khomeini. The Imam didn't run or try to hide his identity," the cleric added. "He told them straight out, 'I'm Khomeini.' Then they took him from this house to Tehran and deported him."

Khomeini spent the next fourteen years in exile, primarily in Iraq. He never forgot that his humiliating banishment—and the selling out of Iran's clergy—was a price the shah had been more than willing to pay for closer relations with the United States.

As Ghazanfari recounted the historic role of Khomeini's home in the revolution, several aging clerics wandered in, sat on the floor and became engrossed in their own discussions.

What did the clerics still do here? I asked Ghazanfari.

"They come here to meet and talk and debate one another. Since Khomeini's death this house has also become a center to provide answers for people who have questions about Islam and Islamic law," he told me.

"There's one cleric who was with the Imam in Iraq and he's particularly familiar with the Imam's thinking. Many people come to consult him about what the Imam had said on a subject or what he might think."

The cleric standing in for Khomeini turned out, of course, to be Ayatollah Khatam Yazdi, the unfriendly tea drinker.

The use of Khomeini's first home in Qom for consultation reflected the power of the Shi'ite clergy. A single individual, usually a grand ayatollah or an imam, can leave a lasting and often authoritarian imprint through his rulings. One man's version of the truth might endure for years, decades, even long after his death.

I asked if Ayatollah Khatam Yazdi received many inquiries.

"Oh yes," Ghazanfari said. "We also have it set up so that anyone with a question can fax here. The number is Qom 744-444."

With obvious pride, he added, "We even take questions in English."

As I left, I wondered how many questions a lone cleric could address, even if he had help. The system in use at Khomeini's home helped explain the slow pace of Islam's evolution. It explained Islam's past.

IN STARK CONTRAST to the simplicity of Khomeini's barren home was a second religious landmark in Qom. The bustling new computer center at the Golpaygani Seminary, an impressively large yellow-brick building with blue-tiled trim, reflected why the pace of Islamic reform had begun to quicken. It was the harbinger of Iran's future.

The center was the brainchild of Ayatollah Ali Korani, a gentle cleric with a white beard and a white turban who hadn't even known how to type when he decided, about the time of Ayatollah Khomeini's death in 1989, that Islam had to meet modernity in the form of computers. The idea grew out of his own rather unusual research.

"Since I was a child I loved Imam Mahdi, our twelfth imam who disappeared," he told me when I called on him at the computer center, where he and a young cleric were engrossed in a new software program.

"Some of us believe from reading Islamic sources that he'll come back at the same time as Jesus. The coming of the Mahdi is certain because the prophet Mohammad said it would happen. He'll come first and go to Qods [Jerusalem]. Then Jesus will appear from heaven and they'll pray in Qods together. And then there will be unity between Christians and Muslims," Korani explained.

"So we began to do research and write books to make our case. We worked on this subject for five years and produced five volumes. But they weren't complete, because we still had many sources to check. About that time I read a magazine about computers and realized a computer would be ideal for us to do more extensive research," he said.

"So I went to [Grand] Ayatollah Golpaygani and explained what we could do if we put all the religious texts and all the writings on Islam and other religions on computer. I said life is so short and it takes such a lot of time to get answers to questions if each person has to go through so many sources. He accepted our argument and ordered that this center be established."

It wasn't easy at first. Many senior clerics protested the idea. Others feared the center was intended to replace serious scholarship—and them.

Korani also had to start from scratch with a lone computer and a few manuals. The first few books that he and his aides programmed each took an average of five hundred hours. Over the next decade, his staff grew to include eighty young clerics, who managed to put some three thousand works on computer—in multiple languages with multilanguage search capabilities.

By the revolution's twentieth anniversary, Qom had seventy centers with computers for religious research. On the day I visited, the room across from Korani's office was packed with turbaned clerics working industriously on three rows of Epson and Philips computers.

"Today one person could do in one month what it took thirty of us five years to do in our research on the Mahdi and Jesus," the ayatollah said.

The initial database included the Koran, the Islamic traditions known as the *hadith* and the works of major religious authorities over the centuries. But it was hardly uniform, identical or monotonous material. The compilation instead illustrated the wide diversity of thought within Islam. Over the centuries, clerics have offered quite disparate answers to questions about the faith; answers to formal queries were a standard means of offering direction or issuing fatwas within Islam.

"To show what we had accomplished, we took the computer to Ayatollah Golpaygani and told him to ask us one question. He did, and in minutes we produced fourteen thousand answers from everyone important who had spoken on the issue," Korani recalled.

Over time, the database went beyond Islam. The ayatollah and his aides also programmed the complete texts of the Torah and the Bible, in both Farsi and Arabic, along with encyclopedias and other academic works on the Jewish and Christian sacred books.

To show me the scope of the database on early Christianity, Korani hit the search function and typed in the word "disciple," which turned up screen after screen of citations—all in Farsi—from twelve hundred different sources.

"We hope Jews and Christians are going to give us other sources so our computers can provide a greater selection of information and thought," Korani said. "Eventually we hope Jews and Christians will have the same kind of thing we've developed so we can compare fatwa and dogma."

Korani had already made inroads when envoys from the Vatican diplomatic mission in Tehran had visited the computer center.

"The world is going toward the scientific," Korani said. "I think computers will help all religions understand one another better."

The even bigger accomplishment, however, may have been winning over his peers.

"Even the old ones are learning how to work with computers," the ayatollah noted, with a small chuckle. "It's now accepted that to be a modern cleric you have to know the computer."

THE CASPIAN

In the rest of Iran the air is dry, limpid; clouds are rare and appear as mere decorations. Here on the contrary your skin and lungs recapture a forgotten flexibility.

—Jean Hureau,
Iran Today[43]

For centuries, Iranians have played hardest in the rolling hills and sandy beaches of the Caspian Sea. The cool, clear air along Iran's northern border offers relief from the heat of Mideast summers. And the lazy pace of Caspian life provides relaxation year-round from the pressures of trade or politics or urban life.

An Iranian friend who grew up spending summers on the Caspian—in her case, before the revolution—recalled her vacations with nostalgia.

"I remember the live music and the disco. The kids played tennis or Ping-Pong or billiards and the adults gambled at the casino. We could wear bikinis at night and make fires beside the sea," she said.

"Many of us had our first loves there, by the sea. I'll always remember this was the place where my father told me that men are like wolves and once they have a woman they don't want her anymore. He said men will tell you anything to get you—that your eyes are beautiful or that your hair is lovely. Then my mother said, 'Go look in the mirror and ask yourself if the things he says are true. If not, you know what he wants.'

"My parents told us those things when we were at the Caspian," she added, "because those were the kinds of things that happened there. The Caspian was about fun and passion and pleasure."

Twenty years after the revolution, the Caspian was still about fun—at least as much fun as the Islamic Republic would tolerate. But most of the passions and symbols of pleasure were long gone.

The fate of Ramsar and Chalus, neighboring resort towns four hours from Tehran on the other side of the Alborz Mountains, was typical. Once among the best places in the entire Mideast for sports, gambling, playing and partying, they had become sleepy towns for picnics, quiet nature walks and family outings.

The pool at the old Chalus Hyatt, renamed the Independent Hotel after the revolution, had been empty and neglected for so long that it had deep, irreparable fissures. Vacationers wandered instead along the shoreline fully covered—women in chadors or *hejab* and men in trousers and long-sleeved shirts. Swimming and sunbathing were no longer options. Tennis and other sports were segregated by gender. The disco had long ago closed, since the revolution had made public dancing and live music illegal.

In Ramsar, the elegant casino had probably been the most notorious of all the Caspian's attractions before the revolution. It once drew patrons from as far away as Europe. The building, commissioned by the first Pahlavi king in 1933, copied a grand European style that belonged more in Monte Carlo or Nice than in the Middle East. It was an apt setting for the clientele—mainly rich, Westernized Iranians and foreigners.

The casino's aging caretaker, Ali Asghar Fili, offered me a tour when I stopped in to see what had happened to it. The building had reopened as a hotel after the revolution, but few Iranians could afford the steep rates anymore, so on that day only two rooms were occupied.

Little had actually changed, except for the addition of a giant picture of Ayatollah Khomeini, whose scowling visage loomed large over the doorway to the casino. The main gaming room still had the big tacky crystal chandeliers and overstuffed leather chairs from the time when the casino was open all night. The teller's window, where the patrons once bought gambling chips, looked as if it might open at any minute.

"For a while, we used to allow people in to see the casino as a sort of museum to evil, but they scratched the leather and put out cigarette butts in the arms," Fili explained. "No respect. Really, it was very sad."

So even the museum of evil had become off-limits.

Ramsar was like the other Caspian towns I visited. Most of it was squeezed onto a single main street that ran parallel to the coast. Several towns were so small that exact addresses were unnecessary. Downtown areas were limited to a restaurant or two, a hotel, a couple of mom-and-pop groceries and an outdoor vegetable market, maybe a clothing or hardware store and, of course, at least one mosque.

Ramsar also had a photo shop. It was run by Hadi Khodaparast, an engaging young photographer who supplemented the sale of video and sound tapes, film, tape cassettes and batteries by taking wedding pictures. Weddings and funerals, he said, had become the high point of local social life.

I asked him what else people did, since most forms of entertainment had been restricted.

"The beauty of the region hasn't changed. It's just twenty minutes from the mountains to the sea, and in between it's so lovely that the newspaper reported the other day that dozens of other towns around the world have been named Ramsar," he said.

Was that enough? I asked.

"We go to relatives' homes. We pool resources. Someone has a satellite dish to get foreign television. And I have videos. We watch whatever we can get," he said.

"But people now know that they should forget the past. What you have in Europe or the West we won't have again," he said, with a shrug of acceptance. "After twenty years, people are used to the boredom."

Besides its beauty, the Caspian is probably still best known for its exquisite caviar, the so-called food of kings that is by many measures the finest roe in the world. The black and coral eggs are produced by the world's most expensive fish, an array of sturgeon unmatched anywhere else on earth. Although Azerbaijan, Kazakhstan, Russia and Turkmenistan also border the Caspian, the layout of the world's largest inland lake has traditionally produced the best caviar on the Iranian side.

Twenty years after the revolution, however, Caspian caviar was another endangered aspect of Iranian life. Indeed, it had become almost rare inside Iran. I heard about the problem at the Massoumeh Brothers corner grocery in Ramsar.

"Some think that people who live on the Caspian eat caviar for breakfast, but it's not like that at all," said Eraj Massoumeh, the young co-owner.

"We eat a lot of fish, but people here haven't acquired a taste for caviar because of the cost. I've never had it."

He then did a quick poll of his half-dozen customers. One couple complained of the high price of caviar—higher after the revolution than during the monarchy.

"Everything's more expensive since the revolution," an older man shot back.

"You see, most people have never had it. Besides," Massoumeh added, "you can't find caviar in the stores here. The government and the smugglers control the business. The people don't get any of it."

In fact, smugglers actually dominated the business. The total annual caviar yield in 1997 was roughly 250 tons, only 50 tons of which was caught legally and sold by the government,[44] mainly for export to earn badly needed foreign currency. The rest was caught and sold illegally on a burgeoning caviar black market.

Caviar cultivation had also been endangered by environmental hazards. By 1998, twenty-three species of caviar-producing sturgeon were facing extinction. Pollution was a growing issue. So was the fact that Iran's neighbors annually poured 350 tons of industrial chemicals—the leading hazard to marine animals—into the sea.[45]

The biggest threat to Iran's caviar industry, however, was the prospect of the world's most promising new oil and gas boom, which had the potential to transform all aspects of life along the sleepy Caspian. Estimates of the quantities were still tentative as the revolution marked two decades. But even cautious predictions suggested that the Caspian basin could have reserves of between 200 billion and 300 billion barrels of oil, making it one of the three largest deposits in the world. In contrast, Saudi Arabia has around 260 billion barrels and the United States less than 30 billion barrels.[46]

Optimistic estimates suggest that by 2010 the new oil from the Caspian region and Central Asia could represent at least 3 to 4 percent and possibly as high as 6 percent of the world's oil supply.[47] If those figures are correct, pessimistic projections predict, the Caspian's caviar and its lazy lifestyle will eventually disappear.

Before leaving the Caspian, I went to the Rooftop of the Caspian, a half-hour cable car ride above towering white birch and pine trees to the top of a mountain some 3,000 feet above sea level. It had become the Caspian's most popular attraction since the revolution. During peak months, the line for the cable car could be several hours long. The sweeping view across the vast sea's soft blue waters, the salty breeze and the crisp air were a powerfully gentling combination. At the top was a forested park with picnic tables, coin-operated telescopes and paths for walking in the woods.

Among the picnickers on a warm autumn day was Bagher Salman-zadeh, a young London-trained economist who had brought his wife and energetic toddler up from Tehran for the weekend. Cocooned in the Caspian from the political and economic turmoil in Tehran, we talked at length about the Islamic Republic at a crossroads—and how Iranians then felt about their revolution. I asked Salmanzadeh whether outgoing, curious and generally fun-loving Iranians were willing to accept indefi-nitely the restrictions and slower pace of an Islamic lifestyle.

"Not completely. That's why things are changing, slowly," he said.

Like a lot of Iranians, he framed his answer in terms of the revolution-ary dress code, the barometer of the Islamic government's flexibility—or lack of it.

"A few years ago I couldn't wear this type of clothing," he said, refer-ring to his fitted jeans and striped rugby shirt.

"At the same time, I don't think the government will ever give up *hejab,* not as long as the clerics and other conservatives still have a role in government," he added, shaking his head.

"You'll never see bikinis back on the Caspian, not in my lifetime."

CHAPTER 7

WHITHER THE REVOLUTION?

Talk about God and don't think about anything else.
— AYATOLLAH KHOMEINI[1]

If the clergy distance themselves from the factual realities of the present-day world, they won't be able to fulfill their role.
— PRESIDENT KHATAMI[2]

I HEARD the demonstrators long before I saw them.

"Allahu Akhbar," the crowd roared in tribute to God's greatness.

In small groups and individually, hundreds of students were heading
toward a green open-back truck parked in the center of Tehran University. It was laden with amplifiers and covered with posters. Students on
the back of the truck were using a bullhorn to rally new arrivals while
others on the ground distributed placards and banners. The sunny, late-
autumn afternoon was perfect for a march through the capital. The atmosphere was almost festive.

"Down with violence," exhorted Ali Tavakoli, a stocky student leader
with a thick brown beard.

"Down, down," the kids shouted back in unison. "Down with violence."

Tavakoli then led the crowd through the litany of the day's political targets.

"Down with monopolists," he yelled—"monopolists" being the conservative camp and its vision of only one "right path" for Iran and Islam.

"Down with Taliban Islam," he cried, denouncing the kind of rigid Islam of neighboring Afghanistan—so strict that it made Iran look wildly liberated.

"Down with American Islam," he shouted, a reference as much to the Islam practiced in Saudi Arabia and other pro-Western states as to America.

"Down with the Great Satan," he yelled, the euphemism for the United States government made famous by Iranian students a generation earlier.

With each cheer, the students chanted rhythmically, "Down, down."

"Khatami," Tavakoli then bellowed through the bullhorn, his arm thrusting into the air. "Khatami is the real face of Islam."

"Khatami," he continued. "Now is the time for a dialogue of civilizations."

"Khatami, Khatami, Khatami," the crowd roared back in an open-ended refrain.

The student demonstration in the first week of November has been an annual event since the 1979 student takeover of the American Embassy. It's held to commemorate the hostage drama that dragged out for 444 days. Almost two decades later, it still had the status of a national holiday.

But in 1998, in keeping with Iran's deeply fragmented political scene, Tehran hosted two rival demonstrations.

The first was on November 2, two days before the real anniversary. It was organized by the Office to Foster Islamic Unity, a well-organized coalition of student groups from fifty campuses all over Iran. It was the renamed, reconfigured heir to the movement that originally seized the sprawling American compound. That much smaller and originally ad hoc group—which nonetheless once ranked as the world's most famous student organization—had called itself Students Following the Imam's Line.

More than the name had changed, however. A generation later, the students' message was quite different too. Or so the signs indicated.

"In the heat of revolutionary fervor, things happen which cannot be fully contained and judged according to usual norms," proclaimed one placard. It was a computer printout on three white pieces of paper mounted on raw cardboard.

A second declared, "Nothing should prevent dialogue and understanding between the Iranian and American nations."

"Terrorism is a product of despotism and nihilism," pronounced a third placard.

But the fourth was the topper. "Not only do we not harbor any ill wishes for the American people, but in fact we consider them to be a great nation," it said.

And there was no danger of mistranslation or misunderstanding a nuance. All the signs were in English.

One of the demonstrators distributing placards was Behzad Nikzad, a lanky industrial-management student with long sideburns and the standard three-day facial stubble who was dressed in a brown-and-beige checked logger's shirt. Nikzad told me that he was twenty-five, making him only six when the embassy was taken. Like all the students I interviewed, he had no memory of the drama. Yet he had nonetheless come from a university near the Caspian Sea for the rally.

"Most of these slogans are the words of President Khatami. But this is also what more than sixty million people are now saying," he offered, as he handed out a placard with another Khatami quote declaring, "No place for absolutism."

"We're beginning to have real freedom in Iran. And after twenty years, we want to avoid any one group's having a political monopoly," he said, the group of boys around him nodding in agreement.

"November 4 is for those who are monopolists, the ones who say 'Death to America.' We like the American people and their history. Students today would like to have relations with America and I'm not afraid to say it," he added.

To preempt the so-called monopolists, the Office to Foster Islamic Unity had mobilized its supporters two days before the annual commemoration. The students wanted to strike first. Their goal, outlined in an advance statement, was to "crush the wall of mistrust," not make it worse.

Why the change of heart? Was America now fully acceptable? I asked the young men who'd surrounded me.

"Oh no, America still owes us an apology," replied Bahman Karimi, a bespectacled senior in literature at Tehran University who carried a fat tome in English entitled *Dictionary of Politics*.

"If America hadn't made the coup in 1953, then we wouldn't have such a situation now," he said, as others nodded.

For Americans, bad relations date to the 1979 embassy seizure. But for Iranians, even those who like the United States, varying degrees of suspicion, animosity and resentment date back to the 1951–53 nationalist movement led by Prime Minister Mohammad Mossadeq that openly confronted the shah and forced him to flee the Peacock Throne for Rome. Alarmed by Mossadeq's nationalization of Iranian oil, his nonaligned foreign policy and the socialists in his broad political coalition, American and British intelligence orchestrated riots that forced the prime minister's resignation.

The Americans who ran the operation were Kermit Roosevelt, grandson of former President Teddy Roosevelt and a longstanding Mideast intelligence specialist, and Norman Schwarzkopf, Sr., father of the general who led Operation Desert Storm against Iraq.[3]

The operation was successful. The shah was back home in less than a week.

Even the former American hostages later acknowledged Washington's role—and Iranian anger that an attempt at evolutionary political change had been blocked.

"One thing that the CIA was good at in those days was organizing opposition groups. General Schwarzkopf's dad went in there with Kermit Roosevelt and handed out money to pro-shah demonstrators and assisted in the ouster of Mossadeq and the return of the shah," Colonel Chuck Scott, a former hostage who oversaw American arms sales to Iran, recalled in 1999.

"From that day on, the people of Iran believed, basically as an article of faith, that the United States was behind the shah, so therefore the shah was a puppet of the United States and we were responsible for all the shah's failings, shortcomings and excesses."[4]

American involvement in the coup d'état marked the first stage of Washington's political intervention in Iran—a fact many Iranians, including Ayatollah Khomeini, never forgot. The embassy seizure was part of the response a quarter century later.

"But circumstances change," reflected Karimi, the bespectacled student demonstrator. "This demonstration is an invitation to the American people for a dialogue. We Iranian students are doing whatever we can. Now it's the turn of American students."

I asked Karimi just what he wanted from his American peers.

"We want them to lead their political officials into having better relations with Iran," he replied.

The orderly crowd soon massed behind the truck and started winding its way around the campus grounds, picking up more and more students coming out of classes. Males were in front, females in the rear in their own section led by their own banners. Then they all hit the streets for the forty-five-minute march along one of Tehran's widest boulevards to the walled-in American diplomatic compound.

Toward the front of the crowd was a short, fiftyish mullah with a white turban, meaning he wasn't a descendant of the prophet Mohammad. A couple of the young men around him tried to shoo me back to the women's section. But Mohammad Araghi, head of the Islamic Propagation Organization, motioned for me to walk with him.

I asked Araghi about the contradictions in the student rhetoric—one minute the crowd condemned the Great Satan and the next called for dialogue and understanding. Not many Americans, I told him, would be interested in dialogue with the prospect of still being condemned in the next breath.

"We shout death to policies, not to the scientists and thinkers of America," he said, as if the difference were obvious and I had to be daft not to understand.

"Even the Imam said the people in the United States are good people. What the United States government has done to Iran is what's bad. That's what we want to end."

The distinction is not new. Both before and after the revolution, Iranians differentiated between a government and its citizens—not only in the United States. It's a common attitude in the broader Middle East and even throughout the Third World.

What did he think of President Khatami's proposal for a dialogue? I asked.

"We think Islam historically has invited all people to a dialogue," he responded, as the mobile phone in a pocket underneath his robe began to ring softly. He answered it and told the caller to wait.

"We hope the new generation of Americans can understand what we say. People, especially students, can help us and the Americans to close the big gap," he added, and then went back to his call.

Since the hostage ordeal had ended in 1981, the American compound had been used as a vocational school by the Revolutionary Guards. The compound, surrounded by a high brick wall, included the ambassador's residence, several sizable staff houses, a chancery, a consulate, a warehouse (nicknamed the Mushroom Inn by the hostages because of its windowless walls and dark, damp atmosphere), an office building, a commissary, a power station, an athletic field large enough for soccer, a couple of tennis courts and a pool, a parking lot and large landscaped areas. I once met a guard who'd taken computer classes in the old chancery, but various attempts I had made over the decades to gain access had failed.

During the revolution's first decade, the perimeter wall had become a street gallery for revolutionary art and graffiti. Several slogans from Ayatollah Khomeini had been painted in huge letters. One declared in both English and Farsi, "We will make America Face a Severe Defeat." Most of the art had long since faded—until this anniversary. The rival rallies had prompted organizers of the second commemoration, scheduled two days hence, to dispatch a crew of artists to create new images.

The most startling addition was a bright cartoon of the Statue of Liberty—with a skeleton's skull rather than a woman's face.

When the students arrived, the truck parked in front of the redecorated fence and the demonstrators, who'd grown to almost three thousand, massed around it. Tavakoli then introduced the rally's featured speaker—one of the original students who had stormed the embassy. Ibrahim Asgharzadeh had probably been the most recognizable figure in the American Embassy seizure. In 1979, he'd been the primary spokesman for Students Following the Imam's Line. He'd often briefed American journalists in front of the same brick wall.

"This takeover is not a game! This is a nest of spies," he'd angrily told reporters that first day.

Now graying, bespectacled and dressed in a charcoal suit, Asgharzadeh had matured into paunchy middle age. His views had also mellowed by 1998.

"Our dealings with the hostages were not directed against the American people and not even against the hostages themselves," he told the crowd. "We're not terrorists. We were wronged. If we hadn't captured the embassy, we couldn't have dried up the root of America in Iran."

But a generation had passed, he said. And different times and different interests called for different attitudes.

"Today we invite all the hostages to return to Iran as our guests," Asgharzadeh told a new generation of students. "Regarding relations with America, we must look to the future and not to the past."

As he spoke, several passersby on the shop-lined sidewalk across from the embassy stopped to listen.

"We have a new language for the world," he continued. "We defend human rights. And we'll try to make Islam such that it won't contradict democracy."

Before Asgharzadeh could finish, the students began cheering wildly— or, as one local journalist later reported it, "they reacted with thunderous applause."[5]

Not everyone agreed, however. On the edge of the crowd, a few dozen Hizbollahis moved in angrily. They were clearly looking for some kind of physical confrontation. They taunted the students as "sissies" and "clowns." And they held up an American flag with the obvious intention of burning it.

From the truck, Tavakoli interrupted to implore the Hizbollahis to stop.

"To burn the American flag is to oppose Khatami," he shouted through the bullhorn. "We beg the other group not to give food to the foreign media.

"The flag is the symbol of a people and we are *not* against the people," he shouted louder.

That's all it took. The defiant Hizbollahis countered with their own chants. "Khamenei, Khamenei, we support you. We follow the orders of Khamenei," they yelled. "We are the Basij. Iran is full of Basij."

Then they set fire to the flag.

Riot police with shields and sticks moved in quickly to separate the two sides. The flag went up in flames so fast that it didn't really matter. But police nonetheless deployed as a wall between the two groups, just in case.

After the police intervention, I went over to talk to one of the Hizbollahis.

Babak Shahrestani, a tall, gaunt student with light-brown hair and a shirt hanging loose over jeans, appeared to be the leader. He wasn't as friendly as the marchers had been, but he wasn't hostile either. He told me he was a major in chemical engineering at Amir Kabir University, one of several universities in Tehran.

I asked what he hoped to achieve. "To defend the Supreme Leader and to defend revolutionary life," he said. "That's our duty now—and in the future."

What did he think of Khatami's call for cultural exchanges and a dialogue of civilizations? I asked.

"If journalists, students, scientists, professors and normal people want to come, that's okay. But we don't want officials here. America didn't have ambassadors in Iran. It had spies. That's what all the embassy documents showed," he said, referring to the thousands of classified papers hastily put through shredders as the embassy was being stormed that were later meticulously reassembled and published by the Students Following the Imam's Line.

"The situation today is still like a wolf and a calf. America still refuses to release our assets," he said, alluding to the protracted court proceedings at the Hague. Since the hostage crisis ended in 1981, a special U.S.–Iranian tribunal had been struggling to settle disputes over Iranian assets in the United States frozen during the hostage crisis and American assets in Iran nationalized by the revolution. Eighteen years later, several cases still had to be resolved.

"If Americans come again to Iran, we're afraid they'll spy again and make conspiracies against the people or try to topple the government or make the nation dependent again," he added, reflecting the paranoia that pervades a new generation too.

"But we warn them: If the Americans try to do any of those things to us, we'll do the same thing again to them too."

The otherwise orderly rally soon broke up and the various students and police departed. Despite the Hizbollah disruption, there was a sense in the air that something had changed, that a moment of history had been made, that the healing process had begun and that rapprochement was around a corner—a distant corner maybe, but a corner.

Two days later, on the official anniversary, I went back to the embassy. This time, streets were clogged with buses that had brought in demonstrators—virtually all schoolchildren had been given time off for the newly declared Pupils' Day. They ranged in age from about eight to seventeen or so. But all had clearly been born after the revolution—and after the hostages were freed.

November 4 had also been officially dubbed Anti–Global Arrogance Day, the kind of belligerently grandiose title that tweaked the revolutionary imagination. Artists had been busy finishing their updates during the intervening two days. A huge American Stars and Stripes, flanked on both sides by large Israeli flags, had been painted across the wide boulevard in front of the embassy. New banners now hung along the road.

One, under a painted version of the famous photo portraying a blindfolded hostage, declared, "We put America under our feet."

Another warned, "Iran will strongly fight against the belligerent policies of the United States."

This demonstration's quite different intent was evident in the theatrics, rhetoric and honored guests. As black smoke rose into a blue sky from burning effigies of Uncle Sam and American flags set ablaze every few minutes, an unnamed official launched the rally with a declaration that "the Iranian nation still considers the arrogant government of America its number-one enemy."

Several conservative members of Parliament, including the Speaker who'd been defeated by President Khatami, were among those who cheered, according to Tehran Radio, although I didn't see them. For security reasons, no one was allowed to watch from the roofs or balconies across from the embassy. The best I could do was peer awkwardly through the lattice grillwork from one of the few business offices that dared to be open on November 4. I ended up back on the street.

This crowd did not, however, include any of the original captors. All but a half dozen of the four hundred students that ended up with major roles in the embassy takeover had joined the Khatami camp. And the rest had apparently decided to keep their distance from this event.

The guest speaker this time was General Mohsen Rezai, who had headed the Revolutionary Guards for more than a decade. A large, thickset man with a black beard and two small pinkie rings, Rezai was widely associated with many of the regime's efforts to export the revolution and other misadventures. He had deployed troops in Lebanon, and at home his forces had helped train Islamic militants from other Muslim states. After Khatami's election, he had been moved to the Expediency Council headed by former President Rafsanjani.

"Our stand against the United States is not a political jest. It's a real struggle to preserve our international prestige," Rezai told the crowd. Yet even he hinted at the eventual possibility of rapprochement—albeit with the emphasis on "possible" and on terms still partially unacceptable to the United States.

"There are four conditions before any negotiations. As long as the Americans don't meet our conditions and don't adopt a more humane approach toward us, negotiations are impossible," he warned.

The first condition was a public statement from Washington at some unspecified "international forum" apologizing for seventy years of "dictatorial behavior." The second was a commitment not to interfere in Iran's internal affairs. The third was a pullout of American naval forces from the Persian Gulf. And the fourth was to release Iran's frozen assets.

"Many of the people who say today, 'Why doesn't Iran establish ties with America?' mainly emphasize the short-term reasons for the embassy takeover," Rezai said.

"But there were bigger, long-term reasons for taking over the den of spies," he said. "And those shouldn't be forgotten!"

For all the anger in words and symbols, however, the second demonstration actually had a carnival atmosphere. The playful, rowdy crowd—probably several times larger than the first rally—was a telling contrast to the serious and orderly march by university students who'd actively chosen to participate, who'd given up something to join the march and who'd listened intently to the speakers. During the second rally, schoolkids wandered down the boulevard chatting, joking, playing—and ignoring virtually everything else. For all the amplifiers, the speakers were sometimes difficult to hear because of the raucous street noise. The schoolchildren, several of them told me, had been rounded up to come. For most, it seemed more like a field trip into history than a protest.

"Who'd object?" said a sixteen-year-old named Nezam who sported the first hint of fuzz on his chin. "It's a day off school and a free trip downtown with my friends. I don't have to go home to chores or class assignments."

A few of the kids had red bandannas tied around their foreheads emblazoned with "God Is Great," the kind of look that had been sported by young Basij volunteers during the war with Iraq. But far more wore T-shirts heralding the Chicago Bulls, the Los Angeles Lakers and a dozen other big-name American teams. A few sported baseball caps worn backward. One teenager had a picture of *Titanic* star Leonardo DiCaprio splashed across his chest.

I asked several of the boys—and this crowd was overwhelmingly male—how they felt about America, about its cultural and sports icons, about the potential for renewed relations. Most expressed interest, some even excitement, about the United States, especially in the context of

American musical groups or CD-ROM games that they reeled off—and that I'd never heard of. I couldn't find one kid who said he'd prefer to stay at the embassy when he was given a choice between the rally or watching an American sports event or movie, even if only on television.

A fifteen-year-old named Hadi pushed his way through the group to ask for help with a visa so that he could study or work in the United States, at which point several of his friends chimed in that they'd like one too.

Throughout the morning, the rally droned on and on, without much order or sense of focus. The young became more distracted, and the speakers more difficult to hear. Afterward, the kids noisily trooped back onto their buses, clogging traffic and leaving behind a thick litter of pennants, miniature posters and other items intended as keepsake souvenirs. It was, in the end, rather anticlimactic.

The two rallies were a microcosm of Iran at a crossroads—the wide domestic political divide, the tough foreign-policy choices and the difficult decisions ahead, all shaped by lingering fears. They also underscored the role of Iran's youth as barometers of the revolution's appeal—and as agents of change.

With more than a bit of irony, the rival rallies also brought Iran full cycle. A generation earlier, at another critical juncture, the debate over the revolution's future course had also played out over the United States.

In 1979, the real issues that had spurred the American Embassy takeover were internal: What a new government would look like and who would control the levers of power. "Power" was the pivotal word. Like other revolutions, the struggle for much of the first two decades pitted power held by a new revolutionary elite against real empowerment of the people.

After Ayatollah Khomeini's dramatic return from his last base of exile in Paris, controversy raged for months among the disparate factions that had once marched together against the shah. The fiercest clashes played out over a new constitution in the fall of 1979. The secular technocrats who ran the first revolutionary government didn't want the clergy to dominate. But militant clerics feared a strong secular leader might open the way for yet another dynasty, as had happened with the last shah's father. Islamic intellectuals wanted religion to be just one element guiding the state. But Islamic zealots wanted Sharia as the only law. Ethnic minorities wanted provisions for political and economic autonomy.

But socialists proposed political centralization and strict regulation of the economy on behalf of the masses.

The divisive process had produced sixty-two draft constitutions and more than four thousand constitutional proposals.[6]

The introduction of an omnipotent Supreme Leader, or Velayat-e Faqih, in the final draft produced a fierce reaction, even among government officials and some clerics. In October 1979, Prime Minister Mehdi Bazargan, a diminutive, French-educated engineer and a leader in Mossadeq's nationalist movement of the 1950s, began warning of a "dictatorship of the clergy."[7] Debate raged as Iranians prepared for a nationwide referendum on the constitution set for December.

As politicians clashed, the population grew visibly weary and wary of the revolution. The anticipated empowerment was proving to be elusive. Instead, a wave of summary trials, political purges and executions spawned widespread public fear. The economy ground to a halt after nationalization of private banks, insurance companies and key industries. Dozens of publications were closed down, while new restrictions made criticism of the revolution, the revolutionaries or Islam punishable with prison terms. Other temporary freedoms evaporated. So did public enthusiasm. The revolution was in trouble.

An almost uncanny confluence of events then diverted attention. The most important was the arrival of Mohammad Reza Shah Pahlavi in the United States for treatment of lymphatic cancer. It was a trip wire for xenophobic fears about Washington's intentions—and for suspicions about a repeat of America's 1953 intervention to restore the monarchy.

In late October, some eighty students assembled in a north Tehran suburb to debate a response. They were enraged by the American decision to take in the dethroned shah. They were also alarmed by political trends at home. After heated debate, they agreed to stage a sit-in at the American Embassy. The timing was deliberate. They set the date for November 4, the fifteenth anniversary of Khomeini's eviction from his homeland—provoked by his protest over new laws granting immunity to Americans from criminal prosecution in Iran.

The students' original plan actually had limited goals. It was also supposed to be more peaceful than the first embassy takeover.* The students only intended to hold out for three to five days.[8]

---

*The embassy takeover on November 4 was actually the second time the United States compound was overrun. On February 14, in the heady and breathless days immediately after Ayatollah

"We weren't supposed to occupy the embassy. We just wanted to protest. We didn't think it was going to last long," Asgharzadeh, the captors' spokesman, recalled a generation later.[9]

"We expected that American youth, seeing how they reacted to Vietnam, would be supportive of us. We took no issue with the United States as a country. We were simply saying that we had a problem with the way the United States treated Iran. We expected Americans to understand this," he added. "But it didn't turn out that way."

What they really didn't expect was Ayatollah Khomeini's reaction, especially in light of his genuine apology after the first embassy takeover.

"The leader of the revolution gave us his blessing," Asgharzadeh said. Several of the hostages later recalled how their captors were stunned by the unexpected announcement on Tehran Radio.[10]

The Imam's intervention quickly transformed a limited student protest into a protracted international crisis.

The calculations were clever. With the constitutional referendum closing in, Ayatollah Khomeini saw an opportunity. The takeover proved to be the stimulus needed to break the political stalemate. Angered by the embassy seizure, Prime Minister Bazargan resigned, leaving the clerics who ran the Revolutionary Council in control. The zealotry that had dissipated since the Imam's return was also whipped up again in demonstrations by tens of thousands in front of the American compound. Whatever their problems, Iranians once again felt that they had gained the upper hand, that they had stood up to another "oppressor." Ayatollah Khomeini was close to the mark when he dubbed the takeover "the second revolution."

Tapping into a fierce nationalism built up over almost three millennia, the Islamic revolution was once again on a roll.

Four weeks later, the Islamic constitution was put to the nation for a vote. The timing—the day after Ashura, when Shi'ite fervor was at its peak—was again deliberate. The new momentum, spurred by religious

---

Khomeini's return, Islamic zealots and leftists stormed the embassy grounds with guns ablazing. With only thirteen Marine guards to cover the whole complex, the Americans soon surrendered. But the takeover lasted only a few hours. Ibrahim Yazdi, a naturalized American pharmacist who returned from Houston, Texas, to be revolutionary Iran's first foreign minister, mobilized a group of Tehran University students to liberate the embassy. Rival groups of Iranians fought for control of the compound. Yazdi's force prevailed. Ayatollah Khomeini later dispatched a delegation of mullahs to the embassy to convey his apologies for actions "contrary to his wishes" and his relief that no one had been hurt. For the next nine months, Iran still sold oil to American companies. Iran, in turn, continued to buy American military equipment. The basic tenets of the long-standing relationship didn't change.

sentiment, pushed the new constitution through with 99 percent of the vote. The militants, the Islamic revolutionaries and the zealots had won.

The embassy takeover was not the last time they would tap into other events to revive public fervor, particularly among young activists who so often proved to be the instruments of the revolution's survival. The regime reaped even bigger benefits after Iraqi troops invaded Iran's western border in 1980. Nationalism rallied public spirit. Attention was diverted this time for eight years. And with the help of millions of young fighters, including the newly created Basij volunteers, the theocrats cemented their control.*

Two decades after the revolution, a new generation of Iranian youth still provided the most important barometer of its appeal. But instead of being the primary instrument of the revolution's survival, a new student movement had become the main agent pressuring for change.

The new activism also returned public focus to the revolution's original goals—and the struggle between power and empowerment.

"This revolution has had some problems," Ali Reza Taheri explained to me quite bluntly. Taheri, an intense Tehran University engineering student who wore aviator glasses and gesticulated with the help of a yellow mechanical pencil, was on the leadership council of the Office to Foster Islamic Unity, the group that had sponsored the first of the two rallies at the American Embassy in 1998. I met him at the group's headquarters, a converted house off one of central Tehran's back alleys. The humble furnishings in the somewhat run-down facility included file cabinets taken years earlier from the American Embassy.

"Our priority for the next ten years will be to correct the inside of the regime, to see changes particularly in politics and culture," Taheri continued.

What kind of corrections? I asked.

"The three goals of our movement are freedom, justice and religion. Democracy is at the top of the list. We want a peaceful space with dialogue—a country that is full of freedom, independence, dignity, dialogue, defending all human beings' rights without harshness. We also want all aspects of the constitution to be practiced, especially those parts that have been forgotten, such as the rules that support civil society."

---

*The same motive was behind Ayatollah Khomeini's 1989 death verdict against Salman Rushdie for blasphemy in *The Satanic Verses*—ten months after the book came out and only after protests had erupted in India, Pakistan and Europe. Sensing another issue to exploit, his fatwa rallied attention when the regime couldn't accommodate public expectations after the war with Iraq ended.

Leaning across a long conference table decorated with a vase of plastic roses, he again offered candidly, "We've had some problems in building a democracy. But with the election of President Khatami we hope finally to spread freedom. We want all people and all political parties who have accepted the constitution to participate freely in activities and have a role in government."

The student movement, which claimed fifty thousand members from universities throughout Iran, considered itself a model of Iranian democracy. It had six coleaders, male and female, who came from different schools. The term of office was one year, with possible reelection for two more years—but no more.

"We have term limits," Taheri stressed. "Every year we have new leadership so no one's influence lasts too long. Also, the students make decisions according to their own time."

Who or what were the obstacles to their goals? I asked.

"The conservatives have been against full democracy," he said.

The students' emphasis on democracy reflected a profound shift on a chicken-and-egg issue that has defined all ideological debate in the twentieth century, not only in Iran: What is the best route to empowerment? And which goal should come first—the political freedom of democracy or the economic equality of socialism?

Although Islam strongly backs the rights of private property, the revolution first called for "social justice" to better the lot of the poor and oppressed. The theocrats had initially argued that redistributing national wealth and creating social justice would eventually empower.

Two decades later, I asked Taheri which was more important—democracy or social justice?

"In terms of values, both are equally important," he replied. "But first we should have democracy. Through democracy, people can achieve social justice."

In terms of both policies and practices, the student movement seemed to have evolved over the years, I commented.

"Today it's not necessary to have such revolutionary behavior. We're looking for peace and security. Now we have the slogan about the rule of law. And we defend the security of all Iranians and all non-Iranians in our country," Taheri responded.

"We're not going to accept the kind of behavior from the beginning of the revolution. If there's a problem with any embassy, the government should solve it. Times have changed."

Taheri paused for a moment. "Like the revolution, we've gone through stages. First we tried to stabilize and reinforce the revolution. When Iraq invaded, many of our members were defending the country. Afterward, we focused on reconstruction," he continued.

"We've only come back in the last few years—now that we have a new mission."

In fact, Iran's student movement was largely dormant, as a political player, after the 1981 hostage release and until the mid-1990s. With a special touch of irony, its revival was due in large part to the urging and aid of Ayatollah Khamenei. The Supreme Leader, who had a limited power base, viewed the students as a potential force to rally behind him and to keep the revolutionary movement on course. To get them started, he provided the building on Shahid Rajab Beghi Street, a little alley named after a martyr in the war with Iraq.

What Ayatollah Khamenei hadn't counted on was how much the revolution had changed Iran's young—and how some changes the revolution considered successes might actually turn around and spark new challenges.

What the revolution produced was the most educated class of young people in Iranian history. From 1979 to 1999, the literacy rate shot up from 58 percent to 82 percent, Iran's Ministry of Education reported.[11] And the number of university graduates soared from 430,000 to more than 4 million.

By the revolution's twentieth anniversary, the first postrevolutionary generation also proved to be the most politically savvy and demanding generation in Iranian history. And they had the numbers to make the demands—especially with voting rights beginning at age fifteen. By the year 2000, more than 30 million people, roughly half the country, were under twenty-one years old. And 65 percent of Iran's population was under twenty-five.

But the largest segment of Iranian society had also been born or brought up after the revolution. The vast majority had no memory of the shah or personal anger about the monarchy. Iran's young were supposed to be the "Islamic generation," but what little they remembered of Ayatollah Khomeini had been relegated to the history of childhood, at best. For most Iranian youth, the unavoidable pull of globalization also relegated religion to just one corner of their lives.

Their pasts were unique. So were their visions of Iran's future—about everything from the foundation of an Islamic state to its relationship with the outside world. Some of their most controversial positions centered on the role of the Supreme Leader.

"His help to us in the past doesn't mean we have to follow him or agree with him on everything. We're independent," explained Ali Tavakoli, the husky, bearded student who'd led the cheers at the first rally. He'd joined us late in the conference room of the student headquarters.

"We had a meeting with the Supreme Leader recently and we told him that when something is not a religious issue, we can come to our own decision. On many issues, we have independence to do what we believe is right," he added.

Had the role of the Supreme Leader changed? Had the position's power changed? I asked.

"When the Imam was alive, because of his special characteristics, no one asked if he was supreme or not. But afterward, people believed that the Supreme Leader should operate according to the constitution—where the duty and position are clear. He's not above the constitution," Tavakoli said. "He's subject to it, like everyone else."

In the late 1990s, the bold defiance of Iran's young became a regular feature of Iranian life—not only during commemorations of the American Embassy takeover. Few issues were off-limits at increasingly frequent public protests.

The arrest of Tehran's reformist mayor, Gholamhossein Karbaschi, sparked a series of angry demonstrations to demand his release—and the resignation of those who arrested him. The first was canceled after student leaders acceded to an appeal from President Khatami to help restore calm to the capital ten days after his arrest on April 4, 1998. But some four thousand students showed up anyway.

At a rally commemorating the first anniversary of President Khatami's election, students boldly shouted for the ouster of Iran's judiciary chief, Ayatollah Mohammad Yazdi, one of the half-dozen most powerful conservatives.

"Resign, Yazdi, resign," the Tehran University students demanded, in a chant that soon became a standard at student rallies.[12]

After the 1999 disclosures that a death squad operating inside Iran's Ministry of Intelligence was responsible for the gruesome assassinations of leading writers and dissidents, hundreds of students dared to take to the streets to demand the firing of Iran's intelligence chief.

"This is the demand of the nation—sacking the intelligence minister," read one of their banners.[13]

Elections also often spawned protests. Several demonstrations demanded that the vetting process for candidates be changed or revoked altogether. Three thousand kids turned out to protest the rejection of several leftist candidates in small parliamentary by-elections in 1998.

"Monopolists want to appoint people to Parliament, not have them freely elected," the demonstrators charged during a march near Tehran University.

"Khatami, we support you," the students then chanted. "You need to be given more authority."[14]

The students even protested the way they were treated at other protests. In Isfahan, a thousand students and professors turned out at the University of Technology on Valentine's Day 1999 to protest the beating of students at another rally earlier in the month. They verbally attacked police for failing to intervene when hard-liners tackled demonstrators.[15]

Even students studying to be mullahs protested. At Shahid Shahabdi Seminary, theology students demanded the dismissal of the head seminarian and lower tuition fees. Female theology students joined the protest to demand an investigation into the poor level of instruction, inexperienced teachers and inadequate research facilities.[16]

Two decades after the revolution, Iran's youth and their demonstrations had become a defining force in the country's political climate—maybe even the defining force.

"Students are the engine of change in Iran. Their sheer numbers give them more weight than in other societies—or even compared with the student movement during the revolution," said Nasser Hadian, the political scientist at Tehran University who has been my longtime guide to the youth movement.

Heshmatollah Tabarzadi, a lean young man with a neat beard who perpetually palmed a set of yellow worry beads in his hand, has organized some of Iran's boldest protests. At one, some two thousand students showed up to demand that women and nonclerics be allowed to run in the 1998 Assembly of Experts election. The assembly selects the Supreme Leader—and is also empowered to dismiss him.

"The purpose of our revolution was to allow us to breathe in a free atmosphere," he had brazenly told the crowd.

The rally had been broken up when Hizbollahi thugs pelted the platform with rocks, lunged for the sound equipment and attacked students. Police had eventually intervened to disperse the crowd.

At another rally that probably ranked as the boldest student protest ever held in revolutionary Iran, Tabarzadi had called for constitutional changes that would let all Iranians elect the Supreme Leader, limit his term of office and better define his role—basically converting the job of Shi'ite pope into a mere political role, and a temporary one at that. He'd even dared to suggest abolition of the Supreme Leader's job altogether.

Tabarzadi kept a bloodied shirt in his office as a souvenir of the aftermath. Young vigilantes raided his office, breaking windows, computers, furniture and other equipment. When I went to see him in 1998, he still bore the scars on the side of his head from their beating. It was the third time he'd been physically injured by Hizbollahis.

"What we wanted in the revolution was freedom and rule of law. But over the past twenty years, we've instead experienced religious totalitarianism," he told me.

Tabarzadi headed the Union of Muslim University Students and Graduates. He was something of a perpetual student who'd been an activist since the revolution—which is why "graduates" had been tagged on to the title. But students still considered him a peer in a society where the young often work for years before going to university. Iranian students aren't always in their teens or twenties.

"What we want now is the rule of law, not the rule of the clerics," he explained. "The clerics are only pretending to have the rule of law, when they really have absolute power."

Tabarzadi had little confidence that Iran's new leadership would be able to solve Iran's mounting problems, even if the conservatives conceded political defeat.

"President Khatami is a positive man, but his actions aren't strong enough," he said, adeptly pushing the yellow beads with his thumb across his palm.

"After all, he's a cleric. He's still one of them."

EIGHT MONTHS AFTER that conversation, Iran erupted. The crisis began with Tabarzadi's arrest. By the summer of 1999, the aging "student" had gone too far. Conservatives apparently decided that if vigilantes couldn't silence him, then the judiciary would. He was picked up on July 6. The charge: insulting the Islamic system.

Tabarzadi's arrest was the first of several moves that inflamed long-sizzling student frustration. The subsequent explosion was arguably the most important week of open confrontation inside Iran since the revolution—or, appropriately, in a generation.

The main spark, however, was press freedom. On July 7, Parliament approved a sweeping new law to muzzle Iran's increasingly outspoken media.

"The press is a gateway for a cultural invasion, so we must take measures to stop it," declared Speaker Ali Akbar Nateq-Nouri from the dais of Iran's ornate Parliament.

"Some people, under the pretext of press freedom, are plotting against the system."

The Ministry of Culture and Islamic Guidance tried to block the move—and warn legislators about the repercussions.

"Freedom can't be repressed by any law. We have to create laws in accordance with freedom, not freedom according to our laws," Mohajerani pleaded with Parliament.

"If a crime is committed, we'll take legal action. But let the people first say what they want to say."[17]

The media had once again become a battleground for a couple of reasons: During President Khatami's first two years in office, the new crop of feistily irreverent newspapers and magazines had arguably become the reform movement's biggest achievement. They not only reported what was really happening, they also defined the third republic's new agenda.

Second, with conservatives controlling the main instruments of power, plus radio and television, the independent dailies, weeklies and monthlies were the reformers' only source of influence. They could challenge the conservative clergy in ways even other mullahs of equal rank could not—at least in public. They dared to snoop and scoop and even spoof the uncompromising and purist theocrats.

But Mohajerani's last-ditch appeal failed decisively. The impact was immediate. Within hours, a special court run by the clergy banned *Salam,* a big supporter of President Khatami. The leftist newspaper was charged with disturbing public opinion, endangering the nation's security and violating Islamic principles—as well as an array of other offenses listed in forty hefty files, the court announced.[18]

What really riled conservatives was a *Salam* scoop. Based on a top-secret document, the paper claimed that the senior intelligence official arrested for organizing the 1998 death squad murders of writers and dissidents had also drawn up a master plan for the press restrictions that

Parliament had just passed. *Salam*'s revelation was explosive because it alleged a central mastermind and base of operations for an orchestrated—and officially sanctioned—campaign against reformers.

It also undermined the intelligence agency's claim that the death squad assassins were renegades who'd acted on their own initiative. (Rather conveniently, the intelligence officer had died mysteriously in prison after ingesting hair remover. His death was ruled a suicide. No one ever bothered to explain how he got access to hair remover.)

The *Salam* story crossed yet another threshold for Iran's media. It meant no branch of government or society was above scrutiny—not even the intelligence community, not even the clergy. It also opened the way for other papers to follow suit.

Students were big readers of *Salam,* and the story aroused fury among Iran's young. It confirmed what many had long suspected.

Not surprisingly, students were also the first to react when conservatives abrogated tentative press freedoms. The new law and the ban on *Salam* signaled an offensive with a transparent goal: to blunt—even bludgeon—the voice of reform in the run-up to the pivotal parliamentary elections in early 2000.

The students' reaction was also immediate. The next day, July 8, undergraduates at the University of Tehran mobilized a protest. It began as a limited rally of only some five hundred or so students on campus—tiny compared with the number involved in the anniversary of the American Embassy takeover. But it quickly became big, and then bloody, when Ansar vigilantes intervened. The thugs attacked students, pelting them with rocks and closing in to beat them up.

Throughout the fracas, police stood nearby and watched, basically giving Ansar a free hand, eyewitnesses reported. Students eventually fled or retreated into campus dormitories.

The disturbance might have remained just another in the growing string of confrontations between Iran's youth and the conservatives' allies and surrogates. But this showdown didn't end after the students dispersed.

In the middle of the night, Ansar thugs and police raided the Tehran University dorms.

"Police knocked in the doors where we were sleeping and attacked us with tear gas," one student told local reporters.[19] Students were then "beaten like lunatics" with iron bars and chains as weapons, he said.

Some were struck as they lay asleep in their rooms. Other students were roused from bed and beaten. A few were pushed from second- and third-floor windows. Even the dorm for foreign students was attacked. Students from Bosnia, Tanzania and India all complained of being "terrorized."

Television coverage and photographs later showed dorm rooms badly trashed and furniture overturned. Windows no longer had panes. Gaping holes in several doors were proof that they'd been kicked in. A few rooms were so badly burned that they were basically gutted.

The dorm attack also produced the first serious casualties. One student was killed. Dozens had to be treated at hospitals for an array of injuries. Hundreds more were arrested.

The next day, a Friday, the deeply divided government turned on itself. The Ministry of Education blasted police for their raids and "violent intervention" in the campus dorms.

"This incident was part of a calculated plan to plunge the country into crisis by a number of willful forces," the ministry charged. It described the students as "wise and pious" and said they didn't deserve "such insulting treatment."

Students went much further. Although the Muslim sabbath is normally a day when Tehran virtually shuts down, thousands of young men and women showed up outside the dorms to show support for their peers. They also demanded the ouster of government hard-liners.

"Death to despotism!" they shouted, their cacophonous cheers echoing for blocks. "Death to dictators!"

They left no question who they meant. "Khamenei must quit," several chanted with reckless abandon.[20]

Again Ansar vigilantes intervened. Again clashes erupted. Again, police basically watched.

But this time the students left something behind before they were forcibly dispersed. In a bold communiqué, they listed fourteen demands, and conditions for ending their protest. They included:

- Reining in police and putting them under control of the government rather than the clergy.
- Opening all trials to the public, ending the use of the judiciary as a political tool and firing Ayatollah Mohammad Yazdi, Iran's chief judge.
- Making secretive state institutions, all the way up to the Assembly of Experts, give full public accountings of their activities and decisions.

- Public investigations into intelligence and security operations against dissidents.
- Freedom for all political prisoners—most notably Tabarzadi and Mohsen Kadivar, the popular young cleric.
- An end to all house arrests, especially for Ayatollah Montazeri, the Imam's former political heir who'd turned into the regime's leading critic—and then been isolated beyond public reach.
- An end to bans on any newspapers, the repeal of the new press law and the firing of the head of Iranian television and radio.

"Those who have based their rule on the principle of conquest or terror are now facing the consequence of their atrocities," the student communiqué declared.

"There is such a volcano of national rage erupting in the university, as the eternal vanguard for freedom, that if the demands of this nation are not heeded by the tyrannical forces, the flame of this inferno shall burn all the present authorities in this regime."[21]

Despite the hyperbole, the student protest was, in fact, not the first shot of a counterrevolution—at least not yet. The vast majority of protesters wanted to change the system from within, not scrap it entirely. In the Islamic Republic, they wanted the main emphasis on "republic" rather than "Islamic."

"We should not assume that this movement could turn into a revolution," editorialized Neshat, the reformist newspaper that was often a mouthpiece for the student movement. "It's neither possible nor desirable."[22]

Yet the summer of 1999 marked a turning point. And by day three, July 10, the students were on a roll. Some ten thousand showed up Saturday for a sit-in on campus. They defiantly shouted at security forces and chanted for the police chief's dismissal.

A second column marched from a dormitory several miles away. Along with banners and posters of President Khatami, several students waved the blood-stained shirts of youths who'd been injured in earlier clashes.

"Students, stand up, your brothers are being killed," they chanted rhythmically over and over, louder and louder.

"Shame on police. End this despotism!"[23]

The police issued a statement charging that they were only doing their duty against an illegal gathering. But it didn't wash.

By day's end, Education Minister Mustafa Moin had resigned. So had the university chancellor. The university's board of directors threatened to quit unless the growing number of detained students were released.

In his resignation letter to President Khatami, Moin apologized to the "innocent students" and charged that the security forces had "paved the way for a national crisis. I consider this incident a suspicious measure aimed at sabotaging the trend of political development."[24]

Emboldened by the growing public furor over the police action, thousands and thousands again rallied on day four, July 11, on Tehran University grounds. Their rhetoric almost taunted hard-liners.

"Either Islam and the law—or another revolution," they chanted.

Others heckled the Supreme Leader.

"Ansar commits crimes and the Leader supports them. Oh, great Leader, shame on you," they jeered.

"Khamenei, show some dignity and leave the people alone!"[25]

Support for the students was widely visible. Drivers caught in traffic as the students marched from campus through city streets honked rhythmically in support. Tehranis who lived along the route offered water to counter the sweltering heat of an Iranian summer. University deans and faculty pledged that they'd stage their own sit-in the next day in sympathy with the students. And journalists on more than twenty newspapers announced a nationwide strike on July 13.

"As a sign of solidarity with their colleagues in *Salam,* they will lay their pens down Tuesday and no newspapers will appear on Wednesday," *Neshat* reported.[26]

With the tide decisively against them, police were ordered to stay away. Without police cover, vigilantes did too. There was no violence.

The first four days of demonstrations were the biggest and boldest challenges to an Iranian government since the revolution. They also had a special legitimacy because many protesters were children of the original revolutionaries. The higher-education system had long given preference to applicants with Islamic "credentials"—the offspring of veterans or "martyrs" from the eight-year war with Iraq as well as children of clerics, civil servants, military officials, bazaar merchants who financed the revolution and the poor in whose name the revolution was undertaken.

"The biggest problem for the regime in general is its own children, who aren't in tune with them," reflected Haleh Esfandiari, a former Iranian journalist who has also been my mentor on Iran.

"It must be chilling to see their own children rising up against them," she added.

Four days of spiraling unrest was more than conservatives could handle. More than one thousand youths had been arrested, yet each day even more students showed up. So police issued a warning: Demonstrations without a government permit would no longer be tolerated.

That's all it took. On July 12, day five, an even larger crowd of students turned out on the streets of Tehran to pledge that they wouldn't give up until their demands were met. The mood was intense and angry.

At one point, an attempt to read a statement from the Supreme Leader was met by shouts of "Down with the dictator" and "Commander-in-chief, resign!"[27]

But the Leader was not the only target.

In a telling moment, many students began a chant directed at the Iranian president. He had so far been unseen and unheard from during the biggest crisis of his presidency.

"Khatami, Khatami, where are you?" students shouted plaintively. "Khatami, your followers are being killed."[28]

With police ringing the campus, helicopters hovering overhead and Ansar vigilantes on motorcycles circling the campus outskirts, a confrontation was inevitable.

Police closed in as soon as students began their march toward the city center, forcing them to scramble back onto campus grounds and barricade themselves inside the university. They set fire to old tires at the tall steel campus gate to hold off police and their allies. But it wasn't enough.

After police fired waves of tear gas onto the campus grounds, vigilantes armed with cables, chains and metal rods went after the protesters—and chaos erupted.[29] At a campus mosque, medical students tried to treat the growing number of injured, although they had little more than water and gauze.

"There's so much tear gas you can hardly breathe," said a local correspondent covering the protest.[30]

In a separate incident downtown, police clashed with a thousand protesters on the Vali-e Asr Square. Riot police wearing shields and helmets beat students into cages mounted on the back of pickup trucks, which took them off to jail. Even photographers were arrested to keep them from capturing the trouble on film.[31]

By day five, unrest was also no longer confined only to Tehran. In more than a dozen cities, from Tabriz in the north to Mashhad in the west and Yazd in the south, students at other universities protested in sympathy with their Tehran brethren. They too demanded further and faster reforms.

As unrest spread nationwide, President Khatami finally made his first public comment. He blasted the dorm attack as one of the most bitter events since the revolution. But then he urged "my children" to respect the law and avoid violence.

"The bulk of the students have shown restraint and prevented [the rallies] from turning into a difficult national question. And they have pushed for demands in a logical way," he said.

"Now students should cooperate with the government and allow law and order to be established in society. You should not commit illegal acts, so that in a calm situation we can make a firm decision in the interests of the system. . . . The important thing is to use this nation's unity for more fundamental goals."[32]

That night, state television's evening news broadcast a tough police ultimatum: Protests must stop—or else. "Police have been ordered to create order and stability—and to prevent *any* unlawful gatherings,"[33] it reported. For good measure, the gates to Tehran University were locked.

It didn't deter the students. On July 13, day six, they massed early outside the university entrance.

"We don't want a government of force," they chanted, in rhythmic repetition. "We don't want a mercenary police."[34]

Crowds of Tehran residents swelled the numbers. To the student cheers, they responded, "Students, students, we support you. Iranians die before they accept humiliation."

Surrounding them all was a full array of Iranian security forces: uniformed and plainclothed police, Revolutionary Guards, riot squads, Basij volunteers plus Ansar vigilantes wielding clubs, stones and even meat cleavers. Helicopters flying low over the campus directed the action from above.

The demonstration quickly disintegrated into street battles after riot squads fired tear gas into the crowd and guns into the air. Basij and Ansar thugs who'd been lurking on the outskirts then went after the students.

"Army brothers, why kill brothers!" students shouted as they tried to hold off the assault.

The chants were an eerie replay of the revolution. The same cry was the rallying slogan for students in 1979 when the caretaker government left behind by the shah relied on the military to beat back demonstrators loyal to Ayatollah Khomeini. That government collapsed a mere eleven days after the Imam's triumphant return—because the army heeded the protesters and announced support, albeit reluctantly, for the opposition. They opted to avoid a wider and prolonged civil conflict.

This time, security forces remained loyal. Riot police surrounding the university campus hauled away both men and women, some by the hair, to waiting vans.

Yet the protests refused to die, as pockets of unrest erupted elsewhere in the capital.

Tehranis, both students and residents, demonstrated outside the Ministry of Interior and *Kayhan* newspaper, Iran's most hard-line paper. They rallied at Revolution Square, the capital's largest intersection. They marched on Val-e Asr Avenue, the tree-lined boulevard that bisects the capital from the cool northern suburbs to the arid southern plains. Each incident also quickly deteriorated into open clashes. Students hurled stones. Riot police blocked off side roads, allowing armed vigilantes on motorbikes to beat, chase, club and knock demonstrators to the ground.[35]

In the commercial district south of the university, shop windows were smashed and a neighborhood bank and empty buses were set afire during the melees. Much of Tehran hurriedly closed—stores rushed to pull down protective steel grates, shopping centers and office buildings locked front doors, gas stations turned away drivers. Public transportation ground to a halt. Even Tehran's legendary bazaar opted to shut down.

Throughout the day, state television and radio repeatedly broadcast a speech by Supreme Leader Khamenei calling for calm and blaming the unrest on foreign enemies, notably the United States. It had limited impact. Tehran echoed most of the day with the whine of ambulances, police sirens, drivers honking in sympathy, students shouting in anger or fear. As the drama unfolded, Tehranis poured onto balconies, windows and rooftops to watch.

By the end of day six, Iran's security forces did regain control. Basij and Ansar patrolled deserted streets throughout the night to ensure no further outbreaks. Several were heard shouting their own chants.

"We donate to the Leader the blood in our veins," they cheered. "Praise to you, Hizbollah."[36]

Students later alleged that their peaceful protests over the previous two days had been infiltrated by provocateurs who'd manipulated confrontations into riots to discredit them. The claims gained widespread credibility among both local and foreign reporters in Tehran.

Either way, Tehran was on the brink.

But the sixth day turned out to be the last day of trouble. Students ceded to President Khatami's appeal for a return to calm. They, too, began to worry about where the spiraling unrest was headed. At least five students had by then been killed, hundreds injured and more than fourteen hundred arrested.

The youths did not, however, abandon their demands. To press their case, the new Select Council of Sit-in Students demanded meetings with Iran's top politicos, including the Supreme Leader.

"The Council will put off a decision to hold any demonstration, gathering or sit-in for the future. So it begs our students and our mature people not to join any demonstration, gathering or sit-in that could be manipulated by anarchists and people who favor violence," declared a four-page communiqué.[37]

The new council, which included representatives from eleven Tehran universities, in turn demanded that the government restrain "paramilitary forces."

In a separate letter delivered to the police chief, Hedayat Lotfian, as well as local papers, the council said it "expected" Lotfian to "bravely resign and bravely admit your mistakes.

"Can you give an answer before God or the Iranian people if you continue your post as chief of this force?" the students demanded. They charged that police under Lotfian's command had joined forces with "vigilante savages."

A student leader warned what could happen if the government didn't listen and act. "If officials don't respond accordingly to this tremendous call for reforms, the door for peaceful negotiations will shut," Ali Afshari told local reporters.

"We may be the last generation that believes in peaceful recourse."[38]

Conservatives ignored the appeal. They instead opted for their own demonstration on July 14, day seven of the unfolding drama.

The hastily organized "national unity" parade was a scene right out of the revolution's early days. Thousands turned out to hail the Supreme Leader and condemn Iran's enemies.

"Death to America! Death to Israel! Death to the Hypocrites!" they chanted.

Posters of the Supreme Leader were handed out to anyone who would hoist, carry or wave them. Long white banners proclaimed, "My life belongs to the Guide." Children were bedecked with headbands that pledged, "Khamenei is our Leader."[39]

In a message read to the rally, Ayatollah Khamenei warned that trouble might not be over, and called for support from his allies.

"My Basij children must reserve the necessary readiness and be present at any scene where they're needed to intimidate and crush the enemies," he said.[40]

Other speakers warned that students detained during the protests could face the death sentence for spreading "corruption" and "fighting God."[41]

But for all the bluster, the rally actually lacked passion and energy. Many, perhaps even most, of those who turned out were government employees and their relatives and friends. Military personnel admitted they'd been given the day off to attend in civilian clothes. The bazaar had been closed down to encourage merchants, businessmen and shoppers to attend.

In a land that loves its rallies, the turnout was also significantly lower than the huge crowd that had celebrated President Khatami's first anniversary in office in 1998. It was tiny compared with the revolutionary demonstrations a generation earlier. And most participants strolled casually, as if on an outing. Many paid little heed to speakers, instead chatting among themselves or window-shopping.[42]

Over the next few weeks, Iran's conservatives, clearly scared, took other steps to strengthen their position.

Parliament first torpedoed a long-negotiated compromise that would have weakened the Council of Guardians' role in screening candidates. It was a major blow to reformers' efforts just to win the right to run for office.

"Absolute vetting power has now been legalized. Parliament has taken the last arrow from its quiver to fire at political progress," lamented the reformist paper *Khordad*.[43]

The judiciary then approved a draconian "thought-crime" law that made virtually any criticism of the state illegal and punishable with stiff sentences. The bill described political crimes as "any violent or peaceful act by a person or group against the regime."

Most ominously, it also made illegal "any contact or exchange of information, interviews or collusion with foreign embassies, organizations, parties or media at whatever level which could be judged harmful to Iran's independence, national unity or the interests of the Islamic republic."

One news outlet compared the proposed bill's sweeping breadth with the thought-crimes depicted in George Orwell's *1984.*[44]

Third, to flex conservative muscle, the Basij carried out the largest military maneuvers ever conducted in the capital. Some fifty thousand young volunteers were hurriedly mobilized in a massive show of strength three weeks after the unrest was put down. They staged drills to quell demonstrations, conducted mock commando raids, held shooting competitions and even ran parachute drops.

"These maneuvers show determination to defend the revolution from the curse that threatens it," a military official told the local press.[45] The "curse" was never specified, but the implication was that it came from inside the country, not outside Iran.

Meanwhile, Ansar vigilantes once again went after individual dissidents. In August, Soroush was attacked as he met with supporters in the eastern city of Mashhad. What made this encounter different—and more menacing—was that the meeting took place inside a private home, not a public venue. Ansar shouldn't have even known about it or had access to it.

Fourth, conservatives continued to arrest students weeks after the unrest ended. In early August, police picked up Ali Tavakoli, the charismatic student leader who'd led the earlier demonstration at the American Embassy.

"Tavakoli faces charges of fanning the unrest through his speeches," reported *Qods,* a leading conservative paper.[46]

Finally, the judiciary tightened its squeeze on the reformist press. The publisher and editors of *Salam* were tried on charges of libel, defaming members of Parliament and publishing state secrets. In August 1999, the Special Court for Clergy ended up banishing *Salam*'s top editors from journalism for several years.

And in September, the judiciary closed *Neshat.* Its offense: "Insulting the sacred decrees of Islam and the Supreme Leader."

The trigger was an article calling for an end to capital punishment and the "eye-for-an-eye" standard of Islamic law.

"Penalty of death by hanging and vengeance laws are not solutions to murders or corruption on earth. And they are not in accordance with the

United Nations' Universal Declaration of Human Rights," *Neshat* pronounced in a bold editorial.[47]

The article enraged Ayatollah Khamenei.

"Anyone who renounces the fundamental precepts of Islam must be seen as an apostate—and death will be his punishment," he shot back.[48]

Neshat was the fourth reformist paper closed in eight months. It was also the third time the same editors and staff who launched *Jameh,* then *Tous* and finally *Neshat,* had been shut down.

Who came out ahead from the historic week of unrest and its aftermath?

Not the students, at least short-term. Nor the reform agenda.

Indeed, the introduction of violence as the students lost control of their protest provided just the pretext conservatives needed to clamp down even harder. The unrest ended up limiting the students' ability to impact the system rather than increasing their clout—at least short term.

The protests also exposed the precariousness of reform. Although 70 percent of Iran's population had voted for change—by electing President Khatami—they didn't have the means to pull it off.

The president once told Iran's soccer team after it qualified for the World Cup, "We're in the same boat, you and I. Only you've been more successful in satisfying the people's expectations. I still have a long way to go."[49]

At the same time, student rage ignited simply by new press restrictions was a harbinger of what could lie ahead if conservatives succeeded in blocking all political openings.

The bottom line: Conservative bullies may have won this battle. But long-term, they were unlikely to win what was becoming an open war over Iran's future.

The real loser, however, was the broader society in Iran. In a deeply divided country, one side had the numbers, the popularity and the vision. The other had the instruments of power.

Without compromise, without change, Iran was increasingly combustible.

ON THE TWENTIETH ANNIVERSARY of Iran's revolution, the most popular new hangout for young Iranians in Tehran was the Argentine Pizzeria, a restaurant with black walls on the corner of Argentine Square.

The dark cul-de-sac side street was one of the liveliest places in the capital on a Thursday or Friday night.

"The pizza's a lot better at other places, but that's not why we come here," explained a tall teenager named Ali who wore a long tunic-like shirt over baggy jeans. He and his friend Ramin came often, despite past arrests.

"The last time, the Basij came and took everyone on this street to the police station in a minibus. They made us all sit on the floor and they wouldn't let us call our parents," Ali recalled.

"We had to write down that we wouldn't do it again. After a few hours, they let us use the phone. The next day we went to a place like a court and again we had to write that we wouldn't do it again. Then my parents paid a fine."

How long ago was that? I asked.

"Last month," Ali replied.

What if he was arrested again?

"Maybe some lashes," he speculated.

As we talked, several clusters of girls sauntered up and down the short street between the cars and the pizzeria, repeatedly pretending that they had just arrived or were just leaving. Only a couple went inside the restaurant. Several girls were dressed daringly by Iranian standards, their scarves pushed back to expose a bit of hair, or tight-fitting jeans visible beneath a *roopoosh,* or bare ankles exposed above platform sneakers.

Most of the boys hovered in groups around cars. Every few minutes, a white Korean-made Kia sedan whizzed down the street, did a sharp U-turn wheelie at the end, then flew back by us. In the midst of the comings and goings, an old man tried to interest the boys on one side of the street and the girls on the other in buying two green parakeets in a tiny cage.

I asked Ali what he and Ramin, a high school senior wearing a navy Adidas sports jacket, got out of it. Was it worth the hassle or danger?

"Sometimes we meet girls. Sometimes a guy will convince some girls to let him give them a ride home. Most of the time we just hang out. The most I usually get is a phone number," Ali said. "But at least a phone number is a way to talk to a girl."

Access to telephone numbers was actually a big deal among Iran's young. And those who didn't get them tried anyway. Prank calls—a risk-free way to find a female to talk to—became a chronic problem in the revolution's second decade. In a nine-month period in 1998, some 56,000 prank calls were registered with authorities in Tehran alone. And it was probably a small fraction of the real number, officials conceded.

Newspaper editorials railed against the practice as immoral. "The telephone, if not used properly, could be a means of violating society's sacred values," warned an editorial in the conservative *Qods* newspaper.

"Alexander Graham Bell would never have thought his great invention would be used one day to create trouble. It's a form of sadism. The people behind these calls are mentally ill."[50]

Parliament even imposed new laws to stop the practice. First came a warning. Then the telephone company disconnected a prankster's telephone for longer and longer periods—a move that in 1998 led to the disconnection of four thousand telephone lines in Tehran alone. Frustrated that the practice only seemed to get worse, Parliament finally passed a new law stipulating prison terms of up to six months for repeat offenders.

But the law had marginal impact on the core problem: Iran's young, who lacked the fear and inhibitions of their elders, were increasingly emboldened to defy both tradition and Islamic laws.

In some ways, it played out fairly innocently. As the 1990s progressed, Tehran was rife with tales of forbidden youthful encounters across the gender barrier. Males and females walked together in parks. They planned picnics in "separate" groups of males and females on blankets positioned just a bit apart. They hung out in malls where the boys might brush by the girls and ask for a telephone number or suggest a meeting somewhere else. They crossed paths at Tehran's new Cyber Café, where the young flocked to surf the Internet and send e-mail over complimentary coffee—albeit on separate floors for the separate sexes.

Young Iranians proved ingenious in their efforts to socialize. One of dozens of tales I heard over the years involved Basij stopping eight kids on the ski slopes reserved for females in the Alborz Mountains. All were covered in the required head covers and body drapes, but facial stubble had given four of them away. Desperate to be with girls, the boys had donned Islamic dress as a disguise.

The bold defiance among Iran's young began to redefine the parameters of public behavior. It also had explosive potential.

The possibilities were visible when Iran became the last of thirty-two teams to qualify for soccer's 1998 World Cup—courtesy of a last-minute two-two draw in a game with Australia played in Melbourne. Tehran literally erupted. The euphoria easily rivaled the jubilation when Ayatollah Khomeini returned. In many ways, it was the same kind of release.

Led by the young, millions poured out of homes, businesses and stores to join spontaneous celebrations on the streets. Teenagers danced atop cars with tape decks blaring. Chants and cheers moved like a wave across crowds—and back again. Girls dared to let headwear slip off to their shoulders. Car caravans honked their way amid both male and female celebrants partying through the night. No one dared stop them. In fact, several young soldiers were seen joining the festivities.

The nightlong revelry in strict Iran cemented the power of the young. The soccer stars quickly gained a kind of stature that rivaled President Khatami's standing—and that clearly surpassed anyone else inside or out of government. Iran had new heroes.

It happened all over again after Iran's first World Cup match in France, when Iran stunned the United States with a two-to-one victory. The government tried to take precautions to prevent another round of revelry. But it was no use. Even though the game didn't begin until almost midnight, Iran's young, some still in nightshirts, poured into the night after it ended.[51]

For good reason, the events became known as the "soccer revolution," the moment when a form of nationalist pride that the regime could no longer manipulate or control prevailed.

The young were so brazenly defiant in large part because the Islamic republic offered so little incentive to obey—or simply because it offered them so little. And what was available was often beyond reach.

For years, the Qods Department Store, a five-story building on Vali-e Asr Avenue that is the local equivalent of Woolworth's, has been one of my barometers of Tehran's economy. During one of the toughest periods of the war, the food section carried little more than ketchup, tea, rice, uneven squares of hard cheese and some scrawny pieces of unidentifiable meat. Even rationed staples were often sold out. Other sections that sold clothes, household appliances, toys, books, handicrafts, luggage and toiletries also had pitifully limited variety.

After the war, in response to a consumer frenzy, Qods stocked up. And as the revolution began its third decade, it was also catching up with what was available elsewhere in the world. The Simpsons had made it to Qods. Masks of Bart and sister Lisa, complete with spiked pastel hairdos, dangled from shelves laden with games in the toy section.

"Children looooove these," a salesgirl told me, as she put one on and bobbed her head to mimic the Simpson kids.

The Ninja Turtles had arrived too. At a stall of video games, a twelve-year-old boy named Shahab who had amazingly long black eyelashes was entranced by a demonstration tape. He was clearly a fan. On his wrist, he wore a plastic digital Mutant Ninja Turtle watch—lift up the shell to tell the time. And his tennis shoes had lime-green turtle laces and encrusted mock turtle shell on the sides.

"The turtles are on his underwear too," his mother volunteered.

Elsewhere, several teenage girls at the cosmetics counter were inspecting nail polishes in funky greens, alluring reds and trendy blacks, with lipsticks to match, of course, plus a rainbow spectrum of mascaras, eye shadows and blushers. Several older teenage males were inspecting sports equipment and looking at books nearby. A nineteen-year-old named Mohammad was leafing through a Persian biography of Albert Einstein. Other young males were in the men's toiletry section where Brut aftershave, Right Guard deodorant and Gillette razors were among dozens of foreign products neatly displayed in glass cases. In the basement, the food market was packed with staples as well as delicacies like salmon, tropical fruits and cream-filled cakes.

The wealth and variety of goods were typical of Iranian tastes—quite worldly. They also reflected Iranian expectations.

The economic reality, however, was something else.

Two decades after the revolution, Iran had to cope with formidable arithmetic: Its population had doubled since 1979, but its oil income had plummeted by two-thirds. Oil that had been selling for $35 a barrel in 1979 had dropped to less than $10 by 1999, the lowest price in a quarter-century. And oil accounted for 80 percent of Iran's exports.

The Islamic republic had a few other money problems too. Its currency was in free fall, having dropped in value from 67 rials to the dollar in 1979 to more than 8,000 to the dollar in 1999. And while people were paid in rials, prices of consumer goods were often pegged to the dollar. The government said inflation hit 24 percent in 1998, but diplomats estimated it was probably closer to 40 percent.[52]

As a result, the average take-home pay of an Iranian civil servant wasn't enough to cover the average family's rent and food.[53] The vast majority of Iranian families couldn't afford the $1 for the Bart Simpson mask, much less the $22 for the imported Ninja Turtles video game.

The job scene was just as bad. Unemployment, officially 10 percent, was unofficially at least 25 percent, with millions underemployed and even more holding down two or three jobs. University professors averaged less than $100 a month, forcing them to tutor, do research for government ministries or advise businesses to supplement unlivable incomes. A young teacher I knew called in sick whenever she got a freelance translation job, which she needed to survive even though she still lived with her parents. Primary school teachers made less than $25 a month in 1999. So many people left early or called in sick at their first jobs in order to be able to work second and third jobs that schools, factories, businesses, shops and government offices all had service, labor or production problems.

Even government officials usually had other jobs. Members of Parliament often worked as teachers, in business, in journalism or at mosques. Several cabinet ministers held outside jobs as heads of associations. So many senior officials worked two and three jobs that Parliament passed a law in 1995 banning members of government from holding more than one official post. But it didn't stop the practice.

The problem of multiple jobs had spillover. After an Iran Air crash killed 132 people in 1993, Tehran's press ran letters to the editor blaming the economy—specifically conditions that forced air controllers to moonlight long hours as cab drivers to make ends meet.

The regime also bore the sapping drain of subsidies of fuel, medicine and foodstuffs such as bread, a measure originally introduced to help the oppressed. But costs soared as Iran's population doubled. Subsidies cost a whopping $11 billion by 1999—when oil income was estimated to earn a mere $12 billion.[54]

Fuel was the most costly subsidy. Iranians paid only between 7 and 10 cents a liter, only about a third the cost of producing it—and the cheapest price to consumers in the world. But fuel consumption multiplied fivefold during the revolution's first two decades. So the world's third-ranking oil exporter, after Saudi Arabia and Norway, actually had to import some $300 million worth of refined oil products—at world market prices—to satisfy domestic consumption in 1999.[55]

Iran's Parliament finally approved a 75 percent price rise in 1999—after rejecting the government's proposed hike of almost 300 percent as grossly inflationary.[56] But the price was still under 20 cents a liter.

The government's problems were exacerbated by the fact that a host of foundations, technically affiliated with the regime but largely self-governing, controlled as much as 40 percent of the economy.[57] The Qods Department Store chain, for example, was run by a foundation. And the foundations were virtually all controlled by conservatives—and loyal to the policies of the Supreme Leader. They made any serious or sweeping economic reforms almost impossible.

Perhaps most embarrassing for the theocrats was the debt issue. In the 1980s, the regime liked to gloat that, despite economic sanctions and diplomatic isolation, it had paid off the $7.4 billion foreign debt accumulated by the Pahlavi Dynasty. Over the same period, the United States became the world's largest debtor.

But in the 1990s, an uncontrolled foreign shopping binge for billions of dollars' worth of consumer goods and postwar rearmament left the theocracy with a far greater debt in 1999 than the monarchy left behind in 1979—and a gap between expectations and reality that had never been wider.

The bottom line was that Iran's economic mess also produced a far greater challenge than its deep political divide.

The economic heart of Tehran, both physically and historically, is in its Great Bazaar, arguably the best of its kind in the Middle East, not only for Persian carpets. A covered maze of dusty alleyways, glittering lights and spicy aromas stretching over six square miles, the bazaar is made up of thousands of large shops and hole-in-the-wall stalls. Iranians say virtually everything can be purchased through Tehran's bazaar and—since much of its business is conducted through a vast and often invisible network of which actual merchandise is but a small part—it's probably true. In shop windows, I've seen the unlikeliest things over the years, from silk carpets woven with the face of the Mona Lisa and a $5 bill to a frisky little red negligee, sheer as chiffon.

On one of my visits in the late 1990s, the bazaar was bustling, as always. At the gold section near the entrance, clutches of women wrapped in chadors peered at gold bracelets, rings, pendants and necklaces in a row of jewelry shops. Iranian jewelers normally thrive in both good times and bad because gold is a form of saving, especially in a country where banks don't give interest because of the Islamic ban on usury. Instead, banks pay "dividends" based on business. Gold also always sells well because even the poorest women are given jewelry to mark a birth or other important personal or family occasions.

But the bustle was deceiving.

"They're just looking," said Ali, the proprietor of a small corner shop, as he put a sugar cube on his tongue and then, Iranian-style, drank a hot cup of tea that dissolved it.

"Everyone in Iran is just looking these days."

True enough, most of the women were peering through windows from outside the stores.

I asked where the money had gone. He wound his finger several times around his head to indicate a turban.

Anger ran deep not just because the clergy had mismanaged Iran's economy and national resources for two decades. Corruption was also so rampant that it had spawned a second black economy. In the minds of many Iranians, the mullahs in power and those around them were the ones profiting the most.

"The clergy tries to keep itself clean. But you can't do anything anymore without paying off this mullah's son or that mullah's brother-in-law—and these days usually both," Ali said.

Historically, bribery has been part of business in the Mideast, even part of the ritual of trade. In Iran, however, it was increasingly becoming the biggest part of a business deal—and a lot of other transactions too. Iranians called it "oiling the mustache." Bribery was commonly practiced during the monarchy too, but before the revolution, payoffs were usually a one-time thing of a known amount. Two decades after the revolution, even the smallest service called for lots of oil on lots of mustaches.

Foreigners also had to oil the mustache. Despite exorbitant overseas telephone charges at hotels, switchboard operators required regular payment to ensure they could make the connection—even though it was all direct dialing. Dozens of diplomats told me how they regularly paid off police to provide protection—even though that's what the Iranian government had already assigned and paid them to do. To ensure a visa extension, a generous gratuity to the local office that stamped it in a passport always helped—even though another government office had already written a formal letter granting it. Problems at customs about a journalist's laptop computer, tape recorder or other equipment could be solved by slipping someone a few thousand rials or, even better, a few dollars—even though the equipment was perfectly legal to import for personal use.

What riled Iranians was that the real workers usually reaped the least, while the significant payoffs went further up the chain of command to the ruling clergy's inner circle.

The dimensions of rot within the system were reflected in the regular buzz on Tehran's grapevine about this top mullah's recent acquisition of a fancy Mercedes or that top cleric's business monopoly on some agricultural or industrial product or a third mullah's palatial new villa near the shah's old palace—questionable purchases for any politician, but particularly for the representatives of God's government. Corruption, after all, had been one of the issues that eventually undid the last shah.

I asked Ali if history was repeating itself.

"I supported the revolution. *Bazaaris* are religious by tradition. They were religious long before the revolution. And if there were no economic difficulties, this system would be good, very good," he replied.

"But the way things are now, we can't go on like this. The cost is too high."

After the trip to the bazaar I stopped by one of my favorite bookstores, where the proprietor is known as a thoughtful pundit on local affairs. I explained what I had just seen and heard.

"Ah yes, don't I know," the proprietor responded. "People are more depressed now than during the war. The economic situation affects us in more ways. We had expected that when the war ended, things would be better. But instead they're worse. You feel it in every aspect of life.

"This is a society that has always loved jokes," the proprietor continued. "Throughout most of the revolution and the war years, people still told wonderful stories. In the end, we could laugh at our troubles. But I don't know how long it's been since I heard a new joke, or reheard an old one. Even parties are boring, because all people can talk about is the economy.

"I'm the same way," the proprietor added. "Do you know that a set of tires now costs more than a million rials, as much as you would have paid for a new car before the revolution? Chicken now is the same price as in Germany, but we're paid Third World salaries. And cars are more expensive than in Europe."

Indeed, Iran's economy was in such bad shape that it was one of the few places in the world where the value of a used car actually went up. At Tehran's Golden Horse dealership, run by a group of retired Revolutionary Guards, the price tag on a 1975 Camaro was over $5,000, while a 1983 Chevy Blazer was going for more than $16,000.

Beginning in the early 1990s, the pressures of a deteriorating economy sporadically exploded in Tehran, Shiraz, Mashhad and Arak. Nationwide, price hikes triggered hundreds of slowdowns and small strikes among workers demanding higher wages. Tens of thousands were involved in pockets of unrest over the years. Individually, they were usually of marginal significance. Together, they represented a serious internal threat.

President Rafsanjani once admitted the dangers—and the stakes. "You have every right to want better living standards," he told thousands assembled at Khomeini's shrine. "The Islamic system has to show that it can provide a decent standard of living."[58]

President Khatami also acknowledged that the economy was "chronically ill." He pledged to "combine fast growth with social justice without imposing hardship on the working population."[59] But it was a virtually impossible task.

As the revolution began its third decade, Tehran did take some drastic steps, such as slashing imports, digging deep into reserves and deferring payments on foreign debt—again. Twice in his first two years in office, President Khatami had to severely cut back the budget because of plummeting oil prices.[60]

But the theocrats also tried some ingenious measures. The regime began selling draft exemptions. In 1998, Iran announced that young males would be able to buy their way out of the mandatory twenty-one-month military service for fees ranging from $1,700 to $5,000.[61]

When families of martyrs killed in the war with Iraq complained, the government extended them 50 percent discounts. But gone was the sense that defending the revolution was the first and foremost duty of every young male.

Iran also turned to tourism—not just the religious pilgrims who'd come by the thousands since the revolution to visit various Shi'ite shrines. Tehran began inviting back the big-buck tourists from the West. That's when the first American tourists returned to Iran. The country once so intent on exporting its revolution also cut back its diplomatic presence abroad.

In an attempt to attract foreign investors, Iran even announced plans to return some assets—including businesses, factories, villas and apartment blocks—that had been confiscated after the revolution. The motive was to convince investors that their money was safe.[62] So much for redistributing the wealth. After a long ban, Iran also revived the lottery—even though games of chance and betting are in principle forbidden by Islam.

None of those measures, however, made much of a difference. The core of Iran's problem really went far deeper: The theocrats knew what kind of political system they wanted, plus or minus. They had a distinct social policy, however unpopular. Their diplomacy had evolved fairly consistently, albeit to the consternation of both neighbors and the wider world. But on economic policy, they hemmed and hawed indecisively and ended up all over the map.

The central conundrum dated back centuries. And it was due in large part to the duality within Islam, which has inbuilt aspects of both capitalism and socialism, not unlike many other major faiths.

On the one hand, the Islamic legal code known as the Sharia rigidly protects the rights of private property and free enterprise. Both are also long-standing traditions in Iran that predate Islam's arrival by centuries. That's why the *bazaaris,* a term that embraces all merchants, have historically been one of the three pillars of Iranian society—on a par with the clergy and the military. Bowing to Iran's past, the Islamic constitution has a section on the rights of the people that guarantees "the prestige, lives, property rights, dwelling places and occupations of people shall be immune against encroachment."

But on the other hand, Islam also emphasizes the need for charity and public welfare. Besides the Iranian state tax, all good Muslims are supposed to pay two stiff religious taxes. *Khums* is an annual tax of 20 percent on seven forms of wealth, including business profits, precious minerals, treasure and war booty. It's for use and distribution by the clergy. *Zakat* is a wealth tax imposed in a complicated formula on gold and silver, agricultural surplus and herds of cows, sheep and camels and paid at the end of the Islamic holy month of Ramadan. It's for charity work, building mosques and schools, helping the poor repay debts and assorted other good deeds.

The idea of social justice is even more central to Shi'ism, a legacy from the persecution or discrimination against Shi'ites by the majority Sunni Muslims. Throughout the Mideast, Shi'ite communities have always established clinics, schools, welfare programs and other services to ensure their brethren were provided for and protected. In Lebanon, Shi'ite-run services were a virtual state-within-a-state. Iran is the world's only overwhelmingly Shi'ite state, so, not surprisingly, the revolution gave enormous emphasis to the oppressed, or *mostazafin.*

In other countries with strong faith, sorting out the contradictions was not as problematic because of the separation between the state and church, temple, synagogue or mosque. But in Iran, the only contemporary theocracy, the state was supposed to provide both. And Iran never figured out how to do that—or at least how to do it well. The result was often a doctrinal deadlock.

In the revolution's first decade, Iran's Parliament tried to pass laws to even out the economic disparities, but the deep rifts between government sectors always reemerged to stymie implementation. In 1980, the then ruling Revolutionary Council approved a land reform law that created such chaos and drew such criticism from the clergy and the landowners that Khomeini suspended it eight months later, and hundreds of thousands of acres were given back to their original owners. Subsequent bills on trade nationalization, expropriating the land of Iranians who had fled the country, urban land use and labor laws were, after long deliberations and compromises, passed by Parliament only to be vetoed by the Council of Guardians.

In the early 1990s, President Rafsanjani tried to push in the other direction, proposing "shock therapy" through privatization, reviving the stock market and subsidy cutbacks. This time, the executive branch's proposals were blocked by Parliament.

In the late 1990s, despite President Khatami's pledge of action, not a single significant bill dealing with the economy was submitted to Parliament during his first two years in office—except the budget.[63] The former culture minister and head of the National Library instead focused his energies and clout on civil society and local elections, perhaps in part because he knew the economy was an issue on which he wouldn't win against the conservatives. His own advisers were also deeply divided.

The toll was hard on all Iranians. But the young took by far the hardest hit of all.

In 1999, a staggering 70 percent of Iran's unemployed were its young aged fifteen to twenty-four. Courtesy of Iran's baby boom, 850,000 young people annually entered the job market—in an economy that could produce only 300,000 jobs for all ages. And those lucky enough to find employment faced the prospect of a per capita income that was only one-quarter of what it had been on the eve of the revolution two decades earlier.[64]

The crunch affected other areas of life. Schools were so overcrowded that most classes ran tightly scheduled double shifts. Universities could provide places for only one out of ten applicants. More than 8 million Iranians of marriageable age were unable to afford the costs of a dowry, *mehr,* a wedding, a spouse, independent living or children.[65]

The result was an increasingly restless generation—millions of young people frustrated in employment, starved socially, dependent on parents well into adulthood and unmarriageable.

And even more dangerous for the Islamic republic's future, their problems were virtually certain to get worse, even if oil prices shot up again. The demographic bulge worked against Iran not only for the new generation but for the generation it would produce as well.

"In ten years, Iran economically is going to look like India or Bangladesh, with a population over a hundred million and severe poverty. The gap between rich and poor will be much wider and the poor will be really poor," predicted Bagher Salmanzadeh, the young economist I'd met with his family on the hilltop overlooking the Caspian Sea.

I asked if he thought Iran's revolution might go the way of the former Soviet Union, a country that once bordered Iran and that spawned the other great revolution of the twentieth century. The Soviet economy had eventually undone its ideology.

"There are two important differences," Salmanzadeh said.

"The one thing we have in Iran that they didn't in the Soviet Union is spiritual morality. The people in Russia were very materialistic. Here there are a number who are spiritual and therefore willing or able to tolerate more hardship. There are also lower expectations. Iran is a developing country, not a superpower.

"Secondly," he continued, "the Soviet Union spent far more on military expenditures. Our budget for education is several times what we spend on defense. This government has also been clever. It ensures that the people have the basics."

So what did that mean for the future of the theocracy in another decade? I asked.

"Ah, the future on all counts will really depend on the young," Salmanzadeh said. "And they are only now coming of age."

The danger was not only that the combustible combination of frustration, disillusionment, anger and rebellion might someday swell up and threaten or even undo the theocracy. The broader danger to Iran was also the erosion of a once great and still proud civilization, one of the world's oldest.

The scope of discontent and the danger of decay were reflected in its growing problem with drugs among the young as the Islamic Republic began its third decade. To understand the potential, I called on Hamid Reza Ghaffarzadeh, an Iranian with a mop of curly hair who was a senior official of the United Nations Development Program in Tehran.

"Iran is sitting next to the drug production center of the world in Afghanistan. It's also the natural corridor from south Asia to Europe and the West. Drugs come across by every means you can imagine, including camel convoys," he explained.

Beyond the centuries-old habit of opium, narcotics had actually taken a long time to spread widely in Iran. The drug barons had promised Tehran that if they were allowed to pass through Iran, then they wouldn't peddle drugs inside the country, Ghaffarzadeh told me. Tehran's efforts to stem drug trafficking in the 1980s were also limited. With a war to fight on its western border with Iraq, it had limited resources to fight the drug traffickers on the eastern frontier.

Then in the 1990s, Iran's young began using heroin. By 1999, the number of drug users was estimated to reach 3 million.[66]

"When a young person doesn't have work and doesn't have hope and there's very little else for him to do, what does he turn to?" Ghaffarzadeh said.

"This is one of the youngest countries in the world. But how many in this sea of youngsters get to go to university? And even if they do get in, most graduates today can't find jobs. We've even produced a lot of doctors who can't find jobs. And the problem is much worse for high school graduates.

"The hope in the future is gone. And with no future here, they try and try and try to get out of the country. You don't know how many thousands of youth want to get out of Iran because there isn't much for them here. But most of them are stuck," he said.

"And all this is combined with the fact there is now a tremendous drug supply here."

Iran was candid about the problem. In 1992, Iran's Drug Control Headquarters launched a massive campaign to counter drug use that blanketed television, radio, billboards and even the back of buses. But the problem only grew worse. A 1997 study at drug rehabilitation centers found that just over half of drug users were aged between sixteen and twenty, while just over 40 percent were between twenty-one to twenty-five—or more than 90 percent born or raised after the revolution.[67]

The Islamic Republic countered with a full-scale war on the narcotics traffic coming from Afghanistan and neighboring Pakistan, deploying troops, tanks and helicopter gunships and erecting military-like barriers on the main arteries. It also cracked down on domestic poppy production, enough to win recognition from the United States. In 1998, the Clinton administration removed Iran from its official list of drug producers. Washington even suggested that collaboration on efforts to stem the narcotics trafficking in south Asia might be a step on the road to rapprochement.

Yet the numbers of users continued to go up. Frustrated by the failure to stem the tide, Iran's chief prosecutor announced in 1998 that anyone caught with more than thirty grams, about an ounce, faced the possibility of a death sentence. In 1999, the problem was so severe that 60 percent of all Iran's inmates were jailed on drug dealing, possession or trafficking offenses.[68]

For a country that considered itself to be one of history's original superpowers and still viewed itself as a rich civilization with renewed purpose, the accumulative problems of the young were ominous signs. Their numbers, their potential spawned by education, their pent-up energy, their financial problems, their nothing-to-lose attitude all promised that much more change is still to come in Iran.

The stunning political upset in 1997 that brought President Khatami to power was first and foremost the result of the young vote. If a new leadership is unable to satisfy the young, then Iran's most important constituency may push for much more serious change. President Khatami was, after all, the byproduct of change, not the leader of it.

Whether or not Iran's revolutionary ideology will survive is thus still up for grabs. The scorecard has yet to be tallied. So far, it gets mixed marks, at best.

If bettering the lot of the oppressed was a prime goal, then the Islamic Republic did passably well in some areas, such as education and child health. But it also failed seriously in others, such as the overall standard of living.

If producing a new society of devout Muslims was a goal, then the Islamic Republic did spur an Islamic consciousness. But it also sparked a deep suspicion about the powers and purity of the clergy.

If empowerment was a goal, then the Islamic Republic made inroads, but often despite the original revolutionaries.

If creating an independent state not beholden to or dependent on any other country was a goal, then the Islamic Republic did fairly well. But as in each other area, the gains were achieved at extraordinary cost.

But then that is the way of revolutions.

All the current signs indicate that the Islamic Republic is not likely to survive in its current form. The turbaned class may manage to hang on to power, although over time they almost certainly will be weakened and probably increasingly will have to work alongside those in hats—and maybe someday even ties. Iran's theocrats, however, could also eventually go the way of France's Jacobins and the Soviet Bolsheviks, fading into history because of their own unacceptable political dogmatism, internal squabbling or economic failings.

Either way, however, the Islamic Republic does deserve credit for one of the twentieth century's most important legacies. In ways never anticipated, Iran's upheaval did succeed in creating a climate for revolutions within the revolution—in women's rights, the arts and social customs, among the young and, most important, within Islam itself. Through these other movements, Iranians took bigger steps in defining a modern Islamic democracy than any other Muslim country.

And those revolutions will survive. They have already permanently changed the face of Iran. And they have planted seeds that are almost certain to influence or eventually help change the face of other Muslim societies too. The revolutions within the revolution, rather than the political system that produced the world's only contemporary theocracy, will be what eventually earn Iran the rank of the Modern Era's last great revolution.

APPENDIX I

IRAN'S TWENTIETH-CENTURY CHRONOLOGY

PRE-REVOLUTION

1905–11

Iranian protests against economic and territorial domination by Britain and Russia lead to the Constitutional Revolution by clerics, merchants and intellectuals, forcing the weak Qajar Dynasty to accept the first constitution and Parliament, which in turn limits the shah's powers.

1925

After the collapse of the Qajar Dynasty, Reza Khan, a semiliterate military officer, seizes power and proclaims himself the first shah of the new Pahlavi Dynasty.

1941

Under pressure from the British and Soviets because of his pro-Nazi sentiments, Shah Reza Pahlavi is forced to abdicate. His twenty-one-year-old son, Mohammad Reza Pahlavi, becomes king.

1951–53

In 1951, Prime Minister Mohammad Mossadeq comes to power and over the next two years nationalizes Iranian oil, moves to limit the shah's power and curtails the role of foreign interests. After the nationalist movement forces the shah to flee to Rome in 1953, American and British intelligence orchestrate riots that bring down the Mossadeq government and allow the shah to return to Tehran.

1961

Mohammad Reza Shah Pahlavi launches the White Revolution to further modernize Iran's economy and social infrastructure, including land reform and women's rights.

1963

Ayatollah Khomeini launches a campaign to oppose the shah's reforms. After calling for Iranians to rise up against the monarchy, he is imprisoned.

1964

The shah deports Ayatollah Khomeini, who ends up in Najaf, the Shi'ite Muslim holy city in southern Iraq.

REVOLUTION

1978

Uprisings against the shah spread throughout the country. Under pressure from Tehran, the Baghdad government forces Ayatollah Khomeini to leave Iraq. He ends up in Paris.

1979

The shah is forced to leave Iran on an "open-ended vacation." Ayatollah Khomeini returns from exile to a triumphant welcome. Iranians overwhelmingly vote to establish an Islamic republic, marking the onset of the revolution's "first republic," which lasts through 1989. After the shah arrives in the United States, militant students seize the American Embassy compound and take fifty-two hostages, who are held for 444 days.

1980

Abolhassan Bani-Sadr is elected the first president of the Islamic Republic of Iran. The shah dies in Cairo. Iraq invades Iran.

1981

After prolonged negotiations, the American hostages are released on the same day President Jimmy Carter leaves office. President Bani-Sadr is forced from power and flees the country. Mohammad Ali Raja'i is elected the Islamic republic's second president. In two of several bloody bombings, the new president, the prime minister, twenty-seven members of Parliament and ten cabinet officials are killed. Iranians elect Ali Khamenei to be the third president.

1982

After Israel's invasion of Lebanon and occupation of the southern half of the country, Iran deploys Revolutionary Guards in Lebanon's eastern Bekaa Valley, a move that in turn gives birth to Hizbollah, or the Party of God. Four Iranian diplomats are taken hostage by the American-backed Phalange militia in Lebanon, triggering retaliatory kidnapping of the first American hostage by a pro-Iranian group—an act that starts a trend. Over the next nine years, more than a hundred Westerners will be abducted by various militias.

1983

Pro-Iranian militias in Lebanon are blamed for the bombing of the American Embassy and the United States Marine barracks in Beirut.

1984

The United States warms up relations with Iraq after a seventeen-year break, a shift that eventually leads to American intelligence assistance to Baghdad in its military campaign against Iran. Pro-Iranian militias are blamed for the bombing of the second American Embassy in Beirut. The war escalates as Iraq launches and Iran responds to strikes on civilian areas and oil tankers in the Persian Gulf. The "tanker war" eventually leads the United States Navy to reflag and escort Kuwaiti oil tankers.

1985

Khamenei is reelected to a second and final term as president. Ayatollah Montazeri is designated as Khomeini's successor.

1986

Reagan administration officials Robert McFarlane and Oliver North conduct secret diplomacy, including a trip to Tehran, to swap arms for American hostages held in Lebanon. Three Americans are freed but three more are soon taken. The war turns in Iran's favor for the first time.

1988

The United States shoots down an Iran Air passenger plane, killing all 290 on board, including 66 children. After a series of devastating defeats, Iran is forced to accept a United Nations resolution ending the war with Iraq. Iran holds parliamentary elections.

1989

Ayatollah Khomeini fires his heir apparent, Ayatollah Ali Montazeri, and condemns author Salman Rushdie to death for his controversial book *The*

Satanic Verses. Khomeini dies. Khamenei is elected by the Assembly of Experts to replace him. Ali Akbar Hashemi Rafsanjani is elected the new president after constitutional amendments strengthen the presidency and eliminate the prime minister. The Rafsanjani presidency, 1989–1997, represents the Islamic republic's "second republic."

1991

After Iraq's invasion of Kuwait, Iran takes a neutral position on the American deployment in the Persian Gulf. Afterward, Tehran facilitates the release of the last American hostages held in Lebanon.

1992

In key parliamentary elections, many of the militants who have dominated Iran since the revolution are replaced by social conservatives who foil President Rafsanjani's political and economic reform efforts and refocus Iran on moral issues.

1993

Rafsanjani is reelected president for his second and final term.

1995

The United States tightens sanctions to enact a total economic embargo against Iran on charges of promoting terrorism.

1996

Conservatives tighten their domination of Parliament in national elections.

1997

In a major upset, dark horse candidate Mohammad Khatami, a former Culture Minister purged in 1992, is elected president, defeating Parliamentary Speaker Ali Akbar Nateq-Nouri. He promises to restore the rule of law and to encourage freedom and civil society. Khatami's election may mark the beginning of the "third republic."

1998

In a CNN interview conducted by Christiane Amanpour, Khatami calls on Iran and the United States to "crack the wall of mistrust." In an address to the United Nations, Khatami calls for a dialogue of civilizations to avert a conflict between Islam and the West. Iran and Britain announce that the death sentence on Salman Rushdie no longer is in force. The government announces that a death squad operating within the Ministry of Intelligence is responsible for the mysterious recent murders of dissidents, intellectuals and writers.

1999

Just after celebrating the revolution's twentieth anniversary, Iran finally holds municipal elections after a twenty-year delay, putting almost 200,000 elected officials into office. The political confrontation between reformers and conservatives escalates.

In response to a new law limiting press freedom and the banning of a reformist paper, students stage six days of demonstrations that escalate as vigilantes and provocateurs intervene and clashes turn bloody. Five are reportedly killed and 1,400 students arrested in the worst unrest since the 1979 revolution.

APPENDIX 2

CAST OF CHARACTERS

Note: Iranian names are spelled according to phonetic transliterations of Farsi, or Persian. Readers may be confused by different spellings of similar names. The Prophet's name, for example, is Mohammed in Arabic but Mohammad in Persian. Although the two languages use the same alphabet, the pronunciation can be different.

ABBAS I: The greatest king of the Safavid Dynasty who ruled in the sixteenth and seventeenth centuries. He made Isfahan the capital of Persia. The dynasty switched the country to Shi'ite Islam, largely to give Persia a separate identity from the neighboring Sunni Muslim Ottoman Empire.

ABBAS-GHOLIZADEH, MAHBOOBEH: Editor of *Farzaneh* magazine and a leading Iranian feminist.

ABDI, AKBAR: Iran's leading comedic actor who broke ground by playing a woman in the controversial movie *The Snowman*.

ALI, IMAM: Son-in-law and cousin of the prophet Mohammad, after whom Shi'ism is named; the Shi'a—or, as originally named, Shi'at Ali—means

295

"followers of Ali." The dispute over leadership of the new Islamic world after the Prophet's death in the seventh century led to the greatest schism ever within Islam.

ANSAR-E HIZBOLLAH: "Helpers of the Party of God" militants.

ARAGHI, MOHAMMAD: Head of the Islamic Propagation Organization.

ASGHARZADEH, IBRAHIM: Spokesman for the students who seized the American Embassy in 1979 who invited the hostages to return in 1998. One of the biggest vote getters in 1999 election to Tehran's city council.

BADR, MOHAMMAD: American-educated business administration professor and executive director of the Islamic Association of U.S. and Canadian Graduates.

BANI-SADR, ABOLHASSAN: First president of the Islamic Republic; ousted in 1981 when he fled to Paris.

BARAHENI, REZA: Avant-garde poet and one of eight drafters of the "We Are Writers" letter.

BAZARGAN, MEHDI: First prime minister after the revolution who resigned after nine months when the American Embassy was seized.

CHAHSADI, ROSTAND: High priest of the Zoroastrian faith.

CYRUS THE GREAT: One of Persia's earliest and greatest kings, he ruled in the sixth century B.C. His conquest of Babylon and freeing of the Jews are recounted in the Bible.

DARIUS I: Great Persian king who ruled in the sixth century B.C. and who ordered construction of Persepolis.

EBTEKAR, MASSOUMEH: American-educated spokesperson for the students who captured the American Embassy in 1979 and took fifty-two Americans hostage. Appointed Iran's first female vice president by President Khatami in 1997.

EKRAMI, SIMIN: Iranian sculptress.

ELIASI, MANOUCHEHR: Jewish representative in Iran's Parliament.

ELIASSIAN, HOSHAY: Senior official for Tehran's Jewish community, employed at the Ministry of Agriculture.

ENAYATI, HASSAN: Groundskeeper at Isfahan's Martyrs' Cemetery.

ESFANDIARI, AMIR: Director of International Affairs at Tehran's Farabi Cinema Foundation.

FARAJI, MORTEZA: Director of Iran's Equestrian and Equine Breeding Organization.

FILI, ALI ASGHAR: Caretaker of the former casino on the Caspian Sea.

FOROUHARY, FEREIDOUN: Doctor and director of Iran's No-Scalpel Vasectomy Clinic.

GHAFFARZADEH, HAMID REZA: Senior official in the Tehran office of the United Nations Development Program.

GHAZANFARI, REZA: Cleric in charge of Ayatollah Khomeini's home in Qom.

GOOLGERI, MASSOUMEH: Instructor at Zahra's Society, a female seminary in the holy city of Qom.

HADIAN, NASSER: Tehran University political scientist and analyst.

HAFEZ, SHAMS AD-DIN MOHAMMAD: Great fourteenth-century poet from Shiraz who is still revered in Iran; his grave is a site of pilgrimage.

HASHEMI, FAEZEH: Editor of Zan, or "Woman," newspaper, member of Parliament and daughter of President Rafsanjani.

HASHEMI, MOHAMMAD: Younger brother of President Rafsanjani and head of Iranian television and radio in the 1980s.

HORMUZI, CYRUS: Priest of the Zoroastrian faith in Tehran.

HOSSEIN, IMAM: Grandson of the prophet Mohammad and son of Imam Ali, the followers of whom founded Shi'ism; martyred in a seventh-century clash with the Sunni Muslim army of the new Umayyad Dynasty at Karbala.

JAFAARI, HASSAN: Public relations officer for the Martyr's Museum in Tehran.

JALAIPOUR, HAMID: Publisher of Jameh, Tous and Neshat, the leading reformist newspapers in Iran, two of which were forced out of business by conservatives. Imprisoned in 1998.

JANNATI, AHMAD: One of the half-dozen leading conservatives and member of the powerful Council of Guardians.

KADIVAR, JAMILEH: Former adviser to President Khatami and among the first Tehran city council representatives. Conservative attempts to have her disqualified were rebuffed. Married to the culture minister, Ataollah Mohajerani, and sister of reformist cleric Mohsen Kadivar, who was imprisoned in 1999.

KARBASCHI, GHOLAMHOSSEIN: Innovative former mayor of Isfahan and, in 1989, Tehran. A major player in Mohammad Khatami's presidential campaign. After conservatives in Parliament linked him to graft, he was convicted of corruption in 1998 and imprisoned in 1999.

KHARRAZI, KAMAL: Iranian ambassador to the United Nations in the 1990s. Appointed foreign minister by President Khatami in 1997.

KHAMENEI, ALI: Third president of the Islamic republic, from 1981 to 1989. Elected by the Assembly of Experts to succeed Ayatollah Khomeini as Supreme Leader in 1989.

KHAMENEI, HADI: A reformist cleric, adviser to President Khatami, editor of *Jahan-e Islam,* or "Word of Islam," and younger brother of the Supreme Leader.

KHATAMI, MOHAMMAD: Former Minister of Culture and Islamic Guidance, purged in 1992. In a stunning upset, elected president on a platform of reform in 1997.

KHAYRANDISH, ELHAM: A young art student at the University of Shiraz and devotee of Hafez.

KHOMEINI, RUHOLLAH: Revolutionary leader who became the Islamic republic's Supreme Leader until his death in 1989. Popularly known as the Imam. Married to Jamileh Kadivar, former adviser to President Khatami and among the first Tehran city council representatives.

KORANI, ALI: Reformist ayatollah who introduced computers to the seminaries in Qom and put Muslim, Christian and Jewish religious works on the Internet.

LATIFI, MALIH: Women's fitness instructor.

MASHALLAH, SHAMSOVAIZIN: Editor of *Jameh, Tous* and *Neshat,* Iran's leading reformist papers, two of which were put out of business by conservatives. Imprisoned in 1998.

MEHRJUI, DARIUSH: Internationally acclaimed movie director, screenwriter and founder of Iran's "New Wave" cinema. Movies were banned by both the monarchy and the theocracy.

MOHAJERANI, ATAOLLAH: Minister of Culture and Islamic Guidance and leading reformer appointed by President Khatami. Parliament's attempt to impeach him in 1999 failed.

MOHAJERI, ABOL FAZL: Instructor in Iran's internationally acclaimed family-planning program.

MOHAQEQDAMAD, MUSTAFA: Head of the Academy of Sciences Department of Islamic Studies and leading reformer on women's, family and social issues.

MONTAZERI, ALI: Selected in 1985 as heir apparent to Ayatollah Khomeini, but fired by Khomeini in 1989 for his criticism of the regime. Subsequent movements restricted.

MOSSADEQ, MOHAMMAD: Leader of a nationalist coalition that came to power between 1951 and 1953. Forced out of power by riots orchestrated by American and British intelligence.

NAGHAVI, MOHSEN: Director of Tehran's Badr Clinic and an innovator in Iran's family-planning program.

NATEQ-NOURI, ALI AKBAR: Elected speaker of Parliament in 1989. Despite strong support of clergy, defeated in 1997 presidential elections by Mohammad Khatami.

NOURI, ABDULLAH: Minister of Interior, which controlled elections and administration of Iran's twenty-six provinces, under President Rafsanjani. Forced out in 1992. Reappointed by President Khatami in 1997, then impeached in 1998 because of his reformist policies. One of the top vote getters in Tehran's first city council election in 1999 and elected council chairman.

OFFICE TO FOSTER ISLAMIC UNITY: Heir to the student group that seized the American Embassy that was revived and reconfigured in the mid-1990s with a reform agenda.

PAHLAVI, MOHAMMAD REZA: Second and last shah of the Pahlavi Dynasty. Forced into exile in 1979; died of cancer in Egypt in 1980.

PAHLAVI, REZA: Semiliterate military officer who as Reza Khan founded the Pahlavi Dynasty. Forced into exile in 1941 and died in South Africa in 1944.

PAHLEVAN, CHANGIZ: Well-known political writer and signatory of the "We the Writers" letter appealing for an end to censorship.

PARNIANPOUR, YAFA: Jewish housewife in Tehran.

PAYGHAMBARY, HOSSEIN: Proprietor of the Nomad Carpet Shop in Isfahan.

QAJAR, MOHAMMAD: Descendant of the last Qajar shah and guide at the Central Bank's museum of crown jewels.

RAFSANJANI, ALI AKBAR HASHEMI: Speaker of Parliament, 1980–89, and president, 1989–1997. Appointed head of the Expediency Council in 1997.

RAHIMIRAD, MUSTAFA: Young Iranian soldier and political science student.

RAIE, MOJTABA: Iranian movie director.

RAVANI, PARVIZ: Zoroastrian member of Parliament from 1992.

REZAIE, MOHSEN: Revolutionary Guard commander in the 1990s. Moved to the Expediency Council after the election of President Khatami.

SADEGHI, LILY: Iranian journalist and interpreter.

SADIGHI, MARZIEH: Conservative politician and American-educated female member of Parliament from Mashhad who won more votes than her husband, Golam Reza Shirazian, also a member of Parliament. First elected in 1996.

SAHABI, EZZATOLLAH: Editor of *Iran-e Farda,* or "Iran of Tomorrow."

SAHIHOLAMAL, AMID: Jewish teenager who was bar mitzvahed in Tehran in 1998.

SALMANZADEH, BAGHER: Iranian economist.

SEMATI, HADI: Tehran University political scientist and analyst.

SHAHRESTANI, BABAK: Student vigilante.

SHAHRIARI, SAFIEH: Female gynecologist and senior expert on family planning in Iran's Health Ministry.

SHIRAZIAN, GOLAM REZA: Husband in one of two husband-and-wife teams in Iran's Parliament. Married to Marzieh Sadeghi. American-educated conservative.

SIRJANI, ALI AKBAR SAIDI: Leading dissident writer detained in 1994 who subsequently died in prison.

SOROUSH, ABDUL KARIM: Iran's leading philosopher and Islamic reformer, sometimes called the Martin Luther of Islam.

STUDENTS FOLLOWING THE IMAM'S LINE: The student group that seized the American Embassy in 1979 and held fifty-two hostages for 444 days. It was later renamed the Office to Foster Islamic Unity.

TABARZADI, HESHMATOLLAH: Head of the Union of Muslim University Students and Graduates who challenged the concept of a Supreme Leader.

TAHERI, ALI REZA: One of six student leaders of the Office to Foster Islamic Unity.

TAVAKOLI, ALI: One of six student leaders of the Office to Foster Islamic Unity.

YAZDI, IBRAHIM: Naturalized American pharmacist from Houston who became the first foreign minister after the revolution; resigned after the 1979 American Embassy takeover and became leader of Iran's Freedom Movement.

YAZDI, MOHAMMAD: Chief of Iran's judiciary and one of a half-dozen leading conservatives.

ZIBAKALAM, SADEQ: Tehran University political scientist and analyst.

ZOROASTER OR ZARATHUSTRA: A "divine helper" who was born in Persia six centuries before Christ and was the founder of the Zoroastrian faith, which was one of the earliest faiths to believe in one God. Its ideas about the devil, hell, a future savior and a worldly struggle between good and evil ending in a day of judgment had great impact on all monotheistic religions.

NOTES

INTRODUCTION

1. Wright, *In the Name of God,* p. 22.
2. St. Vincent, *Iran: Lonely Planet Travel Survival Kit,* pp. 30–31.
3. Ibid., pp. 30–31.

CHAPTER 1

1. Lewis, "Islamic Revolution."
2. Munson, *Islam and Revolution in the Middle East,* pp. 41–45; Limbert, *Iran: At War with History,* pp. 78–82; Fischer, *Iran: From Religious Dispute to Revolution,* pp. 30–31 and 181–84.
3. Munson, *Islam and Revolution in the Middle East.*
4. Bill, *The Eagle and the Lion,* pp. 26–72.
5. Brinton, *The Anatomy of Revolution,* pp. 17–18.
6. Ibid., p. 49.
7. Ibid., p. 269.
8. Hashim, *The Crisis of the Iranian State,* pp. 3–29.
9. Algar, *Islam and Revolution: Writings and Declarations of Imam Khomeini,* p. 48.
10. Benard and Khalilzad, *The Government of God,* p. 110.
11. Ibid., p. 111.
12. "Dual Control," *The Economist Iran Survey,* Jan. 18, 1997, p. 7.
13. Wright, *In the Name of God,* pp. 82–107.

14. Elaine Sciolino, "Montazeri, Khomeini's Designated Successor in Iran, Quits Under Pressure," *New York Times,* March 29, 1989.

15. Kim Murphy, "In Tehran, Veil Lifts, But Slowly," *Los Angeles Times,* May 14, 1992.

16. Robin Wright, "Iran Embraces Paradoxes, If Not Western Culture," *Los Angeles Times World Report,* June 27, 1995, p. 1.

17. Hashim, *Crisis of the Iranian State,* p. 10.

18. Robin Wright, "Dateline Tehran: A Revolution Implodes," *Foreign Policy,* Summer 1996, pp. 161–74.

19. Hashim, *Crisis of the Iranian State.*

20. Brinton, *Anatomy of Revolution,* pp. 272–73.

21. "Iranian Ayatollah Tells Mosques to Keep Noise Down," Agence France-Presse, July 14, 1998.

22. Brinton, *Anatomy of Revolution,* pp. 272–73.

23. Ibid., p. 18.

CHAPTER 2

1. "For the Flower of Freedom," an open letter by Abdul Karim Soroush to Dr. Ali Akbar Velayati, Iranian foreign minister, on Dec. 31, 1995, printed by *The Iranian* on http://iranian.com/Jan96/Opinion/Soroush.html.

2. Speech to the opening session of the United Nations General Assembly, Sept. 21, 1998.

3. Hashim, *Crisis of the Iranian State,* pp. 3–6.

4. Soroush believes liberties are "suprareligious," in that they are issues to be decided before or beyond religion, similar to the issue of whether the human race is predetermined or not.

5. Wright, *Sacred Rage,* pp. 37–38.

6. Wright, *In the Name of God,* pp. 42–46.

7. Algar, *Islam and Revolution,* pp. 169–73.

8. Ibid., pp. 169–73.

9. Ibid., p. 374.

10. Wright, *In the Name of God,* pp. 42–46.

11. Ibid., p. 56.

12. Kayhan, Dec. 26, 1995, from "A Biography of Dr. Abdul Karim Soroush," first draft July 1996, published by web site www:http://dspace.dial.pipex.com/town/parade/ac889/biog.html. Abadan Publishing Co.

13. Letter dated Dec. 31, 1995, reprinted in *The Iranian,* January 1996, on web site: http://Iranian.com/Jan96/Opinion/Soroush.html. The Abadan Publishing Co.

14. "Iran," *Human Rights Watch World Report 1995,* New York: Human Rights Watch 1995.

15. *Soroush Letter to Rafsanjani on Harassment,* in Foreign Broadcast Information Service, May 22, 1996, pp. 76–78, translated from *Akhbar,* May 18, 1996, p. 3.

16. "Islamic Students Say Islamic Thinker Soroush Wants to Topple System," in *Sobh,* May 26, 1996.

17. Robin Wright, "Dateline Tehran: A Revolution Implodes," pp. 161–74.

18. Interview on Iranian television, Nov. 17, 1997.

19. "Iran's Khatami Doffs Clerical Garb to Donate Blood," Reuters, July 30, 1998.

20. "Iran's Media-Savvy President Hosts Radio Phone-in," Reuters, Aug. 27, 1998.

21. "Iran's Khatami Cements 'Rule of Law,' " Jonathan Lyons for Reuters, Aug. 2, 1998.

22. "Iran Crowds Cheer Khatami on Anniversary," Reuters, May 23, 1998; "Iranians Celebrate Anniversary of Khatami's Election," Afshin Valinejad for Associated Press, May 23, 1998.

23. *Excerpts from Speeches and Messages of Imam Khomeini on the Unity of the Muslims,* booklet distributed by the Ministry of Culture and Islamic Guidance, Tehran.

24. Elaine Sciolino, "Iranian President Paints a Picture of Peace and Moderation," *New York Times,* Sept. 22, 1998.

25. "U.N.'s Annan Endorses Iran's Khatami, Peace Process," Paul Taylor for Reuters, Dec. 11, 1997.

26. "Iran Announces Second Extension of Voting," Reuters, Oct. 23, 1998.

27. Jonathan Lyons, "Iran's Clerics Ride Political Machine to Victory," Reuters, Oct. 26, 1998; Scheherezade Faramarzi, "Hardliners Win National Elections for Key Iranian Assembly," Associated Press, Oct. 26, 1998.

28. "Iran: From God or Man?" *Economist,* Oct. 24, 1998, p. 42.

29. Kianouche Dorranie, "Brother of Iran's Supreme Leader Assaulted as Political Violence Continues," Agence France-Presse, Feb. 13, 1999.

CHAPTER 3

1. Douglas Jehl, "Who Says There's No Fun in an Islamic Republic?" *New York Times,* Oct. 13, 1997.

2. Speech at Tehran University in May 1998 on the first anniversary of his election.

3. John Lancaster, "The Global Power of U.S. Culture: Barbie, 'Titanic' Show Good Side of Great Satan," *Washington Post,* Oct. 27, 1998.

4. Ayatollah Ruhollah Khomeini, *Pithy Aphorisms: Wise Sayings and Counsels* (Tehran: Institute for Compilation of Imam Khomeini's Works, 1994), pp. 152–54.

5. Wright, "Dateline Tehran: Testing the Limits of Cultural Freedom," pp. 12–13.

6. Ibid.

7. Robin Wright, "Media: Iran Fighting Back Against Invasion of Satellite Dishes," *Los Angeles Times World Report,* March 14, 1995, p. 1.

8. Peter Waldman, "Iran Fights New Foe: Western Television," *Wall Street Journal,* Aug. 8, 1994.

9. Ibid.

10. "Iranian Parliament Bans Satellite TV Dishes," Reuters, Sept. 20, 1994.

11. "Iran Hauls Satellite TV Gear Smuggled as Tuna," Reuters, Nov. 11, 1998.

12. Afshin Valinejad, "Chador-clad Doll Is Iran's Answer to Barbie," Associated Press, Oct. 24, 1996; Sabrine Hassen, "Mattel Inc.'s Barbie Doll Faces Challenge from Iran's Sara," Bloomberg News, Nov. 19, 1998.

13. "Dirty Dancing Dolls Kick Up Storm In Iran," Agence France-Presse, Sept. 16, 1997.

14. "Stage Embrace Enrages Iranian Students," Reuters, Mar. 10, 1994.

15. Wright, "Testing the Limits," pp. 12–13.

16. "Farsi to Be Purged of Western Words and Expressions," *Compass,* Apr. 12, 1995.

17. Wright, "Testing the Limits," pp. 12–13.

18. "Iran Filmmakers Want Less State Control," Reuters, June 12. 1995.

19. Neil MacFarquhar, "Backlash of Intolerance Stirring Fear in Iran," *New York*

Times, Aug. 20, 1996; Anthony Shadid, "Amid Hard Times, Regime Cracks Down While Iranians Seek Good Life," Associated Press, Sept. 1, 1996.

20. MacFarquhar, "Backlash of Intolerance."

21. Shadid, "Amid Hard Times."

22. "Iran Militants Attack Movie Theater for Film," Reuters, May 6, 1996; "Muslim Activists Assault Moviegoers at Tehran Theater," Associated Press, May 6, 1996.

23. Afshin Valinejad, "Parliament Approves Iran Cabinet After Heated Debate," Associated Press, Aug. 20, 1997; Steven Swindells, "Iran Cabinet Nominees Defend Records," Reuters, Aug. 20, 1997.

24. Mehrdad Balali, "Hollywood Returns to Iran After Two Decades," Agence France-Presse, Apr. 5, 1998; Jonathan Lyons, "Iran's Khatami Cements Rule of Law," Reuters, Aug. 2, 1998; Lancaster, "The Global Power of U.S. Culture."

25. *Tehran Times,* Oct. 24, 1998.

26. *Tehran Times,* Oct. 28, 1998.

27. *Tehran Times,* Oct. 31, 1998.

28. Kianouche Dorranie, "Iranian MPs want Interior Minister Impeached," Agence France-Presse, June 10, 1998; "Iranian Deputies Call for Minister to Be Sacked," Reuters, June 10, 1998.

29. Jonathan Lyons, "Iran Parliament, President Clash Over Minister," Reuters, June 21, 1998.

30. Afshin Valinejad, "Iranian Deputy President, Culture Minister Assaulted by Militants," Associated Press, Sept. 4, 1998.

31. "Court Warns Iranian Newspaper Director Over 'Defamatory' Articles," Agence France-Presse, June 9, 1998.

32. "Iran Newspaper Sales Top Two Million," Reuters, May 12, 1998.

33. "Banned Liberal Paper Reappears Under New Name . . . Again," Agence France-Presse, Aug. 2, 1998.

34. Howard Schneider, "Guessing Wrong What News Was Fit to Print," *Washington Post,* Sept. 28, 1998.

35. "Iranian Cleric Calls for Curbs on Media," Reuters, July 31, 1998.

36. "Banned Liberal Paper Reappears."

37. John Daniszewski, "Fifth Killing of Activist for Change Raises Fears in Iran," *Los Angeles Times,* Dec. 13, 1998.

38. Mehrdad Balali, "Ten Arrested for Murders of Dissidents in Iran," Agence France-Presse, Jan. 12, 1999.

39. Jonathan Lyons, "Khatami Celebrates Iran's Democratic Experiment," Reuters, Apr. 29, 1999; Kianouche Dorranie, "Khatami Denounces Conservatives, Disputed Council Members Take Seats," Agence France-Presse, Apr. 29, 1999.

40. "Kadivar Defends Intellectual Freedom," *Iran Report,* vol. 2. no. 18 (May 3, 1999).

41. "Iranian Cleric Sentenced to 18 Months in Prison," Associated Press, Apr. 21, 1999; "Liberal Iranian Cleric Sentenced to 18 Months in Prison," Agence France-Presse, Apr. 21, 1999.

42. Jonathan Lyons, "Case of Obscure Cleric Exposes Iran Division," Reuters, Apr. 13, 1999.

43. "Tehran Conservatives Want Liberal Minister Impeached," Reuters, Apr. 21, 1999.

44. Mehrdad Balali, "Iran Hardliners Seek to Oust Key Moderate Minister," Reuters, Apr. 30, 1999.

45. Jonathan Lyons, "Khatami Aide: Iran's Cultural Thaw Irreversible," Reuters, Apr. 24, 1999.

46. Ibid.

47. "Cultural Reforms Cannot Be Changed Due to Impeachment," *Ettela'at International,* Apr. 26, 1999, p. 1.

48. Anwar Faruqi, "Iranian Culture Minister Defeats Impeachment Motion," Associated Press, May 1, 1999.

49. Christophe de Roquefeuil, "Iran Reformers Hail Minister's Victory Over Conservatives," Agence France-Presse, May 2, 1999.

50. Ibid.

51. Jonathan Lyons, "Advocate of Tolerance Wins Showdown in Iran," Reuters, May 1, 1999.

52. De Roquefeuil, "Iran Reformers."

53. Ibid.

54. "Iran Considers Ending Satellite TV Ban for Cultural Elite," Agence France-Presse, Mar. 16, 1999.

55. "General Information," in *A Selection of Iranian Films: 1998* (Tehran: Farabi Cinema Foundation), p. 14.

56. Douglas Jehl, "Iranian Film Rocks Hotbed of Tradition," *New York Times,* Jan. 1, 1998.

57. Geraldine Brooks, "In Iran, Quiet Films Can Speak Volumes," *New York Times,* Nov. 8, 1998.

58. Godfrey Cheshire, "Revealing an Iran Where the Chadors Are Most Chic," *New York Times,* Nov. 8, 1998.

59. Lisa Nesselson, "The White Balloon," *Daily Variety,* May 31, 1995.

60. Kate Durbin, "From Tehran With Love," *Mirabella,* January 1999, p. 26.

61. Lesllie Camhi, "Daughter of Iran, Shades of Her Father," *New York Times,* Feb. 21, 1999.

62. Ibid.

63. Afshin Valinejad, "Iranian Film Opens on U.S. Hostage Rescue Mission," Associated Press, Aug. 27, 1997.

64. M. T. Faramarzi, *A Travel Guide to Iran* (Tehran: Yassaman Publications, 1997), p. 59.

65. *International Film: A Cross Cultural Review,* vol. 4, no. 4 (Summer 1997).

66. Interview with Ali Mehran, film critic of *Iran News;* Ali Mehran, "The Envelope, Please: Tandees for Best Film Artists Were Presented at a Ceremony in Vahdat Hall on Thursday," *Iran News,* Oct. 31, 1998.

67. Cheshire, "Revealing an Iran."

68. "Movie Theater Construction Is a Cultural Necessity," *Iran News* editorial, Nov. 20, 1994. "New Iran Film Boss Wants a Movie at Each Park," Reuters, Aug. 17, 1997. "Iranian Minister Calls for Increased Movie Theaters," Compass news service, Aug. 29, 1997; *A Selection of Iranian Films: 1998,* p. 8.

69. "Banoo, a Film with Implied Concepts," *Tehran Times,* Nov. 12, 1998.

70. "De Niro to Feature in Iranian Movie Showcase," Agence France-Presse, Nov. 19, 1998.

CHAPTER 4

1. Speech on the opening day of the 53rd United Nations General Assembly, Sept. 21, 1998.

2. Jere Longman, "Beneath Coat and Scarf, the Freedom to Play: Despite Restrictions Unimaginable in the West, Iranian Women Are Flocking to Sports," *New York Times,* May 26, 1998.

3. Azar Nafisi, "The Veiled Threat," *New Republic,* Feb. 22, 1999, pp. 24–29.

4. Robin Wright, "Iranian Women Lead New Revolution," *Los Angeles Times,* June 23, 1998; "Iranian Leader Warns Women Against Copying Western Feminist Trends," Agence France-Presse, Oct. 22, 1997.

5. Haleh Esfandiari, "Iranian Women in the Public Sphere," paper delivered at the World Bank, May 1998.

6. Esfandiari, "Iranian Women."

7. David Briscoe, "World Sends More of Its Daughters to School, but 51 Countries Lag," Associated Press, Oct. 19, 1998, citing a report by Population Action International, a Washington, D.C., nongovernment organization.

8. "Women to the Forefront of Education Scene in Iran," *Iran News,* May 22, 1995; "Behind the Chador," *Economist,* Jan. 18, 1997, survey insert on Iran.

9. Robin Wright, "Losing Faith," *Los Angeles Times Magazine,* April 23, 1993.

10. Esfandiari, *Reconstructed Lives.*

11. "Policewomen Return to Iran for First Time Since 1979 Revolution," Agence France-Presse, Aug. 4, 1998.

12. "Iran Names Four Judges for the First Time," Agence France-Presse, Dec. 25, 1997; Esfandiari, "The Politics of the Women's Question in the Islamic Republic, 1979–1999."

13. *Tehran Times,* May 5, 1998.

14. The Koran, translated by M. H. Shakir (New York: Tahrike Tarsile Qur'an, Inc., 1997).

15. Elaine Sciolino, "Top Woman in Iran's Government Once Spoke for Hostage-Takers," *New York Times,* Jan. 28, 1998.

16. Wells, *444 Days,* pp. 129–30, 161, 180–81, 421–23, 425.

17. Wells, *444 Days,* p. 161.

18. Massoumeh Ebtekar and Moneer Gorgi, "The Chosen Woman: A Study of the Life and Status of the Virgin Mary (Mariam), the Mother of Christ, in the Holy Koran," *Farzaneh: Journal of Women's Studies and Research,* vol. 1. nos. 2, 3 (Winter and Spring 1994), pp. 67–80.

19. Hayden, a founder of the radical Students for a Democratic Society and one of the Chicago Seven arrested for protesting at the 1968 Democratic Convention, went on to become a California state senator and a candidate for mayor of Los Angeles in 1998. Bobby Rush founded the Illinois branch of the Black Panthers and served six months in prison for weapons possession, but was elected to Congress in 1992 and served for three terms. He lost a bid to become mayor of Chicago in 1999.

20. Esfandiari, "Iran: Women and Parliaments Under the Monarchy and Islamic Republic," pp. 1–24.

21. Fischer, *Iran: From Religious Dispute to Revolution,* pp. 226–27.

22. Esfandiari, "Iran: Women and Parliaments."

23. Esfandiari, *Reconstructed Lives,* pp. 1–9.

24. Esfandiari, "The Politics of the Women's Question in the Islamic Republic, 1979–1999."

25. Esfandiari, *Reconstructed Lives,* pp. 19–51.

26. Ibid.

27. Ibid.

28. Elaine Sciolino, "The Chanel Under the Chador."

29. "Iranian Parliament Bans Pictures of Uncovered Women in Press," Agence France-Presse, Apr. 12, 1998; "Iranian Parliament Bans 'Exploitative' Images of People in the Press," Agence France-Presse, Aug. 12, 1998.

30. "Iran Top Body Objects to a Single-sex Hospitals Law," Reuters, Oct. 13, 1998; "Iranian Authority Rejects Hospital Segregation Bill," Agence France-Presse, Oct. 14, 1998.

CHAPTER 5

1. From 1976 to 1986, the rate of population increase shot up from 2.7 percent to 3.4 percent per year—or 3.9 percent if the huge influx of Afghan refugees was included—which international agencies pegged as among the world's highest.

2. Neil MacFarquhar, "Iran's New Ideal: Small Families," *International Herald Tribune,* Sept. 9, 1996.

3. Statistics from Population Action International in Washington, D.C., 1996 database; "Iran: Fewer Means Better," *Economist,* Aug. 5, 1995, pp. 41–42; "Family Planning a Successful Experience in Iran," *Iran News,* May 15, 1995; "Iran Says Population Growth Sharply Down," Reuters, July 10, 1995; Scheherazade Daneshkhu, "Birth Control Successes Moderate Iran's Stance," *Financial Times,* Sept. 1, 1994; *Country Report on Population, Reproductive Health and Family Planning Program in the Islamic Republic of Iran,* Ministry of Health, Tehran, February 1998.

4. According to figures from Population Action International in Washington, D.C., women in Iran between 1965 and 1970 were having an average of 6.97 children. Between 1970 and 1975, they were having 6.54 children per woman. And for 1975–80, the figure was 6.5, indicating only a marginal reduction during the monarchy.

5. *World Population Growth from Year 0 to Stabilization,* United Nations Population Division. Nov. 11, 1996; J. D. Durand, *Historical Estimates of World Population: An Evaluation,* University of Pennsylvania Population Studies Center, 1974.

6. MacFarquhar, "Iran's New Ideal."

7. Anthony Shadid, *Iran's Population Program Cited as Model,* Associated Press, Feb. 6, 1995.

8. Anwar Faruqi, "Rafsanjani: Men and Women Should Get Together More Often," Associated Press, Dec. 6, 1990.

9. Wright, "A Tehran Summer."

10. "Behind the Chador," *Economist* special section on Iran, Jan. 18, 1997; Esfandiari, "The Politics of the Women's Question in the Islamic Republic, 1979–1990."

11. Robin Wright, "Islam Rising: Ideology," *Los Angeles Times World Report,* Apr. 6, 1993, p. 2.

12. Christiane Amanpour, "Iran Versus Iran," CBS *Sixty Minutes,* May 10, 1998.

13. Robin Wright, "Iranian Women Lead New Revolution," *Los Angeles Times,* June 23, 1998.

CHAPTER 6

1. St. Vincent, *Iran: A Travel Survival Kit,* p. 110.

2. Ibid., p. 111.

3. Robin Wright, "Forget Politics—Tehran's Traffic Can Drive You Mad," *Los Angeles Times World Report,* June 20, 1995, p. 6.

4. Sharon L. Camp, ed., *Population Action International, Cities: Life in the World's 100 Largest Metropolitan Areas* (Washington: Population Action International, 1990), wall chart.

5. "Iran Widens Tehran School Closures Due to Smog," Reuters, Dec. 15, 1998.

6. St. Vincent, *Iran: A Travel Survival Kit,* p. 138.

7. Keddie, *Roots of Revolution.*

8. Kaplan, *The Ends of the Earth,* pp. 195–96; Keddie, *Roots of the Revolution.*

9. Brinton, *The Anatomy of Revolution,* pp. 264–66.

10. Keddie, *Roots of Revolution,* pp. 252–53.

11. M. T. Faramarzi, *A Travel Guide to Iran* (Tehran: Yassaman Publications, 1997), p. 273.

12. It was not the last time the Persians and Jews would ally to balance the numerical or geographic dominance of the Arabs. Iran's last shah also had strong diplomatic and commercial relations with the modern state of Israel.

13. Among Arab states, the Jewish community in Iraq dropped from some 150,000 in 1951 to less than 100 by 1998 and in Morocco from 250,000 in the 1940s to some 8,000 in 1998. By the century's end, Syria, Lebanon, Yemen and Libya had anywhere from a dozen to a few hundred.

14. Armenian Christians, for example, have two members of Parliament. But the religious minorities don't have to vote for one of their own; they have the option of voting with the general population for a Muslim representative.

15. Scheherezade Faramarzi, "Although Regime Anti-Israel, Thousands of Jews Stay on in Iran," Associated Press, Jan. 19, 1998.

16. "Iran Report on Human Rights Practices," in *U.S. Department of State Annual Human Rights Report 1996,* Washington: Bureau of Democracy, Human Rights, and Labor, January 30, 1997.

17. Ann Lolordo, "Being Jewish in a Muslim Theocracy," *Baltimore Sun,* Aug. 12, 1997.

18. Kianouche Dorranie, "Arrest of Jewish 'Spies' Triggers New Round of Factional Fighting in Iran," Agence France-Presse, June 12, 1999.

19. The name Zoroaster is the Greek version of the original Zarathustra. He was born in Mazar-e Sharif in what was then Persia but is today Afghanistan.

20. Severy, ed., *Great Religions of the World,* p. 18.

21. Geoffrey Parrinder, ed., *World Religions: From Ancient History to the Present* (New York: Facts on File, 1983), pp. 177–91.

22. The Baha'is are the largest non-Muslim sect in Iran—and the most persecuted. The Islamic republic views the Baha'is, who number between 300,000 and 350,000, as a "misguided sect" because they rejected the Shi'ite brand of Islam. They have also been suspect politically because the shah employed a few Baha'is in senior positions.

After the revolution, the government banned Baha'is from teaching, practicing their faith or maintaining links with brethren abroad, according to several U.S. State Department Human Rights Reports. Universities denied admittance to Baha'i students. Baha'is have also been regularly denied compensation for injury or criminal victimization. More than two hundred Baha'is have been executed since the revolution, according to human rights groups.

23. Bill, *The Eagle and the Lion*, pp. 183–85.

24. Algar, *Islam and Revolution*, pp. 200–208.

25. Munson, *Islam and Revolution in the Middle East*, p. 20.

26. Ghani, *The Memoirs of Dr. Ghassem Ghani*, p. 18, translation by Gertrude Bell.

27. Translated by John Charles Edward Bowen, in *Iran Today*, by Jean Hureau (Paris: Jeune Afrique, 1972), p. 165.

28. Parrinder, *World Religions*, pp. 493–96.

29. Arberry, *Hafez: Fifty Poems*, p. 118.

30. Ghani, *The Memoirs of Dr. Ghassem Ghani*, p. 16, translation by Gertrude Bell.

31. Arberry, *Hafez: Fifty Poems*, p. 110, translated by R. Le Gallienne.

32. St. Vincent, *Iran: A Travel Survival Kit*, p. 238.

33. M. T. Faramarzi, *A Travel Guide to Iran*, p. 91.

34. Ibid., p. 95.

35. Ibid., p. 101.

36. St. Vincent, *Iran: A Travel Survival Kit*, p. 143.

37. Ibid., p. 141.

38. Wright, *In the Name of God*, p. 50.

39. Amir Taheri, *The Spirit of Allah: Khomeini and the Islamic Revolution* (London: Hutchinson, 1985), p. 19.

40. Ibid., pp. 134–46.

41. Algar, *Islam and Revolution*.

42. Ibid., pp. 181–88.

43. Jean Hureau, *Iran Today* (Paris: Jeune Afrique, 1972), p. 25.

44. Massoumeh Ebtekar, Iran's vice president for the environment, in a speech on Caspian oil sponsored by the Iranian Institute for Energy Studies in Tehran, Nov. 9, 1998.

45. Ibid.

46. British Petroleum Statistical Review of World Energy, graphic reproduced, *San Francisco Chronicle*, Aug. 10, 1998.

47. Speech by Franz B. Ehrhardt, President and Managing Director of Conoco EurAsia at the Caspian Oil and Gas Resources conference in Tehran, Nov. 7, 1998.

CHAPTER 7

1. Sign painted on the exterior wall at Niavaran Palace, one of the shah's former residences.

2. "Khatami Urges Clergy to Take 'Present-Day Realities' into Account," Agence France-Presse, May 26, 1999.

3. Wright, *In the Name of God*, pp. 48–51; Peter Jennings, "The Century: The Evolution of Revolution," ABC News special, Apr. 10, 1999.

4. Jennings, "The Century."

5. Scheherezade Faramarzi, "Mellowed Captors Invite Former U.S. Hostages Back to Iran," Associated Press, Nov. 2, 1998.

6. Bakhash, *The Reign of the Ayatollahs*, p. 75.

7. Milani, *The Making of Iran's Islamic Revolution*, p. 266.

8. Kifner, "How a Sit-in Turned into a Siege"; Robert D. McFadden, Joseph B.

Treaster and Maurice Carroll, eds., *No Hiding Place: The New York Times Inside Report on the Hostage Crisis* (New York: Times Books, 1981), pp. 175–87.

9. Jennings, "The Century."

10. Wells, *444 Days,* pp. 97–176.

11. Statistics are hard to verify. But the United Nations' *Human Development Report 1997* said that Iran's adult literacy went from 29 percent in 1970 to 69 percent by 1994.

12. Mehrdad Balali, "Thousands Throng Tehran University to Celebrate Khatami's Anniversary," Agence France-Presse, May 23, 1998.

13. Afshin Valinejad, "Students Want Intelligence Chief to Resign for Deaths of Dissidents," Associated Press, Jan. 12, 1999.

14. "Four Injured as Students Clash in Tehran University Rally," Agence France-Presse, Mar. 2, 1998.

15. "Iranian Students Stage Protest Against Beatings," Associated Press, Feb. 14, 1999.

16. "Students Call for Change," *Akhbaar News,* vol. 16, no. 36 (May 16, 1995), p. 6.

17. Christophe de Roquefeuil, "Leading Iranian Daily Banned as Conservatives Move to Curb Press," Agence France-Presse, July 7, 1999.

18. "Dozens Hurt as Iran Hardliners Attack Campus," Reuters, July 9, 1999.

19. Christophe de Roquefeuil, "Iran in Turmoil After Three Students Reported Dead in Clashes with Police," Agence France-Presse, July 10, 1999.

20. "Iranians Oppose Hardliners: Thousands of Students Demand Resignation of Ayatollah," news services in the *Washington Post,* July 11, 1999.

21. "Statement in Support of the Spontaneous Movement of Tehran University Students and the Declaration of the Position of the United Student Front," July 10, 1999.

22. Elaine Sciolino, "World Cup '98: Singing, Dancing and Cheering in Streets of Tehran," *New York Times,* June 22, 1998.

23. De Roquefeuil, "Iran in Turmoil."

24. Ali Raiss-Tousi, "Iran Minister Quits Over Student Crackdown," Reuters, July 10, 1999.

25. Mehrdad Balali, "Iranian Students Wind Down Street Protests," Reuters, July 11, 1999; also "The Spark that Ignited Nationwide Student Protests," *The Iranian,* July 12, 1999.

26. Anwar Faruqi, "More than 5,000 University Employees Stage Sit-in in Tehran," Associated Press, July 12, 1999.

27. Jonathan Lyons, "Police Beat Tehran Students, Empty Campus," Reuters, July 12, 1999.

28. Ali Raiss-Tousi, "Police and Students Clash Again in Iran," Reuters, July 12, 1999.

29. Elaine Sciolino, "Iran Protests Spread to 18 Cities; Police Crack Down at University," *New York Times,* July 12, 1999.

30. Lyons, "Police Beat Tehran Students."

31. Sciolino, "Iran Protests Spread."

32. Anwar Faruqi, "Iranian Police Crack Down on Student Protests," Associated Press, July 12, 1999; also Kianouche Dorranie, "Demonstrators Clash with Security Forces in Tehran," Agence France-Presse, July 12, 1999.

33. Jonathan Lyons, "Iran Students in New Clashes with Police," Reuters, July 13, 1999.

34. Jonathan Lyons, "Iran Students in New Clashes with Police"; "Students in Renewed Clashes with Security Forces in Tehran," Agence France-Presse, July 13, 1999;

Elaine Sciolino, "Chaotic Protests Reign in Tehran; Vigilantes Active," *New York Times,* July, 14, 1999.

35. Sciolino, Lyons and Balali, op. cit.

36. Mehrdad Balali, "Security Forces and Vigilantes Control Tehran," Reuters, July 13, 1999.

37. Elaine Sciolino, "Iran Students Suspend Protests but Persist with Demands," *New York Times,* July 18, 1999.

38. Anwar Faruqi, "Iran's Top Military Leaders Warn Khatami," Associated Press, July 22, 1999.

39. Christophe de Roquefeuil, "Islamic Regime Hits Back with Show of Strength on Tehran Streets," Agence France-Presse, July 14, 1999; Sciolino, "Iran Students Suspend."

40. Elaine Sciolino, "Turning Tables in Iran, Crowds Back Old Line," *New York Times,* July 15, 1999.

41. Ali Raiss-Tousi, "Iran Rally Backs Islamic Rule; Rioters Warned," Reuters, July 15, 1999.

42. Sciolino, "Turning Tables in Iran."

43. Jonathan Lyons, "Iran's Clerics Strengthen Grip on Election Process," Reuters, Aug. 12, 1999.

44. Marc Carnegie, "Iran's Judiciary Approves Sweeping 'Thought-Crime' Law," Agence France-Presse, August 3, 1999.

45. "Iran's Islamic Militia Steps Up Show of Force Around Capital," Agence France-Presse, August 5, 1999.

46. "Reformist Student Leader Arrested in Iran," Reuters, August 3, 1999.

47. Marc Carnegie, "Iran Courts Close Down Fourth Pro-Reform Newspaper This Year," Agence France-Presse, Sept. 5, 1999.

48. Carnegie, "Iran's Judiciary."

49. "The People's President," *CNN Perspectives,* August 1, 1999.

50. Kianouche Dorranie, "Prank Calls a Growing Headache in Iran," Agence France-Presse, Mar. 2, 1998.

51. Sciolino, "World Cup '98."

52. Figures from interviews at the United States Department of State, May 1999.

53. "Why Iranians Are So Tired," *Economist Iran Survey,* Jan. 18, 1997, p. 15.

54. Kianouche Dorranie, "Iranian President Submits Austerity Budget to Parliament," Agence France-Presse, Nov. 29, 1998.

55. "Iranian Parliament Approves Petrol Price Rise," Agence France-Presse, Jan. 20, 1999.

56. "Iran Expects to Earn $12 Billion from Oil Exports in 1999," Agence France-Presse, Jan. 20, 1999.

57. Douglas Jehl, "Iran Discontent Rises as Oil-Based Economy Fails," *New York Times,* Dec. 13, 1998.

58. Robin Wright, "Losing Faith," *Los Angeles Times Magazine,* Apr. 25, 1993, pp. 28–43.

59. Jahangir Amuzegar, "Khatami's Iran: One Year Later," *Middle East Policy,* vol. 6, no. 2 (October 1998), pp. 76–94.

60. Jehl, "Iran Discontent Rises."

61. "Iran to Sell Draft Exemptions for $1,700 and Up," Reuters, Nov. 4, 1998.

62. "Iran May Return Some Confiscated Assets—Newspapers," Reuters, May 29, 1999.

63. Christophe de Roquefeuil, "Iran's Reformist President Dogged by Economic Failure," Agence France-Presse, May 22, 1999.

64. "Iran Survey," *Economist,* Jan. 18, 1997; de Roquefeuil, "Iran's Reformist President Dogged by Economic Failure"; "Iran: Survival Against the Odds," *Economist,* Feb. 6, 1999, p. 48; some figures from the U.S. Department of State, May 1999.

65. Kianouche Dorranie, "Marriage Turning into a Crisis for Young Iranians," Agence France-Presse, Dec. 4, 1998.

66. "Drug Use on the Rise Among Young Iranians: Report," Agence France-Presse, Feb. 17, 1999.

67. Drug Control Headquarters document, *Anti-Drug Efforts of the Islamic Republic of Iran in 1997,* Washington, D.C., pp. 40–43.

68. Colin Barraclough, "Iran Confronts a Long-Hidden Problem: Drugs," *New York Times,* Aug. 29, 1999.

SELECT BIBLIOGRAPHY

BOOKS

Abrahamian, Ervand. *Iran Between Two Revolutions.* Princeton, N.J.: Princeton University Press, 1982.

Afshar, Haleh, ed. *Iran: A Revolution in Turmoil.* Albany: State University of New York Press, 1985.

Ahmed, Akbar S. *Postmodernism and Islam: Predicament and Promise.* London: Routledge, 1992.

Akhavi, Sharough, *Religion and Politics in Contemporary Iran.* Albany: State University of New York Press, 1980.

Algar, Hamid, trans. *Islam and Revolution: Writings and Declaration of Imam Khomeini.* Berkeley, Calif.: Mizan Press, 1981.

———. *Religion and State in Iran: 1795–1906.* Berkeley: University of California Press, 1969.

———. *The Roots of the Islam Revolution.* London: Open Press, 1983.

Arberry, A. J., ed. *Hafez: Fifty Poems: Texts and Translations.* London: Cambridge University Press, 1970.

Arendt, Hannah. *On Revolution.* New York: Penguin, 1965.

Arjomand, Said Amir. *The Shadow of God and the Hidden Imam: Religion, Political Order and Societal Change in Shi'ite Iran from the Beginning to 1890.* Chicago: University of Chicago Press, 1984.

————. *The Turban for the Crown: The Islamic Revolution in Iran.* London: Oxford University Press, 1988.

————, ed. *Authority and Political Culture in Islam.* Albany: State University of New York Press, 1988.

Ayoob, Mohammed, ed. *The Politics of Islamic Reassertion.* New York: St. Martin's Press, 1981.

Bakhash, Shaul. *The Reign of the Ayatollahs: Iran and the Islamic Revolution.* New York: Basic Books, 1984.

Bani-Sadr, Abolhassan. *Islamic Government.* Translated by M. R. Ghanoonparva. Lexington, Ky.: Mazda, 1981.

Bayat, Mangol. *Iran's First Revolution: Shi'ism and the Constitutional Revolution of 1905–6.* New York: Oxford University Press, 1991.

Beeman, William O. *Language, Status and Power in Iran.* Bloomington: Indiana University Press, 1986.

Benard, Cheryl, and Zalmay Khalilzad. *The Government of God: Iran's Islamic Republic.* New York: Columbia University Press, 1984.

Bill, James A. *The Eagle and the Lion: The Tragedy of American-Iran Relations.* New Haven, Conn.: Yale University Press, 1988.

Brinton, Crane. *The Anatomy of Revolution.* New York: Vintage Books, 1965.

Christopher, Warren, et al. *American Hostages in Iran: The Conduct of Crisis.* New Haven, Conn.: Yale University Press, 1985.

Chubin, Shahram, and Charles Tripp. *Iran and Iraq at War.* Boulder, Colo.: Westview Press, 1988.

————. *Iran's National Security Policy: Capabilities, Intentions and Impact.* Washington, D.C.: Carnegie Endowment for International Peace, 1994.

Clawson, Patrick; Michael Eisenstadt; Eliayahu Kanovsky; and David Menashri. *Iran Under Khatami: A Political, Economic and Military Assessment.* Washington, D.C.: Washington Institute for Near East Policy, 1998.

Cole, Juan R. I., and Nikki R. Keddie, eds. *Shi'ism and Social Protest.* New Haven, Conn.: Yale University Press, 1986.

Cottam, Richard. *Nationalism in Iran.* Pittsburgh: University of Pittsburgh Press, 1979.

Cottrell, Alvin J., and Michael L. Moodie. *The United States and the Persian Gulf: Past Mistakes, Present Needs.* New York: National Strategy Information Center, 1984.

Dabashi, Hamid. *Theology of Discontent: The Ideological Foundations of the Islamic Revolution in Iran.* New York: New York University Press, 1993.

Durraj, Manocher. *From Zarathustra to Khomeini: Populism and Dissent in Iran.* Boulder, Colo.: Lynne Rienner Publishers, 1990.

Esfandiari, Haleh. *Reconstructed Lives: Women & Iran's Islamic Revolution.* Baltimore: Johns Hopkins University Press. 1997.

Esposito, John L. *The Iranian Revolution: Its Global Impact.* Miami: Florida International University Press, 1990.

———. *Islam and Politics.* Syracuse, N.Y.: Syracuse University Press, 1984.

———. *The Islamic Threat: Myth or Reality?* New York: Oxford University Press, 1995.

———. *Voices of Resurgent Islam.* Oxford: Oxford University Press, 1983.

Faramarzi, M. T. *A Travel Guide to Iran.* Tehran: Yassaman Publications, 1997.

Farman Farmaian, Sattareh. *Daughter of Persia: A Woman's Journey from Her Father's Harem Through the Islamic Revolution.* New York: Crown, 1992.

Fischer, Michael M. J. *Iran: From Religious Dispute to Revolution.* Cambridge, Mass.: Harvard University Press, 1984.

Fukuyama, Francis. *The End of History and the Last Man.* New York: Free Press, 1992.

Ghani, Ghassem. *The Memoirs of Dr. Ghassem Ghani.* Ithaca, N.Y.: Ithaca Press, 1981.

Gibb, H. A. R. *Islam: An Historical Survey.* New York: Oxford University Press, 1949.

Green, Jerrold D. *Revolution in Iran: The Politics of Countermobilization.* New York: Praeger Publishers, 1982.

Guillaume, Alfred. *Islam.* New York: Penguin Books, 1954.

Haeri, Shahla. *Law of Desire: Temporary Marriage in Shi'i Iran.* Syracuse, N.Y.: Syracuse University Press, 1989.

Hafez. *Teachings of Hafez,* translated by Gertrude Bell. London: Sufi Trust and Octagon Press, 1979.

Halliday, Fred. *Iran: Dictatorship and Development.* London: Penguin Books, 1979.

Hashim, Ahmad. *The Crisis of the Iranian State: Domestic, Foreign and Security Policies in Post-Khomeini Iran,* Adelphi Paper 296. London: International Institute for Strategic Studies, 1995.

Hendra, Tony, ed. *Sayings of Ayatollah Khomeini.* New York: Bantam Books, 1979.

Hiro, Dilip. *Iran Under the Ayatollahs.* London: Routledge & Kegan Paul, 1985.

Huntington, Samuel P. *The Clash of Civilizations and the Remaking of World Order.* New York: Simon & Schuster, 1996.

Huyser, General Robert E. *Mission to Tehran.* New York: Harper & Row, 1986.

Islamic Student Followers of the Imam's Line. *Revelations from the Nest of Espionage.* Approximately 35 volumes to date. N.p., n.d. In English and Persian.

Jansen, Godrrey H. *Militant Islam.* London: Pan Books, 1979.

Kaplan, Robert D. *The Ends of the Earth: A Journey to the Frontiers of Anarchy.* New York: Vintage Books, 1996.

Keddie, Nikki R. *Roots of Revolution: An Interpretive History of Modern Iran.* New Haven, Conn.: Yale University Press, 1981.

———, ed. *Religion and Politics in Iran: Shi'ism from Quietism to Revolution.* New Haven, Conn.: Yale University Press. 1983.

——— and Eric Hooglund, eds. *The Iranian Revolution and the Islamic Republic.* Syracuse, N.Y.: Syracuse University Press, 1986.

Kemp, Geoffrey. *America and Iran: Road Maps and Realism.* Washington, D.C.: Nixon Center, 1998.

―――. *Forever Enemies? American Policy and the Islamic Republic of Iran.* Washington, D.C.: Carnegie Endowment for International Peace, 1994.

Khatami, Mohammad. *Hope and Challenge: The Iranian President Speaks.* Translated by Hossein Kamaly. Binghamton, N.Y.: Binghamton University Institute of Global Cultural Studies, 1997.

―――. *Islam, Liberty and Development.* Translated by Hossein Kamaly. Binghamton, N.Y.: Binghamton University Institute of Global Cultural Studies, 1998.

Khomeini, Ayatollah Ruhollah. *Islam and Revolution: Writings and Declarations of Imam Khomeini.* Translated by Hami Algar. Berkeley, Calif.: Mizan Press, 1981.

Lewis, Bernard. *Islam in History.* New York: Library Press, 1973.

―――. *The Political Language of Islam.* Chicago: University of Chicago Press, 1988.

Limbert, John W. *Iran: At War with History.* Boulder, Colo.: Westview Press, 1987.

Masci, David. *Reform in Iran,* CQ Research. Washington, D.C.: Congressional Research Service, 1998.

Milani, Mohsen M. *The Making of Iran's Islamic Revolution: From Monarchy to Islamic Republic.* Boulder, Colo.: Westview Press, 1988.

Miller, Judith. *God Has Ninety-nine Names: Reporting from a Militant Middle East.* New York: Simon & Schuster, 1996.

Mortimer, Edward. *Faith and Power: The Politics of Islam.* New York: Vintage Books, 1982.

Morton, Elaine. *U.S. Policy Toward Iran: Where Has It Been? Where Is It Going?* Washington, D.C.: Petroleum Finance Company, 1998.

Mottahedeh, Roy P. *The Mantle of the Prophet.* New York: Pantheon, 1986.

Munson, Henry, Jr. *Islam and Revolution in the Middle East: Religion and Politics in Iran.* New Haven, Conn.: Yale University Press, 1987.

Pipes, Daniel. *In the Path of God: Islam and Political Power.* New York: Basic Books, 1983.

―――. *The Rushdie Affair: The Novel, the Ayatollah and the West.* New York: Birch Lane Press, 1990.

Piscatori, James P. *Islam in the Political Process.* Cambridge: Cambridge University Press, 1983.

Ramazani, Rouhollah K. *Revolutionary Iran: Challenge and Response in the Middle East.* Baltimore: Johns Hopkins University Press, 1986.

Roosevelt, Kermit. *Countercoup: The Struggle for Control in Iran.* New York: McGraw-Hill, 1979.

Rosen, Barry M., ed. *Iran Since the Revolution.* New York: Brooklyn College Program on Society in Change, 1985.

Roy, Olivier. *The Failure of Political Islam.* Translated by Carol Volk. Cambridge, Mass.: Harvard University Press, 1994.

Rubin, Barry. *Paved with Good Intentions: The American Experience in Iran.* New York: Penguin Books, 1981.

Ruthven, Malise. *Islam in the World.* New York: Penguin Books, 1984.

St. Vincent, David. *Iran: A Travel Survival Kit.* Berkeley, Calif.: Lonely Planet Publications, 1992.

Scott, Col. Charles W. *Pieces of the Game.* Atlanta: Peachtree Publishers, 1984.

Severy, Merele, ed. *Great Religions of the World.* Washington, D.C.: National Geographic Society, 1971.

Shaban, Hussein, and Robert Johnston. *The Fall of Theocracy in Iran.* Hamilton, Ontario: McMaster University, Press, 1994.

Shariati, Ali. *On the Sociology of Islam.* Berkeley, Calif.: Mizan Press, 1979.

Sick, Gary. *All Fall Down.* New York: Random House, 1985.

Simpson, John. *Inside Iran: Life Under Khomeini's Regime.* New York: St. Martin's Press, 1988.

Sivan, Emmanuel. *Radical Islam: Medieval Theology and Modern Politics.* New Haven, Conn.: Yale University Press, 1985.

Stempel, John D. *Inside the Iranian Revolution.* Bloomington: Indiana University Press, 1981.

Sullivan, William H. *Mission to Iran.* New York: W. W. Norton, 1981.

Vakili, Valla. *The Political Thought of Abdolkarim Soroush: A Commentary on Religion and Politics in Iran.* Oxford: St. Antony's College, Oxford University, March 1996.

Voll, John Obert. *Islam: Continuity and Change in the Modern World.* Syracuse, N.Y.: Syracuse University Press, 1994.

Wadud-Muhsin, Amina. *Quran and Woman.* Kuala Lumpur: Penerbit Fajar Bakti Sdn. Bhd., 1992.

Wells, Tim. *444 Days: The Hostages Remember.* New York: Harcourt Brace Jovanovich, 1985.

Wright, Robin. *In the Name of God: The Khomeini Decade.* New York: Simon & Schuster, 1989.

———. *Sacred Rage: The Wrath of Militant Islam.* New York: Simon & Schuster, 1985.

ARTICLES

Afkhami, Mahnaz. "A Future in the Past: The Pre-Revolutionary Women's Movement," in Robin Morgan, ed., *Sisterhood Is Global: An International Women's Movement Anthology.* New York: Doubleday, 1984.

Bakhash, Shaul. "Iran's Unlikely President." *New York Review of Books,* Nov. 5, 1998.

———. "Prisoners of the Ayatollah." *New York Review of Books,* Apr. 11, 1994.

———. "The Politics of Land, Law and Social Justice in Iran." *Middle East Journal,* vol. 43, no. 2 (Spring 1989), pp. 186–201.

Banuazizi, Ali. "Iran's Revolutionary Impasse: Political Factionalism and Societal Resistance." *Middle East Report,* vol. 24, no. 6. (November–December 1994), pp. 2–8.

Boroujerdi, Mehrzad. "Iran's Elections: Implications for U.S. Policy." Paper delivered at the Middle East Institute, July 30, 1997.

Chubin, Shahram, and Jerrold D. Green, "Engaging Iran: A U.S. Strategy." *Survival,* vol. 40, no. 3 (1998), pp. 153–69.

Cottam, Richard W. "Inside Revolutionary Iran." *Middle East Journal,* vol. 43. no. 2 (Spring 1989), pp. 168–85.

Esfandiarai, Haleh. "Iran: Women and Parliaments Under Monarchy and Islamic Republic." *Princeton Papers in Near Eastern Studies 2,* 1993.

———. "The Politics of the Women's Question in the Islamic Republic, 1979–1999." Paper delivered at a joint Georgetown University and Middle East Institute conference on Iran's twentieth anniversary in Washington, D.C., on Feb. 11, 1999.

Fairbanks, Stephen C. "A New Era for Iran?" *Middle East Policy,* vol. 5, no. 3 (September 1997).

Kifner, John. "How a Sit-in Turned into a Siege." *New York Times Magazine,* May 17, 1981. p. 54.

Lewis, Bernard. "Islamic Revolution." *New York Review of Books,* Jan. 21, 1988.

Ramazani, Nesta. "Women in Iran: The Revolutionary Ebb and Flow." *Middle East Journal,* vol. 47, no. 3 (Summer 1993), pp. 409–28.

Ramazani, R. K., ed. *Iran's Revolution: The Search for Consensus.* Bloomington: Indiana University Press, 1990.

Rouleau, Eric. "The Islamic Republic of Iran: Paradoxes and Contradictions in a Changing Society." *Le Monde Diplomatique,* June 1995.

Sciolino, Elaine. "The Chanel Under the Chador." *New York Times Magazine,* May 4, 1997.

Soroush, Abdul Karim. "Cultural Pillars of Democracy," paper lent to the author.

———. "Perplexity and Faith," paper lent to the author.

———. "A Religious Democratic Government?" Human Rights Seminar in Hamburg, Sept. 22–24, 1992.

———. "Science as the Privileged Component of Modernity," paper lent to the author.

Wright, Robin. "Dateline Tehran: A Revolution Implodes." *Foreign Policy,* Summer 1996.

———. "Dateline Tehran: Testing the Limits of Cultural Freedom." *Civilization,* March–April 1995.

———. "The Faded Remnants of Iran's Last Dynasty." *Civilization,* March 1996.

———. "Iran's Greatest Political Challenge." *World Policy Journal,* Summer 1997.

———. "The Islamic Reformation and Democracy." *Journal of Democracy,* April 1996.

———. "A Teheran Spring." *The New Yorker,* June 22, 1992.

———. "A Teheran Summer." *The New Yorker,* Sept. 5, 1988.

——— and Shaul Bakhash. "The U.S. and Iran: An Offer They Can't Refuse." *Foreign Policy,* Fall 1997.

ACKNOWLEDGMENTS

I AM PROFOUNDLY GRATEFUL to Haleh Esfandiari of the Woodrow Wilson International Center for Scholars and Shaul Bakhash of George Mason University, who have long been my mentors and guides to Iran. Both have been incredibly thoughtful and generous with their time, knowledge, unique insights and experience. Haleh has been an endless source of information, big and small, and she also went over the manuscript with the fine eye of an expert and an editor, while Shaul has talked me through many of the pivotal issues and turning points in Iran's revolution over the years. I am indeed fortunate to have such marvelous friends.

In international affairs, Iran is among the most hotly debated issues. Twenty years after the revolution, feelings still run deep—and in different directions. Some experts now believe that the revolution was an important event and that the Islamic republic is gradually transforming itself into a system the world will be able to accept. Other specialists believe the theocracy is still among the most dangerous political systems in the world and little can redeem it. Most are somewhere in between. Over the past two decades, each of the experts has in some way enriched my understanding of Iran and the issues that have made the revolution a regular focus of the world's attention.

Among academics and think tank analysts, they include Gary Sick of the Gulf 2000 Project at Columbia University; Ambassador Richard Murphy at the Council on Foreign Relations; Nikkie Keddie of the University of California, Los Angeles; R. K. Ramazani and Scott Harrop at the University of Virginia;

Roy Mottahedeh at Harvard University; Augustus Richard Norton of Boston University; Jerrold Green, Graham Fuller, Zalmay Khalilzad and Bruce Hoffman at the Rand Corporation; Judith Kipper and Anthony Cordesman, codirectors of the Middle East Program at the Center for Strategic and International Studies in Washington; Mark Juergensmeyer at the University of California, Santa Barbara; Thomas H. Henriksen at Stanford University; John Esposito and John Voll at Georgetown University Center for Christian–Muslim Understanding; James Bill at William and Mary University; Andrew Parasiliti and Ambassador Roscoe Suddarth at the Middle East Institute in Washington; Shahram Chubin, executive director of the Geneva Center for Security Policy in Switzerland; Ken Katzman of Congressional Research Service; Patrick Clawson and Kenneth Pollack of the Washington Institute for Near East Policy; and Daniel Pipes, director of the Middle East Forum in Philadelphia and editor of *Middle East Quarterly.* Gerald Linderman, my wonderful history professor at the University of Michigan, also thoughtfully and thoroughly advised me on the chapter about revolutions—a subject he first taught me and inspired me to pursue.

Over the past twenty years, various American officials have generously offered me their time and perspective on Iran. They include former National Security Advisers Brent Scowcroft, Zbigniew Brzezinski and Robert McFarlane. At the National Security Council, I am particularly indebted to current and past senior officials Jim Steinberg, Bruce Riedel, Richard Haass, Ambassador Robert Oakley, Geoffrey Kemp, William Quandt and Ellen Laipson.

At the State Department, I have benefitted from the knowledge and policy perspective of several Assistant Secretaries of State for Near East Affairs, including Ambassadors Edward P. Djerejian, Martin Indyk and Robert Pelletreau. Other senior State Department officials who have talked me through issues involving Iran and Islam include Ambassador L. Paul Bremer III at Counterterrorism; Legal Adviser Abraham Sofar, who administered the Iran–United States financial claims; Ambassador Robin Raphel, who began her diplomatic career in Iran before the revolution; Steve Grumman and Henri Barkey at Policy Planning; Steve Fairbanks at Intelligence and Research; and Chris Stephens of the Iran Desk.

I've had support and encouragement as well from former hostages, particularly Bruce Laingen, Mike Metrinko, John Limbert and Colonel Leland Holland. They have all surprised me with their ongoing fascination with a country that treated them so poorly. Their love for the people says a lot about the potential of Iran, whoever is in power.

I owe a great deal to many of my colleagues as well. One of the interesting things about American coverage of Iran is the number of female correspondents who have been drawn to Iran again and again—and again. Their observations and stories have greatly added to my understanding. Among them are Christiane Amanpour of CNN and CBS, Caryle Murphy of the *Washington Post,* Elaine Sciolino and Judith Miller of the *New York Times,* Geraldine Brooks of the *Wall Street Journal,* Susan Sachs of *Newsday,* Kim Murphy of the *Los Angeles Times,* Jackie Lieden of National Public Radio, Carol Morello of the *Philadelphia*

Inquirer and Barbara Slavin of *USA Today.* William Royce at the Voice of America has also been wonderful in keeping me posted on the inside stories about Iran.

Both personally and professionally, I'm particularly grateful to the Mac-Arthur Foundation, *The New Yorker,* the *Los Angeles Times, The Sunday Times* of London and the Carnegie Endowment for International Peace for backing my adventures in Iran. The John D. and Catherine T. MacArthur Foundation gener-ously funded my expeditions in and around Iran that were critical to both this book and my book on the revolution's first ten years, *In the Name of God: The Khomeini Decade.*

At the *Los Angeles Times,* I owe a great deal to the encouragement of Editor Michael Parks and former Editor Shelby Coffey III, National Editor Scott Kraft, Washington Bureau Chiefs Doyle McManus and Jack Nelson, Foreign Editor Simon Li and National Security Editors Warren Vieth, Drex Heikes and Joel Havemann.

At the Carnegie Endowment for International Peace, Thomas Hughes and Larry Fabian allowed me two marvelously tranquil years to explore the growth of Islam as a new idiom of political opposition. Pauline Baker, now President of the Fund for Peace, was then a marvelous colleague, reader, editor and sounding board.

At *The New Yorker,* I'll always be grateful to Robert Gottlieb, David Rem-nick and John Bennet for sending me to Iran at critical junctures, particularly as the Mideast's bloodiest war came to a climax, and for their efforts at teaching me to write in ways that draw people to subjects about which they might otherwise not care. Many of my trips to Iran in the 1980s were during my years as the Beirut correspondent for *The Sunday Times* of London. James Adams never hesitated to allow a female to make those journeys at times other editors wouldn't allow women to go to either Beirut or Iran.

I've also benefitted from the editorial guidance and feedback from editors who've published other pieces I've written about Iran and the emergence of political Islam in *Foreign Affairs, Foreign Policy,* the *Journal of Democracy, World Policy Journal,* the *Middle East Journal* and *Civilization.*

During the quarter-century I've covered Iran, I've had other institutional affiliations that have helped me build on my Iran experience. The *Christian Science Monitor* sent me to Tehran for the first time in 1973. Duke University's Insti-tute for Policy Studies gave me a wonderful year as a visiting fellow to write my first book, *Sacred Rage: The Wrath of Militant Islam.* Stanford University and the University of California, Santa Barbara, also offered me time away from journalism to write, research and reflect on Iran.

Needless to say, this book could not have been written without access to or assistance from hundreds and hundreds of Iranians who've provided me excep-tional access and assistance, opening their homes, businesses and, most of all, their hearts over the past quarter-century, often at great personal risk and in defi-ance of official policy toward the United States. My dear friend Lily Sadeghi, with whom I've shared many adventures and whose journalistic and translation skills were essential in navigating Iran, is at the top of the list. Nasser Hadian and Hadi Semati, both professors at Tehran University, have also been wonderful advisers about political, economic and social trends. Others came from all strata of society and all walks of life. For understandable reasons, most prefer not to be named. They deserve so much more than this simple line of deep gratitude.

My literary agent Esther Newberg has, as always, been a wonderful shoulder. And at Alfred A. Knopf, Victoria Wilson has been a delight to work with.

Last but never least, Phyllis Wright, my mother and the most important person in my life, deserves the greatest thanks. Throughout my life, she has been the inspiration and catalyst to do things I didn't think I was capable of, and her inexhaustible love sustained me through all my far-flung adventures. So often she told me, "The only thing that separates us is miles." I owe her so much.

INDEX

A Note on the Type

The text of this book was set in a typeface called Times New Roman, designed by Stanley Morison (1889–1967) for *The Times* (London) and first introduced by that newspaper in 1932. Among typographers and designers of the twentieth century, Stanley Morison was a strong forming influence—as a typographical adviser to the Monotype Corporation, as a director of two distinguished publishing houses, and as a writer of sensibility, erudition, and keen practical sense.

Composed by Creative Graphics,
Allentown, Pennsylvania

Printed and bound by Quebecor Printing,
Fairfield, Pennsylvania

Designed by Cassandra J. Pappas